Dramas of Nationhood

THE LEWIS HENRY MORGAN LECTURES / 2001

Presented at The University of Rochester, Rochester, New York

Dramas of Nationhood

The Politics of Television in Egypt

LILA ABU-LUGHOD

WITH A FOREWORD BY ANTHONY T. CARTER

The University of Chicago Press
Chicago and London

The University of Chicago Press, Chicago 60637
The University of Chicago Press, Ltd., London
© 2005 by The University of Chicago
All rights reserved. Published 2005
Printed in the United States of America

14 13 12 11 10 09 08   3 4 5

ISBN: 0-226-00196-2   (cloth)
ISBN: 0-226-00197-0   (paper)

Library of Congress Cataloging-in-Publication Data
Abu-Lughod, Lila.
    Dramas of nationhood : the politics of television in Egypt / Lila Abu-Lughod;
with a foreword by Anthony T. Carter.
        p.   cm. — (The Lewis Henry Morgan lectures ; 2001)
    Includes bibliographical references and index.
        ISBN 0-226-00196-2 (hardcover : alk. paper)—ISBN 0-226-00197-0
(pbk. : alk. paper)
    1. Television broadcasting—Social aspects—Egypt.   2. Television and
culture—Egypt.   I. Title.   II. Series.
HE8700.9.E3A28   2005
302.23'45'0962—dc22

                                                            2004001470

FOR TIM

Contents

Foreword

LILA ABU-LUGHOD delivered the Lewis Henry Morgan Lectures on which this book is based at the University of Rochester in October 2001. They were the thirty-ninth in a series offered annually by the Department of Anthropology to the public and to students and faculty at the university. The fortieth lectures were delivered in 2002 by Deborah Gewertz and Frederick Errington, and the forty-first were presented in 2003 by Elinore Ochs. Paul Farmer will give the forty-second Morgan Lectures in 2004.

The lectures honor Lewis Henry Morgan. In addition to playing a signal role in the creation of modern anthropology, Morgan was a prominent Rochester attorney and a benefactor of the University of Rochester from its beginning. At the end of his life, he left the university money for a women's college as well as his manuscripts and library.

In *Dramas of Nationhood: The Politics of Television in Egypt,* Lila Abu-Lughod introduces us to Egyptian debates concerning the people's identities as members of a late twentieth-century, postcolonial nation-state by examining the cultural knowledges circulating in and around the popular dramatic serials broadcast on state-owned television during the Muslim holy month of Ramadan. *Dramas of Nationhood* thus bears an interesting relationship with Sherry Ortner's *Sherpas through Their Rituals,* which employed an examination of key rituals to introduce us to Sherpa ideas concerning their own identities. Of course, neither the topics nor the analyses of these important books are entirely analogous, but the contrasts between them serve to highlight some of what Abu-Lughod has accomplished. As one shifts from rituals performed in a small, face-to-face Sherpa village community to dramatic serials broadcast over national TV channels and viewed and discussed throughout Egypt, the density of action thins considerably. And Egyptian debates about their national identities are notably contentious, the partici-

ix

pants having very different perspectives and participation statuses. More-over, the quarter century separating the two studies has seen many impor-tant shifts in anthropological theory. Where Ortner analyzed Sherpa rituals in terms of widely shared key symbols, Abu-Lughod writes "against cul-ture," focusing on conversations or debates in which, as Ulf Hannerz, an-other recent Morgan Lecturer put it, cultural forms and ideas are distrib-uted rather than shared. All this presents enormous challenges to participant observation.

Abu-Lughod manages these challenges through an innovative multi-site methodology. One site of her research is the interlocking networks of writ-ers, directors, producers, actors, government officials, and critics who make serials, put them on the air, and debate their significance in publications and social gatherings. The second research site is a peri-urban village near Luxor, in Upper Egypt. This community is deeply involved in the tourist industry bringing visitors to ancient Egyptian sites, but it is on the margins of the contemporary Egyptian state. The third "site" comprises conversations with a selection of impoverished women household workers in Cairo—women who, though regarded as the stereotypical audience of dramatic serials, have a marginal place in the rural communities from which most of them come and in the city in which they are employed. Working in the first of these sites, Abu-Lughod is doing what Laura Nader called "studying up," moving among and listening to those who have a major role in producing and dis-tributing representations that define and redefine the Egyptian nation. By focusing considerable attention on the second and third sites, she provides subaltern perspectives on these elite representations. Together these several perspectives allow her to thicken her description of the production of Egyp-tian national culture.

Television was introduced in Egypt in 1960. At that time, it was explicitly tied to the nationalist and developmentalist aims of the government under President Nasser. It was seen as a means of disseminating public informa-tion and educational materials and of creating citizens. Much had changed by the 1990s, the turbulent decade of Abu-Lughod's research. Discourses of national development were being challenged by globalization, on the one hand, and Islamism, on the other. The Egyptian government was espousing a program of privatization and market reform, cutting its support for edu-cation, health care, and other development programs. Accompanied by in-creasing amounts of advertising, television serials were addressed to imag-ined consumers rather than to citizens. Tracing the manner in which the makers of dramatic serials have responded to these developments, Abu-

Lughod finds that the nation remains a salient horizon of meaning in Egyptian discussions of their identity.

Though the cultural texts circulated on television and in other mass media have enormous power, it does not follow that viewers are passive recipients, reliably shaped by the messages and information they contain. The Upper Egyptian villagers and Cairo domestic servants with whom Abu-Lughod worked were, she argues, already cosmopolitan, familiar in their various ways with many different cultures and points of view, including the asymmetries of power and information that separated them from the elite makers of dramatic serials. Like advertising in the United States, Egyptian dramatic serials "regularly miscommunicate by addressing an audience different from the actual audience."[1] Their messages are, as Abu-Lugod puts it, "deflected" as they enter the everyday lives of viewers.

Dramas of Nationhood is a notable example of an anthropology that, as the title of a recent project of the Royal Anthropological Institute put it, is "exotic no more." Agencies of the United States government have long participated in debates about identity in Egypt and elsewhere in the Middle East. Leaving aside the role of the US Agency for International Development in the design of the public health messages inserted in Egyptian television serials, Abu-Lughod delivered her Morgan Lectures in the month following the destruction of the World Trade Center, an event that served to underline U.S. interest in the views of Islamicists. As *Dramas of Nationhood* goes to press, the United States has occupied Iraq and inserted itself into debates concerning national identity in that country and its Arabic-speaking neighbors. A U.S. Army "psy-ops" team is helping Iraqia, an American-funded TV channel broadcasting from Mosul, increase its audience by airing *Talents,* a show based on the Fox Network's reality show *American Idol.*[2] On February 4, 2004, President Bush announced the creation of Al Hurra (Arabic for "the free one"), a Virginia-based, Arabic-language satellite television station broadcasting throughout the Middle East to compete with Al Jazeera and Al Arabiya, the satellite channels based in Qatar and Dubai.[3]

And it is not as if American identities were firmly settled and noncontroversial. Parallel debates concerning who Americans are or should be occur in the United States, as in other imagined national communities. Just as Egyptian commentators debate the merits of the Ramadan serials, so, for example, American commentators vigorously discuss the meanings of TV programs such as *The West Wing* and *The Simpsons* and films such as Michael Moore's *Bowling for Columbine* and Mel Gibson's *The Passion of the Christ.*

Abu-Lughod also shares with the authors of *Exotic No More* a concern to help solve social problems as well as describe and analyze them. She shares the social and feminist concerns of many of those involved in the making of dramatic TV serials in Egypt and, as an expert, moves in overlapping social networks. In giving voice to the Upper Egyptian villagers and urban domestic workers with whom she watched and discussed television, she hopes to make her elite interlocutors aware of the ways in which their work appears unrealistic and patronizing to and miscommunicates with much of its target audience.

Nevertheless, as the historian of science Steven Shapin observes,[4] in the modern era we all learn a great deal of what we know about the world from impersonal communication with anonymous and/or remote experts. Professional anthropologists have some power in expert circles, but the gulf between the producers of dramatic TV serials and the experts with whom they may interact, on the one hand, and the bulk of the television audience, on the other, is enormous, in the United States as well as Egypt. It is some comfort, therefore, that viewers may be expected to retain the critical defenses they derive from their cosmopolitan awareness of the worlds around them and their places in it.

Anthony T. Carter, Editor
The Lewis Henry Morgan Lectures

NOTES

1. M. Schudson, *Advertising, The Uneasy Persuasion* (New York: Basic Books, 1984), 4.

2. A. Garrels, "Iraq Gets TV Update with 'Idol' Clone," *All Things Considered,* January 28, 2004; online at www.npr.org/rundowns/rundown.php?prgId=2&prgDate=28-Jan-2004.

3. T. Regan, "US Image Abroad Will 'Take Years' to Repair," *Christian Science Monitor,* February 9, 2004; online at www.csmonitor.com/2004/0209/dailyUpdate.html?s=entt.

4. S. Shapin, *A Social History of Truth* (Chicago: University of Chicago Press, 1995).

Acknowledgments

I BEGAN EXPLORING the world of Egyptian television in late 1989 and have accumulated an enormous set of debts since that time. I would like to thank all the people who have contributed to the making of this book, though I can mention by name only some of them.

Without the people in Egypt who shared their lives with me and helped me understand a little of what television meant to them, I never would have been able to write anything. I owe a very special debt to two remarkable women, Samira Muhammad and Hamida 'Abd al-Majid, both strong spirited and intelligent, who taught me patiently. In Upper Egypt the whole Salim family, young and old; Zaynab Ramadan and her brothers and sisters; Umm Kulthum Lam'i; Nafissa Ibrahim; Yamna Ali and her children; Shahhat Shhittu and family; the Muntalibs; Hasan Murad and his family; Khayri Muhammad and his mother, Fatma; and the family of Muhammad 'Abdellahi, among others in the village of B'erat, were especially helpful, making me and my family always feel welcome and giving me insight into their worlds. In Cairo the working women, especially Sabrine, Zaynab, Madame Fatma, Sa'diyya, Na'ima, Samah, and Sahar, were wonderfully generous with time and knowledge. I hope the respect and affection I feel for all of them come through in the way they are portrayed and quoted.

I made five trips to Egypt while working on this book; the longest was nine months, the shortest three weeks. All but the first time, I came with my young children. This presented special challenges along with the obvious pleasures. For logistical help and generous hospitality along with good intellectual company, contacts, leads, clippings, and references, I want to thank Soraya Altorki, Elwi Captan, Ferial Ghazoul, Nicholas Hopkins, Siona Jenkins, Hind Khattab, Huda Lutfi, Samia Mehrez, Hasna Mekdashi, Cynthia Nelson, Reem Saad, Olivier Sidnaoui, David Sims, and Elizabeth

Wickett. There is no way to measure my debts to an extraordinary friend, Dr. Boutros Wadieh, for great conversation, admirable dedication, incisive explanations of everything from Egyptian political economy to village history, and brilliant medical advice to the whole family.

On one research trip, I was fortunate to have as a supervising colleague Faruq al-Rashidi, of the Higher Institute of Cinema in Cairo. He introduced me to many of his colleagues and opened up research opportunities among television professionals. So many of these busy professionals gave generously of their time; I am most grateful to Usama Anwar 'Ukasha, Muhammad Fadil, and Fathiyya Al-'Assal, who granted me interviews and invited me to sit in on rehearsals and watch filming on sets, giving me access to not only the views of committed and talented television professionals but also the everyday worlds of making serials. I also learned much about this world from Salwa Bakr, Abbas Fahmy, Layla Kamil, Wafiyya Kheiry, Mamduh al-Laythi, Basim Mahfuz 'Abd al-Rahman, Mustafa Muharram, Amal Ramsees, Nur al-Sharif, and Muna Zaki. Don Heisel and Sahar El-Tawila at the Social Research Center were helpful in sharing their research on television serials. The American Research Center in Egypt kindly arranged for my research permissions and provided a base on the longer trips. Amira Khattab and later her son Amir deserve special mention in this regard. Ann Radwan, director of the Fulbright Commission, was extremely helpful twice in providing housing and other assistance to a Fulbright alumna.

Over the years I was also lucky to have had so many people in Cairo and New York willing to assist me with my research. They tracked down periodical sources, searched for references, and valiantly helped with translations. Some were highly overqualified for this work, and I am a grateful beneficiary of their amazing efforts. I want to thank in particular Kamal Abdel Malik, Hala Abu-Khatwa, Omnia El Shakry, Iman Farid Basyouni, Dalia Essam Wahdan, Maha Mahfouz 'Abd al-Rahman, Sonali Pahwa, Elizabeth Smith, and Mohammad Tabishat.

It is hard to imagine how I would have found the courage to embark on this project in the first place if not for Arjun Appadurai and Carol Breckenridge, then at the University of Pennsylvania. They were just beginning their public culture project when I met them in 1987, and they helped me understand that the topic I wanted to study could actually be a serious endeavor. Also helpful was Margaret Mills, herself at the university during the year that I spent there as a Mellon Fellow, getting familiar with folklore and postcolonial studies alongside this new idea of transnational cultural studies.

This research project pretty much coincided with my years in the wonderful anthropology department at New York University, which followed a fruitful year at Princeton University, where I was fortunate to have had so many great colleagues. From Faye Ginsburg, Fred Myers, Susan Rogers, and Bambi Schieffelin I received excellent ideas and criticism. The unique Program in Culture and Media directed by Faye Ginsburg provided an ideal context for thinking about television. I learned as much from my graduate students as I taught them; especially valuable to my work on Egypt and television were Amahl Bishara, Tejaswini Ganti, Sherine Hamdy, Brian Larkin, Ayse Parla, Elizabeth Smith, and Jessica Winegar. In my last years at New York University, the scholarly community built around Middle East studies was excellent—Jenine Abboushi, Khaled Fahmy, Michael Gilsenan, and Zachary Lockman were especially important interlocutors. Ella Shohat and Shiva Balaghi helped organize film festivals from which I learned a lot, including one in which Walter Armbrust and Viola Shafik, generous to me in other contexts as well, participated.

I have been very fortunate in the institutional support I have received for my work over the years. This has included fellowships in 1989–90 from the American Research Center in Egypt and the Near and Middle East Committee of the Social Science Research Council; in 1993 and 1995 from New York University; in 1996–97 from the John Simon Guggenheim Foundation and the National Endowment for the Humanities; and a teaching leave from Columbia University in 2000–2001. This support enabled me to do precious long-term research as well as to find time to write. I am deeply grateful to these institutions and organizations, and to all those reviewers who found my project worthy. I hope the other projects I worked on along the way—edited collections on feminism and modernity in the Middle East and on the anthropology of media—are sufficient excuse for my delay in completing this one.

To Anthony Carter and the anthropology faculty at Rochester University, who honored me with an invitation to give the Lewis Henry Morgan Lectures in 2001, I am deeply grateful, because they gave me the opportunity to pull this research together and frame it in terms of the anthropology of nations. The experience of presenting my work to this group was very stimulating, and I am especially grateful for thoughtful engagement with it by Mohammad Bamyeh, Lisa Cartwright, Ayala Emmet, Robert Foster, and Robert Gibson.

Although I presented early versions of chapters 4, 6, and 7 as part of the Morgan Lectures, and wrote chapter 8 for presentation as well, this book consists of much more. This expansion was necessary, I felt, to give an adequate sense of the relationship between nationhood and television drama in Egypt. Five chapters are new and previously unpublished (1, 4, 7, 8, 9); two chapters have been revised significantly from earlier published versions (3, 6); and two have been slightly updated only (2, 5). Chapter 2 is a slightly modified version of "The Interpretation of Culture(s) After Television," in *The Fate of "Culture": Geertz and Beyond*, edited by Sherry Ortner, 110–35 (Berkeley and Los Angeles: University of California Press, 1999). Copyright © 1999, The Regents of the University of California. Reprinted with permission of the University of California Press. Chapter 5 is a slightly modified version of "Modern Subjects: Egyptian Melodrama and Postcolonial Difference," in *Questions of Modernity*, edited by Timothy Mitchell, 87–114 (Minneapolis: University of Minnesota Press, 2000). Copyright © 2000, The Regents of the University of Minnesota. Reprinted with permission of the University of Minnesota Press.

I have presented parts of this book in earlier versions at more colloquia and conferences than I can remember. I am grateful to all those who invited me and asked good questions at the American Research Center in Egypt; Columbia; Duke; Harvard; the London School of Economics; Michigan State; MIT; the New School for Social Research; New York University; Princeton; Rutgers; St. Catherine's College; Smith; the University of California campuses at Santa Barbara, Santa Cruz, and Berkeley; the University of Iowa; the University of Michigan, including its Institute for the Humanities; the University of Minnesota; the University of North Carolina at Chapel Hill; the University of Pennsylvania; the University of Texas; and Yale. I also found extremely helpful the comments of those attending the conference on rural Egypt in Aswan organized by Nicholas Hopkins and Kirsten Westergaard; "Questions of Modernity," two conferences I organized with Tim Mitchell; the Association of Social Anthropologists' decennial conference in Oxford; two conferences on nationalism, one at Brown and the other at UCLA; and two conferences on globalization, one at the Five Colleges, Amherst, and the other at the University of Karlsruhe, Germany.

Very special thanks must be reserved for Ayse Parla, Catherine Lutz, Jessica Winegar, Reem Saad, Elizabeth Smith, and Walter Armbrust, who generously and meticulously commented on a draft of the whole manuscript. I was inspired by their comments, though unable to follow through with all their fine suggestions. I did sharpen my arguments, correct errors, and try to infuse the book with more passion and more endnotes; I am sure they will see their imprints here. Excellent comments on or contributions to particular chapters or issues also have come from Janet Abu-Lughod, Ann Allison,

Talal Asad, Amrita Basu, Carol Breckenridge, Kamari Maxine Clarke, Nicholas Dirks, Richard Fox, Farha Ghannam, Faye Ginsburg, Joel Gordon, Gail Hershatter, Nicholas Hopkins, Suad Joseph, Brian Larkin, Catherine Lutz, Saba Mahmood, Purnima Mankekar, Justine and Claire Mitchell, Afsaneh Najmabadi, Danny Miller, Toby Miller, Tim Mitchell, Sherry Ortner, Gyan Prakash, Anupama Rao, Rayna Rapp, Dwight Reynolds, Susan Slyomovics, Ted Swedenburg, and Lisa Wedeen. The sophisticated and intellectually generous students in my NYU seminar, "Culture and the Nation," and my Columbia seminar, "National Ethnography," also got me thinking along certain lines. And I am grateful to Mary Cross for her good company and generosity over the years as well as for the use of some of the great photographs she took when she visited us in Egypt.

In the endless details of preparing the final manuscript, I benefited from a series of smart friends and students: Lori Allen, Hamdi Attia, Karen Austrian, James Conlon, Ilana Fischer, Megan Huston, Haley Olsen-Acre, and Naomi Schiller. Nadia Guessous provided the superb index. At the University of Chicago Press, T. David Brent and Elizabeth Branch Dyson shepherded the manuscript through the publication process with positive efficiency. I am also grateful to Sandra Hazel for excellent copyediting.

It is sad to think that my father, who now lies buried in Jaffa, in his beloved Palestine, will not see this book. He and my mother were the ones who introduced me to Egypt, where I have since spent so many wonderful years. Both of them also pushed and supported me, providing different models of committed scholarship. Some of the moral outrage I feel about the inequities within Egypt and describe in this book must come from them. Finally, I thank Tim Mitchell, who has shared in so much of its research, though he didn't get as much pleasure from the television soaps as I did. It was his project that led me to Upper Egypt and all the friends we made there. As "Father of the cats" to my "Mother of the cats" (the "cats" being our twins, Adie and JJ, who have so enriched our lives even as they endured our work schedules), he has made all the difference in life and work, even though we no longer have time to read each other's every word. I dedicate this book to him.

[PART ONE]

Anthropology and National Media

Playing soccer in the parking lot in front of the temple of Madinet Habu,
Upper Egypt, 2001. Photograph courtesy of Mary Cross.

[1]

Ethnography of a Nation

FOR MUCH OF THE DAY, tour buses fill the new parking lot in front of the Pharaonic temple at the center of the small Upper Egyptian hamlet in which I have worked for the last decade. European tourists in shorts and sunburns and Egyptian schoolchildren dressed in their best clothes spill out of the vehicles and are herded back in. Some buy potato chips from makeshift stands set up by local women (the Antiquities Organization that controls the area will not authorize new vendors' permits). Some get drinks, including bottled water, at one of the cafés that compete for their business. Some look suspiciously at replicas of Pharaonic cats and ibises that local guys furtively unwrap for them. Most dutifully make the tour of the temple, one of several sites across the Theban necropolis they will visit that long day.

At 4:30, as closing time nears at the temple, bored security guards in bulletproof vests begin to get restless. The young men of the village now drift into the parking lot. As the shadows lengthen and the sun begins to sink, jeeps carry off the guards, who have been posted here ever since Islamic militants began targeting tourists. Hiking up their *gallabiyyas* (long robes) to reveal shorts, the young men pull out a ball and begin to play soccer. The hamlet is returned to the comings and goings of its residents. Sheep are brought in for the night; empty donkey carts head home; people put on their visiting clothes and head off to call on the sick. There is a lot of movement on the road and in the lanes until the first of the evening television serials starts, about 7:30. Then it goes quiet again, and all one hears is barking dogs and the muffled sound of television sets.

This is just one small community in a region marked by its difference from the more populated north, with its cosmopolitan urban centers of Cairo and Alexandria, in a country that itself is sometimes counted as peripheral, part of what used to be called the Third World but is now known

3

as the global South. Yet this evening moment reveals much about the kind of world anthropologists find themselves working in, a world quite different from that in which the discipline was formed. We find people living among ruins of earlier civilizations that now stand as commodified symbols of human heritage. We find people's everyday lives, from their rhythms to their incomes, shaped by the structural adjustment policies enforced by international lending institutions that make tourism, including that organized around this heritage, a crucial but very vulnerable part of national economies. We find young men playing soccer, a game they experience intensely in parking lots and playing fields but also passionately follow in the televised rivalries between Egyptian teams and even among different countries, as in qualifying matches for the World Cup. Indoors, we find the sisters of these young men doing homework in front of the television set, their plain school uniforms and regulation white head scarves neatly set aside and replaced by comfortable long housedresses, while their mothers scold them for not helping around the house more. It is a world, as the soccer and homework examples suggest, in which national television is a significant presence in quotidian life.

What does this world mean for anthropologists? For me, doing fieldwork in the last decade of the twentieth century, it meant trying to understand something about the place of this ubiquitous form of mass media in people's social lives and imaginations. This in turn led to a set of questions, to be explored later, about the role of television culture in the hegemony of the nation-state and in relation to what are widely described as the forces of globalization. In Egypt since the late 1970s, political shifts have taken the form of assaults on public industry, on state support for social welfare, including education and health, and on the connected nationalist ideologies of what might be called developmentalism.

A NATION'S SALIENT INSTITUTIONS

Perhaps this set of questions about national processes was inevitable, given the starting point for my fieldwork. I had been puzzled in the late 1980s by the controversial appeal of melodramatic radio serials broadcast from and based on life in Cairo among the adolescent girls in the Awlad 'Ali Bedouin community in Egypt's Western Desert, where I had been doing fieldwork off and on since the late 1970s. In a family with almost no access to television (because the father considered it corrupting) and where only one girl had completed high school, in a community in which many adults proudly resisted institutions and ideologies of an alien Egyptian state associated with "people of the Nile Valley," afternoons in the mid-1980s found the young women huddled around a radio, shrugging off their mothers' rebukes, to listen to love stories involving computer dating or office romance in an urban dialect that they all associated with an elsewhere. This attraction to mass-mediated stories of life-worlds that so little resembled their own was curious to me. Enmeshed as their parents had not been in the pedagogic institutions of the state, the girls were well within reach of national forms of mediated popular culture, not just radio soap operas but pop music. Later for these girls, this culture would include television, although already in the Bedouin towns of the northwest coast television sets were common, and television serials (formally known as *musalsalat* and colloquially as *tamsiliyyat*), the successors to radio serials, much watched.

At the time, I saw the Awlad 'Ali girls' interest in radio serials as an instance of a cross-cultural encounter. What could it mean when girls living in a desert region with barely a shop nearby, restricted to relatives in their social encounters, caught up in the social and cultural worlds of their community, knowing they would have almost no say in whatever marriages their families arranged for them, listened to such stories of a foreign existence? Were they doing ethnography among their Egyptian neighbors when they followed the radio serials? Were they aspiring to the urbane modernity represented by the lifestyles of these fictive characters? The beginnings of consumer desires for lipstick and lingerie hinted at that, as did the budding interest in the markers of Islamic piety.[1]

What in fact was causing all this fuss? I began to want to know what the girls were listening to, who produced these serials, and who was the intended audience. What did it mean to have national radio broadcasts, an industrial form of cultural production that, unlike the community-based songs and poems I had been studying among the Awlad 'Ali that were passed on from person to person, had its locus in the urban national capital and was broadcast through national channels across diverse communities within the nation-state? The fact that the "culture" the girls encountered on the radio provoked generational conflict, their parents perceiving the serials as threatening, suggested something further. For them, Cairene culture, like the dialect, modes of dress, habits, and values associated with it, was not just that of a people socially and morally different from the Awlad 'Ali; in addition, the beaming of the serials into the community was seen as an aggressive attempt to assimilate the distinct community into a nation-state that already dominated in the urban centers and now was reaching out through a variety of institutions, especially schools, into such rural areas. Mass media forms, in other words, as perceived by the older generation who had grown up with a certain independence from the state, came not just from a particular sociocultural milieu but also were connected to the powerful institutions of the state.

This encounter with radio soap operas in the Western Desert led me quite quickly to television, because everywhere else in the country, it was the more popular media form: by the midnineties, almost all Egyptian households were said to have television sets.[2] I also was led to my focus on the dramatic serials shown on the two main state-operated channels, because even with the multiplication by the late 1990s of terrestrial channels to include five new regional channels (nevertheless still under the control of the Egyptian Union of Television and Radio, like the original three in place through the 1980s) and the introduction of satellite (whose use has remained limited relative to other Arab countries), the vast majority of the 69 million Egyptians leading such different lives—business tycoons and tenant farmers, Bedouin and urban aristocrats, Islamists and leftists, mothers and movie stars, peddlers and professors—still tend to watch more or less the same television serials every evening. This is especially true during the month of Ramadan, when people avidly watch some of the most captivating serials broadcast each year.[3] Television serials, more popular than their counterparts on radio and arguably the most popular genre of television, are addressed to multiple audiences, given their regional reach as a form of programming whose export to other Arab countries is financially essential. Yet I will argue that their primary imagined audience is the Egyptian citizen.

In her study of the crucial importance of the institution and practices of archaeology to national self-fashioning in Israel, Nadia Abu El-Haj has argued that "particular *domains* become profoundly *salient* sites for the production of *specific* national cultures."[4] Other anthropologists who have attempted to write ethnographies of nations have also focused on particular institutions. Catherine Lutz has shown, through her study of the microcosm of one southern city that hosts an army base, how the military and the compulsion for military preparedness it pressures for have formed and deformed the history and social life of the United States.[5] Katherine Verdery's classic study of nationalist ideology looked to intellectuals and the academy for insight into how nationalism gained such force in Nicolae Ceauşescu's socialist Romania, attending to the strange refractions in intellectual discourses of the dynamics of competition over resources and jockeying with the regime.[6] In a somewhat broader frame, Liisa Malkki examined the social and material conditions (specifically, refugee camps versus urban living) that predisposed certain Hutu refugees in Tanzania to the moral categorical thinking of mytho-historical consciousness essential to nationalism and a sense of peoplehood, while others adopted a more cosmopolitan, antinational sensibility.[7]

My argument in this book is that, for various reasons, television is a key institution for the production of national culture in Egypt; it is certainly an institution whose careful exploration allows us to write an ethnography of the Egyptian nation. At the simplest level, it is salient in national processes because of the special place it seems to have in defining Egypt as a unique cultural center, dominant in the Arab region. As the premier producer of film and television in the Arab world, Egypt played host in 1995 to the first Arab Television Festival, where its own films and television serials won most of the prizes. It is acknowledged locally that Lebanon, Syria, Jordan, and some of the Arab Gulf states produce excellent serials as well and are beginning to compete. But in terms of scale and seniority, Egypt is unrivalled. People in Egypt know this, just as they know that most of the stars who fill their fan magazines are Egyptian; that the Egyptian broadcasts on their own screens are also watched enthusiastically across the Arab world; and that many singers and actors from elsewhere come to live and work in Egypt.

As an outsider rather new to Egyptian television who has immersed herself in and derived pleasures from its serial programming only for a decade or so, I can confirm that there is good reason for this national pride. In spite of yet thanks to state support, the best television serials are gripping spectacles with moral truths that move their audience to tears, tensions and plots that keep them interested, loveable characters who make them laugh, brilliant lines that are worth repeating, music that embeds the shows in the memory, and characters who forge with viewers long-lasting attachments. Although some people express more excitement over the violent action and extravagant song of Indian films that are broadcast as special Ramadan treats, or fascination with the fabulous lifestyles, strange morality, and clean streets of American soap operas and films (and some critics, as we will see, disdain the homegrown products "irrigated by the waters of the Nile" for their obsession with local social and political issues), the engagement with these familiar household experiences is for everyone part of being a nation that has the capacity and talent for quality television drama.

A second reason to look to television as a salient national institution in Egypt follows from Benedict Anderson's suggestion that insofar as nations are "imagined communities," mass media, from the novels and newspapers he discusses to the television broadcasts analyzed in this book, might have roles to play in producing nations and national feelings and in shaping national imaginaries.[8] Just as scholars have looked at the power of romantic fiction in Latin America, mass advertised consumer goods in Papua New Guinea, and displays of cultural patrimony in museums and architectural preservation in Quebec in forging national sensibilities, so, too, they might well look at television serials.[9]

In the introduction to "Screening Politics in the Nation-State," the special section of *Public Culture* in which I published my first long article on television in Egypt, I argued that anthropologists had not, until recently, been much concerned with nationalism and national processes.[10] Before the late 1980s, when an explosion of anthropological publishing on these topics occurred, heralded by Richard Fox's collection on nationalist ideologies, there was surprisingly little literature.[11] I mentioned in the article as an exception the New Nations project at the University of Chicago in the 1960s in which Clifford Geertz participated. But there was another important precedent that I missed, one even closer to my own project in the way it conjoined the study of media and the nation. Unlike decolonization and independence movements, which inspired the study of "new nations," or the rise of ethnic nationalisms coinciding with the end of the Cold War that may have inspired something of the current wave of interest in nationalism, the political turmoil of the Second World War gave rise to this earlier project. From the late 1940s a set of studies conceived of as about "national character" and using techniques for studying "culture at a distance" that included media and film analysis was carried out by Margaret Mead, Ruth Benedict, Gregory Bateson, Geoffrey Gorer, and other key figures of American anthropology.[12]

The flaws in Mead et al.'s approach are obvious now: on the one hand they reduced and reified nations and peoples by granting them the qualities of an individual personality; on the other hand, they minimized the complexity of the dynamics of media production. Unlike them, I will not in this book seek out any kind of timeless native culture or national character in Egypt's television productions (the local popularity and mobilization of stereotyped notions like "the Egyptian personality/character" [*al-shakhsiyya al-misriyya*] notwithstanding).[13] Rather, I will investigate the relationship of some aspects of what we might call, following Adorno, the Egyptian "culture industry" to the social and imaginative lives of diverse people in Egypt at a particularly volatile political-historical moment, the 1990s.[14]

Nation-states can be looked at both as cultural artifacts whose technologies of production and imagination can be analyzed and as modes of ordering everyday life that can be ethnographically investigated. In Egypt, these technologies and modes of organization include national museums, military parades, flags, national anthems sung in every schoolyard, architecture, school curricula, bureaucracies of taxation and licensing, military conscription, security police, public companies, mosques, consumption goods, and much more. Television may be one of the richest and most intriguing technologies of nation building in Egypt, because it works at both the cultural and sociopolitical levels, and it weaves its magic through pleasures and subliminal framings.

HEGEMONY AND NATIONAL DEVELOPMENT

Anderson's popular formulation of the nation as an "imagined community" has come under increasing criticism for leading scholars with a cultural bent to eviscerate the nation, deflecting attention from the power that is used to keep citizens in line and regimes in control and the ideologies that mask inequalities (the vertical tensions rather than horizontal fraternities) and force national homogeneity over deep cultural differences—racial, ethnic, gendered, or other.[15] As the Awlad 'Ali parents' disapproval of radio soap operas first alerted me, studying television serials in Egypt necessarily entails examining a "national space" rife with tensions, inequalities, and regionally configured power systems, to use Claudio Lomnitz-Adler's formulation, or "the nation and its fragments," to use Partha Chatterjee's felicitous concept.[16] If, as Gramsci notes, "[e]very relationship of 'hegemony' is necessarily an educational relationship and occurs not only within a nation, between the various forces of which the nation is composed, but in the inter-national and world-wide field, between complexes of national and continental civilisations,"[17] then our task is to ask how television serials might work as a fraught means of educating subjects in the unequal world of which Egypt is a part. Gramsci's special concern was the intellectual and how he (and I will add *she,* since I consider feminist television producers as well) contributed to "the process by which power is produced and reproduced or transformed."

This is a concern that must be at the heart of any study of national television, since one could argue that those who produce and criticize television, at least in Egypt, are part of the intelligentsia.[18]

More attuned than Anderson to the power entailed in creating national citizens, Etienne Balibar has noted that the family and the school are the primary institutions of the propagation of the illusion of the nation and the socialization of individuals to be nationals.[19] Television and radio, in Egypt and elsewhere, sit in the home, at the heart of families. But television in Egypt also has a direct relationship to schooling, itself promoted as part of the development of the new independent nation in the 1950s. Radio transmissions of President Gamal Abdel Nasser's charismatic speeches, and even the mesmerizing concerts of the legendary singer Umm Kulthum, remain iconic of Egyptian national and nationalist sentiment.[20] Yet the new government in Egypt pushed mass media overtly as a means of "citizen education" and as an "agent of public information and education," rapidly increasing broadcast hours and subsidizing radio receivers in the late 1950s and introducing television on July 21, 1960.[21] Under a mandate to educate and inform, Nasser's government invested in television, beginning with three channels catering to slightly different audiences. To provide television access in rural areas, the government even subsidized television sets for cooperatives and village councils. A major part of programming included shows with developmental and educational themes.[22]

The specific historical association in Egypt, as in many Third World countries, of television drama with national pedagogy is the subject of this book, but especially the two chapters that make up the second section. These chapters explore television's engagement with the two groups that since the early part of the twentieth century have been, as Omnia El Shakry shows, major objects of social reform, uplift, and modernization in Egypt: peasants and women.[23] Television followed different trajectories from those of the United States and even first world nations like Britain, where public broadcasting dominated until recently. In Egypt, as in India, for example, television was introduced at the start of the 1960s, centralized and linked to the state, and took off in the 1980s with advertising. As I will explore more fully in a later chapter, it was being transformed by the end of the 1990s with neoliberal reforms, greater privatization, and competition from satellite.

As in many other postcolonial nations, the purpose of national media in Egypt had never been justified in commercial terms. It was yoked to political and social projects, even if the technology and expertise had initially come from the U.S. company RCA and entertainment was and continues to be part of its mission.[24] The addressee was the citizen, not the consumer. Audiences were to be brought into national and international political consciousness, mobilized, modernized, and culturally uplifted. As Muhammad Fadil, a major television director since the 1960s, put it, one goal was to eliminate cultural illiteracy.[25] The uneducated and uncultured masses were to be introduced to literature and made aware of the larger world. Even the broadcast of televised soccer matches, those vivid spectacles of local and national identity, were defended to me by the famous actor Nur al-Sharif as having been part of this attempt at modernization.[26] Although programming today consists of many genres, including talk shows, news, sports, religious programs (Qur'anic recitation opening and closing the day), children's programs, comedy selections, music videos, imported soap operas and cartoons, and local serials and films, with special seasonal showings of parliamentary debates, riddle shows, and celebrity game shows, a significant amount of airtime is still devoted to educational or service programs. As late as 1986, about 17% of weekly programs were "developmental": either educational (literacy, math, science, culture) or concerned with health, agriculture, or social welfare (having to do with youth, the law, family, tourism, or money).[27] Despite the commercialization of television, the official didactic ideology of the medium persisted into the 1990s, as the following comments by Mamduh al-Laythi, then director of the Egyptian Union of Radio and Television's film and serial production sector, reveal. He explained to me,

Egypt is a developing nation, and we as a country are very concerned with the cultural education of our people. . . . Our most important goal in relation to the citizens is to help individuals become cultured. We must educate them, teach them the basics of morality and religious duty. The individual needs guidance. He needs information, and we need to inculcate the spirit of patriotism, morality, religion, courage, and enterprise. We have found that the best means to reach the individual is through drama. It works like magic.[28]

It is helpful in this context, however, to think in terms of Homi Bhabha's formulation that in nations, the people are both pedagogical objects and performative subjects.[29] In this spirit I have treated the relationship between television and its national audiences as a series of encounters. These encounters are between the television dramas that seek to shape, inform, and educate and those who are the intended objects of this molding. However, I have staged the encounters between mass media and the people not as ones between abstract pedagogical forces emanating from some disembodied state or nation and its objects but as between two sorts of performative subjects—a certain elite who, among other things, produces national television for imagined audiences, and various subalterns who not only appreciate and enjoy but critically interpret, select, and evaluate what the elites produce, always in the context of their everyday lives. Although I recognize that the middle class is as important an audience for television produced by its members, and I do not want to artificially divide subaltern viewers from elite producers, my methodological decision to work with the urban intelligentsia that produces and comments on television and with only some marginal social groups (such as villagers in a disadvantaged region of Egypt that has long been discriminated against or women forced to work as domestics in the urban metropolis of Cairo) allows me to highlight how this pedagogical encounter is related to class and gender, and how national ideologies are themselves related to power.

In the chapters of the second section in particular, I examine various aspects of these encounters, trying to detail the ways television dramas construct images of the good nation and citizen, call (in the Althusserian sense) viewers to that vision, and groom them for the role. I discuss from among the many serials produced and aired each year those in which these pedagogical intents were particularly apparent. I did not have to dig deep or choose obscure productions: these serials had, with one or two exceptions, great popular appeal. They were written and directed by some of the major players in Egyptian television and included the popular stars whom audiences want to see. Many were aired during the prestigious Ramadan season. They are thus significant works, many remembered, and rerun, for years.

Selecting particular serials produced by particular members of the culture industry allows me to move beyond simply accusing state-controlled media of doing the bidding of the regime, even if we must take into account that the Minister of Information supervises it. Most radio and television around the world has been state controlled or in the hands of culture industry professionals who, as Stuart Hall (1980) has argued, tend to share the "dominant codes" of the nation-state. Censorship and anticipatory self-censorship are the norms. Whether to create loyalty, shape political understandings, foster national development, modernize, promote family planning, teach privatization and the capitalist ethos, make good socialists, or innocuously entertain, mass media have been viewed as powerful tools for social engineering. But producers are critical mediators, articulating and translating larger projects. They are also creative individuals, working not only with their own professional codes and generic conventions but also with their own career interests and visions, sometimes oppositional because of training under earlier and different conditions or because they represent a new generation with changed circumstances or influences.[30] There is a good deal of room for slippage in this mediation by professionals, slippage that is worth documenting and that keeps one true to the principle that all the people of a nation are performative subjects.

In Egypt, as I discovered, many television writers and directors position themselves as critics of the regime and of its policies; some seek to be the voice of the people. Even though I did not document anything as blatantly counterhegemonic to certain state and national interests as described elsewhere—for example, when a Bolivian television host used the popular base created by his program to create a new political party which he headed; or when activist video makers from indigenous groups rejected national television in favor of their own productions or made political points through documenting their own protests of national projects; or most famously when clerics in Iran in the late 1970s used "small media" like audiocassettes to mobilize people for a revolution against the shah—I still have tried to respect the ways in which individuals in this group have acted as political critics.[31] I analyze throughout the tensions and alignments between those who make television programs and those who defend the nation-state and regime, recognizing the role of intellectuals, in Gramsci's formulation, in a social hegemony that is distinct from, even if related to, the domination of the state.[32]

At the same time, since my most intense fieldwork and my primary sympathies were with viewers of television, I have been especially concerned with how particular communities and individuals both have been subjected to and have responded to the calls of television and its entertaining serials. In this book I explore how they have reacted with their situated knowledge and desires and how they have taken captivating television dramas and characters (not to mention stars and all those aesthetic features from which serials are constructed) into their lives. These are lives, in Egypt, for which there are real limits placed, for economic, political, and social reasons, on the possibility of achieving certain ideals and becoming the subjects of national pedagogy. For those who do not have access to the education that marks the good upright citizen or the emancipated woman; for those whose livelihoods are so precarious that they cannot dream of the comforts that allow art, beauty, and modernity to become the terms of value; for those whose experiences of the nation-state have tended to be more through police violence, official corruption, security surveillance, or the maltreatment of conscription than through the privileges of office, income, and social standing, one needs to ask how the messages of developmentalism and good citizenship are assimilated. How "available," to use Daniel's term, is the nation to these groups?[33] I argue that the way people respond depends both on the experiences they have on the ground and the alternative discourses they have available to them.

NATIONS IN HISTORICAL TIME:

THE EROSION OF NATIONAL PEDAGOGY

Unlike Mead's national culture studies or even many more recent general studies of nationalism, I argue in this book that rather than studying "the nation" or any particular nation, we must admit that we are always studying nations at particular moments in their histories. The dynamics within and the forces that shape a nation are always in flux, even if there are periods of relative stability. The 1990s signify a particularly complex political moment in Egypt's national history when the hegemony of one vision, of which state media was to be an instrument, was seriously eroding. Particular changes were set in motion in the 1970s that unfolded especially starkly over the course of the 1990s, making Islamism and globalization, to use the shorthands of local political discourse, serious competitors for the developmentalism that was integral to the earlier pedagogical moment.

This book therefore paints a portrait of the Egyptian nation as it has been refashioned in the crosscurrents of particular political and economic trends. Television serials and the debates about them, ephemeral and continuously unfolding, give us, I argue, special access to the rough processes involved in nation making and national cultural formation in changing circumstances. Any suspicions I might have harbored that television serials were simply escapist entertainment were quickly put down in my first years of studying television. At least some serials were closely tied to contemporary political debate, as I learned from the Ramadan serial that most riveted audiences and provoked national discussion in the late 1980s and early 1990s. *Layali al-Hilmiyya* (Hilmiyya nights) was written by Egypt's most popular television writer, Usama Anwar 'Ukasha, someone who had studied sociology in college, written literature, and then realized he could reach more people through television. The serial was unusual for a number of features, including its having been a brilliant historical epic of modern Egypt that started in the 1940s and took viewers into the present, over the course of five annual installments beginning in 1988. It was quickly embroiled in public debate. The merits of the serial were discussed in newspapers and magazines, and a leading intellectual, Sayed Yassin, even used it as a metaphor for "Egypt's real abilities," contrasting its excellent script, capable director, talented and devoted actors, and involved audience with the failures of current political activity in Egypt. He suggested that what Egypt needed was a better text to guide its director (the president), more respect for its citizens, and the introduction of new political actors.[34]

Not everyone was so positive, and the debates in the press focused squarely on why: the political perspective presented in this large spectacle. As one headline in the newspaper *Al-Wafd* bluntly asked, "Does the Author of *Hilmiyya Nights* Have the Right to Write History from the Nasserites' Perspective?"[35] The writer of the article used the serial as the occasion to set the public straight about the reign of Egypt's first president. In the same newspaper, the leading establishment historian of Anwar al-Sadat's presidency (the period being depicted in that year's installment) explained why he had not criticized the serial. He argued that the scriptwriter had merely presented the period as those living through it had perceived it, explaining that the people had worshipped Nasser for achieving so many of their dreams: a republic, land reform, socialism, a strong army, and Arab unity. They had not realized, he continued, that what Nasser had created was a military dictatorship. And because of media disinformation, they knew little about how many Egyptian thinkers of the Left and Right he had imprisoned.[36] Others of the same persuasion criticized the slighting of the October 1973 war with Israel, accusing the writer of belittling not just Sadat's achievement but that of all the people who fought.

The serial was criticized from other political perspectives as well. In the leftist newspaper *Al-Ahali*, 'Ukasha was asked why he made the capitalist pasha such a sympathetic character and ignored the everyday problems of ordinary people. In another opposition newspaper, later banned, that had included the viewpoint of the Muslim Brotherhood, the paper's editor, 'Adil Husayn, defended *Hilmiyya Nights* and praised its writer for depicting everyday religiosity, noting that he had earlier criticized the serial, like all

Stills from *Hilmiyya Nights:* above, working-class home (Sayyid 'Azmi and Magda Zaki); below, aristocratic home (Hisham Salim and Ilham Shahin). Photographs courtesy of the Egyptian Radio and Television Union.

television drama, for never showing Islamic religious practices as part of daily life.

Those sympathetic to 'Ukasha's politics wrote articles complimenting the serial for its brilliance, invoking a discourse of art over politics or openly supporting his political perspective. They decried the much-publicized state censorship with which he had been threatened. This suppression is exercised in Egypt in the name of protecting the public from the morally, politically, or religiously offensive. *Hilmiyya Nights* had tested the limits of the more generous freedom of the media that has been President Muhammad Hosni Mubarak's public policy.[37] The writer had clashed with the television censors, who not only commented on the screenplay but also required cuts after the filming was complete. Many of the cuts requested by the censorship office were finally overridden on the personal authority of the Minister of Information and the head of the television sector responsible for the production of films and serials.

From the internal records of this clash over the serial's third installment, which covered the 1970s, it is clear that most of the censors' objections were political.[38] Although they had asked for one sexually suggestive scene to be cut, the balance of the censors' requests focused on removing lines in which President Nasser was praised or defended by sympathetic characters. They also objected to scenes suggesting criticism of President Sadat and his policies. For example, they requested more balance in the reaction of the characters to Sadat's visit to Israel in 1977. They asked the writer to change the timing of a scene in which the neighborhood coffee shop of a beloved patriotic character is sold; by having it coincide with Sadat's visit, they felt he implied that it was Egypt being sold. And, for reasons that I will detail more fully in the chapter on media and Islamism, they asked that all dialogue be removed from a scene in a mosque, saying, "We don't want any discussion of religion and the role of fundamentalists." Ironically, the censors also objected to a scene in which a newspaper editor cuts part of a journalist's story that he considers too dangerous. They insisted that this was inaccurate; there had been no censorship at the time of Sadat.

It is clear that *Hilmiyya Nights* was caught in the political tug-of-war between those with different views of the regime that had overturned many of the policies of Nasserism and was still, under President Mubarak, in power. The scriptwriter accused the censors of "destroying the work on grounds that to criticize the Sadat period is to be against the current regime in the country."[39] In short, *Hilmiyya Nights,* a serial that showed how political events at the national level affected the lives of individuals and communities, a serial in which personal histories, fortunes, and tragedies were directly related to policies and events, was meant and was taken as a direct intervention into contemporary political debate.

This serial and the debate it spawned gave me clues about the significance of television drama for changing national policies. During the austere era of the 1960s when the excesses of a corrupt overthrown monarchy and aristocracy were vilified and the promises of a better life were being offered to the poor, the prevailing political ideology stressed secularism and the larger social good, encouraging only a sensible consumption as part of good citizenship. The television industry in Egypt mirrored and promoted this ideology, as can still be seen in the pedagogical serials produced by veterans of the television world, serials I discuss in part 2. In the 1980s and '90s, the public service ideology of television weakened precipitously. Granted, providing entertainment had never been denied as part of the state media industry. Among the first regular programs on television, I recall from childhood visits, was the imported situation comedy *I Love Lucy*—hardly pedagogical. Television always had a great tradition and good backlog of feature films, including comedies and musicals, on which to draw to fill airtime.[40] But one can see today significant shifts in the content and styles of the serials alongside significant changes in the organization of the industry (including some privatization) that indicate a serious transition.

Whereas television was introduced at the same time that Nasser nationalized industry, mandated mass public education and welfare, redistributed land, discouraged imports, and called for Arab socialism, it now operates in an environment much changed by regimes since his death in 1970. Many of the policies have been or are being reversed as the country is opened up for private, local, and transnational capitalism. The effects can be seen everywhere in Egypt as the processes begun by Sadat's "economic liberalization" or "open-door policy" in the 1970s have escalated, with the money to be made by entrepreneurs and multinational corporations taking advantage of conditions imposed by the International Monetary Fund (IMF).

What happens when state interests are complex and contradictory, as they are in many of the countries in which anthropologists work today— places where, as in Egypt, neoliberalism or structural adjustment policies have been adopted or where socialism is being replaced by "reform" or "transition to the market"?[41] Supporting privatization and multinational corporations does not sit easily with a governing elite's self-justification in terms of a continuing rhetoric of national development whose keystone was social development and the wider social good. These uneven political and economic transformations are linked particularly to a transformation in the worlds of consumption.

Television, I argue, plays a part in this shifting national story. In the chapters of part 3, I use television melodramas to analyze modern forms of selfhood forged at the intersection of competing discourses and projects; to explore the ambivalent reactions of the poor to the rearguard actions of television producers who attempt to invoke national culture through the mobilization of discourses of authenticity in the face of threats of globalization and Islamism; to trace out the consequences for a sense of the nation of the heavy-handed responses by state media and the intelligentsia to the challenge of the religious extremism and communal conflict that seemed to threaten the Egyptian nation; and to note the uneven development of the consumerism and extremes of wealth and poverty associated with the new economic policies. In these studies of the genre of melodrama, serials that seek to construct a national cultural identity, serials that focus on religion, and the advertisements and glitzy serials that have increasingly come to dominate television, I attempt to uncover the particular cleavages, exclusions, and forces at work in the Egyptian nation today and the relationship of television to internal national politics.

METHODS FOR THE ETHNOGRAPHY OF NATIONAL TELEVISION

Even if we grant that television is a central institution that can help one grasp the dynamics of national life, how can one possibly claim to write an ethnography of such a vast and complex object as the nation as it shifts over time? How should we do ethnography in or of nations, in a world of nation-states, and in a world where the nation is a powerful frame for the imagination? In an early programmatic statement on the subject, Lloyd Fallers asserted, in his Lewis Henry Morgan Lectures published in 1974, that anthropology was "the science of the sociocultural microcosm"; even when studying the nation-state, anthropologists had to concern themselves with the life-worlds of face-to-face communities of people engaged in meaningful acts within the boundaries of the nation-state.[42] As for the cleavages of class or religion, or other "primordial solidarities" that differentiated citizens, these, Fallers argued, would "appear in everyday life in the structure of the complexes of microcosms" and would "enter into the worlds of meaning which inform social interaction within microcosms."[43] They were not themselves microcosms that could be subjected to ethnography.

While holding on to the basic method of anthropology—close engagement with the everyday life-worlds of people and participant observation within particular settings—George Marcus in a more recent set of programmatic statements has articulated two useful developments for someone who would like to take up the mediated nation as her object of study. First, he has argued that a new kind of mobile ethnography "moves out from the single sites and local situations of conventional research designs to examine the circulation of cultural meanings, objects, and identities in diffuse time-space."[44] Second, what he then labels as multi-sited ethnography depends on doing ethnographies of "life-worlds" in several locations—not haphazardly, but with the intention of revealing the connections among them as the logic of larger systems within which particular lives unfold. The nation, it could be argued, is such a system.

With these methodological thoughts in mind, I want to describe the fieldwork I undertook for this book. First, I took as fundamental the circulation of television programs, not in some abstract sense but in particular locations. I use the dramatic television serials of the 1990s, especially the popular and high-quality productions shown during the Ramadan months (but always rerun later), to explore the role of television in national debates about key social and political issues and in the lives and imaginations of two groups who could be considered as living at the margins of the nation: women in a village in the disadvantaged region of Upper Egypt and women who work, out of necessity, as domestic servants in Cairo. I do not speculate about such things as whether television as a technology shapes affect, attention, brain waves, modes of perception, or senses of the self. Nor do I want to write about how it reshapes social life in general, atomizing society or binding individuals into deterritorialized communities, although these are worthy subjects.[45] Rather, following the lead of viewers and producers of television dramas, I take seriously the content of television programs, especially the dramatic plots, characters, and emotions, in the conviction that since these are the aspects of television serials with which viewers themselves are imaginatively engaged and in which writers and directors invest enormous creative effort, they deserve our attention. As I explore in much more detail in the next chapter, I ask about how these messages circulate from Cairo television studios to various types of homes, from particular producers to particular audiences.

I chose to concentrate on a single genre of television programming in Egypt for similar reasons, guided by the people with whom I have been working. There is little doubt that the dramatic serials, a genre begun in the 1960s that—unlike long-running American, Australian, or British soap operas, or even the more finite Brazilian or Mexican telenovelas, whose episodes reach over a hundred—generally consists of fifteen episodes (though running to thirty when intended for Ramadan broadcast) broadcast on consecutive evenings, are the most popular television shows in Egypt and the Arab world. They are rivaled only by films (shown on but until recently not made for television) and, for men, by the more sporadically televised national and international soccer matches. Not only do people watch in vast numbers, as people in other parts of the world watch their counterparts—American, British, and Australian soap operas, telenovelas in Latin America, and teleserials in India—but these serials are the subject of commentary in the press, as well as on television and radio. Unlike many other Egyptian television programs, the serials are exported to other Arab countries and now broadcast on satellite, where they reach beyond to Europe and the United States. In London or New Jersey, one can even rent videos of the serials.

Although the televisual texts, with the messages they contain, are central to my analysis, as they are in the work of other anthropologists who have studied television serials, such as Purnima Mankekar, who has written a study of Indian teleserials (including religious ones), my approach is not literary but ethnographic and social.[46] I am most interested in how the television texts articulate with what we might, in another moment, have thought of as their contexts but, as Arvind Rajagopal indicates, might better be thought of as "inter-animating" each other.[47] These contexts are of different orders, but all of them are amenable to ethnographic study. I have chosen to do fieldwork in multiple sites that are deeply significant for any argument about the Egyptian nation. I do not presume the existence of abstract forces like the world system, capitalism, or fascism as either contexts or determinants, as even someone as sophisticated as Adorno does in his ruminations on the culture industry.[48] Instead, I look for a variety of more localizable and tangible contexts that reveal what the Egyptian nation is and illuminate television's place in it. These include immediate viewing contexts, contexts of television production in studios and intellectual and literary worlds, social contexts of village or urban life in the Egyptian nation-state with its own governmental institutions, and contexts of a less face-to-face and partly imaginative national life, accessed through public forms including newspapers and other media and through people's talk, whether about the stars or the stories.

The method advocated by many media ethnographers like Lull, Morley, and Silverstone is to study the local or immediate viewing contexts of television, getting a sense of the place of television in viewing situations and everyday social lives.[49] As Ien Ang, one of the most compelling advocates of the ethnographic turn in media studies, argues, we need to ask how "people encounter, use, interpret, enjoy, think and talk about television," looking at microsituations and actual audiences.[50] The problem is that these immediate local contexts are so varied that not one of them could stand in for the whole or give a picture of what television means in a country like Egypt. In my field notes and memories are situations as varied as the following: (1) As I stand in early evening on the east bank of the Nile in Luxor, waiting for the ferry to take us across, I see one of the tourist cruise boats moored. On the upper deck, a young European couple gaze at the setting sun, arm in arm. Down below, the music of the popular evening serial *Hilmiyya Nights* has drawn all the young male Egyptian crew. From the ferry dock a local woman in black strains to watch the distant screen. (2) On a winter evening I join our village neighbors to watch the new serial in their mud brick home. I find the adult women of the household sitting on the floor together, sifting flour that has just come back in large sacks from the mill. The flicker of the television screen and the faint illumination of a bare light bulb reveal that each shakes a large sieve. Their faces are ghostly with flour dust as they watch an odd serial set in a circus. There is a poignancy to the event, since this serial had suddenly been aired in place of a serial about Upper Egypt that they had been looking forward to: its star, Karam Mutawi', had just passed away. In his role of a professor, this actor gives a speech about art and beauty that is as incongruous in this harsh setting as the lions and trapeze artists of the circus. (3) One afternoon in a modern Cairo apartment with a tree or two rustling outside, an American-trained Egyptian architect runs from her modern kitchen into the living room to videotape a new serial she wants to follow, set in Upper Egypt. Her son plays computer games in the next room. (4) On a high floor in Maspero, the building that houses the television and radio bureaucracy as well as the old studios, the head of the Production Sector responsible for serials and entertainment watches multiple screens simultaneously and anxiously grills everyone who comes into his office about which serials they are watching this Ramadan.

As if the settings for television viewing were not diverse enough, there are also variations in viewer habits, even among the same viewers. Often when I watched television with a large village family in Upper Egypt, they would laugh and comment on what was going on; sometimes they were completely silent. Frequently they would lounge with their feet up or sit on the ground; at other times, when they had a guest, for example, they might sit up primly on benches, the young women turning their heads slightly so as not to be too visible. Sometimes the adults might talk over the sound of the television, ignoring it; sometimes they would all watch in silence.

It is impossible to generalize even about the social configurations in which people watch television. In Egypt, they tend to watch with their families at home; but there are also many public settings in which television sets are on: doormen in the cities watch with their colleagues from their street-level rooms, shopkeepers watch with their customers, cafés often have a television going, and friends get together to watch at each others' homes. Unlike U.S. soap operas, the Egyptian television serials are not primarily aimed at and watched by women; women may be more attached to the shows and more likely to watch regularly, but men watch as well, and the major Ramadan serials tend to have wide and mixed followings, as evidenced by the critical discussions and debates, primarily among men, that flow from them in the newspapers and magazines. Except for a minority who claim to disapprove of television in general, some because they are intellectuals and some because they are insistently pious, only a bad serial, work demands, or organized socializing keeps people away from their sets. And though there is no way to judge the kinds of statistics thrown around, television sets are to be found in anywhere from 70% to 93% of households. This is partly a function of the labor migration to Iraq, Jordan, and the Gulf states in the 1980s, even though many of the poor have to buy theirs on credit and still had to make do with black and white, at least in the early 1990s.

So, these immediate viewing contexts, fascinating as they are, are neither sufficient nor sufficiently interesting. Therefore, I tried to explore more fully the relationship between particular television serials and the everyday worlds in which people live their lives by using the discussions and commentary on programs that occurred outside of viewing times, among people or with me directly. Gillespie has described this as TV talk.[51] Moreover, I have not hesitated to draw associations and analyze relationships that I observe between everyday lives and what people are watching on television, even when no individual commented specifically on the program. As Ang has recognized, even if we are interested in the microsituations of actual audiences, we have to realize that television is regulated by institutions (in Egypt, broadcast and government) and by what she calls "traces of cultural positionings and identifications that people 'bring into' and actualize within concrete situations . . . as well as cultural ideologies as to the meaning of television as a social and aesthetic phenomenon." [52]

The most radical departure from my previous research is in the variety of locations in which I worked. Although my most intimate and grounded understanding of the place of television in everyday lives comes from the time I spent in a small hamlet in Upper Egypt, I interviewed many other people in connection with this project. On what is known by media scholars as the "reception" side, to get some sense of the urban poor I talked, sometimes at great length and over the period of a decade, with women working as domestics in Cairo. Socially and economically marginal like the rural villagers and yet close to and personally familiar with the urban worlds depicted in the serials, such women provided glimpses of another important "fragment" of the nation. Mostly I talked with them as individuals, though occasionally with a small group of friends. I never set up focus groups, ethnographic or not.[53] Reading the national press on the subject of television serials provided access to the national public sphere, a sphere peopled by the educated middle class and the intelligentsia. Although I did not have the time, qualifications, or inclination to do an ethnography of television production, to demystify the production process I attended some script readings and shooting sessions and interviewed numerous television personnel including bureaucrats, writers, directors, and actors, all in Cairo. Luckily, producers can be accessed also through their creative products, and thus my method of examining the aesthetics and messages of television drama can be considered an important aspect of my research on an urban intelligentsia bound in complex and sometimes adversarial ways to the government.

The "sites" of my ethnography are obviously deeply incommensurate. However unevenly studied, though, they can at least illuminate the tensions of national life by marking, as I explore more fully in chapter 2, crucial nodes in a circuit. Although unable to match the wonderfully complex and multi-sited ethnographies of science, such as Emily Martin's work on AIDS and Rayna Rapp's on amniocentesis, I hope that my juxtapositions will allow what Marcus calls "an explicit, posited logic of association or connection . . . that in fact defines the argument of the ethnography." [54] The argument goes something like this: the nation is an often tense intersection of multiple communities or microcosms, divided and crosscut by region, religious affiliation, urban or rural habits, class, gender, and power. National television is imbricated in deeply political efforts to make nations into legitimate units, dominated by particular groups and with specific images of and visions for themselves and for their citizens.

TOWARD AN ANTHROPOLOGY OF NATIONAL MEDIA

Anthropologists have only recently begun to attend to forms of mass media like television, despite the fact that media technologies have been with us for quite some time and have increasingly infiltrated the everyday worlds of even the "remotest" groups, whether Amazonian Indians or Australian aboriginals.[55] As much as the spread of mass and small media around the globe, the shifts in the intellectual terrain of anthropological theory and research have set the stage for this endeavor. As part of the creation of an "anthropology of the present"[56] or an "anthropology of contemporary change and transformation,"[57] an earlier interest in kinship systems has been displaced by the study of gender or redirected by the unsettling possibilities opened up by the new reproductive technologies; the study of religion and cosmology transformed into the analysis of communal politics or fundamentalist ideologies; the comparative study of political systems replaced by explorations of the cultural construction of ethnicity, the meaning (or not) of violence, the workings of governmentality, or the interactions among local, national, and transnational organizations; and the study of cultures as wholes, and even culture itself, put under suspicion for homogenizing and fixing groups, denying people their histories, reifying practices, and exoticizing.[58] Culture is set aside in favor of explorations of internal differences, such as those based on race or other forms of identity, historical transformations, or the link between power and the making of culture and cultures. Finally, in recognition of the importance of technology to the lives of all, whether scientists working in laboratories or indigenous groups contesting pharmaceutical companies who want to patent what is in their environment, the anthropology of science has taken off.

The anthropology of media, rejecting the tradition/modernity dichotomy and the disciplinary division of labor that oriented anthropological work, has risen from the ashes of these critiques and on the wings of these new possibilities—based on a recognition that we all are "modern" and that mediascapes, to use Arjun Appadurai's confection, lie within the purview of this discipline that claims contemporary humanity as its object.[59] But what significance to give to media and how to study it anthropologically are still being worked out. This book is a contribution to that effort, one that focuses not on mass media's technological innovations or its transnational circulation but on its national dimension.

Running through the text is the question of effects that persistently haunts all those who produce and study media and is, in the end, unanswerable.[60] In this case, how effective are state media products in achieving their hegemonic goals of influencing audiences and incorporating them into national life on their own terms? It will become clear from the close examination of serials and lives to follow that we need to reframe the question. Assessing the impact of television, or any cultural or ideological apparatus, is difficult. Instead, we would do better to explore the multiple levels at which failures and successes occur by studying the social fields that structure these engagements and the actual ways that people and groups relate to media. Anthropologists have revealed ironies such as the way commercial broadcasts uncontrolled by the state or not linked directly to state interests can have the unintended consequences of bolstering national identity or pride.[61] But they have also examined the way particular programs or projects have backfired.[62] In the final chapter of this book, I consider carefully the special nature of national forms like the television serials that are the subjects of this book—forms that are meant to entertain while they teach and that use complex means, including actors who become celebrities, to mobilize fantasies, pleasure, and emotion, sometimes undermining their own intentions with their excess. What this study of national media can do is to trace both how and why media messages go awry and yet how the television serials that are so central in Egypt do shape lives and may help create a national habitus, recognizing that television is generated out of complex interests and that audiences are neither resistant heroes to be celebrated nor duped victims to be pitied. I have tried to trace these processes through an ethnography of the multiple microcosms and various subjects of one nation in flux, as a contribution to our understanding of mass media and the processes, powers, and resistances that produce nations and national subjects.

Although I recognize that no nation is isolated and that, perhaps more than ever, the boundaries of nations are fluid, I am convinced from my study of television in Egypt that we must remain concerned with the nation. This is not because territorial boundaries are natural or define entities with certain characters but because "the nation" continues to be a powerful concept, internally and externally in the world of nation-states and because the nation-state remains the primary context, at least in Egypt, for the everyday lives and imaginations of most of the people who produce media and constitute their audiences. Even if people consider themselves to belong primarily to (and to engage with media as) subnational or transnational communities, and nations are always in contact with other nations and transnational entities or ideas (and may, as anthropologists Arjun Appadurai and Ulf Hannerz along with others argue, be losing sovereignty and power), the national is still a potent frame of reference, especially in the many countries where the state has been the prime actor in the creation and regulation of media.[63]

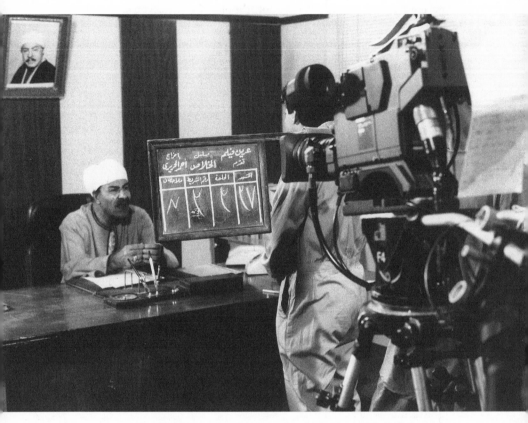

Shooting a scene of a privately produced television serial, *Al-khalas* (Deliverance), written by Fathiyya al-'Assal and directed by Ahmad al-Hariri, Zamalek. Cairo. Lila Abu-Lughod/Anthro-Photo.

[2]

Interpreting Culture(s) after Television
On Method

IF I WERE TO OPEN, as Clifford Geertz did one of his most celebrated (not to mention controversial) essays, with a story about how I began my fieldwork in the village, there would be telling differences.[1] I would confess that rather than walking around the Upper Egyptian village with the feeling that people were looking through us as if we were "gusts of wind," my spouse and I were immediately recognized and firmly placed—in a social network of Canadian, American, and French scholars, journalists, and archaeologists whom the villagers had known. On the west bank of the Nile and a ferry ride from Luxor, the hamlet was in and among the Pharaonic temples that for over a century archaeologists had been unearthing and tourists—now in air-conditioned buses or riding donkeys or bicycles—had been admiring.

When I arrived in the spring of 1990, the friendly welcome I received was also due to intense curiosity. Here finally was "the wife." My husband had preceded me there, following the trail of an American writer who in 1978 had published a popular life story of a village youth. This was a story that had (too) closely echoed earlier accounts by Jesuits and Orientalists of "the Egyptian peasant," a timeless creature of habit and violence.[2] My husband had sought out a few individuals whom a friend of ours from Cairo, a folklorist writing a dissertation on Upper Egyptian funeral laments, had told him about and to whom she had sent greetings. He had made a special point of meeting Zaynab, whose household had been our friend's haven.[3]

I, in turn, found Zaynab serious and gracious. Her weathered face and unkempt hair, peeking out from her patterned black head shawl, betrayed exposure to the sun and the pressures of being a mother of six (at that time) whose husband had migrated to the city. She asked for news of her folklorist friend, as she would do every time I arrived in the village over the next decade, whether from Cairo or the United States. I shared what information I had, even as I tried to distance myself from other foreigners Zaynab knew whose morals and behavior in the village could not be guaranteed. I emphasized my half-Palestinian identity to distinguish myself. But in the end, Zaynab knew I was from the world of the foreigners she had met, and she took advantage of our time together to improve her understanding of fellowships, dissertations, the cost of living in the United States, research, and books, among other more troubling aspects of Euro-American life. I was a message bearer and informant as well as a researcher.

In my story of rapport, moreover, instead of Geertz's description of a dramatic police raid on an illegal cockfight that people passionately cared about, I would have to make do with telling of the quiet pleasure of recognition that Zaynab and her children, like most families, evinced when I professed an interest in television. Would I like to watch? They brought out their little television set. They apologized, as they fiddled with its homemade aerial, because it was black and white. And they invited me to come watch with them any evening, pitying me for not having access to a television set of my own. Television bonded us. And this bond began to separate me from other foreigners, people who generally, as the villagers knew, did not follow the Egyptian television melodramas they loved.

THICK DESCRIPTION, STILL . . .

Despite the differences my story suggests in the kinds of worlds people now inhabit (more interconnected) and, not unrelated, the kinds of subjects anthropologists find worth studying (mass media), I want to argue that Geertz's call for thick description as the method of ethnography is still compelling.[4] But it needs some creative stretching to fit mass-mediated lives.

Many of the studies of popular culture, and especially television, that I have come across are disappointing. They do not seem to be trying to offer profound insights into the human condition, or even into the social, cultural, and political dynamics of particular communities—goals anthropology has always, perhaps with hubris, set for itself. Is it the object, television, that thwarts us? We are not dealing with intricate rituals or complex kinship systems, or even with histories and structures of conjuncture in colonial moments, all of which have deep traditions in the discipline. Television partakes of the ephemerality of the postmodern and is associated, whether here or there, as Geertz likes to put it, with the kind of ordinary people some call the masses.[5] It is also associated with either commercial entertainment or state propaganda, both always suspect. Does the taint of lowbrow status and the apparent banality of television rub off on those who study it? Or is it, as Jean Baudrillard might have it, that in a world of simulation and simulacra, of which television is such a conspicuous part, notions like the human condition have become hopelessly obsolete?[6]

I would like to argue something else here: that we are only beginning to find the right point of entry for the ethnographic work—in the field and in our studies—that it would take to draw out the significance of television's existence as a ubiquitous presence in the lives and imaginaries of people in the contemporary world. In a recent review of some studies of "resistance," Sherry Ortner diagnosed their weaknesses as being caused by "ethnographic refusal." This strikes me as an apt diagnosis for media studies as well. If there is one theme that has dominated the study of media, especially television, in the last two decades, it is resistance. And if there is one thing that can be said about these studies, it is that despite their considerable theoretical sophistication they are ethnographically thin, rarely giving a larger sense of the lives and concerns of the people who are the media consumers.[7]

Ironically, for the last decade in cultural studies, the calls for ethnography as the solution have been insistent. Janice Radway's study of romance readers is hailed as a classic that proved the value of ethnography in analyzing popular culture.[8] Yet researchers seem reluctant to heed the call. Books with promising titles like *Television and Everyday Life* intelligently criticize the finest examples of what are known in the business as reception and audience studies and propose that more ethnographic (and psychoanalytic) case studies are needed. The author of this particular book then argues that "an enquiry into the audience should be an enquiry, not into a set of preconstituted individuals or rigidly defined social groups, but into a set of daily practices and discourses within which the complex act of watching television is placed alongside others, and through which that complex act is itself constituted."[9] The book's author, however, does nothing of the sort. Making appropriate excuses, he avoids the practical engagement this would require in order to pursue some (culture-bound) general theorizing about suburbia, modernity, and domesticity. When researchers do pursue ethnography, as one of the most persuasive and subtle advocates of "the ethnographic turn" admits, they use a notion of ethnography that little resembles the anthropological ideal.[10]

What can anthropologists offer when we begin to take television seriously? In her early overview of the emergent field of the anthropology of media, Debra Spitulnik claimed that anthropologists "have in some way already bypassed many of the debates within media studies . . . because they implicitly theorize media processes, products, and uses as complex parts of social reality, and expect to locate media power and value in a more diffuse, rather than direct and causal, sense." [11] In her "(mild) polemic" on the same subject, Faye Ginsburg locates anthropologists' distinctiveness in their less ethnocentric stance, their attention to the contexts of media texts, and their recognition of "the complex ways in which people are engaged in processes of making and interpreting media works in relation to their cultural, social and historical circumstances." [12]

And indeed, the theoretical arguments by anthropologists for careful ethnography—ethnography that illuminates what Brian Larkin calls "the social space" of television—are promising. [13] In a powerful analysis of the politics and interpretations of a television soap opera that gripped China in 1991, Lisa Rofel argues that ethnography—defined as "attention to the contingent way in which all social categories emerge, become naturalized, and intersect in people's conception of themselves and their world, and further, an emphasis on how these categories are produced through everyday practice," is necessary to the study of encounters with media because "the moments of immersion in a particular cultural artifact are necessarily enmeshed within other social fields of meaning and power." [14] Drawing more directly on the insights of cultural studies, Purnima Mankekar's first article on women television viewers in New Delhi, India, showed how "their interpretations are profoundly influenced by the broader social discourses [primarily those on gender and nationalism] in which they are interpellated; they are shaped by events in the viewers' lives and by the relationships in which those viewers define themselves." [15]

But just how do we trace this enmeshment of television in other social fields? [16] The key, I would argue, is to experiment with ways of placing television more seamlessly within the sort of rich social and cultural context that the sustained anthropological fieldwork that has been our ideal since Bronislaw Malinowski is uniquely able to provide. The special challenge we face in doing so is that the cultural forms transmitted by television have no obvious and simple community and are always only a part—sometimes larger, sometimes smaller—of people's complex lives. Moreover, they are produced deliberately for people, under conditions that vary politically and historically.

Anthropologists are probably best prepared to study what in media studies is narrowly called reception. But how can we get more than a fragmentary sense of the everyday lives, social connections, and concerns of the people interviewed, or of the diversity of viewing communities?[17] What we often have is only the anecdote or the fragmentary quotation of a decontextualized television watcher. In the more thorough audience studies by media researchers, on the other hand, how can we get more than a partial sense of the everyday lives, social connections, concerns, and complexities of the people quoted, not to mention of the much larger group who consume the cultural forms and share the nation or community?

Television's messages, I will argue throughout this book, are deflected by the way people frame their television experiences and by the way powerful everyday realities inflect and offset those messages.[18] Roger Silverstone's image of the television audience as positioned in multiple spaces and times suggests how daunting the task of fully contextualizing television is. He notes that people "live in different overlapping but not always overdetermining spaces and times: domestic spaces; national spaces; broadcasting and narrowcasting spaces; biographical times; daily times; scheduled, spontaneous but also socio-geological times."[19] Which means we should somehow try to include these various spaces and times in our thick descriptions of people who watch television.

Yet even this is not enough. Anthropologists cannot dispense with "textual" analysis, the equivalent of the symbolic analyses of rituals and myths that have illuminated so much. Even more important, they need to do ethnographies of production. Television programs are produced not just by specialists of a different social status than viewers, like priests and bards, but by professionals of a different class—often urban, rather than rural, with national and sometimes transnational identities and social ties—who are working within structures of power and organizations that are tied to and doing the work of national or commercial interests. For a truly thick description, we need to find ways to interrelate these various nodes of the "social life of television."[20]

When I argue that part of the solution to the thinness of studies of popular culture lies in returning to the insights of Geertz's "Thick Description," I do not mean that our goal is necessarily the same as his was—to develop an interpretive theory of culture or to translate cultures—even though I share Geertz's faith that a good analysis demonstrates "the power of the scientific imagination to bring us in touch with the lives of strangers."[21] Rather, I think we need to recall that when Geertz calls for microscopic ethnographic description, he justifies these "protracted descriptions" of distant events as—to borrow a phrase from someone he considers irredeemably wrongheaded—good to think. Thick descriptions of social discourses in particular places have general relevance, he argues, because "they present the sociological mind with bodied stuff on which to feed." With their specific knowledges, anthropologists can think intelligently about, and imaginatively with, the megaconcepts of social science.[22] Or of the humanities, one might now add. Along the same lines, Geertz warns that though anthropologists often study *in* villages, they don't study villages. They confront the same grand realities and big words as other social scientists—but in homely locations and forms.[23]

Extending these ideas, I want to suggest that we can still profit from trying to use careful contextualizations of small facts and events—in this case of television consumption in particular places, including homely villages in Upper Egypt—to help us reflect on some big issues, particularly those concerning the nation-state. If television seems banal, then one of Michel Foucault's most memorable phrases should inspire us: "What we have to do with banal facts is to discover—or try to discover—which specific and perhaps original problem is connected with them."[24]

In this chapter, I will focus on one of the problems that stories about women and television in an Upper Egyptian village can speak to (or be made to speak to, as Geertz reminds us): the nature of "culture," and "cultures" under the conditions of what many would call postcolonial postmodernity. This chapter will also explore more fully a method for studying national media, offering a kind of appropriate technology of media studies. In later chapters, the focus will shift to issues of national pedagogy and the changing configurations of power and culture in Egypt. Yet I also want, in this chapter, to begin to show why the study of television, especially in places like Egypt, where it is tied up with national projects, encourages an anthropology that engages not just with academic questions but with other social fields of the world in which we work.

CULTURAL TEXTS AND "MULTI-SITED" ETHNOGRAPHY[25]

In January 1996, when I was on a short visit to the Upper Egyptian village I had been working in intermittently since 1990, I watched with various friends some episodes of the current television serial, *Ummahat fi bayt al-hubb* (Mothers in the house of love), which is set in a retirement home for women. The program's central drama concerns an attempt by the unscrupulous brother-in-law of the widow who runs the place to take it over so he can achieve his dream of building a twenty-two-story hotel. Armed with a newfound purpose, the women residents band together to defend their threatened home. They forget their squabbles about which television programs to watch, mobilize their talents to raise the money to buy out his share, and stand up to him.

The serial had been written a few years earlier by Fathiyya al-'Assal, a vibrant and self-confident writer, and one of only a handful of women of her generation writing television dramas in Egypt. Active in the Egyptian leftist party, she had occasionally been jailed and had had numerous story ideas tabled and serials cancelled by the television censors—civil servants working for state-owned television—and even by those higher up in the government. Her serials were known for their social concerns, and she considered women's issues critical. She had also done some ethnography in a retirement home to make her script more realistic.

How to study the encounter between some Upper Egyptian village women and this television serial? With television programs, one is forced to talk not so much about cultures-as-texts, as Geertz might have, as about discrete cultural texts that are produced, circulated, and consumed. Thick description of television therefore invites, as I argued earlier, a multi-sited ethnography wherein, as George Marcus has put it regarding commodities in a world system, one can "follow the thing." [26] The relevant system here is national, rather than global. Therefore, I will start with the villagers and their responses to the television serial, using this close look at one serial to introduce them and open up the basic structures and meanings in their lives. But I also want to keep tracing the serial back to Cairo, where it was produced in a very different milieu by a leftist intellectual and some urban professionals working with and against a state-controlled medium and with imagined audiences for their work. This approach will, in the end, allow us some insight into the dynamics of the culture of national television.

I watched several episodes of *Mothers in the House of Love* with my neighbors, who, though intrigued, kept up a running commentary, laughing at ludicrous characters like the compulsive knitter of pullovers. Although viewers know perfectly well that television characters are fictional stereotypes, they still respond to the dilemmas they face and use them to talk about life. After an episode in which a widow finally consents to marry an old sweetheart, one person joked, "Now all sixty-year-old women will want to marry." The next day, though, Zaynab commented more realistically on the episode, simply contrasting it with local attitudes. "We say when a girl is past thirty she won't marry. . . . It is shameful. If a woman over thirty does marry, she'll do it quietly, far away, without a wedding celebration."

Zaynab's comment was revealing in so many ways. Directed at me, it posited the difference between the villagers (and Upper Egyptians in general, by extension) and the urban, wealthy Alexandrian women of the television serial as a cultural difference within a moral frame. This construction of difference was partly for the edification of the anthropologist. Zaynab's long years of watching her mother's wealth of funeral laments being carefully noted by our folklorist friend as well as her regular experiences of being photographed by tourists had no doubt helped her objectify her own culture. Her gifts to me over the years suggested she had learned her lessons well. Her first gift was a crude earthenware casserole dish of the sort locally made and used. The second was a traditional piece of black cloth, offered with the confident announcement that she had got me something I would really like, something rare nowadays. The third was a black shawl, the latest local design for what "traditional" women wore on their heads. Each represented something unique to Upper Egypt and something that those eager to become more sophisticated—like her daughter—would have rejected as old-fashioned.

Yet for Zaynab, a woman very much at home in her social world, a little old before her time and confident as one of the adult women of the village who took her social duties—sick visits and funerals, for example—very seriously, the cultural differences within which she framed her response to the serial were also personally meaningful. Her own experience of marriage was very different from what she saw on television. Like most women in the village, she had had an arranged marriage—but, following the lines of closest practical kinship, it was to a maternal, not a paternal, cousin. Zaynab's mother had been a second and younger wife, widowed shortly after she gave birth to her only child. Not close to her own husband's patrilineage, she had turned to her relatives for support and eventually for a husband for her daughter. She had inherited from her father some land, on which she and Zaynab later built a two-story mud-brick home. Zaynab's husband had worked on and off in Cairo since he was fourteen, leaving her mostly alone with her mother to raise her children. Secretly, he had married a second wife in Cairo; Zaynab now knew about this and was resigned to the fact that he would probably never return to live in the village.

As the years went by and Zaynab had more children, conceived on her husband's visits home, she had a harder time coping. It was tough as her milk dried up after she gave birth to twins. Not long after that, she and her mother were forced to sell all their livestock because they couldn't take care of them. Then her mother died, leaving Zaynab on her own.

One cannot ignore the possibility that Zaynab had remarked on the episode of the older widow's wedding because it was meaningful to her own personal situation. She was alone, managing a complex household, and her children provided her with her only company most evenings (when they all watched television together). She had no man to help her make decisions about the children's schooling, about what crops to plant and harvest on which strips of land, and about which domestic livestock to buy or sell. For help with the work in the fields, she had to call on young male relatives or pay for labor. Certainly she had no one for companionship or love. She said about her husband's visits home: "He's like a guest; he doesn't know anything about our lives."

In fact, a recurrent theme in my conversations with Zaynab was the situation of the older women from Switzerland, Germany, and the United States, who had married—or had affairs with—local village youths they met while on holiday. Some were divorcées with grown children, as Zaynab noted. Using me as an informant about the strange behavior of foreigners, she would ask me how these women could do it. She was puzzled about how their behavior might be acceptable, especially to their children. She was not the only village woman to talk to me about this phenomenon, but I wondered if her curiosity about these older women who had had second lives, second chances at love or sex, might not have had a special resonance. Nevertheless, as a woman whose respectability rested on her marriage, she distanced herself in moral language from what she perceived as a cultural difference between life here, in Upper Egyptian villages, and there, in Alexandria, Cairo, or other cities.

Zaynab could not even begin to recognize that for the Cairene writer of *Mothers in the House of Love,* a progressive activist engaged in arguments with more conservative intellectuals and politicians, this episode about the value of love in the face of social pressure was not meant as a simple portrayal of the middle-class values of Alexandrian society but as a universally applicable revolutionary alternative to enhance women's status and lives.

Another serial of which al-'Assal was proud was about a woman who, rejected by her husband because she is uneducated, goes out and gets herself an education. When her husband then wants to take her back, she refuses, even though they have a son together. Al-'Assal said of this serial, "My point was to emphasize the value of a home as a home. That is to say, a man and woman should only enter on condition that they love one another." [27] Marriage, she contended, should be first and foremost about mutual understanding and love. She contrasted her ideas about companionate marriage with prevailing values that place financial considerations first. Her reference point was urban and middle class and her views were those of the most progressive and modernist end of a continuum. While the ideal of the bourgeois couple and some version of the idea of companionate marriage have been increasingly idealized and realized by the middle classes in twentieth-century Egypt, Al-'Assal's stress on the equality of husband and wife was meant to be more radical than the mainstream middle-class vision.[28] Yet Zaynab's marriage did not even fit the ordinary middle-class ideal; the vocabulary of rights to love and personal happiness was foreign to her.

There are other examples of how the serials both raised relevant issues for village viewers and yet were inassimilable because of fundamental differences of perspective related to social location. In one of the first conversations I had while watching television with Zaynab, she animatedly told me about the program that had just come on the air. This extraordinary weekly interview show, which was to be removed from the air a few years later, was called *Al-muwajaha* (The confrontation) and consisted of interviews—more like interrogations—of actual criminals serving prison sentences. Imitating the Cairene dialect, Zaynab recounted a memorable interview with a woman drug dealer. When the interviewer asked if she would do it again, the woman had replied, "Of course. As soon as I get out I'll deal in drugs again." Asked why, she replied, "I have to eat." Zaynab added that the woman had become used to a certain way of life and so had to keep it up. Zaynab quoted her again, "They'll jail me and I'll get out and deal. They'll put me in prison, I'll get out and do it again. That's how I make a living."

That Zaynab found this female criminal so compelling seems as significant as the fact that she responded to the television theme of marriage at a late age. The woman drug dealer, trying to make a living, must have represented something intriguing for this person of great integrity insulted by any hint of disrespect. Zaynab's whole life was organized around trying to feed herself and her family—in the larger sense of managing a household and educating, clothing, and raising her children. She farmed three small plots of land (each far apart from the others), as well as raising sheep, a water buffalo, chickens, ducks, and pigeons. She baked bread. Work and economic struggles were the most persistent themes in her conversations with others and the main concerns in her day-to-day life.

The television serial we watched in January (*Mothers in the House of Love*) also treated this theme. But the way women's work and usefulness were framed made them awkward for someone like Zaynab to assimilate. One of al-'Assal's goals in writing this serial was to show that perceptions of "old age" and "senility" in women were, at least in part, the result of their not having had any social role. As she put it,

I wanted to create a new role for older women. . . . In the retirement home itself, they started a class for teaching English, because one woman had been an English professor; another woman who had been a silversmith opened a small silver workshop and taught women the skills needed for this work. They participated in the eradication of illiteracy by teaching neighborhood girls to read and write. They also gave classes on household management, and even agriculture. . . . My message is that women can still learn at this age, and we can still benefit from what they have to teach us as well.

The dynamic Cairene writer claimed to speak from her own experience, explaining,

I am sixty years old now. In the past, when a woman was sixty she was supposed to sit at home waiting to die, having already married off her children. I now have four children and eight grandchildren, but because I have my own concerns and ambitions as a writer and a politician, I do not feel that I am getting older. I wanted to communicate this in a serial.[29]

Al-'Assal's socialist feminist message—advocating socially useful roles for women, skills and activities that could take them beyond their place in the family and home, and economic independence that would alleviate the worst effects of male domination—is impressive. Going somewhat against the grain of current conservative sentiments being voiced in the media and Parliament in favor of women's return to the home (at a time when large numbers of women must work out of financial necessity and professional careers are common), this politically motivated position is underwritten by Al-'Assal's own anger. Her father was a wealthy businessman who, very unusually, had married twenty different women after his marriage to (and eventual divorce from) her mother, a housewife without the power to object. Al-'Assal was determined to become educated herself and still believes in education as the key for women—and for social progress. Historically, this is a political position that had its origins at the turn of the century, when elite and some middle-class reformists (both male and female) began advocating women's education. But it was given real support by Nasserist programs to provide mass education in the 1960s.[30] It was in that era that Al-'Assal began her career as a serial writer—when she found that the students she was teaching to read and write would desert the classroom to listen, with the janitor, to the melodramatic serials on the radio. She still tries to work the importance of literacy into many of her plots (as do others, as the analysis of a television film about a domestic servant's infatuation with school in chapter 4 shows) and proudly told me about one serial she wrote about a woman of fifty whose husband has run off with another woman, leaving her with no skills or identity. As al-'Assal described it,

It was about how she was able to deal with life, how she refused to ever return to be-ing the wife of so-and-so, how she had to become a person in her own right, how she worked in a publishing house and read and expanded her horizons, and finally how she wrote stories and won a prize for them. The serial ended up on that note, in or-der to show how she was able to win the prize herself—she was the sole master of the victory.[31]

How might a theme like becoming literate affect Zaynab? Just the year before *Mothers in the House of Love* was broadcast, government-sponsored literacy classes for women had been set up in and around her village. At-tending was out of the question for someone as busy as Zaynab. Women went for a variety of reasons, but all those who attended had two things in common: they had no children (or only a few that someone else could watch for a while) and their family situations were such that they could be released from work for a few hours in the afternoon.

When I went to pay a visit to Umm Ahmad, another woman I knew and liked, to make conversation I asked if she was going to the classes. With her eyes bright and a big smile, she said she really wanted to; she was dying to learn to read and she hated it that she couldn't even sign her own name (she had been trying to collect her recently deceased father's pension). "But can I learn?" she asked me dubiously. "No, I'm too old. I've got no brain," she laughed. Then she added, "An old woman—why, they'll talk. They'll say, 'Why does she need to go and learn?'" I asked her who would talk, and she said, "The men. The men will talk."[32]

When her son, a young man in his early thirties and the father of two young children, walked into the room, I teased, "Hey, you should let her go to the literacy classes." He replied, "Fine, that's fine. She can go." Turning to her with a smile, he added, "In fact, I'll get you a book bag." This was an amusing idea, since village women never carry satchels or handbags. If they go to market or visiting, they carry a basket on their heads. Otherwise, what they need is tucked inside their long black overdresses. Only schoolchildren and city people carry bags.

But Umm Ahmad was no downtrodden, superannuated old woman lacking any socially useful role or skills, as al-'Assal might have feared. She was a grandmother, but a wiry and energetic one—working in the fields, caring for her water buffalo, and selling cheese and butter locally. Her situation was somewhat unusual, but in my experience everyone's story in the village was unique. She had had a bad marriage and returned to live in her father's household. She had only one son, who, also unusually, lived with her and worked her father's fields while holding a night job as a guard at a nearby Pharaonic temple. For years she had taken care of her father, who was in poor health and not always lucid. A founder of the hamlet in which they lived, he had been an important figure. Umm Ahmad had been in charge of running her father's household and farming enterprise, especially the livestock, while her son was growing up as well as after he left, desperate for income, to work briefly for a Lebanese-owned chicken-breeding outfit near Alexandria.

What significance could a group of wealthy or formerly wealthy women, sitting around a comfortable retirement home and suddenly putting aside their individual troubles and overcoming their sense of helplessness and uselessness, have for Umm Ahmad? What about the modernist feminist ideal of women's rights to education and a meaningful career, or at least socially useful work? What about the idea of winning a prize for writing? Umm Ahmad had to contend with a gender system that constrained women, but this was hardly her main impediment to securing a decent life. Other concerns were more pressing: the cost of farming with more expensive fertilizer, the depressed prices the government paid for crops, the IMF-enforced lifting of subsidies for wheat that made provisioning households with bread a strain for most local families, the higher cost of living in an area where hotels catering to tourists drove up prices, the felt need to get children educated so they might find employment, and the vast inequalities between large landlords and the majority of households.

What possibilities did Umm Ahmad or other village women have for careers that would provide personal fulfillment and the financial independence necessary for a marriage based on equality when even the most educated local men might have to content themselves with being foremen at archaeological sites? Or perhaps with waiting for five or six years after graduating from teaching college for a government job as a librarian in the local high school, working for a couple of hours a day and making barely enough to pay for cigarettes (but getting benefits)?

The problem is that al-'Assal values certain ideals for women and men over others—literacy over ignorance, individual fulfillment and achievement over family unity, national development over communal integrity. This is not just because cultural producers like al-ʿAssal come from a different social class than these village women who watch her programs, though this is significant. Nor is it a matter of the difference between urban and rural experiences, however considerable. Al-ʿAssal has actually tried to bridge this kind of difference by writing a serial, *Harvest of Love,* broadcast in 1993, about rural Upper Egypt. The serial shows the cruelty and power of large landlords and the powerlessness of peasants who don't seek common cause. But the main theme is revenge (the feud), the metonym by which Upper Egypt has been known to generations of northern Egyptian writers (the violence it signifies now transferred neatly, as I explore in chapter 7, onto Muslim militants and terrorists whose strongholds are located there).[33]

Al-ʿAssal wrote this serial out of genuine concern. She even spent three months living with a rural family to prepare herself to write the script, just as she had studied a retirement home to write *Mothers in the House of Love.* As a radical politician who was later to run for office, as I describe in the conclusion, she was deeply concerned with social conditions and the terrible poverty of the region. But her focus on vengeance and the solution she offered reproduced a very old and common discourse of enlightened modernity against backward customs that continues to denigrate Upper Egyptians, men and women. The hero and heroine of the program are a young couple, a latter-day Romeo and Juliet, whose modern education and enlightened ideas lead them to reject the feud (a "backward" tradition still nurtured by older women) and to attempt to break the hold of the feudal lords (and their wives) by supporting the peasants' efforts to set up a collectively owned factory.

The trouble is that Al-ʿAssal's feminism, like her progressive politics, is part of a powerful public national discourse of reform and uplift whose contours can be traced to colonial and anticolonial nationalist efforts to transform Egypt into a modern place and whose objectives are supported by state institutions set up especially under President Nasser in the 1950s and 1960s. Tempered by ethnography and broad sympathy in al-ʿAssal's case, this general attitude of knowing what is good for "society" (seen as an object to be manipulated by one's expertise) underlies the work of many of the writers of television serials, just as it shapes the myriad projects of reform, from schooling to public health plans, in which villagers find themselves involved. In places like Egypt, television is the main instrument for the trans mission of both expertise and these public narratives of the state and the urban middle classes.[34]

Such discourses of enlightenment have their dark side. Had Umm Ahmad been able to attend her local literacy classes, she would have learned to read and write using the textbooks I describe in chapter 3, textbooks filled with didactic stories about the value of small families, neighborly cooperation, and national responsibility. Until she gets her book bag, she is subjected to this pedagogic discourse mostly by watching television, which she does. How does this discourse help her place herself? As someone who could carry a book bag? As someone whose life is different from the ones portrayed? Or as someone whose life is hopelessly inferior?

/ / /

Television makes obvious the fact that the same cultural texts have different imports in different contexts. When Zaynab interprets a scene like the marriage of a sixty-year-old as a matter of cultural difference—linked to region, way of life, and morality—this is because she is so disadvantaged in terms of class and education that she cannot fully appreciate the intentions of the more privileged creator of the program. For al-'Assal—working as an oppositional politician within the national context of a postcolonial state and arguing with fellow intellectuals, critics, and politicians in Cairo and across the Arab world while trying to reform the public—this episode was meant to represent a revolutionary and enlightened feminist option. Only a mobile ethnography can do justice to the ways these different worlds intersect in the nation. And this intersection must be part of any thick description of television and any ethnography of the nation.

This extended reflection on the encounter between some village women and a television serial has attempted to suggest how stories about book bags, marrying at sixty, and television can speak, as Geertz suggested, to megaconcepts. Taking television seriously forces us to think about "culture" not so much as a system of meaning or even a way of life but as something whose elements are produced, censored, paid for, and broadcast across a nation, even across national boundaries. The hegemonic or ideological—and thus power-related—nature of mass-mediated cultural texts in the service of national, class, or commercial projects is undeniable. This, in turn, should lead us to think about the ways that aspects of what we used to think of as local culture, such as moral values about the proper age of marriage or the pro-

priety of women's education, are themselves not neutral features to be interpreted but the sometimes contested result of other, more local, projects of
power that are worth analyzing.[35]

FROM CULTURES TO COSMOPOLITANS

More interesting, perhaps, is the way ethnographies of television—because
its cultural texts are produced elsewhere and inserted into local households,
communities, and nations—confirm for us the need to rethink the notion
of culture in the singular, as a shared set of meanings, distinct from those
held by other communities sometimes called "cultures." This observation
has become something of a commonplace in anthropology. Ulf Hannerz
uses the term *cultural complexity* and has developed a distributive theory of
culture to capture the ways that culture is not necessarily shared.[36] Critiques
of the way the culture concept has tended to homogenize communities and
create false boundaries (perhaps articulated most eloquently by James Clifford) appear in introductions to major interdisciplinary readers and in
arguments like Arjun Appadurai's that "natives"—people incarcerated in
place and in modes of thought—are fictions of the anthropological imagination.[37] They form the basis of earlier Marxist arguments like Eric Wolf's
about "the people without history."[38] In my own argument for "writing
against culture," I, too, registered discomfort with the internal homoge-
nization produced by the culture concept.[39] I explored ways to write against
the typifying of communities that results from thinking of them as "cultures," and I tried to highlight the contestatory nature of discourses within
communities.[40]

This is not to deny that the notion of having a culture, or being a culture,
has become politically crucial to many communities previously labeled
"cultures" by anthropologists—Solomon Islanders invoking *kastom*, dias-
pora Indians supporting fundamentalist religious organizations that glorify
Hindu culture, Catalonians and Jordanians setting up national or regional
folklore museums as part of what could be called the heritage industry. As
Marshall Sahlins, following Norbert Elias and others, has noted about the
origins of the culture concept, it is related to relative disadvantage. It developed in Germany, "a relatively underdeveloped region [as opposed to the
imperial and colonial powers of western Europe] and as an expression of
that comparative backwardness, or of its nationalist demands."[41] The similarities to the conditions in regions where today the idea of culture is gain-

ing currency are obvious. Appadurai has called this phenomenon "cultural-ism," in which identities are mobilized in the context of nation-states, mass mediation, migration, and globalization.[42] It is no accident that in the Up-per Egyptian village where I worked, it was Zaynab, a woman with strong ex-perience with foreigners, who knew what kinds of gifts I would appreciate: objects from a distinct local "culture." The "culturing" process is related to encounters with others, many of whom arrive already primed with notions of culture.

However, these reactive processes are balanced by many others that un-settle the boundaries of cultures. Much has been written on travel or migra-tion, which has certainly been a growing part of Upper Egyptian reality—Zaynab's husband, for example, joining generations of Upper Egyptians in the city of Cairo, long dotted with clubs devoted to migrants from particular villages. Much, too, could be written about colonialism and other forms of political and economic interpenetration. In Upper Egypt, the best examples are the royal family's large nineteenth-century estates turned to sugarcane production, which remains the major crop in this village.[43]

But television is an extraordinary technology for breaching boundaries and intensifying and multiplying encounters among life-worlds, sensibili-ties, and ideas. Television brings into Zaynab's home, her conversations, and her imagination a range of visions, ideas, perspectives, and experiences orig-inating outside her community in such places as Cairo, Alexandria, Holly-wood, Bombay, and even Tokyo. At the same time it places her in a particu-lar relation to them. And with UNESCO's 1993 estimate of more than six million television sets in Egypt, and other estimates of access putting televi-sion watching at anywhere from 93% to 98% of the population, Zaynab's ex-posure is hardly unusual.[44]

What is critical is that television's meanings are produced somewhere—for most viewers, somewhere else—and consumed locally in a variety of lo-calities. Even if it ultimately helps create something of a "national habitus," as this book argues, or hints of a transnational habitus, television is most in-teresting because of the way it provides material which is then inserted into, interpreted with, and mixed up with local but themselves socially differen-tiated knowledges, discourses, and meaning systems.[45] Television, as media theorists have amply demonstrated, does not preclude active engagement with or creative appropriations of these visions. My own work in the village has shown that individuals have different levels of attachments to the world of television, different degrees of knowledge about what they see, and dif-ferent reactions to what they watch.

Thinking about Zaynab watching Egyptian dramatic serials and films, interviews with criminals, broadcasts of Parliament in session, American soap operas, imported nature programs that take her to the Caribbean or the Serengeti Plain, and advertisements for candy, ceramic toilets, chicken stock cubes, and Coca-Cola leads me to begin thinking about her and others in this village not as members of some kind of unified Egyptian, or Upper Egyptian, peasant culture—one in which it is improper for women over thirty to marry or older women to be out and about going to school—but in terms of the cosmopolitanism they might represent.

The introduction here of the concept of cosmopolitanism might seem surprising or glib. Since it is generally associated with those who travel, those who feel at home in several parts of the world, and those who are professionals, the concept would seem to apply more readily to the progressive television writer al-'Assal.[46] Although her political and social concerns are passionately focused on Egypt, her political vocabulary is international; she is well aware of foreign literature, film, and media; she has grown children who work in Finland and France; and she expresses frustration that the work of many fine Egyptian women writers is not translated into foreign languages. She reads television texts in terms of their political perspectives, criticizing fellow writers for being conservative or caving in to government expectations. She worries about television's social impact, disapproving of an American soap opera like *The Bold and the Beautiful* for the immorality it normalizes.

However, what village women like Zaynab, her daughter Sumaya, and her neighbor Fayruz can help us understand is how wealth, education, and particular experiences in everyday life combine with television to mark out other varieties of cosmopolitanism. These are the kinds of cosmopolitanisms one finds in many rural areas around the postcolonial world and that confound the concept of "cultures." Poverty, for example, impedes full access to the consumer culture and commodification of signs that are so conspicuously a part of a postmodern cosmopolitan's life. Yet Zaynab's life is not untouched by these features of cosmopolitanism that will be discussed more fully when I discuss consumerism. Television advertisements in Egypt insistently traffic in such signs, their jingles—written by advertising firms with names like Americana—enticing people to buy brand-name shampoos and yogurt. Unlike her children, Zaynab remains fairly unmoved by these advertisements, but this does not imply that Zaynab's imagination is not broad or that she does not have great knowledge of other worlds, gleaned not just from television but from foreign friends. The hamlet she lives in, with its European and American folklorists, journalists, political scientists, tourists, and aging divorcees, is only an extreme version of the kinds of communities in which many villagers in Egypt and elsewhere live. Migrating husbands and imported fans and television sets (brought back from wealthy labor-importing countries) are also familiar figures and objects—the products of unequal economies, nations, and states. The postcolonial state is there, too, very present in a national curriculum disseminated by newly literate teachers in overcrowded classrooms with barely any resources; in literacy textbooks promulgating family planning messages; and in television serials promoting modernist ideals forged in the anticolonial nationalist movements of the first half of the twentieth century.

Yet Zaynab's life is anchored by economic constraints in her house, family, and village; the aspiration to educate her children is the only modernist national ideal within her reach, and, like most village parents, as I will argue, she sacrifices much for it. Zaynab has spent time in Cairo, getting medical treatment for her son. While there, she stayed in the Canadian folklorist's apartment—which was decorated with Egyptian antiques, folk art, and Bedouin rugs, but also boasted a transcriber, cassette player, and lots of books. Zaynab's subaltern relationship to this metropolitan world, related to her poverty and lack of education, is symbolized best by what she wore in Cairo. Despite her versatile knowledge, she wore the only clothes she had—clothes that announced her regional and rural origins.

This is in contrast with the form of cosmopolitanism that characterizes her wealthy neighbor, Fayruz. The first time I heard about this young woman was from her mother, the wife of the largest landowner in the village. During our first visit in 1990, I had talked to the mother about *The White Flag*, a television serial about the struggles of a retired diplomat to save his historic villa from destruction by a nouveau riche developer. She told me how some Egyptian tourists, finding themselves still on the west bank of the Nile when it came time for the serial, had knocked on her daughter's door and begged to watch the program there. Her daughter Fayruz, she proudly said, had cooked them dinner. She implied that Fayruz possessed the sophistication to feel comfortable with these urban types as well as the traditional generosity to invite them to a meal.

Fayruz lives around the corner from Zaynab in a house that looks quite different. In front sits a small shop, its shelves stocked with the usual contents of a local store anywhere in rural Egypt—laundry soaps, cans of tomato sauce, halvah, cooking oil, cigarettes, and candies. The shop is also the center for an immense wholesale grocery business, which, combined with

their agricultural efforts and a monopoly on government-ration distri-
bution, has helped her husband and his brother consolidate their father's
wealth.

Down the driveway is an odd structure that says worlds about Fayruz's
social location. A mud-brick house adjoins a concrete-and-brick house,
complete with a balcony. This is the type of "villa" people with money now
aspire to build. When I first met Fayruz, she lived in the spacious and tidy
mud-brick house. Like all village women, she baked bread in her outdoor
oven. But her house looked cleaner, because she did not need to keep livestock to boost the household income. When I returned in 1996, she had
moved into the adjoining structure, with its stone floor tiles and bright
blue ceramic-tiled bathroom, complete with toilet and bathtub. She showed
me around the house so I could see all the furniture—beds, wardrobes,
couches, armchairs, and side tables. (In contrast, Zaynab owns only a couple
of locally made benches, a low table for eating, one large wooden bed, and a
number of other small beds made from palm reeds pruned from her four
trees.) The new "modern" house had been prepared for Fayruz's younger,
educated brother-in-law. But when he finally found a bride, a girl from a local wealthy family in Luxor, she refused to live in the village—even in what
locals might have considered a sophisticated "palace." She insisted on living
in an apartment across the river in Luxor.

Compared to the distinctions that can be marked by goods in a city like
Cairo, where the wealthy, educated cosmopolitan elite can have the best
imported appliances and furniture and where distinctions of taste can be
subtly marked (decorating at least one room with Arabesque furniture was
common among the "cultured" in the 1970s and 1980s, a symbolism I discuss in chapter 6 that analyzes a serial by that name; in the 1990s folk arts
were popular), the distinctions in a provincial area like Luxor are cruder.
Fayruz's household had furniture, a telephone, and a color television set.
These set its members apart as people with money and a "modern," worldly
—not rural and backward—orientation. In contrast, her father (from an
older generation and, like Zaynab, more locally oriented), though perfectly
willing to invest in tractors and harvesters for his agricultural enterprise,
would not consider moving from his mud-brick house or buying a bigger
television set even if he was eventually persuaded to build a villa for his
younger son.[47]

When Fayruz unlocked her wardrobe and started pulling out dresses to
show me, I understood even better how her wealth enabled a different form
of cosmopolitanism than Zaynab's, while her lack of education and her lo-

cation in the provinces still distinguished her from urban professional cosmopolitans like those involved in television. Fayruz showed me amazing dresses of chiffon and satin, with sequins and gold buttons, all long and with long sleeves (only the urban upper classes and movie stars would wear anything more revealing)—some with surprisingly curved bodices and extravagant flounces. I was surprised, because around the village she wore the usual black head covering and an overdress only slightly more sophisticated than most women's.

This ornate wardrobe full of extraordinary dresses out of a lavish television serial like *Hilmiyya Nights* (discussed in chapter 1) reveals a great deal about urbanity, class distinction, and the national context in which these figure for a provincial. When Fayruz went to Cairo to get medical treatment for her migraines, she stayed, unlike Zaynab, in a shabby part of town where few foreigners would live. She and her husband called on business contacts her brother-in-law had developed while attending the business school run (as part of its parallel educational system) by the venerable mosque-university Al-Azhar. Whereas Zaynab, despite her contact with foreign cosmopolitans, had worn her village clothes, Fayruz, whose knowledge of other worlds came from television and Upper Egyptians with urban experience or aspirations, plucked her eyebrows, wore makeup, and put on some of the more modest dresses she had in her wardrobe. She also replaced her black head cloth with the *hijab*—the head covering associated with modest Islamic dress—thereby erasing her village identity. This adoption of the *hijab* is not surprising. For rural Egyptians, as for urban lower- and middle-class women since the 1980s, to become "modern" and urbane has meant taking on a more identifiably "Islamic" look and sound.[48]

We can read in these differences a contrast of cosmopolitanisms: between the resolutely national frame of an up-and-coming provincial and the sharp juxtapositions produced for a poor woman by the intersection of neo-colonial travel by folklorists, anthropologists, and tourists; postcolonial nationalist modernization projects; and transnational flows of television programs. Fayruz, with her chiffon dresses and *hijab,* can more easily imagine herself in the Egyptian serialized melodramas than can Zaynab, who distinguishes the moralities of marriage at sixty. Yet because she has neither the education nor the real urban experience of serial writers like al-'Assal (a staunch opponent of the new veiling), Fayruz asserts her sophistication by placing herself in the middle-class moral world symbolized by veiling.

Fayruz's imaginative participation in the nation, with its power centers in the cities, will be intensified if she continues with her literacy classes. But it should be noted that she is attending more out of wounded pride (and loneliness) than any desire for female emancipation or desires for full citizenship in the nation. When her brother-in-law's new bride refused to stay in the household with her, the bride apparently put on airs because of her education. Telling me these stories, Fayruz fumed, "Is she better than me?" Look at who my father is, she would add. Yet the bride's claims to superiority rested in part on her school diploma. In the national context, where standards are set by the urban and where television glorifies the educated and cultured, as the next two chapters will detail, Fayruz realized she could not rely only on her wealth and family name for status.

For yet a third type of village cosmopolitanism, let us consider Zaynab's twenty-year-old daughter, Sumaya. She has the education Fayruz lacks without the wealth that enables Fayruz to live in a "modern" house and have a wardrobe full of dresses that cannot be worn in the village. Because of her education (she has completed agricultural secondary school), she, too, wears a version of the *hijab* when she goes to school or dresses up, replacing the locally tailored gowns she ordinarily wears with a bright polyester store-bought outfit and high heels. She saves up to buy face creams she has seen advertised on television, and she knows how to bake "cakes" because of her home economics classes. She occasionally reads the newspaper and plans to have a small family, as national propaganda urges. Sumaya's first gift to me, so different from her mother's, bespoke her generation's form of cosmopolitanism. Shyly, she presented me with a color postcard framed with green and blue twisted yarn. The postcard—outdated, printed in Italy, and of the type widely circulated across Egypt—portrayed a European bride and groom gazing into each other's eyes. The frame was her own handiwork, a design no doubt learned in her home economics classes at school using materials only the teachers could provide. A gift her mother could not appreciate, it was a homegrown amalgam of elements originating in various communities and places, expressing her romantic fantasies (encouraged by television) and signifying her modern, state-initiated vocational education.

What the situations, cultural knowledges, code-switching abilities, and imaginative possibilities of these three women mean for the interpretation of culture(s) after television—and everything that has made television possible and widely present in villages around the globe—is not only that (post)colonial processes of cultural hybridization have undermined the utility of more static and homogenizing conceptions of culture(s).[49] Nor is it just that these multiple situations, knowledges, and abilities confirm the importance of, as Bruce Robbins so nicely puts it, attending to "discrepant cosmopolitanisms."[50] Rather, it is that the hybridizations and cosmopolitanisms are worth specifying (Fayruz's, Zaynab's, Sumaya's, and al-'Assal's each being different), and that the effects of media on what Appadurai calls "the work of the imagination" and "self-fabrication" are worth tracing to particular configurations of power, education, age, and wealth in particular places—like an agricultural village in the heart of the tourist industry in a disadvantaged region in Egypt in the 1990s.[51]

ANTHROPOLOGY FOR WHOM?

If, as I have shown, thick descriptions of television can be made to speak to broad issues and concepts, we are still left with the question of which issues to choose and whether, in the end, it is only to colleagues concerned with them that we want to speak. The dilemma goes back at least as far as Max Weber, who, of course, noted that our questions about the flow of life were set by our value orientations.[52] As Ien Ang puts it now, in advocating radical contextualization as the method for critical television studies, it is difficult to know where to stop or where to focus.[53] In this post-Orientalist, post-colonial-critique-of-anthropology, post-crisis-of-the authority-of-science age, Geertz's formulation of the anthropologist's vocation as placing in the consultable record the answers others have given to our deepest questions seems less complete than it used to.[54] Closer to home, and apropos of the development of critical audience studies, Ang's call to recognize that we offer only partial and positioned truths takes us not much further.[55]

My own inclination has been to approach television as just one aspect of late twentieth-century lives, just as I approached the poetry of the Awlad 'Ali Bedouin as an aspect of their everyday lives, rather than as the object of a study of poetics.[56] One of the benefits of working on television as a way into these lives—as opposed, for example, to focusing on poetry, religion, kinship, or political economy—is that it offers particular contemporary possibilities for critical intervention.[57] It does so both in the way it enables us to represent to outsiders people in places like Egypt and, what is more appealing, in the way it enables us to work as intellectuals within the national frame that is such a crucial context today for most people, including the women and men in this Upper Egyptian village.

In *Writing Women's Worlds,* I suggest that we can write critical ethnographies that go "against the grain" of global inequalities, even as we must remain modest in our claims to radicalism and realistic about the impacts of these ethnographies.[58] Television, I believe, is particularly useful for writing against the grain because it forces us to represent people in distant villages as part of the same cultural worlds we inhabit—worlds of mass media, consumption, and dispersed communities of the imagination, where the national figures strongly. To write about television in Egypt, or Indonesia, or Brazil is to write about the articulation of the transnational, the national, the local, and the personal. Television is not the only way to do this, of course; Anna Tsing's reflections on marginality in a remote region of Indonesia and her attention to people like Uma Adang—a singular woman who brilliantly hybridized national, local, and foreign discourses to establish herself as a shaman—were developed without talking about television.[59] But television makes it especially difficult to write as if culture and cultures, despite their "infirmities," were the most powerful ways to make sense of the world.[60]

Working on television also makes possible more local interventions—at the national level, with intellectuals who are our peers and counterparts. These are people I can admire or disagree with, and who themselves can read, criticize, and debate my work. If through my thick descriptions of television in particular places I can begin to tease apart the structures of power within which subaltern groups live their lives and the ways television is now a part of that—in households, in communities, in imaginations—perhaps I can also then enter into debate with concerned writers like al-'Assal, whose work was analyzed in this chapter; Usama Anwar 'Ukasha, the author of *Hilmiyya Nights* discussed in the previous chapter; and many others whose serials are discussed in the pages to follow. They are, as I will show, often nationalists and modernists, and I am concerned about how they think about their audiences and their political projects.

I would like to engage in this debate because I respect their social concern, but I also know from fieldwork that from the vantage of Upper Egyptian villagers like Zaynab and Umm Ahmad, the answers they offer to social problems facing ordinary people often appear unrealistic or patronizing. As I will explore further in the next two chapters, television intersects with and extends the discourse of experts. It is directed at stereotyped audiences, the same generalized objects targeted by social reformers. Is there a way thick descriptions of such communities could complicate urban intellectuals' understanding of Egyptian villagers? Or lead them to take more seriously the complexity of the forms of cosmopolitanisms found across Egypt? Is there a way to begin to question modernist nationalist dogmas about literacy, education, and companionate marriage as panaceas? To al-'Assal's credit, one of her aims in writing the serial on Upper Egypt was to show, as she put it, "that the real vengeance would be to lash out [through development] against the circumstances that have led them to be attached to the vendetta in the first place." But by continuing to subsume much more complex stories of rural life under the utterly familiar modernizing trope of a negative "tradition" and "backwardness," she, like many Egyptian intellectuals, risks reaffirming the marginality of such women as Zaynab and other poor and rural uneducated women and men across the nation.

PART TWO

National Pedagogy

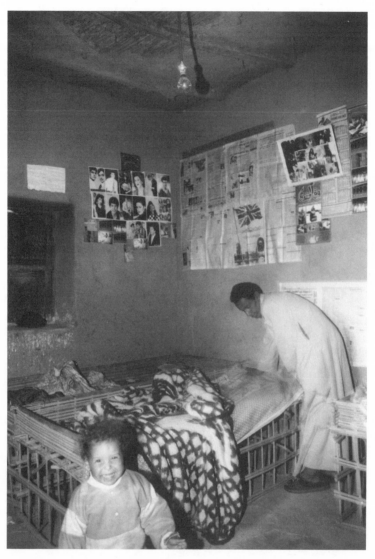

Newspapers, religious prints, and posters of actors, pop stars,
and soccer players mingle on the walls of a village bedroom,
Upper Egypt, 1996. Lila Abu-Lughod/Anthro-Photo.

[3]

Rural "Ignorance" and the Virtues of Education

REPRESENTING THE SAʿID

In 1997, first on Nile TV (the new satellite channel made freely available in the major cities and offering subtitled films and serials for tourists) and several months later on the main government channel, a dramatic serial called *Hilm al-janubi* (Dream of the southerner) was broadcast. The opening episodes, set in and around Luxor, reproduce common images of rural Upper Egyptians, *Saʿidis*. There are violent and dumb peasants, some who refuse to pay the rent for the land they are farming and others loyal henchmen of important men. There is a wealthy but illiterate local man who has worked in tourism but has become rich by digging beneath his house and unearthing Pharaonic antiquities. A poorly informed tour guide whose English is weak misleads tourists about ancient inscriptions, and another character—who becomes the real villain of the serial—has just returned from the oil-rich Gulf states, bringing gifts for the unprincipled school principal to get his teaching position back. The actors all attempted Saʿidi dialect, using characteristic pronunciations and words; mostly, however, they thought to make themselves into Saʿidis by speaking gruffly.

These stereotypical characters are pitted against the unique character, Nasr. He is a cultured local teacher who lectures his high-school students on the history of the great civilization of ancient Egypt, although it was not in the curriculum, and spends his afternoons studying his archaeology books in Karnak Temple, the magnificent Pharaonic temple on the east bank of the Nile in Luxor. He defends the rights of the sons of poor men to have an education, in one case loaning a boy the money to cover his school activity fees. The boy whom he helps counters the principal's threat to expel him with a defense of the rights laid down during the Nasser era, when mass education was instituted: "Education," he declares, "is free in Egypt."

As is true of the best Egyptian television serials—and this one has an unusually complex set of social themes, exciting footage shot on location, colorful characters, and nice dramatic tension—claims to social verisimilitude were made, even if everyone from journalists to businessmen regularly criticize television serials for their inaccurate portrayals of members of their professions or classes. The writer, Muhammad Safa' 'Amir, boasted that he wrote about what he knew and had lived.[1] He himself was born in Upper Egypt, near Qina, though he has spent most of his life in Alexandria, the other setting for *Dream of the Southerner.* Yet despite grains of ethnographic truth in the serial, including the use of genuine Sa'idi entertainers in a wedding celebration scene, the writer had deployed many of the stock themes of rural backwardness and Upper Egyptian violence, familiar from television, film, and literature. Not only are there the stupid and angry locals, but also the worn theme of arbitrary patriarchal authority. The latter is expressed most often in the control over women and the institution of forced arranged marriage, both part of the plot of *Dream of the Southerner,* like this writer's earlier television success, *Dhi'ab al-jabal* (Mountain wolves).[2]

An even more hackneyed theme is the tension between the selfish tomb robber who wants to sell antiquities to foreigners and the cultured Nasr who appreciates antiquities as part of a national heritage. Again, the writer insisted that the figure of the man who gets rich by digging for antiquities under his house is based on a real person he had heard about as a boy. Yet the popular association of tomb robbing with the residents of the Luxor area, and especially Gurna, which I will discuss shortly, has a long history. It is commemorated in two important nationalist films of the 1960s loosely based on real incidents: the 1965 *Al-Jabal* (The mountain), directed by Khalil Shawqi and adapted from a story by Fathi Ghanem about the attempt in the 1940s to relocate the residents of Gurna to a new village built by the vernacular architect Hassan Fathy; and *Yawm an tuhsa al-sinin: Al-mumiya* (The night of counting the years: The mummy), directed by Shadi 'Abd al-Salam in 1967 but not released until 1975. Set in 1881, the latter concerns the revelation to the Antiquities Service of the location of a cache of mummies that for generations had been the secret means of livelihood for local families in Gurna, on the Theban Hills. Like *Dream of the Southerner,* these films pit "ignorant," uneducated Upper Egyptian clans involved in desecrating Pharaonic tombs and selling Egypt's patrimony to foreigners against patriotic, educated modernizers, either those involved in the Antiquities Service or engineers involved in building the new village. These outsiders serve as models for local protagonists who, under their tutelage, eventually break with the negative traditions of their kin.[3] The difference in the 1990s televi-

sion serial is that a local Saʻidi has himself become the educated patriot and
preserver of the nation; there are no outsiders from the urban North involved in the local struggle, even if Nasr later allies with and receives help
from an archaeology professor and his daughter (also studying archaeology,
a role played by the unlikely pop singer Simone) in Alexandria.

The serial also reprises a new theme that was becoming conventional by
the late 1990s. As will be discussed in more detail in chapter 7, like so many
serials since the 1993 media policy of "confronting extremism," this one includes a group of closed-minded, intolerant, and violent Islamists. They are
hoodwinked by our hero's rival into mistaking the protagonist's scholarly
interest in Egyptology for idol worship and so set fire to his house, burning
his precious collection of scholarly books and, as it happens, a papyrus document that is the key to the location of Alexander's lost tomb. (This papyrus
is presented as a priceless national treasure that our hero had refused to return to the self-interested tomb robber who found it; Nasr is horrified, of
course, that this ignorant man had wanted to sell it to foreigners.) When the
producers of *Dream of the Southerner* were challenged about the accuracy of
Luxor as a setting for such militant groups, the writer defended his script by
arguing that all around that city, from Armant to Najʻ Hammadi, were the
sugarcane fields in which terrorists hid.[4] The actor who played the lead role
quickly added that geography was not the issue anyway; it was the danger
these groups posed that the drama wanted to convey. The serial thus reproduces and reinforces the common northern association of religious violence
with the marginality of Upper Egypt.[5]

The only stock element that seems to be missing at first in *Dream of the
Southerner* is the vendetta (*tha'r*), the long-familiar trope for Upper Egypt.
To the writer's credit, this image is self-consciously mocked when the owner
of an Alexandria apartment building does not want to rent to our noble
hero because he is a bachelor from the Saʻid. She worries that he might be
involved in a vendetta and does not want trouble. "You know the way you
Saʻidis are," she apologizes. But the plot, gripping and passionate as it is,
eventually does come to turn on revenge. Our hero's most dangerous foe
becomes his former colleague from the school, the returned migrant, who
marries the tomb robber's niece (for her money), only to discover that she
is in love with the cultured teacher. Out of wounded pride he joins his in-
law, bent on revenge for the financial loss of the precious papyrus. So the violent vendetta is there, but cheapened by being rooted not in grief and the
fierce love of family but in competitiveness, pride, and greed.

Unlike many television serials, *Dream of the Southerner* balances these negative figures with good Sa'idis who are able to join forces with honest and patriotic urban Alexandrians in a black and white morality play. There are two simple but loyal and honest servants: one a country bumpkin, and the other distinguished by his integrity in friendship. And there is the young woman—the love object—who wants to defy custom and ends up bravely saving the day. But the two main protagonists are rural Upper Egyptians who have been redeemed by true education. Nasr has differentiated himself from others around him by his love of learning and selfless devotion to his civilization and nation. His main protector and friend is a wise retired judge, whose cultural taste and knowledge is symbolized by the framed reproduction of the Mona Lisa hanging in his home.

In such representations, *Dream of the Southerner* follows the pattern of many television serials, part of a larger modernist discourse dominant in state culture for much of the twentieth century: the educated cultured individual represents the good, the law, culture, national responsibility, and pride in the greatness of the nation's heritage.[6] An article in *Radio and Television Magazine,* which described the serial as a "television ode to the love of the nation," quoted the scriptwriter as saying that the serial was not so much about the theft of antiquities as the larger question of the integrity or authenticity of the Egyptian character (*asalat al-shakhsiyya al-misriyya*).[7] In a seminar sponsored by the same magazine after the serial was broadcast, he explained that he had tackled five dangerous elements: religious extremism, foreign power, the class driven only by personal interest, government corruption, and personal envy. He had done so, however, and perhaps unthinkingly (so conventional is the theme), by glorifying true education and patriotism.

RURAL CITIZENS AS SUBJECTS OF EDUCATION

The actor who played the role of Nasr defended the Manichean morality of the serial on the grounds that "[t]elevision drama is important, dear to people, and the teacher of the new generation."[8] What *Dream of the Southerner* and numerous other television serials teach is the value of education and devotion to the nation. The same lessons are taught in the schools, and are part of what might be called state culture. Although there are differences in the ways people take in the messages of television and of school, the latter associated with authority and the former with entertainment, the cross-references and similarities make them worth juxtaposing for a sense of the elements of national pedagogy.[9]

For many rural and uneducated Upper Egyptian villagers, encountering state culture means being put in one's place as inferior (as these television characters show and the outside examiners who visit Upper Egyptian schools make the secondary schools' students feel); as people who are at times unsophisticated enough to need television to show them things; and as people who have little access to the kinds of lives depicted in schoolbooks or on television, particularly nowadays, with the explosion of television advertisements for water heaters and toilet bowl cleaners. State culture positions the rural and uneducated as people who must be taught the most basic things in the name of national development.

The families living on the west bank of the Nile across from Luxor with whom I have spoken and watched television appreciate the fact that television serials, produced for state television and approved by censors, are meant to be not just entertaining but didactic. People talked about how "television shows people things." It shows people principles such as good and evil (*khayr wa sharr*), how things work (bribery is given as an example), and that the government is always there. The latter was expressed especially in relation to a favorite documentary program called *Al-muwajaha* (The confrontation), in which criminals are interviewed. As village women excitedly told me about various people who had appeared on this program ("none from around here—they are all from Giza, Asyut, Minya, and other places," they quickly pointed out) they explained that the show teaches people that if they do wrong, the government will find them out. As examples, they described a woman who had drowned two children because she was angry with their family. She tried to make it look as if it had been a robbery, "but the government knew immediately." They also recounted the story of a man who had murdered someone and then tried to destroy any evidence by putting the body inside a rubber tire which he set on fire with kerosene. But he forgot to burn the gloves he was wearing at the scene of the crime. "The government" found them, fingerprinted all the neighbors, and caught him. The women were amazed ("*subhan Allah!*" they exclaimed) at how the government could track down the culprits.[10]

Many viewers also remarked on the educational value of television. One man explained that through television "people become aware (*wa'iyin*)." His wife agreed: "The importance of television is that people like us learn things from it." When she says "like us" she means Upper Egyptian peasants who are not educated or well traveled. This echoed the sentiments of her similarly unlettered sister-in-law, who had compared the present to the past. "People like me," she said, "are angry with our parents for not giving us an education. Now, after schools and television, people know a lot more."

This is certainly the intention of many involved in writing and producing for television and the perception of other viewers across Egypt, including the urban viewers interviewed by Martha Diase in her study of a foreign-funded enter-educate (entertainment-education) television serial aired in 1994.[11] The television producers often couch their discussions in the language of "making people aware." [12] The interviews with the writer of *Dream of the Southerner* and some of the actors who participated in it are typical. One actor described how newspapers each day uncover crimes committed by people who care only to make themselves rich by destroying the Egyptian heritage. He concluded, "The serial has an important role in making people aware of our history and our priceless antiquities." The scriptwriter was even more ambitious. By means of this serial on antiquities theft, he said he wanted to expose all the problems blocking the progress and potential of Egypt.[13]

The most socially concerned television writers see the medium as a means to both educate and communicate the value of modern education. They do not work alone. Adult literacy classes, for example, are seen in the same way. The textbooks produced for these classes, which were so central to the idealism of the Nasser period but gained new momentum in the late 1990s under the encouragement of First Lady Suzanne Mubarak, are intended to teach people to read and write. They also exemplify the efforts of state culture to promote certain values. In the Upper Egyptian village in which I worked, literacy classes for women were begun in 1995. Some local women, unemployed graduates of technical institutes, were hired as teachers. In one class that I attended, the teacher drilled twenty-five students, mostly adult women in their twenties and thirties (with a sprinkling of younger girls who never had an opportunity to go to school), using the same techniques of sing-song repetition used on schoolchildren. She worked with a text whose intention of teaching basic citizens' rights alongside literacy was in many ways admirable but whose condescending presumptions about the students' simplicity were distressing and whose messages could be read as propaganda.

Entitled *Ata'allam wa atanawwar* (I learn and become enlightened), the book begins with lessons that place individuals first as citizens. One is called "My Identity Card."

My name is on my identity card.
My occupation is on the card.
On my card is my place of residence.
On my card is a number.

It also teaches women some basic rights that are at odds with local custom in much of rural Egypt, where families organize marriages. For example, there is this lesson on "The Marriage Contract."

Marriage is God's way.
The family comes into being with the marriage contract.
For the contract you need two witnesses.
This contract exists with the bride's consent.
The consent of the bride is a precondition of marriage.

Later lessons build vocabulary while promoting certain ideas about hygiene and health. They do not miss the opportunity to push family planning—a value, like education, crucial to ideas about making Egyptians modern and developed that can end up devaluing rural women, whose identities are caught up in larger social and familial worlds, as well as furthering the capacities and reach of governmental control, as Kamran Ali has argued in his book, *Planning the Family in Egypt*.[14] Lesson 8 is not subtle.

Kamil loves his family.
Habiba is Kamil's wife.
Kamil loves his wife and Habiba loves her husband.
Tariq is Kamil's son and Samah is Kamil's daughter.
Tariq and Samah are Kamil's children.
Kamil's family is small.
Kamil's family is small and happy.

At the bottom of the page, in small print, the aim of the lesson is spelled out for the teacher: "To deepen the feelings of love among family members and to grasp the connection between the small number of family members and their happiness."

This is a lesson that television would have reinforced for rural viewers. An excellent example is a serial of the mid-1990s set in rural Egypt. Called *Wa ma zala al-Nil yajri* (And the Nile flows on), it was written by the celebrated Usama Anwar 'Ukasha and directed by Muhammad Fadil. These two

Director Muhammad Fadil on the outdoor set of a historical serial, 1997.
Lila Abu-Lughod/Anthro-Photo.

had collaborated on many superb serials in the late 1980s and early 1990s,[15]
but this one was not particularly popular, despite the complex plot, lovely
cinematography, and realistic village setting. The serial was unusual because
partially funded by the US Agency for International Development and produced in collaboration with the State Information Service/Information, Education and Communication Center. The model was, however, soon to be
replicated by a private production company, the Center for Development
Communication, in a serial promoting public health messages that included
family planning, funded by the Ford Foundation, the International Development Research Center, and the Johns Hopkins University's Population
Communication Services.[16]

The SIS/IEC Center had previously developed many radio serials and
a number of television programs to promote family planning (including
minidrama spots and contests like *Wedding of the Month*), and USAID had
over the previous decade helped fund eighty-six health spots on family
planning subjects. This was, however, their first attempt to develop a dramatic serial, in a sense returning to the roots of Third World soap opera,
which was developed for family planning purposes in Mexico and then
adopted widely in India, Pakistan, Indonesia, and other countries.[17] Al-

though 'Ukasha claims they were left absolutely free to determine the script, the USAID population planning officer revealed that at least the initial scenario was discussed by the agency. The Americans were somewhat dismayed to find that the only character who used birth control was to be killed in the end. The report by the Information, Education and Communication Center claims that the strategy for the production was based on the results of field research and surveys in addition to the writer's own vast experience.

Both director and writer were slightly defensive about the serial, because critics attacked it for being didactic. Postviewing surveys revealed that it was far less popular among educated than noneducated viewers; the former felt they did not need the information it contained. Many others defended it with statements about the necessity of producing educational material for the uneducated. The director was quick to correct me when I described the serial as about family planning, a personal issue that is controversial for religious and other reasons. He said it was about the population problem, implying that his concerns were social and national. The writer answered my queries by saying, "I wrote on family planning because I believe overpopulation is a serious economic problem. Writing about this issue is a national duty." The reason this project might have appealed to him is clear from what he said at a symposium, "Scriptwriting for Development Film," in 1997.[18] There 'Ukasha stated that he did not know what was meant by a development film, because "all good art is for development."

Many of the messages of *And the Nile Flows On* are worthy and some of the issues it tackles take courage. The serial criticizes underage marriage and marital rape. A grim picture of the exploitation of women is presented as well as the violence of the landowning class, themes already quite familiar to Egyptians from films and literature. But the serial paints the rural masses as benighted. The problem for rural women was that they were being exploited by ignorant rural men, not that all labored under hardships. And the main protagonist is a physician (played by Fardows 'Abd al-Hamid, a venerable actress who is also the director's wife) who, beautifully dressed and coiffed, supports women against their men. In the opening episode, she is shown delivering a baby. When she discovers it is the seventh in the family, she sighs and regards the poor peasant women ululating outside the shack with pity and disdain. She is especially attached to one young village woman. At one point she says of her, "She is the symbol of what I dream of for every woman and girl in the village. She's educated through middle school, she understands and is aware." Then she describes how this young woman has only one child and a good husband, "a family that makes one happy."

When the literacy textbook directly affirms the value of education, it links individual and national needs, as in following lesson:

Illiteracy is dangerous.
Illiteracy is a threat to production.
Illiteracy is dangerous for people.
Illiteracy is dangerous and a big waste for all.
I am fighting illiteracy . . . I am getting educated.
I am getting educated . . . I am fighting illiteracy.

In principle it is difficult to argue with the virtues of literacy and education, or knowledge of the rights and responsibilities of citizenship, even when couched in the overbearing language of national development. There is little doubt that education, when of high quality, opens possibilities, and knowledge of rights protects women. However, in what follows, I want to explore some of the problems posed by the subjection of rural villagers to such educational messages and messages about education in a national context in which quality education, like other resources, is not equally available to all citizens. I will first show how little these cultural productions reflect of the actual lives and problems of late twentieth-century rural Upper Egyptians, something that may not be all that surprising for the genre of soap operas but is nevertheless disturbing. Then I will try to suggest some of the silencing effects on villagers of such well-meaning discourses. However, I will also argue that the most significant impact of these discourses and the images they support is on those who have the power to reshape the lives of the rural poor.

TEXTS AND LIVES

Do the women in these literacy classes, so eager to learn and write (and to spend their afternoons together working away amidst jokes and chat, escaping the daily chores of the household and the tired company of their families), juxtapose what they memorize and what they actually know? I never heard anyone make fun of the lessons even though the picture of Egyptian society and what the government provides for its citizens must strike them as idealized. The lesson on the right of all citizens to free health care (something USAID is working hard to end) must seem hollow to women who often complain bitterly that when they go to the underfinanced government clinics, the wait will be long and the "free" medicines more likely than not unavailable.

Even more farfetched are the rosy lessons about Egypt's new cities and communities in the desert. One lesson brags about the work opportunities in these new communities, going on to explain the equal rights of male and female workers and the role of the union in defending workers' rights. The teacher who led the chanting repetition of the lesson knows how few work opportunities there are generally, having explained to me in another context that only those with connections can possibly hope to get the secretarial jobs for which they are trained. All the women in the class have brothers or cousins who have graduated from technical schools or colleges and sit unemployed, waiting for seven or eight years to be assigned to positions. As for the less-educated men in their families, the lucky ones get waged employment in restoration or guarding Pharaonic temples. Their salaries are L.E. 120 (120 Egyptian pounds, or $36 US) per month. If fortunate enough to have some land, they work it in the afternoons, plowing, planting, irrigating, and harvesting. The ones who make it are those who somehow link themselves up with tourism, selling things to them, making things for them, feeding or housing them, and befriending or marrying them. Salaries from government jobs, when available, are nothing more than helpful cash supplements—useful to cover children's school expenses and medicines. Village women simply do not work outside their households. Girls who have graduated from the local agricultural high school lose touch with their friends, staying at home to help their mothers until it is time to get married. Only in the very late 1990s did this begin to change in the area where I was working. Young women had begun to seek and find jobs in shops or enterprises that had opened up; some even hoped to get jobs in the offices of the Antiquities Organization that is such a big local employer. But such jobs, poorly paid and part time, still require connections. How relevant to any of these is the next lesson in the textbook that teaches students how to fill out the civil service form requesting a vacation? There are no vacations from low-paid and insecure jobs, not to mention from getting fodder for the sheep or sweeping, cooking, or childcare.

The text teaches reading and writing through essays promoting notions specific to a modern capitalist economy. One of these is about savings accounts. One lesson reads,

Did you know?
That opening a savings account is free?

That you can open a savings account at the Post Office with a pound?

That your money in the account increases?

That the savings account helps protect your money from confiscation?

That a savings account is tax-free?

That in a savings account your money quickly grows and that saving is a security
  for the family and society?

This lesson, transcribed dutifully into school notebooks, is for women whose families frequently have difficulty even keeping up with the monthly expenses, often having to borrow until they can sell a calf or goat. These are women who may have some savings in their gold necklaces and earrings but who invest, if they have anything extra, in livestock. As I explain in more detail in chapter 8, the advantage of livestock is that they increase, even if they require a lot of care. Many women spend their mornings cutting clover (*barsim*) or corn for their sheep and goats. Morning and evening they take them to graze on the stubble or grasses that grow on the edge of the desert. They get water for them to drink. At the end of each day they move them from outside pens to the safety of indoors. Some of these women also care for the family water buffalo or cow, looking forward to calves that can be sold for cash and the supply of milk that will nourish their children and nieces and nephews.

The messages about education are the most unrealistic. Lesson 11 echoes the message of the television serial *Dream of the Southerner*. It repeats the dogma of the old Nasserist state and the values of intellectuals who link development and education.

Education is the right of all.

Education is the right of every citizen.

Education is the duty of every citizen.

I am getting educated.

I am progressing.

I am becoming enlightened.

I am going to continue learning.

I am going to continue learning for free.

It is true that the literacy classes are more or less free, though students must provide their own notebooks and pencils. But that education more broadly is free is simply not the case, as every village family knows. Parents are so convinced that education will provide a future for their children that they deny themselves much to be able to afford it. They forfeit the children's labor, in some cases completely. In other cases, the children have to help before they leave for school or after they return, depending on which shift they are on. Especially at the start of the school year, parents feel the cost of schooling. They will endlessly count and recount the expenses—for new clothes, notebooks, pens, book bags, books, and daily allowances for snacks or transport, not to mention the private lessons later in the year as it becomes apparent that their children are failing. Multiply these costs by the number of children—usually no fewer than three and up to six or seven—and you have some staggering figures, given household incomes.

If you talk to the children, even knowing their biases, you get a fairly dismal view of the "free" education provided to them in this era of structural adjustment; despite continuing proclamations about the value of education, the government devotes nowhere near enough resources to it. Although many children love school, even though it only lasts four or five hours a day because of the shift system needed to relieve overcrowding, most older students had stories about unqualified or unmotivated teachers, from the ones who write English on the blackboard sometimes from right to left and other times from left to right, to the ones who skip classes to go home and cook. Students sometimes contrast the good and bad teachers, the good ones being those who help them cheat when it comes time for exams. Exams are always supervised by outsiders, teachers or inspectors from other schools, but somehow the "good" teachers manage to get in to tell them the answers.

In the schools run by the mosque-university Al-Azhar that many locals prefer, in part because they are not coeducational and in part because they teach more religion and involve less expense, things are no better. One young woman complained that the teachers didn't explain things properly. They went quickly through the lessons, solving the easy questions in class and giving the hard ones as homework. The students were frustrated, but the teachers just yelled at them. In one confrontation, she said, a student challenged the teacher, saying if he treated the class with respect and politeness, the class would respond in kind. The result was that the student was ignored for the rest of the year. Teachers enforce a cultural violence, demanding that children use proper Islamic salutations rather than those of the local dialect. They also use physical violence. That this happens in the local schools became clear in the stories of an excited seven-year-old. Competitive with her cousin, she bragged that her school, the Azhar school, was better. She learned more there than in the state primary school where she had begun. With bright eyes, she explained that she used to be good at reading and Arabic but not the Qur'an. Then the teacher stood her in the doorway and beat her feet. With a proud laugh she said, "Then I learned!"

The classrooms are overcrowded and the teachers grossly underpaid. This leads to the notorious system of private lessons, which the teachers need in order to survive and the parents must pay for if they want their children to pass, a situation as ubiquitous and deplored in Cairo as it is in the village.[19] But an even more egregious example of the failure of the government to adequately fund the educational system can be seen in the stories high-school students tell of what happens when outside examiners come in to administer the year-end exams. Each student is required to contribute 40 LE, not a small amount for them. They must also lend blankets and bedding. What makes the students livid is that they perceive this as a boondoggle for the teachers, at their expense. The visitors are fed chicken and meat every day (when most local households can afford it only once a week), with the local teachers, janitors, and wives all sharing. The students complain that the teachers use this as an opportunity for a vacation, touring all the Pharaonic sites.

The question that needs to be asked is whether, given how understaffed and underfinanced the schools are and how few children can actually succeed there, all the efforts toward schooling are worth it. Even if the family has sacrificed to send their children to an institute or college, they will most likely remain unemployed, especially now that the government has ended its policy of guaranteed employment for graduates. For decades in other parts of Egypt, where schooling was much more available, education had not actually translated into income, and the social mobility it used to promise has become somewhat frozen.[20] Not many local people ask the question; they see no other way, given how little land there is. Those lucky families who have any land find it split more and more ways with each generation. They say that even the most basic jobs now require a diploma. Moreover, they want the social capital that education provides in the local community and marriage market. They have been taught, by television serials like *Dream of a Southerner* and the wider state discourse of which it is a part, that to be respected, to be a national hero, one must be educated.

Only Zaynab, the sharp woman whose life I outlined in chapter 2, expressed any doubt to me.[21] She once asked, "Why is it that even though I never learned to read or write, I understand most things? More than my children who are in school?"

Zaynab's remark brings us to the second problem with the literacy textbooks and television serials. The villagers I know are all more sophisticated than urban intellectuals imagine. Their knowledge comes from their close involvement in the management of daily life in their households and wider families; their detailed knowledge of the experiences of many neighbors, relatives, and other more distant subjects of gossip and discussion; and, it must be admitted, their exposure to school and television. In chapter 2 I even described some of these women as cosmopolitans, to suggest some of the breadth of their knowledge.[22] Their complex situations suggest that the kinds of ignorant rural Egyptians imagined as subjects and citizens by state officials and urban intellectuals, including television and textbook writers, do not exist despite pronouncements as late as 2001 by the writer of *Dream of the Southerner* that the world of Upper Egypt, even in "the age of open skies," was a closed world in which there were limits to the cultural, economic, and behavioral changes that had occurred.[23]

TO WHAT EFFECT?

What effects do such distorted images of the rural and uneducated and such unrealistic messages about the values of education and national development have? As I will argue throughout this study, it is impossible to determine the effects of media. Nevertheless, one can assume that there are some, intended or not, and begin to seek out the domains in which these effects might occur. In this case I would argue that we need to look in two directions. First, one must consider the audiences to whom such images are directed. Then, one must ask about those who already share these values and are in a position to enact policies affecting the lives of rural villagers. It could be argued that the ubiquity, authoritativeness, and pleasure association of these now conventional images may work together in a political process that helps keep rural Egyptians in their place as inadequate and inferior citizens whose rights and needs come second, but who find it difficult to articulate opposition, especially given the repression of political alternatives in Egypt.

As my descriptions of village women's acceptance of the textbooks and the general belief that television is good because it "increases awareness" suggest, people who are disadvantaged do not seem to articulate the criticism that the gap between the messages they receive and the lives they live might be expected to generate. It is surprising to me, for example, that the faith in education is so widespread given that there is so little decent employment for the educated, and that the overtaxed educational system is so poor. Unlike the disaffected urban middle-class youth that Walter Armbrust worked with, who in the early 1990s appreciated the "vulgar" films that were breaking with the modernist nationalist code and were cynical about the touted value of education, people in the village rarely expressed serious doubts about the value of education.[24]

In part, this absence of a critical discourse based on the knowledge of the gap between state rhetoric and everyday experience can surely be related to television. Television upholds these linked values of education and development not just obliquely through dramas like *Dream of the Southerner* and many others with educated protagonists, but directly.[25] A classic example is a program called *100 per cent.* Intended to encourage 100% literacy in Egypt, the program hammers home the value of education in part by shaming those who are not going to school. One evening the host set off to the car mechanics' street in Cairo. He interrogated garage owners about whether they hired underage labor. They all denied it. Then, just as belligerently, he interviewed young mechanics' apprentices about why they had dropped out of school. In most cases, the boys cited "circumstances." When pressed, they explained that financial circumstances in their families had forced them to leave school and begin working. They said that they gave their wages (most said they made L.E. 6 [less than $2 US] per day) to their mothers. The interviewer then taunted them: Don't you think you would make more money if you were educated? Aren't you just being lazy? Just because you didn't like school doesn't mean you shouldn't try. What kind of future do you think you will have?

Yet it is not just bombardment by authoritative discourses of more educated northerners (some associated with the government that had based its legitimacy in part on claims to provide education and social mobility) that prevents the development of critique. I think a more subtle process—in part psychological—is at work. It reveals itself in the absence of open resistance to the mischaracterization of rural lives. Intellectuals from Upper Egypt can be critical of the snobbery and disdain of the urban educated for the countryside, and the association of the north with educated urbanity and the south with uneducated backwardness. Some like 'Abd al-Rahman al-Abnudi have brought to the mainstream folk traditions such as the epic of Abu-Zayd al-Hilali (as discussed in chapter 5), while others have attempted to counter the prevailing discourse by valorizing local knowledges and artistic traditions, and even the lowbrow appeal of television, that they themselves have left behind in their move to the city and higher education.[26] And some local intellectuals can be cynical about the state, as was one engineer in Luxor about the dubious origins of the hero of a television serial about an Egyptian spy in Israel. But I have heard of only two communities, one in Sinai and another in Upper Egypt, that have raised lawsuits against television serials for defamation of character. In the second case, according to Muhammad Safa' 'Amir, the writer of the serial *Dhi'ab al-jabal* (Mountain wolves), the case was dropped as soon as people actually saw the serial.[27] As he described what happened, a group of Hawwara from Upper Egypt had gathered from the media that a serial about them was being filmed and had protested. They were, however, happy with their representation in what turned out to be an extremely popular serial widely praised by ordinary people across Egypt as authentic.

Those villagers with whom I have watched serials set in Upper Egypt never voiced objections to the disfigurement of their dialect or the negative depiction of their fellow Sa'idis even if articles appear in the urban press critical of television peasants. One that was published in *Radio and Television Magazine* in 1997, for example, criticized serials for inaccuracies of dress and dialect and quoted peasant women who found fault with the makeup, long nails, and life of ease of their television counterparts.[28] Some of the lack of criticism I encountered might be explained by the very conventionality, carried over from film to television, of media depictions of peasants. Some might be due to my own presence as an outsider. It was striking, however, that in my experience with women and young people in the village, inaccurate television dialogue prompted only discussion of the differences among dialects from village to village.[29] Negative characters were simply hated for being bad people, like any villains. People actually enjoyed recognizing places or bits of clothing and were glad to be included in the television world they loved. Many told me excitedly about a film that was shot in their villages in the late 1980s and about others shot on location more recently. One filmed in the temple of Madinet Habu in the fall of 1996 included scenes of some local women performing funeral laments, just as *Dream of the Southerner* had included women singing wedding songs.

Nevertheless, serials like *Dream of the Southerner* place villagers in a double bind. Ordinary villagers easily distance themselves from tomb robbers and materialistic teachers, interpreting serials with such moralistic messages as useful because they show viewers the difference between good and evil. They readily identify with morality and integrity. And yet, uneducated or undereducated villagers might find it hard to identify with the cultured and educated history teacher of *Dream of the Southerner,* dressed in the trousers and shirt of the "effendi," the educated class that has long been placed as the superior of the peasant. The serial thus positions them to identify with the moral hero, a position they accept because they see themselves as good people; but if they try to identify with such a protagonist, with all the other values s/he represents, they must realize their own inadequacy as people who have not achieved the protagonist's level of education, culture, and commitment to the nation. Serials like *Dream of the Southerner* might thus encourage them to feel their inferiority because of this promotion of the modernist values of education. Because this whole process takes place in a context of pleasure, since people genuinely enjoy watching television serials, it is difficult to be critical either of the didactic messages or the misrepresentations of themselves.

To suggest that as Sa'idis identify with the good they may be stifled from developing a critical alternative is not to say that they are defenseless against the ideological onslaught. This would be to presume a too-simple dynamic of identification with television characters. Television serials are widely recognized to have generic conventions of theme, setting, and emotionality, as will be detailed in later chapters. They are also recognized as fiction, compartmentalized as a sphere of entertainment with particular hours and forms of engagement, even if very much part of everyday routines and cultural imaginations. This creates certain resistances to messages and their personal implications. I observed that people seemed to resist the most insulting of the representations by simply continuing to go about their lives as if they had value. The pride in being a Sa'idi still exists. In the smallest of ways it is revealed in comments like that of a woman who watched my four-year-old son vigorously weeding in a field. She complimented him by saying, "He's a real Sa'idi!" Manhood, toughness, and skill were all implied. Moreover, people often suggested that Sa'idis were more moral than their northern or urban compatriots—both for the behavior of women and the virtues of poverty and hard work, claims that found some corroboration in the ambivalent depictions of peasants or Upper Egyptians purveyed in films and television serials, as I will describe in more detail in chapter 7.

What strikes me as best revealing that such villagers escape some of the negative entailments for their sense of self, despite their apparent lack of cynicism about the messages of state culture, backed by the presence of the state institutions in which they are so enmeshed now, is the very fact that they persist in being fully involved in the unfolding events and social life of their own community. Although this face-to-face community has its fair share of backbiting, bitter conflicts among neighbors and kin, and envy, along with some seedy morality linked to sex tourism in this part of Egypt, with its long history of involvement with foreigners, people continue to use a language of good and bad that is their own. They may identify with some of the morality of television serials when these exonerate authentic ordinary Egyptians—people with integrity, generosity, and old-fashioned values. But they do not, in their own interactions, immediately appropriate for their own use the values of being educated and cultured presented in serials such as *Dream of the Southerner*. Instead, they judge educated individuals, like anyone else, by their behavior. They recognize that some educated persons, whether outsiders or native sons and daughters, treat others with respect and have something to offer; others are arrogant, put on airs, or are effete. Nor do they necessarily suspect those uneducated who have suddenly become wealthy, even though these nouveaux riches, like the Hagga Fadda of *The White Flag,* have become the favorite villains of many television serials in the 1980s and 1990s since neoliberal reforms took off. Zaynab, for example, once praised a neighbor whose family had succeeded fabulously in tourism. She whispered about the briefcases stuffed with money that one son brought home every day from his concession at Karnak. But she insisted on what a good woman his mother was: she always said yes if you asked her for a loan and when you came to repay it she would ask with concern, "Are you sure you don't need it anymore?" This was a woman, Zaynab implied, who understood the plight of her neighbors.

IMAGES AND POLICIES

State officials and urban intellectuals, on the other hand, do not always share this rich woman's empathetic concern for her rural neighbors. When they are insensitive to the plight of the rural poor, even in social welfare projects directed at the peasantry, it may be related to the virtually unchallenged way that they represent them even in sympathetic serials like *Dream of the Southerner*. This serial was, after all, only a recent variation on numerous novels, short stories, and films that have depicted rural peasants negatively. The most consequential effect of the ways that Sa'idis and other rural and uneducated people are placed by condescending or negative discourses, I would argue, is that officials and educated intellectuals, despite their differences, end up colluding in projects that, sometimes inadvertently, have painful consequences for such people.[30]

The representation of rural peasants as ignorant and in need of education has a long genealogy in Egyptian political life. Michael Gasper has traced the beginnings of the conceptual frame that pitted elites against peasants to the nineteenth-century Islamic reform movement, where the general problem of the "ignorance" of the Muslim population was felt to be keenest in rural areas. There, superstition was thought to be rife, fatalism rampant, and awareness of the world most limited. For these reformers, education was the key to moral and religious reform and the alleviation of this ignorance, which stood in the way of national prosperity and progress.[31] Nathan Brown has analyzed the way peasants were viewed as obstacles to development of the Egyptian state in the early twentieth century.[32] Similarly, Omnia El Shakry's work on social reformers and social engineering projects of the midtwentieth century has shown how nationalist writings "valorized the peasantry as the 'true sons' of Egypt, the repository of national cultural values, but also localized them as a sphere of backwardness to be uplifted and modernized."[33] Elliott Colla's work on the ideological movement of territorial nationalism that organized itself around links to Pharaonic civilization in the period between 1915 and 1940 (and was revived to some extent under President Sadat) reveals, too, the special ambivalence toward the Upper Egyptian peasant. As Colla notes, using as evidence the work of writers such as Tawfiq al-Hakim and Salama Musa, the peasant's proximity to the monuments of ancient Egypt made him (and it was usually a him) "the unconscious inheritor of Pharaonic culture," while his ignorance of its significance made him the inferior of the urban, secular, modern, and patriotic intellectual, who, like the European colonialists, appreciated this heritage, but unlike the European, saw it as his own and the basis for a united nation.[34]

During the Nasser period, the peasant and the worker became symbols of the composition of the nation and were affirmed as keys to its development. At the same time, mass education was instituted as part of state building and national development and at least in popular culture, as we saw with the films *The Night of Counting the Years* and *The Mountain,* the rural peasant was associated with a backward tradition in need of modernization. The value of labor and peasant productivity that was so central to the ideology of socialism has been undermined in the past few decades with the change of regime, as has the state's commitment to mass education, full employment, and health care. But as I will argue in chapter 7, the positive value of local peasant cultures, even in Upper Egypt, is being revived to counter the ideological pull of Islamism. So the ambivalence continues, with television serials such as *Dream of a Southerner* perpetuating the older elite discourse on peasant ignorance as a social and national problem.

The negative views of rural Egyptians that are associated with the positive view of modernity and education continue to underwrite projects that could have difficult consequences for particular communities. A good example is the project that has been under way since the mid-1990s to remove the population living adjacent to, or on top of, Pharaonic ruins, in particular the people of Gurna. This project of the Luxor City Council is supported by the Supreme Council for Antiquities as well as many urban intellectuals who write in the press, although a few dissenters have championed the locals.[35] The project is defended in the name of many of the same values infusing the serial *Dream of the Southerner*. The residents of Gurna are accused of tomb robbing and illegal trafficking in antiquities, just as they have been since 1828, when the European Egyptologist Jean-Francois Champollion wrote a memo to Mehmet 'Ali, the governor of Egypt, deploring the peasants' devastation of the monuments and greedy desire for European money.[36] The locals, now as then, are accused of destroying the archaeological sites that are not just part of the wider national heritage but world heritage. Just as the antiquities dealers and collectors were not blamed in the last century, nothing is said about the buses that rumble up and down the new roads, idle in large parking lots, and spew exhaust into the air, surely damaging the monuments as much as the village households. Few consider the impact of the tourists' breath and perspiration on tombs that have survived for many thousands of years but are now vulnerable to decay. No one dares complain, in the wake of Islamic militants' attacks on tourists, about the investment made to spruce up ancient temples by installing spotlights that bathe them in light all night long. And no one says anything about the army and security forces that have set up what look like permanent camps up in the Theban hills, gashing steps directly into the ancient mountains and stringing electric lights across them.

The villagers' desires to stay in their own houses, on their own land, and in their old community is represented as selfish and individualistic. In the interest of the wider good of preserving the antiquities and making them attractive to the public, the villagers are being asked to move far away from their friends and family, their palm trees, and their work. For the residents of the hamlet near Madinet Habu, they are being asked to move away from the rest of the village of which they are a part. What is being offered to them is a chance to resettle in small concrete houses in an exposed and barren area at the edge of the desert, away from markets and kin as well as access to the tourist income. Having heard the rumors about relocation, the distraught villagers first used to protest to one another, "They can't move us. We have title to the land." But over the past years, despite some very nasty confrontations in which people have been killed, many from Gurna, at least, have moved to the larger houses offered to them, the agreement being that their original family houses will be razed as soon as they move.[37]

It is difficult to separate patriotic concern for the preservation of Egypt's heritage from desires to increase tourism and the income it generates for the state and private investors.[38] The plan to relocate the villagers is in line with proposals of an earlier 1970s World Bank scheme for the development of tourism in Luxor and other plans going back to the 1940s, which involved the infamous construction of New Gurna, the mud-brick village designed by the architect Hassan Fathy and sabotaged by the locals.[39] As Minister of Tourism Mamduh Al-Beltagi states regarding the plan, "This goes again with the development of archaeology in Egypt. It is a very good project to make Luxor into an international museum for everyone."[40]

There is no doubt that the preservation of Egypt's extraordinary treasures is important, and the problems of balancing this goal with the needs of ordinary people who live near them are thorny. But that their needs are so easily brushed aside cannot be unrelated to the ways in which such people are perceived. Their removal has been openly justified in terms of the kinds of backward lives these villagers live. Such villagers do not present to the outside world, especially in the form of the millions of foreign tourists who visit Luxor to see the Pharaonic monuments, the right image of Egypt. They live in shabby houses, they bring their water up in barrels on donkey carts (no piped water is allowed in Gurna), they take their water buffalo to the irrigation canals to bathe, they wear *gallabiyyas,* and they look poor. *Dream of the Southerner* reconfirms that many are stupid and uneducated, crudely sucking sugarcane and unable to read Arabic, even less appreciate Pharaonic inscriptions. Worst of all, their scruffy children beg. The best thing is to get them out of the way so that no one will have to see this embarrassing face of Egypt.[41] One rumor circulating in the late 1990s was that the plan is to preserve some of their houses as artists' studios, while in others actors dressed in Pharaonic costumes will reenact the lives and ways of the ancient Egyptians. A clue to the priorities is that the only locals to be allowed to remain were to be the manufacturers of objects like alabaster vases and painted papyrus for sale to the tourists.

Like the makers of *Dream of the Southerner,* many involved in this project of relocation are sophisticated and socially concerned. They may even be sympathetic to the locals. Yet they cannot help seeing the solution in terms of a particular set of values and priorities, tied to a vision of national modernity that has a long, if uneven, history in twentieth-century Egypt. Television, literacy classes, and other forms of state culture try to promote and encourage these values of education and national modernity. The problem is that unless the basic structures of economic and political life that could sustain such values are put into place more universally in Egypt, the values themselves come only to symbolize a lack on the part of many rural villagers: their inability to measure up to the ideals. This, I have argued, has consequences for their own self-images as well as for wider policies affecting them.

The peculiar effect, even on the most well-meaning of the intelligentsia, of the powerful association of education, modernity, and national progress will be explored in chapter 4, where we consider how women are faring. As many have noted, alongside peasants, they have been the enduring objects of uplift and subjects of national pedagogy in the twentieth century.

Women and girls attending a literacy class in rural Upper Egypt, 1996.
Lila Abu-Lughod/Anthro-Photo.

[4]

Development Realism, "Real Melodrama," and the Problem of Feminism

THE AESTHETIC governing most serious television serials in Egypt might be called "development realism," distinguishable from the other major media aesthetics Michael Schudson identified for the First and Second Worlds. Socialist realism, he noted, was "designed to dignify the simplicity of human labor in the service of the state"; capitalist realism, to glorify "the pleasures and freedoms of consumer choice in defense of the virtues of private life and material ambitions."[1] As the analyses of pedagogic serials in previous chapters have revealed, development realism idealizes education, progress, and modernity within the nation. The aesthetic is connected to an ideology of social welfare and uplift for the benefit of a nation in need of development. It can be thought of as the cultural counterpart of the social welfare policies that initially were considered crucial for national development—an aesthetic and ideology, as I will show in the next few chapters, now eroding in many parts of the world facing the tyranny of new notions of purely economic development in a global capitalist context.[2]

If peasants were one of the targets of uplift and objects of welfare for national development, women were another. In Egypt, as in many parts of the postcolonial world, local feminists have tried to link the advancement of women to national development and progress; we need to examine how they have done this along with the minefields threatening such an enterprise. In this chapter, I will analyze more components of development realism using as a starting point the somewhat complex case of an Egyptian television adaptation of a short story by a progressive woman writer. The story is about a domestic servant, so it is worth shifting viewership from Upper Egyptian villagers to domestic servants in the city of Cairo to see how they respond not just to the values promoted by the developmentalist project but to its paternalism. I examine the ways this paternalism is reflected in television dramas but also in other genres of compelling programs that might be classified as "melodramas of the real." I will argue that such programs are problematic because they encourage viewers, including such women who share the widespread discourse of morality that also undergirds serious serials, to have faith in authority. They then frame their dissatisfactions in the language of complaint about those who do not offer a helping hand, again appealing to morality. Not only are contemporary viewers bound to be disappointed as government policies about social welfare shift because of structural adjustment policies but, as I want to show, they now resist the very structure of the developmentalist discourse, especially in its feminist inflection, which tends to be middle-class in values. This resistance comes both from the demeaning ways middle-class feminists position poor or rural women and from the availability of alternative discourses that offer different constructions of selfhood and community belonging. In Egypt today, the most powerful alternative discourses are religious.

Because I have been working with two sets of viewers who live in tough situations—rural women in a disadvantaged region and domestic workers in Cairo—I keep being drawn into these women's main concerns and trying to understand how television relates to them: to their exclusion from economic security or respectability, their frustrations and thwarted aspirations, their encounters with authority, and their moral and religious identity. This chapter is part of my attempt to discern the political and economic dynamics (national and international) that make their lives what they are, grasped ethnographically through their mediation by that portion of the intelligentsia who claim to speak to and for the poor. And, as I have been arguing in this book, among the more influential of the intelligentsia are those who work in television.

For a discussion of women, the most interesting of these culture producers are those who could be called "feminists"—even if they might deny the label.[3] These are people concerned with women's issues and improving the status of women in Egypt. There are not many of them—five or six major scriptwriters and a few directors—but they are productive and committed. Finding myself simultaneously sympathetic to and uncomfortable with their projects, I use this chapter to explore why someone whose ethnographic work has focused on women who are the targets of these cultural producers' good intentions might find herself ambivalent about progressive causes she otherwise supports. It is not my intention to make here the common and loaded charge that feminism is problematic in Egypt because it is Western. I, like others, have written elsewhere against that simplistic position for its false binarism, among other problems.[4] The excellent scholarship on Egyptian feminism has shown that from its beginnings it has been nationalist, has consisted of many varieties, and has accommodated Islam in multiple ways, even if the general tendency from the 1950s and '60s in the era of state feminism was secular.[5] This chapter will concentrate on a different problem. Although I acknowledge that there are many different kinds of feminism in Egypt—liberal, socialist, Islamist, and local hybrids (to use crude labels only for heuristic purposes)—the kind that concerns me here is that which has been able to penetrate the medium of state television. It is a feminism co-opted by developmentalism, whose basic problem is a middle-class bias.

VOICINGS OF THE DOWNTRODDEN

When they heard I was doing research on television serials, a number of progressive intellectuals in Cairo insisted that I see a television film called *Nuna al-sha'nuna*. They first told me it is based on a short story by a fine woman writer. One told me the film had been awarded second prize at a television festival, though it deserved first, only because "Mamduh al-Laythi [then head of television drama production and regarded by many as crass] doesn't like this sort of thing." She pointed out that the drama was directed by In'am Muhammad 'Ali, a highly respected woman director who was one of the first generation of television professionals. A young actress who, like so many others, denigrated contemporary cinema and television in favor of the old black and white films also spontaneously mentioned the woman scriptwriter of this program, Lamis Gabir, as an example of the few fine writers working in television today.[6]

The television drama is based on a short story about a rural girl who is sent by her father to Cairo to work as a maid. Written by Salwa Bakr, known for "promoting the unheard voices of underprivileged women from the lower classes," as one feminist critic put it, the story had been published in 1986, about ten years before the television production aired.[7] The title of this story, *Nuna al-sha'nuna*, has been translated variously into English as "Dotty Nuna" or "Noony the Loony," referencing both the citified (and silly) nickname given the girl by her employers and the impression she makes on the woman she works for—eccentric or nutty. These translations do not capture the full connotations of *sha'nuna*, which also include "untamed."[8] Nuna's odd behavior (jumping around the kitchen doing exer-

cises, repeating phrases of classical Arabic poetry that she does not understand, letting the water in the sink overflow, or looking intently at onions as
she cooks) actually comes from her obsession with the school next door.
Through the kitchen window she can overhear the lessons and see the activities of a girls' school. She is entranced and confused by this magical
world and spends whatever time she can listening and learning—lines of
classical poetry she finds beautiful but can find no one to explain to her,
chemistry (which is why she is trying to find the hydrogen sulfate in the
onions), and the square root of 25. She is slapped when she can't help cor-
recting the lazy and stupid son of the household during his private tutoring
session in math.

Nuna runs away the day after her father comes to Cairo to take her back
to the village to be married. She has been there for three years. Her father
proudly tells her a suitor has come for her—a man who has returned from
working in Saudi Arabia with enough money to furnish a whole room and
to buy her a pair of gold earrings for her dowry. The reader is less puzzled
than the father or the girl's employers about why she might have fled, a
puzzlement expressed in their confused discussions with the investigating
police where it becomes clear that the employers have had so little concern
for her that they cannot even describe her features. We are privy to her
dream on the final night before her disappearance, when, after laying awake
for hours thinking about how she did not want to return to the village "to
live in filth and fleas" or to marry and "end up like her sisters, sunk neck
deep in hardship and misery," she "dreamt of the school, the girls, the officer's son whom she had slapped—in her dream many times, because he did
not know the square root of 25. She also saw Aytalah [one of the mysterious
words in the line of poetry] and he turned out to be a beautiful being. She
was not sure whether he was human or jinn [a spirit]: he was white, as white
as cotton flowers; he had two wings, beautiful with the colours of the rain-
bow." She clung to them and Aytalah flew with her "far away until she
reached the sky and saw the golden stars."[9]

One admirer of the short story, Ferial Ghazoul, professor of comparative
literature at the American University in Cairo, argues that Bakr in this story
has created both a popular realism and a popular symbolism that reflect the
way the marginal or oppressed, usually silenced, contest dominant discourses.[10] She argues that the dream is a crucial aspect of the story. It symbolizes Nuna's longing for a kind of beauty absent in the oppressive society
in which she finds herself, just as her escape is her resistance against having her destiny decided for her. Both events are ambiguous, however. In not

knowing what happened to Nuna, we might have hope for her future (but we might not). The symbolic ambiguity of the dream is likewise telling. Ghazoul sees the uncertainties and multiple meanings of this creature with rainbow-colored wings that is the means of Nuna's transcendence as reflective of the kinds of vague visions the oppressed have. Ghazoul thus argues that Salwa Bakr, a marginal writer who allows the marginal and the oppressed (those who have a greater understanding of the ways systems benefit people unequally) to speak, has produced "the eloquence/rhetoric of the downtrodden."

The story addresses, with brilliant economy and simplicity, a formidable range of issues from the exploitation of rural girls to the cruelty of class relations in Egypt. Most strikingly, it manages to create at its center a humane image of the innocent openness of a young girl deprived. As Bakr explained,

I wanted to talk about the little village girls exploited from childhood working in houses—how they are dispossessed because their families are the ones who take their salaries . . . , how the girls are subject to the worst kinds of insult and unfair treatment, ranging from rape to being treated as slaves. . . . I spoke about the theft of their identity. . . . When the girl comes to Cairo as a maid they have her hair cut and change her name and this confuses her values so she becomes transformed . . . neither an urban nor rural being. I also wanted to speak about how girls are bound by the chains of slavery through marriage because soon after the girl reaches puberty (twelve to fourteen), they get her married so that her father can take her dowry and get rid of her. Then her husband takes over exploiting her.[11]

In having Nuna's younger sister replace her in the household, Bakr wanted finally to show how "the circle of backwardness reproduces itself."

The unfairness and inhumanity of such practices is drawn in the story by the contrast between Nuna's actual curiosity and desire for knowledge and education and the way she is reduced to her value as a worker. Her mistress describes her to friends as "an eager beaver and . . . as strong as an ox."[12] Bakr explained that she got the idea for the theme of the school (and, as one magazine article described the film character, being "crazy about knowledge") from an experience she had visiting a village with a friend of hers, the daughter of the landowning family. The friend had bought a television for her mother and all the peasant women gathered around, completely mesmerized by the science education program on the air. They did not understand it and saw it instead as a world of magic.[13] She said she asked herself if it really is true that all these illiterate people have no interest in education.

She has found, on the contrary, that they always have a strong desire for education but that for political reasons they are denied it. In support of this argument, she recounted her experience of participating in a literacy program as a university student in the late '60s and early '70s. She described how her group was going to Qaha, a village now famous for its jam factory. "At that time, the landowners who had planted cotton were fighting the literacy program. We were teaching the peasants in the evenings. The landowners did not want the peasants to stay up late because they wanted them to rise early to work. They turned the electricity off. So, the landowners were conspiring against the laborers."

In her short story, Salwa Bakr seems to go beyond the usual liberal and progressive discourses about education in Egypt. Most of those who came of age during the Nasser era, when mass education was instituted, and especially those from nonelite families who benefited from such education (as are many of the major players in television) share a faith in education as the solution to Egypt's backwardness. As I have discussed in previous chapters, education is a central trope for all who talk about Egypt as an underdeveloped nation lagging behind the West and express desires for national development, progress, and enlightenment. Instead of this conventional discourse of development, Bakr gives us a personalized story where education has content. While she understands lack of access to education as political and decries the current inequalities in educational opportunities (a gap she rightly notes is widening precipitously with the removal of support for public education), her short story paints education and knowledge not so much as a means to social mobility but as personally emancipatory and expansive of experience. Most radically, she tries to show how the life of the mind enriches or allows an escape from a life of drudgery. It is the servant girl's poverty of experience and lack of skills that make Bakr feel her lot is so bad.[14] Her newfound world of knowledge, which is also a world of fantasy, is what the servant Nuna does not want to give up by returning to the village.

This feminist approach to education, seeing in it the means for individual growth and personal emancipation, can be found in other works, such as Fathiyya Al-'Assal's favorite serial, *She and the Impossible*.[15] But a story that humanizes a servant girl by showing that she is more than an ox and wants to have a life of the mind implies an unstated corollary: that the underprivileged, the downtrodden, and the marginal would not in the course of their ordinary lives have rich experiences, mental or emotional. The secular intellectual thus speaks, at least in this short story, for the subaltern in a voice that is ultimately middle class and wedded to a modernist set of values that include education, science, and knowledge. Nuna is redeemed by her brightness, curiosity, and desire for education. She desires enlightenment. Were she uninterested in this, desiring instead, for example, to go back to the village to marry and have a family, to help a husband work the land to feed those children, to live among her loved ones, family, and neighbors in "the filth and the fleas," or to restrict her knowledge to local knowledges, including popular Islam, she would not have been a heroine. Nuna's family barely figures in the story. Mostly it is represented in the person of her father, who is an agent of her exploitation, not a victim of a system that keeps some people poor. We get only a hint of the affection that might exist among family members in a passing reference to how Nuna misses her mother and sisters and a wistful remark her father makes to the investigating officer.

Rather than presenting what Ghazoul has called "the eloquence of the downtrodden" (*balaghat al-ghalaba*), I would suggest that Bakr, as an educated intellectual, however radical, feminist, and sympathetic to the socially marginal, cannot escape what we might call instead "the rhetoric of development" (*balaghat al-tanmiya*). And it is the elements in the story that conform to the rhetoric of development that explain why it could have been taken up by television. The story is not just about the feminist and leftist topics of class and gender exploitation, which had gone out of favor by the 1990s and may have been behind the initial opposition to producing the film; it also is about education and that noble goal, enlightenment. In this area, Bakr shares something important with her nonfeminist peers for whom, as we have seen, education is still presented as central to ideals of modernity and national development. This venerable theme made the story, despite certain objections, ripe for television adaptation. The condition of a poor servant girl becoming a subject and citizen is that she renounce her family, her roots—and if not the idiocy, as Marx would have it, of rural life, then its ignorance.

TELEVISION'S PRESSURES

Like many intellectuals who are not involved in television production, Bakr is critical of the medium for cultural and political reasons. In a short story translated into English as "Filching of a Soul," she presents television as responsible for destroying culture and the arts (by replacing reading and cinema-, concert-, and theatergoing) and promoting bourgeois consumerism.

The couple who are the story's protagonists become convinced by television that they must have gadgets "indispensable in the modern home" as well as wall-to-wall carpeting, and so they divert all their resources to such projects.[16] In her interview with me, Bakr focused on another objection she had to television: its political role. She described the medium as simply an arm of the state in Third World countries. In Egypt she sees it as having taken the place of political parties, themselves now extraordinarily weak and ineffectual. No opposition parties are allowed expression on television, she claimed, and all programming, including drama and entertainment, is carefully directed according to political vision. Finally, she maintained that those who work in television are chosen not for their abilities and experience but for their loyalty to the state.

This is a harsh judgment that underestimates the complex way state television works in places like Egypt, even while capturing something of the truth of its use as an instrument of hegemony. Television is indeed a government-funded medium (although increasingly benefiting from advertising revenues) overseen by the Minister of Information (not the Minister of Culture) with its own censorship bureau. Its charter in 1971, eleven years after its founding, declared its goals to be serving the people, national interests, and socialist transformation; participating in expressing the demands of the masses and their daily problems; preserving the national heritage; encouraging free and honest expression; and determining the moral values that should govern broadcast material.[17] However, to ignore the negotiations, struggles, and dynamics of a state-run culture industry is to flatten out the processes that shape its products and thus to miss the ways in which it is not simply hegemonic. Because it takes many talented people to produce television, who come into the production process with different ideas, politics, and aspirations; because television programs always encounter audiences who are interpreting actively in terms of diverse life experiences; and —as I will argue later, in my discussion of a shift away from the developmentalist aesthetic—because the state is not sure what is in its interest, television is always contaminated by that which is counterhegemonic, oppositional, or simply misfitting.

In fact, Salwa Bakr was not unhappy with the way the television adaptation of *Nuna al-sha'nuna* turned out. Although there was indeed opposition to the idea of producing this film, the censors refusing it initially, the director (a woman whose interest in presenting work on women's issues dates back to the late 1960s) fought for it, using her personal influence and standing in the field to persuade the Production Sector to allow her to proceed. As often happens in the case of major directors and writers, she was finally permitted to produce the film. However, the major differences between the short story and the film lead one to appreciate that it was the familiar and well-meaning nationalist message about education and development that enabled her to produce and show the film, and for it to find favor among the progressive intellectuals who recommended it to me. The theme of education was expanded and modified to remove any ambiguities. And though the progressive messages about class exploitation and even gender remained, they were muted and ultimately undermined by the validation of an educated, enlightened middle class.

Not all the changes to the plotline need to be understood as ideological or political. Some of the differences between story and film are the inevitable results of having to spin a spare story of about eight pages into a two-hour film. For example, content was filled in concerning the number of children in the village from which Nuna comes; the reason her father sends her to work in Cairo (so he can purchase some land and a color television); and how she learns city and upper-middle-class ways (quickly picking up the difference between *escalope panné* and *biftek,* learning the names of imported cheeses, and making trips to the dry cleaner's).

The major differences, however, are ones that turned a story that is ambiguous and fundamentally critical of the class system into a television production that was didactic, moralistic, and hopeful for the future. Literary critics condemned some of the artistic choices made by the scriptwriter to render the story more accessible. Safi Naz Kazim was furious that the screenwriter had replaced an exquisite line of pre-Islamic Arabic poetry by Imra' al-Qays that puzzled Nuna with a rather ordinary word, *zanabiq* (lily), that was only slightly unusual and known in many quarters.[18] For Ferial Ghazoul, the real loss was the excision of the important dream sequence that she regarded as representing the confused emancipatory fantasies of the subaltern. Instead of this dream of a winged creature, the film included only short, realistic daydreams in which Nuna sees herself as one of the schoolgirls.

More significant to my mind was that a portion of the bourgeoisie was exonerated. As is the case with many serials of the late 1980s and 1990s produced by the old generation of television professionals, the new capitalists are targeted for criticism. The head of the household was turned from the officer of the short story into a capitalist contractor making money by building tourist villages (although with connections to government officials). He is not evil, but interested in profit, rather than social development. The upper-middle-class Egyptian household is represented in the television film by an idle mistress concerned with her mink coat and the latest in cosmetic surgery; self-absorbed, elite women who hire fortunetellers to solve their marital problems; and spoiled and flighty children who get lavish birthday parties and excessive allowances.

Yet the message about class so unambiguous in the short story is undermined by the creation of a key character for the television adaptation: the sister of the materialistic mistress of the house. She is an educated woman who has just returned from the United States after specializing in occupational safety. She has refused lucrative jobs in America because she wants to return to her own country. She has lots of books, she exercises for health, she refuses the hierarchies by getting her own breakfast, she argues for the rights of workers and servants to decent treatment and conditions, and she is kindly toward Nuna. Not only is she kindly but she actually discovers Nuna's secret and nourishes her desire for education. She buys her books and teaches her to read. This leads her into serious conflict with her sister, who does not want her interfering. When Nuna runs away, she eventually appears at this woman's door. The woman nurses her back to health and finds her a job working in a school, where she will eventually be allowed to study. The enlightened middle-class woman thus rescues Nuna and helps her achieve her dream of education.

The rosy ending might be explained away by the observation many seasoned television serial watchers make: "Arabic serials can't have bad endings." But the introduction of this new character is more crucial. It changes the whole story by framing it as one of morality and paternalism. Not only is this character moralistic in the way she lectures her sister and brother-in-law about their materialism, lack of social conscience, and exploitation of inferiors. By her very existence she proves that social injustice is a moral, not a class, problem. Not all members of the bourgeoisie are to be blamed, this character demonstrates. In fact, the educated and enlightened members of this class are those who will expose the mistreatment of the downtrodden and will help uplift them. In this alteration of the short story, a powerful and longstanding narrative convention has intervened—one that has run through numerous films and television serials, associating the Europeanized upper classes with immorality and the educated middle class (and those from the upper classes redeemed by education) with patriotism and social concern for inferiors.[19]

In this television adaptation of the short story, expression is given to the paternalism (which includes, in Spivak's terms, the maternalism of feminism) endemic to the discourse of national development, the primary language, as I have noted, of this postcolonial state.[20] Those in authority—and that includes those in government and intellectuals, as long as they are honest, loyal to their nation, and with conscience (and therefore do not abuse their positions)—are there to ensure social justice, to help those in need, and generally to improve society. This message is repeated in most television programming, from talk shows with officials to the popular evening serials. And it is this message, with its moral framework, that is probably the most powerful means through which television contributes to the hegemony of the state and the bourgeoisie, despite the claims to oppositionality or social criticism of so many of the finest writers and directors.

The moral framework and the heroism of the educated, enlightened middle class are found in many different types of serials, from ones that are condemned as too obviously didactic to those that, as I discuss in chapter 8, flirt with the glitz of American soaps by taking us into the lives of the extremely wealthy nouveau riche (but whose basic theme is still the evils of corruption). An example of a serial critics found too didactic, as I noted in chapter 3, is the 1991 production *Wa ma zala al-nil yajri* (And the Nile flows on), about "the population problem." The serial's protagonist, Dr. Omayma, is a nicely dressed woman physician with lipstick and not a hair out of place who supports local women against the abuses of their men. Caring doctors are not the only authorities the serial presents as saviors fighting uphill battles. Given the opposition to family planning by many local religious authorities and a widely popular belief that birth control is contrary to God's will, it was important to present a religious counterweight. The other important protagonist is thus an enlightened government-appointed shaykh (learned religious leader) who supports family planning. Played by a popular and handsome actor (Hisham Salim), this religious authority is the voice of compassion and reason.

The State Information Service/Information, Education and Communication Center that sponsored the serial patted itself on the back and considered the production successful in part because its immediate postviewing interviews revealed that what generally attracted viewers to the serial were these two characters of the doctor and the shaykh.[21] In both cases, as is often true with viewers who are pretty sophisticated consumers of drama, the major reason given for liking the characters was good acting. But other reasons given, for the doctor, were that she stands on the side of the oppressed, is considerate, is passionate about her mission, and has important information on family planning. The religious figure was appealing because he understands religion correctly, he solves problems in a good and open way, and he understands family planning well. The popularity of these two characters, the report argued, was to be viewed positively, since the doctor and the shaykh "are the voices of reason and truth and hold sound opinions regarding the population problem." [22] The follow-up survey of six hundred conducted in 1993, a year later, by the Center for Communication Programs at the Johns Hopkins School of Public Health revealed that the less educated were more likely to identify with and think they would turn to the doctor figure for help, suggesting how well the lessons of the goodness of authority figures have been learned. [23]

Few serials have been as openly pedagogical as *And the Nile Flows On*, but many of the important ones since the end of the 1960s that have tried to address women's issues share the basic moral frame and the glorification of education. Among the many serials In'am Muhammad 'Ali has directed are ones addressing the problems of women's illiteracy, the usefulness of women's work and its contribution to a good marriage ("women's work is not a luxury but important for developing societies that cannot be advanced if one half of the society supports the other half"), the economic problems of women-headed households, and the denials of women's rights in marriage that unreformed personal status laws represent. [24] Many of these serials were written by women scriptwriters like Fathiyya al-'Assal and Wafiyya Khayri, who, although quite different in their political visions and social impulses, as I discuss elsewhere, [25] nevertheless push for women's independence, commitment to work as a means to development, transcendence of the role of wife and mother, and rejection of the patriarchal social pressures and "traditions" that limit women's possibilities, suppress their creativity, and prevent them from developing loving, equal relationships with men.

If, as television writer Wafiyya Khayri told me, the pressures of a growing Islamism make it impossible now to produce a bold comedy serial like the 1970 hit *Sayyidati anisati* (Mrs. and Misses) that she worked on—a serial that ridicules the absurdity of social conventions and "traditions that control and impair our lives through their irrational pressures" in favor of a more liberal modernity—it is still the case, as I showed in my analysis of *Mothers in the House of Love* (the serial about women in an old-age home), that serials produced by such women and progressive men continue to show the value of education and work for women.[26] In a wonderful moment of intertextual reference, a character in the film about the maid, *Nuna al-sha'nuna,* is shown watching a television serial. It is another serial directed by In'am Muhammad 'Ali called *Damir abla Hikmat* (The conscience of Headmistress Hikmat), whose protagonist is the headmistress of a girl's school threatened by the collapse of values in contemporary society. This intertextual moment is a perfect index of the entanglement of feminist ideals of personal emancipation with the patronizing developmentalism that makes education not just a means for personal growth but the measure of authority.

LIVES OF THE POOR AND MELODRAMAS OF THE REAL

Both the paternalism/maternalism and the construction of morality and enlightenment that infuse so many of the highest quality television serials, feminist and not, are subtly at work in a kind of television program that seemingly rivals the serials in popularity among the kind of women Nuna is supposed to represent: poor women working in domestic service. I want to turn now to such women as television viewers, to begin to explore how this development realism is received. I will discuss some women in Cairo who work as maids or nannies. Such women, along with doormen's (*bawwab*) wives, are those usually brought up by writers and television producers when they want to show the impact of their work, inadvertently betraying the classist character of their pedagogy. Salwa Bakr, for example, to illustrate the impact of *Nuna,* told me about her doorman's wife, who always asked for hand-me-down Mickey Mouse comics. "After she saw the film, she came to tell me that she had wanted to stay in school, but her father had forced her to quit. This means that the film provoked some wishes and questioning."[27] The scenarist Fathiyya al-'Assal similarly told me an anecdote about a maid to show the importance of writing television drama. She once overheard her maid in the kitchen shouting, "Hit him, you fool." When she came in to see what it was about, the maid complained that in the serial she was watching, a man was beating a woman, and she just let him do it. This story of feminist awakening pleased al-'Assal because she said these were the people she wanted to teach.

I suspect such women are used as evidence of the impact of television because they are, in Egypt, the members of the poor and working classes with whom urban middle- and upper-middle-class people have the most contact. But they are also stereotyped by the middle classes as devoted fans of television serials, although it seems clear to me that television producers have in mind as audiences not just these viewers but critics and fellow intellectuals as well. For such reasons, and because they are women who have the closest contact with other worlds, moving as they do between their popular neighborhoods and own social milieus to the very different social worlds of middle- and upper-middle-class households in the wealthier sections of Cairo, as they move back and forth from their ordinary lives to the very different worlds depicted on television, their reactions to television are particularly interesting.[28]

In 1997 the program that seemed to have most captured their imaginations and their feelings was a short-lived, unscripted show called *Min al-sabab?* (Who is to blame?), hosted by Tariq 'Allam, a young television personality already famous from his pioneering and popular street-quiz-cum-charity show, *Kalam min dhahab* (Words of gold).[29] *Who Is to Blame?* was a program focusing on real individuals with terrible problems. These individuals described their plights, usually the result of mistreatment by parents, spouses, children, bureaucratic institutions, or commercial firms. Relevant others, from relatives to authorities or experts, were questioned about the situation. The goal was to expose the problem, lay blame, and find a solution. Along the way, as I will suggest, viewers were given moral lessons.

I learned about the program when, trying to talk to domestics about television serials that summer, they kept changing the subject, spontaneously telling me instead about what they had seen on this program. From their descriptions, it is clear that *Who Is to Blame?,* which can be thought of as offering "melodrama of the real," was compelling for the way it took to extremes some of what people were accustomed to from serials. It allowed people to glimpse—and even become involved in—a much more amazing range of human relationships and human misery. At the same time, despite the populism of its format as unscripted television and the threatening criticism of government inaction or welfare agencies' ineptitude in alleviating the troubles of the nation's poor, from the perspective of those who talked to me about it, it reaffirmed the values of a strong morality, backed by the authority of the educated.[30]

When talking to me about her own tribulations in life, trying to raise children and support herself after her husband had left her twenty-seven years earlier, Samira, an older educated woman who ran a home daycare center, suddenly brought up *Who Is to Blame?* She told me I should definitely watch it. "True, it makes one cry," she said, "but it is really good. It is powerful." She then went on for half an hour about the situations she had seen revealed on the program. She began with and several times returned to the most recent program, about a man intercepted on his way to an orphanage, where he planned to leave his seven-year-old son. When questioned by the announcer about why he was doing this, he claimed that the boy was naughty. The boy, for his part, said he had done nothing. "It is because Dad left Mom and both of them remarried and my father's wife beats me. So I want to see my Mom. That's why I skip school and go to see her." Another program was about a young man who cried on the air, talking about how his father had left the family and married a new wife. The young man, who had a very young sister, claimed that his father was waiting until his mother had finished raising the children, whereupon he planned to take the apartment. As Samira commented, "Here it is the law that the woman gets thrown out into the street. The mother herself said, 'What can we do?' The young man was crying, the mother was crying. Even the little girl was crying. It was terrible." That was not all. There was a man of eighty who had a tiny shop. He said that his daughter was a deputy minister, but she never brought him anything, not even to eat.

In Samira's recounting of the long, sad story of another old woman she had seen on the show, a crucial element of the program became clear. That is the role of the experts who sit there in judgment, to give advice and draw moral conclusions. Samira told the story this way:

She said her husband had divorced her. She raised her daughter until she grew up and graduated from university. The daughter found someone from the university she wanted to marry. Her mother told her daughter, "But he's flunking. You can get married when he graduates." The girl said "No, I want to marry him." So she went to her father, whom she hadn't seen since the day she was born. . . . Her father, just to annoy the mother, let her marry the boy she wanted. At first they lived in an apartment, but it turned out it was not his—it belonged to his parents. When his mother found out he was living in their apartment, she returned from Saudi Arabia and kicked them out. What should they do? The girl went back to her mother and persuaded her to let them live with her. She gave birth to a boy. Then her husband said, "If you don't make your mother leave, I'm going to divorce you." And the apartment belonged to the mother. So she begged her mother and said she'd pay her the money to move to an old people's home. And she went. They paid every month and she left them the apartment. But then the woman became paralyzed. The home gave her medical treatment, but whenever they were late with their payments, she said, "I want to come back and live in my apartment." She [the mother] talked, crying, crying, and crying. *And the woman sitting there told her, "You should return to your apartment and kick them out. She and her husband should fend for themselves."* Wow, for an apartment she kicked her mother out. The one who raised her. You see, her mother had never remarried and had worked hard just to raise her. (My emphasis)

In this episode, there to corroborate the old woman's story was the nursing home director, who told other horror stories about old people in her charge whose families neglected them. The most important figures in every install-ment of *Who Is to Blame?* are the authorities, who ask questions and make comments. Several times Samira repeated, with approval, what had been said to the doctor planning to dump his child in the orphanage. She de-scribed them—two doctors and one woman doctor (the term *doctor* is used for respected educated professionals, not necessarily physicians) as sitting there crying as they heard the boy tell how his father and stepmother had burned him and beaten him with a hose.

The woman sitting there said, "You burn him and beat him with a hose? Why? Why? How can you mistreat people like this?" . . . When the man protested that she was being too harsh, she said to him "Not a word! You don't even deserve to be talked to." And it was true, a waste. She said to him, "You're a doctor? If you were a peddler or a garbage collector, if you were not educated, we might understand. But you are educated! What did you learn in university? How could you go so wrong?"

Other domestic servants who told me about the show described this woman as an important lady (*min al-sittat al-kubar*) and as a tough lady (*sitt gamda*).

The program clearly has affinities with American talk shows like *Dona-hue* and *Oprah*.[31] People experiencing a problem or an unusual situation are brought before an audience, who are shocked, titillated, and aroused by their accounts of their circumstances, given in intimate, self-exposing detail. But the differences between these American programs and the Egyptian one are telling. In the American ones, there is an apparent populism. People in the television studio audience give their opinions and judge. They argue, and do not agree with one another or with the people who have talked about their situation. As one might expect in a consumer society, people are presented as free to choose. Morality is less certain because many issues are presented as differences in "lifestyle." In the Egyptian program, on the other hand, au-thorities with the last word intervene to judge, and even scold; the im-morality and inhumanity of the persons at fault are made absolutely clear.[32]

The real television audience seems to agree with the authorities about situations that are black and white. When I asked Samira what the program was trying to show, she said (thinking I was referring only to the episode about the mistreated boy), "They want to make people aware. Don't re-marry. They are saying that if someone has children, he should not remarry. Either he or she should live for the children. It is wrong. If the mother mar-ries and the father marries, the children are the victims." When I asked if they had said so explicitly on the television program, she said, "Yes, they said it. The three of them said, 'Have compassion for your children. It is wrong to bring children into the world and then abuse them. There are people who can't have children.'" Furthermore, since this is a program of "charity," other kinds of help besides advice are given. In the case of the fatherless family threatened with eviction, the Minister of Housing offered them an apart-ment. Authority figures, in other words, step in not just to judge but to assist.

Other programs that poor women spontaneously mentioned as ones they watched or listened to regularly, and liked as much as the serials (which are, as one woman said, "only acting"), were other television and radio shows presenting people's real problems. One woman mentioned *I'tirafat layliyya* (Night confessions), in which people phoned in and confessed ter-rible secret things they had done, like a woman who admitted that her new baby was not her husband's.[33] In another program, this one on television, people came with complaints about how they can't make ends meet, they have been swindled in apartment contracts, or they have failed to get any-one to repair their streets. I also was told about a late-night television pro-gram that presented issues such as the complexes produced in children of divorced parents who hate each other. When they talked about these pro-grams, women often also recalled the television program mentioned in the village as well: *Al-muwajaha* (The confrontation), which presented jailed criminals being questioned roughly about their crimes. It had been popular but seemed by the late 1990s to have gone off the air, as did *Night Confessions*, which was cancelled after six years when its hostess, Bouthayna Kamel, re-fused to include authoritative experts.[34]

In all these cases of "melodramas of the real" or what some call "com-passion spectacles," the struggling women I spoke with were gripped and moved by what they saw of human tragedy and immorality.[35] They had compassion for the plight of those less fortunate than themselves. I sensed that they were moved also because they had their own experiences of pain and victimization. As one might expect in a country where the life of a maid reputedly involves the humiliations described in *Nuna al-sha'nuna* and where it is not respectable for women to work in other people's homes, every domestic worker I spoke with had a story of hardship that explained why she was in such a position—a father who died when she was young, a failed marriage, widowhood, a disabled husband. Many had stories about continuing hardship, despite the fact that most of them worked for foreigners and were relatively well paid.

These women often related what they saw on such television programs to their own situations. Discussing *Who is to Blame?* and the story about the old woman sent to the nursing home, Amira, an unmarried maid whose life story I discuss in chapter 5, told me about another person whom she had heard about at her sister's. This was a woman who had worked as a servant all her life to raise her son, and when he married, he and his wife forced her out of the apartment. She had to live under the stairs, and when people were kind enough to give her a little money, her son took it. Amira commented, "You see what the world is like? You think because we aren't married and haven't had children we're missing something. People say we should. But then look at those who marry and have kids. Look what happens. Their sons beat them and throw them out, because of their wives." She then reminded me about her own brother, still in the countryside, and how he was more concerned about his wife's needs than his mother's. "Once a man marries," she said, "he no longer cares about his mother or his sister, or even the blue devil." She had told me earlier how he had confined his mother to one room in the family house, and that his wife was no longer cooking for her. Amira, who was supporting her with her wages, was worried sick about her mother because, to make things worse, she had diabetes.

Amira's good friend Naima, also unmarried and from the same rural area, was part of this conversation. After listening to this real-life melodrama, she began a long tale about her own tribulations over a rent-controlled apartment she had finally been hounded out of by the landlord after a series of conflicts. He kept wanting more money and was angry that she rarely used the place because she slept at her job. Amira berated her for backing down and giving up her rights. They argued back and forth, as they had over this issue for years. At the end, as if to defend herself, Naima mentioned that she had heard many similar stories about apartments on a radio show she always listened to on Fridays.

Naima, who was quite devoted to these "real melodramas" and who felt most strongly that the world had changed and that people no longer cared about one another, also had the sorriest tales to tell. She now lived in a small furnished room on the roof of a building. Her health was poor and she only worked intermittently. She survived on a small pension she had inherited when her mother died, a pension that had been her father's, a former customs officer who had died when she was very young. Somewhat like Nuna, she had come to Cairo as a young girl of eight or nine to work. Instead of working for strangers, however, her employers were maternal relatives. As she told it, "My mother's relatives asked her to let me come stay with them. 'She'll learn to cook and do housework so when she gets married it will be useful.' So I went with them. I was so young I used to sit and cry. I used to sit on the balcony and cry. I didn't want to leave my mother alone. How could I leave my mother? I used to cry about everything."

The poignancy of her circumstances is brought out by her stories about why she did not marry when she was young. Her mother had gone to a matchmaker and they had found someone, but Naima had refused to go back and marry in the village. She said, "I preferred to stay here with my relatives, happily living. I used to cook and help them with the housework. We worked together. And then we'd go out and have fun. We'd go to the movies; we'd go to the parks. It was not like today. It wasn't crowded. I was just a child. I didn't know what would be good or bad for me. I was happy running and playing with the kids in the family." To show how wrong she had been not to notice the differences in their circumstances, she said, "Now they've all graduated from university and entered professions—one is a lawyer, one a doctor. The kids I lived with."

Like many domestics who come from rural areas, she returned to the village to live with her mother when the family no longer needed her, then came back to Cairo to work for another family, relatives of an agricultural engineer based in her region. She stayed there for five years until again the children grew up. This time she did not return home. She found a menial job in a health club, followed by work as a live-in maid. She hated the low salary and could not bear the confinement of living in. "I want to have my freedom to go see a friend and sit and talk with her, or whatever. It drives me crazy not to go out and see people." Since then, she has worked only occasionally. Even so, out of duty she supported a nephew who came to Cairo to study. He shared her little room and she cooked for him.

Naima suffered in love as well, telling stories that rivaled the "melodramas of the real" that she and her friend watched on television. Her brief marriage at thirty-five was a nightmare, convincing her that she would remain single forever. She had married a difficult man more than twenty years her senior because she hoped to be able to stop working. But he was bad-tempered, and when she became unwell, hemorrhaging so much she was forced to stay in bed, he did nothing to care for her. Living in his basement flat with no sun or air, she always felt cold. Her husband complained that he might as well be a bachelor and sent her back to her village to get some rest. Because he disgusted her, she said she didn't mind. He was old, scarred, and filthy. She also recalled that he didn't wash his hands and his breath made her sick. To top it off, he was, as she put it, miserly. They lived on almost nothing. In the six months she was married, she ended up spending all the savings she had—the returned key money from the rent-controlled apartment—on medicines and an operation.

In short, Naima had good reason to feel for others who had been wronged in life. What struck me so forcefully about her, though, was that she maintained at the same time a firm sense of the moral that also made her identify with the judgments of the authorities. She frequently remarked to me that people in the past had been good to and concerned about one another, a sentiment she heard in the especially appealing sermons one preacher gave at a mosque she frequented with Amira. There, she said, the shaykh advised them about right and wrong and how to live a good life: "Lies are wrong, one shouldn't gossip about anyone. We should be good to our neighbors. If someone is ill we should visit them. We should visit our brothers and sisters, because this is a connection through the womb, and it is wrong for anyone to sever it." Perhaps because of her vulnerable position as a poor single woman, she was especially sensitive about gossip and argued ferociously that people should not talk about one another behind their backs. But the other moral ideals, especially those about caring about others, were ones that she would have grown up with and then had reinforced both in the mosque and in the real or in fictional melodramas of the secular mass media.

COMPLAINT

I would argue that along with the lure of drama and spectacle, the shared language of morality is what draws people like Naima into television melodramas. But because these media forms associate moral judgments with educated and enlightened figures of authority, they establish dependence as the proper mode of relations between the disempowered and the state or the educated classes. Instead of a language of criticism of those in power, or even a language of rights—both of which are found among the more educated and those with more social capital, as expressed in political opposition and some writing in the press—women like Naima are led to fall back on the language of complaint about those who do not help them.[36] This discourse is the other side of paternalism/maternalism. It does not threaten, or question, the basic inequalities or structures of political power and class.

This interpretation of what goes on in society leads women like Fatma, an intelligent, lively, and somewhat cynical widowed mother of five adult children, to lay much of the blame for problems she experiences on members of her own class and those inching their way out of it. Several incidents she recounted illustrate this position. One of her complaints about television was that it presented false information. She complained not only about its depiction of crowds cheering the president but also about its ads for family planning.[37] Having heard all this positive talk about family planning, she told me, she decided to take her younger daughter, who had recently had a baby, to the clinic. She described what happened to her there:

I saw [on television] those who said how you get service and they care about the women who come to them. So I went with my daughter. She's a bit simple, so I had to go with her. But you know, they don't even let you see the doctors. The doctors are people of standing. They say "Yes" and "As you wish." But the ones below them, the ones in charge at the desk, they won't even let you get to see the doctors. "Come back tomorrow," "Come back on such and such a day." I say, "Lady, I'm not free. I have work to do." But I brought my daughter the next day and I don't know what the problem was then. I said to them, "By the time you let her see the doctors, the girl will have got pregnant again!"

Fatma then told me about a time she had spent in the hospital. The staff ran around putting nice clean sheets on the beds just before the doctors' rounds at ten o'clock. As soon as the doctor left, they stripped the sheets off and stuck them back under the mattresses, leaving the patients to lie in filth. When I asked who was to blame, she said, "The nurses. They are the worst." She then launched into a story, from television, about how nurses had been substituting water for medicine in the injections they gave. She even complained that nurses reused syringes and needles when they immunized children in the public clinics. Significantly, she added that it was a doctor who had exposed these practices on television.

It is not just the nurses (a very low occupational category in Egypt) but other low-paid white-collar workers that she criticized. A long story about her frustrating attempt to make good on an offer of a subsidized refrigerator made by the national company had a similar moral. Not only did the deliverymen insist on being paid privately, but the company engineer who came when she complained that the refrigerator was not working blamed the weak electricity in her neighborhood. And then he had the nerve to want to be paid for his trouble. Finally, when she went to the headquarters, the women employees sent her from one desk to another. She ended up furious and nearly in tears, threatening to scream if they did not let her speak to the director. "He came out to me and asked, 'What is it you need, Madam?' I told him, look at this. This room is full and that room full of women. If I go to one, she is busy making herself a sandwich. The other is sipping a glass of tea and they are talking about food and drinks and savings associations and what they did. I said, look, the truth is that I work. I'm not free to do this, and I've been coming here for three or four days now." He finished the papers for her refund.

And again, Fatma's long descriptions of the horrendous conditions under which army conscripts live (conditions that she had been forced to see firsthand, because one of her sons was serving his time in the army) placed the blame not on the officers—"the educated one doesn't beat, he just yells" —but on the trainers. As her son told her, they tell you in training camp, "If you have any dignity, wrap it up and put it away so you can take it with you when you get out of the army."

By co-opting the popular language of morality and linking it to an educated elite, television serials and other media programs contribute to the exemption from criticism of such people as officers and doctors. It is not that Fatma, Samira, or Amira were wholly uncritical of the government. Fatma was the most outspoken. She disapproved of the fact that the government paid army conscripts only 5 L.E. (less than $2 US) per month and did not give them enough food to live on. She was disappointed in the government for its failure to provide decent jobs for ordinary graduates of medical school, like her daughter. As I describe in chapter 6, she even accused government officials of absconding with aid meant for the poor and for pocketing income instead of creating jobs and projects to help the underprivileged. But more than anything, like Amira, who had spent months trying to get electricity connected to a new house she was building on the outskirts of Cairo and had to give bribe after bribe, Fatma was angry at the bribes one needed to give in order to obtain things that one was entitled to, like her daughter's graduation certificate. Both women were most frustrated by their encounters with those on the lower rungs with whom they have their most direct dealings. Many of these people are from the same class as the domestics, but with enough education or skill to have attained salaried positions in overextended public institutions. They somehow expected more generosity and integrity from elites.

Thus, along with the glimpses real melodramas and serialized dramas offer into the lives of the less fortunate, the more victimized, and the more heartless, women like Samira, Amira, and Naima are asked to imbibe a faith in the goodness of the enlightened middle-class authorities who voice the judgments they would want to make themselves. One important corollary of this faith, which brings us back to the serial *Nuna al-sha'nuna,* is that education is a virtue that justifies hierarchy. Everyone shares a belief that education is necessary, despite plenty of evidence that for any but the elites these days, with civil service shrinking and being very poorly paid, education rarely guarantees anything.[38] Television films like *Nuna al-sha'nuna* that celebrate education contribute to such continuing beliefs in education in the face of dwindling opportunities, even as they specifically encourage the education of girls. I have discussed in chapter 3 the way this faith in education works in the countryside. Here I want to consider some of the impact of such media-supported notions on urban domestics who mostly buy into, but find themselves unable to attain, the ideals of education for development.

The two older unmarried maids discussed above both expressed regret at not having been educated. Naima said her mother refused to get her educated or trained with a skill with the words "I don't have daughters that get educated. A girl should marry and care for her home." Yet she often commented that people who were educated understood more. Amira noted that when she was young she hadn't understood the value of an education. "I didn't like school, so I used to escape and play with the kids. My sister's house was right next to the school. So I'd go there and stay until the other kids got out of school, and then I'd walk home with them. Four years in school and I couldn't even write my name . . . I didn't know how important it would be. I thought I was going to stay in the village. I didn't know I'd be going to Cairo. And actually, even back home it is useful to be educated. You can teach your children. And girls get diplomas and work, in factories and lots of places. I didn't know that."

When we watched *Nuna al-sha'nuna* together, Amira said it was unrealistic to think that a servant could get educated like that, even though she did recognize many elements of the film from her own experience (the girl's initial fear of traffic, her sleeping on a mattress in the kitchen, her surprise that people ate meat every day of the week, and her difficulties learning the difference between beefsteak and breaded veal when all one had known at home were chunks of meat). She described her own recent efforts to attend literacy classes not through government programs but through the mosque, which was now taking over many of the services that the state used to provide. She did not find the classes good. But she also blamed herself: "My brain is thick, it forgets. And you need time to study. You need time for the lessons, time to study. If I were to do all the work of studying and preparing for class, I wouldn't be able to do my job. I tried for two years. . . . Because one is an adult, one has a lot on one's mind. At the lessons I'd be thinking about errands I had to do for work, like going to the market to get vegetables. You need a clear mind to learn." Although she believed that Nuna could learn because she was young, she also noted that in the past, when maids lived in like Nuna, they wouldn't have had time. She insisted that such girls used to work until ten or eleven at night and then had to be up early to help get the children to school. There would be no time for learning to read.

Another woman, kindly, dignified, and educated through the sixth grade who was working as a domestic to help cover the costs of educating her children, agreed that it might be possible for someone young to learn to read. What it took was real desire. On the other hand, she thought it was hopeless for older women. Perhaps she shared the prejudices of those who told the village woman Umm Ahmad (chapter 2) that she was too old to learn. Like Amira, who had failed in her own efforts, she said older women had too much on their minds, giving the example of her sister, to whom she had given a notebook and pencil with instructions to learn just one letter each day. "One day she writes. Ten days she doesn't. She's gotten old, it's over."

There is a problem in Egypt today with faith in education as central to progress, individual advancement, and the nation that arises from the everyday experiences of the kinds of women discussed here. For all the older women I knew, raising and educating their children were their primary concerns, and they had vague feelings of having been betrayed by their government. Most were heartbroken because their sons, and sometimes their daughters, found it so difficult to find jobs despite their qualifications. For Samira, herself French-educated and someone who had once lived a fine life but had fallen on hard times when her foreign husband had suddenly fled the country, the pain was seeing her children denied jobs that she believed their peers got easily. Salwa's eldest sons had decided to open a coffeehouse, following the line of work of their father's family. They hung their college diplomas on the wall. Fatma's oldest son had emigrated to Italy because he found no work as an agricultural engineer. When he returned to Egypt, only his foreign-language skills were useful, so he was working in a hotel. Her other son, like two of Samira's, was unemployed.

The women did not know whom to blame or have much sense of the policies and economic transformations that were causing the education dream to go wrong. They felt, as they did about many of their problems, that since they worked so hard, they deserved better. The government, or someone, should help. Television drama as well as the developmentalist rhetoric elsewhere in their worlds has led them, I would argue, to expect that a helping hand should be forthcoming. However, with the economic liberalization policies of the state and the imperatives of structural adjustment and privatization, the government and the elite are no longer so sure that they should justify themselves in terms of providing this helping hand.

THE ALTERNATIVES

Although increasingly dominating television, as I will discuss in chapter 8, the capitalist realism of advertisements and the many new serials that go along with the policies of economic liberalization are not the only alternative to developmentalism in Egyptian cultural life. There are signs, for example, of a nihilistic rejection by the disillusioned of the earlier developmentalist ideology of the state. As Armbrust has argued, commercial cinema and music began in the 1980s to expose the humiliations of ordinary people at the hands of the state and its bureaucracies; they also began to celebrate the violence and meaninglessness of lower-class urban life.[39] A spate of recent films such as 'Afarit al-asfalt (Road devils) and Thalatha 'ala al-tariq (Three on the road) offer antiheroes who are hustlers and prostitutes and are shockingly explicit for those more accustomed to the chastity of most contemporary television serials. Among small segments of urban youth, one finds other signs of rebellion. As the bizarre and much publicized 1997 crackdown on so-called Satan worshippers revealed, Egypt even has a few young heavy-metal fans who defy convention by sporting black shirts and earrings, hanging out in front of McDonald's, and mocking religion, just as the hysterical 2001 crackdown on gays revealed another subculture.[40]

But these alternatives are not appealing to poor women like the ones I have discussed in this chapter, women who are trying to support themselves and their families and are concerned about their respectability. More significant for them, and for many others, is the Islamic alternative. It is religious discourse that has appropriated the language of morality being ceded by the state as it pushes for privatization and other capitalist projects that do not find their justification in the language of morality. The domestics discussed in this chapter are as uncomfortable with the antivalues of the new cinema as with the new capitalism. They find more sense in the mosque lessons they now attend.[41] They may be frightened, as were Amira and Fatma, by the intimidation of religious fanatics in their popular neighborhoods. Such zealots had knocked on their doors to make sure that their husbands were going to the mosque to pray and had left notes under their doors demanding that they get their sons serving in the security forces to help imprisoned Islamist comrades. These women may even defiantly resist, as did Salwa, the unreasonable demands of religious teachers who tell them to quit work to attend classes. But the moral language of religion that Naima described above—where people are entreated to care about one another—resonates with them, especially in their neediness. They are somewhat persuaded about the evils of consumption (to which they have so little access), illicit desire (which goes against their upbringing), and even television, which is sometimes branded by religious authorities as immoral for its commercials and dancing and sometimes condemned by these same figures as a time waster. They sometimes find comfort in religious practice. One young maid, abandoned by her husband and working to support two young children, told me how insomnia and nightmares had troubled her until a religious teacher advised her to throw away her popular music tapes and play instead cassettes of Qur'anic recitation at bedtime. It worked wonders.

For these women, the ideals of religious piety (which do not exclude education—after all, Amira's literacy classes were held at the mosque) seem more vibrant than others. These ideals promise community and demand only a disciplining of the self, not consumption, as I explore further in chapter 5. Moreover, those who promote this path will always have the moral high ground in a nation that has never doubted religion, either officially or in the lives of ordinary people, even if it went through a period under Nasser that pushed secular ideals. When Amira watched the scene in *Nuna al-Sha'nuna* in which the enlightened middle-class woman tells Nuna not to call her by the honorific she had been taught by her mistress (*ya sitt*, or *hadritik*) but to use instead more neutral terms like *abla* (referring to her status as teacher), she had something to add: "But now the Muslims [the more pious] say you should not say *sitt*. Religious people say they'll have to pay for the sin of being called this. They say you should say *hagga* (the term for someone who has been on the pilgrimage) or something else. There is no *sitt* or *sidi* (the masculine equivalent) in Islam. Everyone is equal."

This kind of rhetoric of Muslim equality, even though produced in the context of a hierarchy with religious authorities and men at the top and sometimes pushed in authoritarian ways, offers something beyond the rhetoric of development and the increasingly absent helping hand in national

projects of uplift. As Saba Mahmood argues, the goals of the piety movement are to encourage people to cultivate virtuous selves, and beyond that
to create a virtuous Islamic society.[42] Those who teach use the language of
sisterhood and brotherhood, not paternalism and maternalism. For example, a prominent religious authority responsible for many of the "conversions" of actresses and dancers in the early 1990s talks about them as his
"sisters."[43] Given the structures of power, the continuing control of families
over the lives and reputations of women, and the very real social and economic inequalities in Egypt, their messages may resonate with many more
women than feminist developmentalism, with its calls to empowerment
through (a selfish) individual advancement and (an unattainable or disappointing) education and its maternalistic reinforcement of the authority of
the educated middle class. Moreover, the language of piety may seem more
familiar than the secular language of rights and choice used by feminist developmentalists including the writers and directors of television productions like *Nuna al-shaʿnuna* or by the family planning enterprise represented by *And the Nile Flows On*, which, Kamran Ali has argued, through a
language of choice and health of the individual, asks women "to abandon
familial and domestic concerns, and to enter as individuals the realm of the
universal and the civil, the domain of impending citizenship."[44]

I cringe to think what some of these poor working women would think
if they could read the well-meaning but patronizing study by Dr. Nadya
Radwan entitled *The Role of Television Drama in Building Women's Awareness*.[45] Her field study, based in two Cairo neighborhoods, reveals not only
the existence of deplorable class difference in levels of education for women
but the interesting fact that illiterate women tell researchers that television is
their main source of knowledge and information, confirming what television personnel always claim.[46] Like so many of her peers, Radwan views illiteracy as one of the most important problems facing Egyptian women and
society. As she notes, "Through education the individual is able to play his
role in production; education is one of the types of development of human
resources which allows for raising the power, skills and knowledge on which
a high standard of living and strong economy depends." She justifies education for women not just so that they can be the equals of men but for the
advancement of the nation.[47] In an argument that would make most of the
women discussed in this book feel ashamed if not angry, she blames illiteracy for the low level of awareness that leads to so many wrong practices in
Egypt. Among these she counts cousin marriage, ignorance about family
planning and health care, obsession with honor and revenge in the country-

side, drug addiction, polygamy, backward customs such as female circumcision, and male dominance.[48]

Although Radwan sensibly calls for more education for women, she also says that television drama has a role to play in changing values, given the high dependence of illiterate women on it. She argues, for example, that such programming has a responsibility to shed light on a range of issues. Her list includes issues of marriage and childbearing such as marital choice, marital age, equality, bride price, equal value of boys and girls, importance of family planning, feeding children well and vaccinating them; marital issues such as polygamy, divorce, women's rights to be educated and to work, insurance, pensions, and inheritance; issues related to health awareness; and issues of social upbringing, including inculcation of the values of honesty, beauty, love for others, civic consciousness, environmental protection, respect for elders, generosity to the poor, patience, and democracy. Furthermore, she charges television with the task of working on the problem of overpopulation, closing the gap between leaders and ordinary individuals in society, wiping out superstition, and combating antisocial behaviors including noise pollution, bribery, and wasting time at work (!). She even suggests that television help people learn the proper treatment of tourists, a particular concern for a country whose economy depends so heavily on this industry, which was, for this reason, targeted by Islamic extremists in their campaign to undermine the current regime.[49]

Radwan's staggering list reveals clearly the educated middle-class values that she is confident are right for all Egyptian women. As I have shown in this and previous chapters, television already treats many of these themes through the developmentalist voices of its progressive writers and directors, especially those who are women. And what I have tried to describe in this chapter is how such consciousness-raising projects, even when promoting worthy ideals, are first of all usually patronizing, reaffirming the superiority of the middle classes; second, mostly misleading because of the current political-economic circumstances of life in Egypt; and third, sometimes received ambivalently, especially because there are other alternatives, including the Islamic piety movement. As I show in later chapters, the hegemony of the aesthetic of "development realism" that dominated Egyptian television, like much media in the Third World, is eroding as we begin the twenty-first century. For feminists, these alternatives, like religious revival and capitalist consumption, look troubling, but I hope I have shown that the way feminist developmentalism has positioned the poor and uneducated women it has championed has itself not been without problems.

PART THREE

The Eroding Hegemony of Developmentalism

Karima Mukhtar and Hala Fakhir in a melodramatic scene from the historical serial *Al-Shari' al-jadid* (The new street), directed by Muhammad Fadil. Karima Mukhtar has also starred in televised public health spots since the mid-1980s. Photograph courtesy of Fayiq Salah al-Din, 1997.

[5]

Modern Subjects?
Egyptian Melodrama and Postcolonial Difference

IN THE LATE 1980s, a group of critical young university-educated Egyptians performed for their friends in Cairo a clever satire of local television. Recordings of the show later circulated informally on audiocassettes.[1] The performance made fun of the language of state officials and religious authorities, whose frequent appearances on discussion programs are seldom popular. The final three sketches on the tape, however, took on Egyptian television's most popular programming, the dramatic serials and films. Two of these stories are set in the countryside, where the misdeeds of foolish or violent peasants are easily found out by more-educated officers of nonrural origins. The third sketch entices its viewers with a film that promises to be "full of tears and surprises." This story opens with two sweethearts declaring their mutual love. When the man suggests that they get married, the woman protests that they are from different classes, yet admits that she has longed for the kind hand that would rescue her from the society that despises her. (She explains that she was forced to become a dancer when she was driven out of her father's home by a stepmother.) So the couple go off to the religious cleric to marry. There they discover that they have the same last name. The young man is distraught: "The only woman I've ever loved turns out to be my sister?!"

The satire mocks the major interpersonal themes of television melodrama and old films—love, family, and class differences—and recapitulates the politics that inform them: evil is represented as rural backwardness and good as urban modernity. It parodies the unlikely coincidences on which melodrama thrives, but in mimicking the expressive music and heightened emotionality of speech on which the effectiveness of these moral dramas depends, it also nicely captures two other key features—a strong moral message and what seems to be, to the smart university-educated satirists and to anyone more familiar with Western television drama, an excess of emotion.

Although in chapter 4 I described the aesthetic of Egyptian television serials as that of development realism, the nature of the genre itself has so far gone unexamined. In this chapter, I consider its qualities as melodrama and its possible effects, following Raymond Williams, in melodramatizing consciousness. Melodrama has been the subject of a great deal of literary and media theory. The touchstone is Peter Brooks's *The Melodramatic Imagination,* which made a powerful case for the significance of melodrama as a literary/theatrical genre associated with the upheavals of the French Revolution and the onset of the crisis of modernity.[2] Brooks argued persuasively for a particular definition and understanding of the melodramatic imagination—as concerned with the revelation of the moral order in the everyday in a "post-sacred era."[3] Most intriguing was his claim that melodrama was "the central fact of the modern sensibility."[4]

What can the satirical performance in Cairo by a talented group of university students tell us about melodrama and modernity in Egypt? Brooks was concerned with theater and novels in nineteenth-century Europe. In the twentieth century melodrama is more closely associated with forms of mass media like radio, film, and television. And in Egypt, as in other postcolonial contexts, cultural forms like television melodrama, projected by national television industries, are seen by state officials and middle-class professional producers as particularly effective instruments of social development, national consolidation, and "modernization."[5] This raises the question of what sorts of "modern sensibilities" television melodrama might mark in a place like contemporary Egypt, where those who make melodrama see themselves as trying to produce modern citizens and subjects.

I should note that there remains a good deal of confusion—or at least an enormous range of possibility—in the usage of the term *melodrama* in literary, film, and television studies. There is some justification for questioning whether the term actually designates a single genre at all.[6] For Egypt, I would be happy to call television serials domestic dramas. But it is useful to keep the term *melodrama* to remind us of a few features. First, these serials are unquestionably "modern" in drawing directly upon modernist literature, film, and radio. They are mostly about the everyday and involve ordinary people. Their characters are not the universally known heroes of epic poetry or folktales but representations of the common citizen. Like Latin American *telenovelas* and unlike British, Australian, and American soap operas, the Egyptian serials are finite, generally running to either fifteen or thirty episodes. Like melodrama, they come to a resolution, something that some scholars of media consider crucial to ideological clarity.[7] What the television parody captured exquisitely, however, is that they are also more emotional and forthright in their moral lessons than contemporary Euro-American television dramas.[8]

It is the significance of these latter two qualities—the unapologetic moralism (apparent in the plots and storylines) and the quality of emotionality, with affect located in ordinary life (apparent in the genre conventions)—that this chapter explores as part of the way Egyptian television serials might be part of an attempt to create a "modern sensibility." But I will also explore the difference it makes when a modern sensibility is being crafted in a society for which notions of national development remain strong as part of a political legacy, where the embeddedness of individuals in kin and family remains ideal, and where secularism has been only ambivalently constructed as essential to modernity.[9]

Television serials in Egypt, I will argue, work with modernist projects at two levels: intentionally, through disseminating moral messages inflected by local political ideologies, thus attempting to set the terms of social and political debate; but also more subtly, through popularizing a distinctive configuration of narrative and emotionality. It is in this latter way, as a genre with certain conventions, that television melodrama in Egypt might be understood most directly as a technology for the production of new kinds of selves.[10] It is a technology, I will suggest, for staging interiorities (through heightened emotionalism) and thus constructing and encouraging the individuality of ordinary people.

Yet I also want to show that this technology is put to work in a local social and political context that differs in many ways from the context of soap opera production and viewing in Europe or the United States, particularly in the overt projects to produce citizens of the nation in a society in which kinship remains important and other forms of community and morality exist.[11] Moreover, the growing relevance of religious identity and the practices of self-monitoring being encouraged place the genre of television melodrama, though popular, in a field of other technologies of modern self-making, some pulling in the same direction, some not. This suggests that we should be wary of telling any unilineal stories of personhood and the coming to modernity even when confronted with a genre that resembles others elsewhere.

MORAL VISION AS POLITICAL IDEOLOGY

In keeping with media ideology in postcolonial nations, television drama is viewed by most of its producers in Egypt not simply as entertainment but as a means to mold the national community. As Veena Das and others have begun to explore, national cinemas often represent and even help produce the sense of nationhood.[12] What has not been explored is how this ideology shapes the morality of melodrama. The Egyptian serials are concerned with morality—as Brooks's theory might lead us to expect—but this morality is social or community-oriented and thoroughly imbricated with the available political discourses. Like the Cameroonian mini-series, *Miseria,* described by Sheila Petty, and perhaps much officially sanctioned Third World drama, many Egyptian serials privilege "dogmatic concerns at a social level." The morality is not so much that of the individual as the social. Or as Paul Willemen says of Indian cinematic melodrama, of the individual as a member of a society undergoing transformations.[13]

A comparison of the storylines of Egyptian television writers illustrates the way morality is made social and the social is constructed in terms of differing political ideologies that could be characterized (too) simply as liberal, progressive, and conservative.[14] For a liberal feminist writer like Wafiyya Khayri, who has written serials about women and work and the impact of migration to the Gulf, it is the educated middle classes or those whom she calls "the cultural elite"—families with long familiarity with literature and other cultural forms—who represent the embattled values.[15] She dreads the boor as much as the nouveau riche. For a more progressive or populist writer like Usama Anwar 'Ukasha, the hope in his serials usually lies in an alliance between the good authentic people—artisans, the honest hardworking poor devoted to family and community—and the modern educated classes with a commitment to progress, morality, and the good of the nation. Even aristocrats, such as "the pasha" in his most magnificent serial, *Hilmiyya Nights,* can be redeemed by nationalist sentiment, following a storyline already familiar from nationalist Egyptian cinema.[16] Many of 'Ukasha's serials are concerned with the struggles of middle-class people to maintain principles and values, and they often portray the poor as virtuous. Some of his serials even relate individual lives to political events such as

the Palestinian *intifada,* the Gulf War, and the peace agreement with Israel. His intertextual references are with the political discourse of speeches,
newspapers, and historical memory. He shares with other progressive producers like Muhammad Fadil, the director with whom he often collaborates,
a sense that his art is for the "development" of Egypt. For example, in discussing a television film on the 1956 nationalization of the Suez Canal that
he was directing in 1993, Fadil explained that his intention in portraying this
historic national event was "to provide viewers with a sense of hope by com-
municating that, as Egyptians, we are capable of accomplishing things." The
responsibility of art, he added, was to portray reality "as it ought to be." [17]

The link between moral vision and political stance is just as clear in the
serials of a conservative writer like Tharwat Abaza. His work is distinguishable from the serials of liberal and progressive writers like 'Ukasha and
Khayri by its avoidance of reference to the national question, its nostalgia for
patriarchy and feudal values, and its commerce with religion. Abaza frequently uses stories from the Qur'an or from Islamic history as inspira-
tion—as in his 1990 *Ghufran,* based on the story of Joseph, following plots
or moral themes loosely while setting the stories in the present, complete
with infertility clinics, apartments in Europe, Mercedes cars, land seizures,
and crooked businesses. He generally ignores in his stories the anxieties and
struggles associated with modernity or the burning social issues of the day
that so intrigue writers like 'Ukasha and Khayri. His politics are to appear
distant from "the political"—as it is conventionally conceived in Egypt. He
tends to avoid in his stories any reference to Egypt as a nation, or to its place
in a larger world, and thus the main concern of contemporary political discourse—nationalism. If for other writers the city—the space of the modern—is the primary setting for the moral struggles of a complex new world,
Abaza usually prefers the countryside, which can become a timeless, seemingly apolitical locale for the play of good and evil, couched in the comfort-
ing tones of a moderate religious discourse.[18] Abaza is from one of the
politically prominent old landowning families of Egypt, but his own background is no less modern than that of Khayri or 'Ukasha. He is a graduate
of the Law Faculty of Cairo University and was in the early 1990s head of the
Writer's Union. His nostalgia is a defensive product of the social and political transformations of the postcolonial age.

The three writers attribute good and evil to different social classes, de-
ploy nationalist and religious discourses differently, and represent the past
and future differently. In short, their visions of the moral order—that
which Brooks saw as essential to melodrama—differ. This is evidence that

the melodramatic genre may be a key site for contending visions of a moral universe, visions refracted, as in Egypt in the medium of state television, through the competing political ideologies of the age in that particular nation.

Because television is an (albeit complex) instrument of a state that is more ambivalently secular than the Europe Brooks described as the context of the birth of melodrama, its drama does not always exclude religious referents or place morality solely within the nonsacred realm, as Abaza's serials show.[19] But on the whole, the moral visions are not defined by reference to religious truths. In fact, although many political ideologies do not find expression on state television, the most obvious exclusion is that of the Islamists, who, since media war was declared on them in 1993, are regularly represented in dramas as violent, immoral, and ignorant of religion (see chapter 7). However, what seems distinctive about the moral referents of the Egyptian serials, compared to most U.S. melodrama, is that they are tied, in keeping with the sanctioned political ideologies, to the larger social good and the community. With consequences I will take up below, Egyptian television serials, modernist in their secularism and their concern for the nation, explicitly worried about the moral ills threatening the social fabric, also tend to place individual characters very much within their families and their communities.

MELODRAMATIC EMOTIONS

Viewers, whether ordinary television watchers or critics, recognize to varying degrees the ideologies informing these melodramas and react to them—either sympathetically or with hostility, depending on their own situations and political visions. Yet what viewers may be less conscious of—and thus less able to resist—is another aspect of televised melodramas that is actually widely shared: its placing of strong emotion in the everyday interpersonal world. This is a generic convention that cuts across content, that has its source in the genre itself (as adapted and developed over thirty years in Egypt) but is underwritten by the educated middle-class assumptions of those who produce television. This aspect of melodrama may be even more important to the projects of modernity than are the conscious political messages of the serials, because of the way it stages, and perhaps shapes, selfhood.

This is not the place to discuss general debates about reception and the effects of media, among the thorniest problems in media studies. I think it is abundantly clear that melodramatic texts can work on viewers in multiple ways. One cannot simply analyze the overt messages of plot and character. For example, one real possibility is that Egyptian television dramas whose storylines promote nationalist sentiment might fall on deaf ears yet be, as part of a national viewing experience, engendering a certain sense of national affiliation.

What I want to explore here is how melodrama in Egypt might work on people's senses of self by the very way it represents characters as emotional. I will ask, in other words, about one of the distinctive features of melodrama: the purloined letter of its high emotionalism. Feuer, in her classic article on melodrama, has described American prime-time soap opera acting as Wagnerian.[20] She argues that this overwrought acting style is necessary to distill and intensify emotion. Brooks, more cerebral, argued that the exaggerated emotions of early nineteenth-century melodramatic acting were expressionistic, their purpose being to clarify the moral message.[21] I think he overlooked the independent effects—or at least implications—of witnessing such "excessive" affect.

The conventions of Egyptian acting are easily as melodramatic as those that provoked Feuer and Brooks to think about emotion and morality. Critics in Egypt are fond of complaining about their television. Some express weariness with the *nakad*—an untranslatable word referring to the piling on of troubles that I will translate as misery—calling for more comedy, more musicals. Cartoonists, often the most astute commentators on Egyptian life, caricature the experience of watching soap operas as being tied up with tears. Television writers even make fun of themselves about this. In a self-referential moment, one serial scripted a maid (the stereotypical soap opera viewer) inviting a student to come watch the serial with her so they could "get miserable together." But *nakad* is merely an aspect of the general emotionality of Egyptian television melodrama. Although Ien Ang notes that melodrama may be characterized by its "tragic structure of feeling" and the sense that characters are "victims of forces that lie beyond their control"—favorite themes in the many Egyptian television dramas that treat the tribulations of good families facing the problems created by the shortage of housing, a Kafkaesque bureaucracy, or the forces of corruption—the most powerful and appealing dramas actually display a wide range of emotions.[22] Many people with whom I spoke described the good television serial as one that "pulls" (*bitshidd*). It not only "pulls" audiences in, but "pulls" on their feelings. As one television producer put it, misery is just the easiest way to pull on the emotions.

This emotionality, I believe, adds a crucial lesson to melodramas. Not only are they about the moral (and thus the social and political) order, as suggested above, but they provide an education in sentiment. By this I do not mean that they teach people how to feel. That is probably too crude, although they might indeed encourage certain public expressions of emotion or even sentimentality.[23] Rather, by attaching these strong sentiments to characters in everyday life, melodramas fashion ordinary characters whose personhood is defined by what seems a rich inner life and an intense individuality.

This focus on the emotionally laden interpersonal domestic world, what in the United States and Europe is thought of as the women's world, is what has made feminist media scholars take soap opera so seriously.[24] Yet the significance of the location of sentiment in the sphere of interpersonal relations has gone almost unremarked, perhaps because it is so taken for granted in our society, where women and emotion are so ideologically conjoined.[25] Tanya Modleski comes closest to noting what I would like to consider in more detail.[26] In her analysis of the link between daytime television and women's work, she argues that the narrative structures and close-up shots so favored by soap operas exercise women viewers' abilities to read how intimates are feeling. Their viewing experiences thus replicate their primary emotional work in the family—anticipating the needs and desires of others.

These ideas about emotions and personhood can be linked to Raymond Williams's hypothesis that the unprecedented exposure to drama that television has allowed has led to a "dramatisation of consciousness."[27] By this he means that television has led us to see our own daily lives as dramas. Although I would caution against some aspects of this, citing the methodological impossibility of gaining access to people's "consciousness" and a discomfort with the humanist assumptions of an unproblematized inner life such a term suggests, I think Williams's great insight is to suggest that something novel happens to subjectivity as a result of television drama.[28] And in Egypt the question is whether there has not developed a melodramatization of consciousness.

In other words, can the growing cultural hegemony of television melodrama (following along lines laid down by radio serials and films) be engendering new modes of subjectivity and new discourses on personhood, ones that we could recognize as "modern" in their emphasis on the individual? The main features of the modern subject as it has been understood in the West—autonomous, bounded, self-activating, verbalizing him/herself —have been delineated in the philosophical and historical literature, with

Foucault offering us the most interesting theories of the development of the technologies of the modern (bourgeois) self and their links to new forms of power.[29] In the introduction to the second volume of *The History of Sexuality,* he suggested that the discourse on sexuality has been crucial to the development of the modern self; one becomes the subject of one's sexuality. In later lectures he speculated on the relationship between the confession in Christianity and the modern forms of hermeneutics of the self.[30] Psychologizing, buttressed by the whole discourse of psychoanalysis with its vivid conjuring of a rich and conflictual inner world, is also instrumental in constructing modern subjects. And the discourse of feelings and emotion—the very stuff of melodrama—is essential to the psychological.[31]

What is interesting about Modleski's argument about television soap opera as that which trains women for interpersonal work is the assumptions it makes about selves and emotion. It presumes women who live in modern bourgeois families and have a vocabulary of sentiment attached to gesture. It also takes for granted that when sentiments are found, they are expressive of the inner feelings and personal truths of others. This set of assumptions about emotion and personhood must be recognized as historically and culturally specific. As Ann Cvetkovich notes, nineteenth-century mass and popular culture played an important role in constructing the discourse of affect crucial to establishing the middle-class hegemony of a "gendered division between public and private spheres and the assignment of women to the affective tasks of the household."[32]

The untheorized corollary, however, of the discourse of affect is the discourse of the individual who is the subject of these emotions. It is, I want to suggest, the individual who is being highlighted in the heightening of emotionality in Egyptian melodrama. The serials are not only directed at women but men as well. And though they mark men as, on the whole, less emotional than women and the upper classes as less emotional than the lower, all characters are more emotional than might be thought appropriate by a bourgeois European or American self.

In part, the extreme staging of melodramatic selves may seem necessary for those whose goal is to "modernize" a society whose dominant social form is still the family and kin network and whose cultural forms until quite recently (and even contemporaneously in some regions) could be understood to work in different ways and with differing constructions of personhood. So I first want to contrast the melodramatic "structures of feeling" with those of some other popular Arab cultural forms that might previously have provided materials for constructing or conceptualizing selves. One goal is to reveal the particularity of the relationship between modernity and melodrama in the formation of subjectivity. I further want to suggest that the forms of melodrama in Egypt, like the structures of the social and economic worlds in which people there find themselves, differ in crucial ways from the forms and the contexts of Western soap opera and life. In the final section of the essay, I will turn to the sensibilities and the life stories of a woman who was extraordinarily enmeshed in the world of television and radio serials in order to suggest how we might trace the distinctive affective and narrative forms of melodrama into forms of personal subjectivity in Egypt. I will also show, however, how other aspects of Egyptian modernity bolster, or undermine, the work of television melodrama.

DISTINCTIVE SUBJECTIVITIES

Whatever its interreferences with or roots in other forms of cultural expression, Egyptian television melodrama is distinct in its structure and sentiment. The serials are created by people versed in modern literature, theater, and film—Egyptian, Arab, and European.[33] Although occasionally drawing on what they would consider "folk" traditions for local color or regional identification, or to invoke the authentic (as when they have "simple" protagonists reciting proverbs), the primarily urban, middle-class producers of melodrama distinguish their work unambiguously from "traditional" Egyptian and Arab forms of cultural expression that have been, until quite recently, the popular and familiar forms in rural areas and among the uneducated. And the differences between the emotional styles and imaginaries created by these narrative and poetic traditions and those of television melodrama are striking.

This difference can be seen especially clearly in the adaptations to television of local folk forms. This happened in 1997 with the serialized dramatization during the month of Ramadan of the epic of Abu Zayd al-Hilali, considered by many the most magnificent work of Arab oral narrative poetry. The epic, which in its entirety runs to thousands of verses, follows the adventures across North Africa of the Bani Hilal, a Bedouin tribe driven by drought from their home in the Arabian Peninsula. As described by Susan Slyomovics for Upper Egypt and Dwight Reynolds for Lower Egypt, it is recited professionally by socially marginal poets with astonishing verbal talents, not to mention prodigious memories.[34] Widely familiar, it is never performed in its entirety; but when listeners hear their favorite segments, they know the context and the shadow whole is evoked.[35]

In her analysis of the differences between oral and printed versions of the epic, Slyomovics has noted not only that printed versions (or studio-produced commercial recordings) are complete and sequential, rather than segmented and partial, but that they lack the elaborate punning of the performed. This absence of punning indicates two things: a declining attention to the language itself, or poetics, in the printed versions; and a greater reliance on the story, rather than the multiple meanings of the puns, for establishing character.[36]

The television drama shares with the printed versions (on which the scriptwriter relied) a chronological development and decreasing attention to linguistic play, and to the verbal itself. It further transforms the epic by turning it into a melodrama about interpersonal relationships and individual longings and passions, many set in the domestic sphere. The best illustration of these transformations—and thus the genre conventions of serialized melodramas—is how the serial dramatizes the birth of the hero Abu Zayd. This opening section of the epic (rarely performed in Upper Egypt, according to Slyomovics, because it is never requested by local audiences—yet popular, according to Reynolds, in lower Egypt)[37] constitutes the first and crucial week of the television serial, drawing viewers in. The story of Abu Zayd is that he is the son of Rizq of the Hilali Bedouin tribe and Khadra Sharifa, the daughter of the Sharif of Mecca, a descendent of the Prophet. Khadra is barren for many years (in some versions it is seven, in some eleven). Despite their happiness with each other, husband and wife are miserable because of the absence of a son. Finally, Khadra is taken to a pool to supplicate. She sees a powerful black bird driving away the other birds. She prays for a son as strong and ferocious as this bird. She then does miraculously bear a son—Abu Zayd, the hero of the epic. In the version performed for Slyomovics by an Upper Egyptian poet, the pregnancy and birth are described quickly, the love scene after Khadra's visit to the pool being slightly more elaborate:

Khadra Sharifa had stopped bearing, but weak with desire she came to the royal bed yearning.
Rizq son of Nayil came to her after the evening prayer.
Khadra wore silk brocade, she sat with him, she wore brocade of silk, her best clothing.

Rizq asked for union with her.
She was happy! And the Lord of the Throne sent her an infant who vexes the
    enemy!
She bore an infant who vexes valiant men!
Khadra passed the full nine months.
They approached the Emir Abu Zayd, Emir of valiant men,
they found the Emir Abu Zayd was blue-black, not resembling his father,
they found the hero, Abu Zayd the Hilali, the color of a black slave.[38]

In a version recorded by Reynolds, the narrative is more elaborate and
dramatic, but the focus is on the reactions of others to the black infant and
the anger and accusations of Rizq.[39] Neither version dwells on the emotions
of the protagonists just before the birth.

In the televised episode of the birth, covered in the Upper Egyptian performance in just the last six lines, we see Khadra going into labor, the anxious father just outside her door awaiting the birth, a desperate fight in the
streets over the midwife (who is needed in three places at once), more ago-
nies of labor, the husband praying to God, and later, when he hears the child
has been born, falling to his knees, tears in his eyes, and raising his arms to
praise and thank God. Then we see hushed arguments in Khadra's room between the midwife and the attendant women, the midwife refusing to give
the father the news. What's wrong? The midwife points and says, "Look."
They carefully lift the cover off the baby. In close-up, with music, we see a
black baby. The mother is sleeping, beatific. When she sits up and is confronted with this, she holds the baby lovingly, innocently saying, "The boy
is our son, mine and Rizq's. Whether light or dark, he is a gift from God
whom we accept." But then she, too, becomes alarmed. It dawns on her that
the others are worried that she will be accused of adultery.

It is not that the television drama is emotional and the performed epic
not. The performed epic, too, describes feelings, in the conventional for-
mulas for such things. In an earlier segment, for example, Rizq and his wife
Khadra cry over their inability to have a son. After several lines recounting
how Rizq watched other men play with their sons, the Upper Egyptian poet's
version continues,

Rizq the Hilali eyed them and his wound increased
Inside his tent tears poured again
inside his tent tears poured again
he cried, wet his cheeks and his handkerchief

Khadra Sharifa left, her tears a canal.
Beautiful as she was, she loved him to the point of death
beautiful as she was, by God, unique
she cried and felt hardship each night he was absent:
"Tell me what is the reason for laments, O love, O Rizq, you cry why, why?"

Similarly, a version recorded by Reynolds has Rizq saying,

I am the last of my line, my spirit is broken
I have spent my life and not seen a son, prosperous
I have taken of women, eight maidens,
And eleven daughters followed, princesses true!
This bearing of womenfolk, ah!, has broken my spirit
I weep and the tears of my eyes on my cheek do flow.[40]

But the televised drama focuses on the relationships among characters and the shifting emotions of a set of characters who often stare off into space while music evokes their inner feelings. Instead of formulaic phrases about tears and their plenitude, what could be thought of as the phenomenology of emotion itself, television drama tries to produce the inner beings who feel these emotions through close-ups of facial expressions and melodramatic acting. Moreover, the serial brings the mythic heroes down to earth and makes them ordinary people in line with the process of "descending" individualization Foucault has described as so characteristic of modern disciplinary regimes.[41] This is reinforced by the overwhelming visual presence of interior worlds and domestic spaces (always the case, of course, with soap operas, for obvious budgetary and technical reasons).[42]

Like all "folk" traditions, the oral epic's main intent is not the development of the inner life of characters. Most of the epic, like folktales told all over Egypt, consists of what characters did and said and includes little "emotion language" or the gestures and music that substitute for it in melodrama. This is not to say that one cannot find in the cultural traditions the elaboration of sentiment. The poetic, rather than the narrative, genres are the place to look for this. Yet I would argue for a fundamental difference in the localization—or locatability—of the emotions in melodrama and poetry. For example, the *ghinnaawa*s, or little songs, of the Awlad 'Ali Bedouin that I have written about are short expressions of sentiment.[43] Although people recite them as part of stories, to express the sentiments of particular characters, and otherwise in the contexts of intimates to express their own

sentiments about particular life events, they are conventional and formulaic. They are thus, in a sense, depersonalized. They are repeated and appropriated by others and thus are also disembodied. Furthermore, much of
the appreciation of these poems—like the performed Hilali epic—comes
from the poetry of their language.

Ritual lamentation of the dead in Egypt, as in other parts of the Arab and
circum-Mediterranean world, is another highly developed poetic art that is
quintessentially emotional.[44] In Upper Egypt, where many of the television
viewers with whom I had been working live, the 'adida, as the lament is
called, is performed at funerals by women specialists. The mournful chanting is extremely emotional in its presentation, and also evokes strong sentiment through its imagery. However, as Elizabeth Wickett has shown, despite this potent imagery, "few references to emotional states can be found
in the laments, either ascribed to the lamenter or to the feelings of the deceased after death."[45] Laments are, she adds, "ritual texts performed in an
emotional arena" and therefore, I would argue, differ significantly from
melodrama in being limited in context and sentiment. They are specific to
the ritualized context of the funeral. In contrast, the emotions of melodrama cover a wide range and are attached to individuals and embedded in
the everyday, the ordinary, and the domestic.

By establishing these contrasts, I am not trying to assert the existence of
a rigid distinction between modernity and tradition, the "folk" art inhabit-
ing (and defining) the traditional past and the melodrama the contemporary present. All sorts of cross-referencing and transformations occur,
especially as "traditional" forms aggressively enter the mass media world
contemporaneous with the melodrama.[46] What I am saying is that television
melodramas offer distinctive constructions of the world and images of persons, especially within a context defined by "traditional" forms and "traditional ways of life" from which modernist writers and directors are distanc-
ing themselves. Their specificity is in the emotionalization of the quotidian
world, which in turn works to enforce a sense of the importance of the individual subject—the locus and source of all these strong feelings.

HEROINE OF HER OWN MELODRAMA

One evening, as I sat watching television with a poor Upper Egyptian village
family in the midst of various crises, the mother joked, "We are a soap opera!" (*ihna tamthiliyya*). In this comment, one can see that television melo-

drama had come to inform her perceptions of her own life. I think this occurs on a much more intimate and individual level as well. To illustrate how
this might work, I want to discuss a person I knew in Egypt who was deeply
involved with television and radio melodramas: the unmarried domestic
servant in Cairo I call Amira. She listened to her transistor radio while she
cooked for her employers. When she could, she stopped to watch the noon
serial on television. She always watched the evening serials when she got
home. She was knowledgeable about the actors and actresses; she had
watched most serials and films. Intelligent and articulate, she could sum-
marize plots easily and remember most. She rarely watched foreign imports,
although she admitted that the American serial *Knots Landing,* which she
claimed to have been able to understand even though she could not read the
subtitles, had been an exception.

Unmarried and with no children, Amira was both freer to follow television and more dependent on it for companionship and emotional-social
involvement than most women I knew in Egypt. She was somewhat isolated
socially because she lived on her own. Her mother and brothers still lived in
the countryside in Manufiyya. She had two sisters in Cairo. One was married with children and she saw her little. Besides the people she worked for,
some of whom she could not communicate with (they did not speak Arabic), her main contacts seemed to be her unmarried sister, with whom, however, she had frequent conflicts, and her friend Naima, also a single woman
who had come to Cairo from the countryside and like her worked as a domestic servant. With both, she watched television.

Amira was both more sentimental and more volatile than many women
I had come to know. She was often moved by the serials she watched. When
we watched television together, her explanations of who particular characters were carried moral and emotional valences. This scene, she once said
of an episode of *Hilmiyya Nights* (a serial she had watched several times,
though it ran to over a hundred episodes), reveals the worthy from the un-
worthy. With pity she explained to me who a character in another serial
written by 'Ukasha (*Al-shahd wa al-dumu'* [Honey and tears]) was: a poor
young man who is sickly because his mother keeps marrying and abandon-
ing him, putting herself first. When she gets divorced she takes him back;
but then goes and marries again. This has ruined his health and made him
very sensitive. Amira had concluded her summary of the plot of this serial
with admiration for the heroine: "Zaynab is strong and willful in the cause
of right. She's not strong for an immoral end."

But this sentimentality extended to other areas. Once when we turned on the television in 1990 and saw a clip of people in Iran crying after an earthquake, this triggered her memory of having wept "for an hour" after the Egyptian soccer team lost the World Cup match. She had kept herself awake until the early hours of the morning to watch the game on television. She was upset because "they worked so hard and got so tired and then God didn't reward them." She had wept when they lost, and then wept again when she saw the Egyptian players crying. "It really hurt."

Amira was also often embroiled in conflicts and arguments—with her sister, her employers, and her neighbors. She told stories about how angry she was, how wronged she had been. Her neighbors kept a dog on the roof who bothered her. She fought with her landlords because she had to wake up at 3 a.m. to fill her water cans and haul them up to the third story. There was no water at other times in her building. She fought with employers who left her sitting on their doorstep with cooked food for a party, having refused to give her a key to their apartment and having promised to be home to receive the food.

Although I cannot argue for a direct causal link between her involvement with television serials and her emotionality, I suspect there is one. There is, however, another more obvious link between television melodrama and the ways she constructed herself as a subject. This link is through the ways she made herself the subject of her own life stories. I found it striking that of all the women whose life stories I have heard, Amira was the one whose tales took most clearly the form of melodrama. Hers was a Manichean world with good, kind people who helped her and were generous, and greedy, stingy, or cruel people who victimized her.

One can see this in the way she constructed her story of coming to Cairo to find a better life. A local labor contractor found her her first job. She came from a poor family and she had worked on construction sites, hauling dirt and sand, for a daily wage. She wanted to go to Cairo because she saw her sisters, who had gone there to find work, coming home dressed well and wearing gold. She was nineteen when she first went. But she lasted only a month in the first job. The family mistreated her. They woke her up at six in the morning, they didn't feed her, and they kept the food locked up. She was paid five or six pounds per month (about $9 US at that time). She cried and cried and finally persuaded her sister to call and say that she was needed back at home to tend a sick relative. She found another employer and another. Each time, she would find some excuse to go home to the village and she would not return. Eventually she found a job with a good family as a cook and stayed with them for eight years. The themes repeat: exploited and mistreated, the innocent victim escapes until fate deals her some kind people.

It is when Amira talked about her brief marriage, however, that all the elements of drama crystallize. At thirty-seven, she realized that she was too old to hope for marriage. She declared herself ugly anyway—"Who would want to marry me?" But someone did, in 1985, when she was about thirty. The marriage lasted twenty-nine days and she had to get her sister's husband to pay the man a thousand pounds (approximately $700 US at the time) to divorce her. She told the story easily; perhaps it was a well-rehearsed story. He was a plumber who saw her at work. When he asked her about the possibility of marriage, she sent him to discuss it with her brother-in-law. They were engaged for four months, but she never went anywhere with him. When she would suggest it, he would refuse. She claimed it was because he didn't want her to know what he was like or to know anything about him.

Once they were married, he was violent with her. He wanted her to hand over her wages. She refused, saying she had a loan to pay off and then she planned to stay at home. A man, she explained, is supposed to support his wife. He locked her in the house. All she wanted was to be rid of him, and so she got her brother-in-law—whom she held responsible since he was supposed to have looked into the man's background—to pay him money to leave her alone. It turned out he was a tough from a poor quarter. Amira was convinced that he wanted to kill her to take her apartment.

Bitterly she added that Egyptian men are no good. Lots of men have asked her to marry them. Men on the streets, men she meets at work. But they all wanted her money. Actually, it was her apartment they wanted. When they discovered that she had an apartment and furniture, they knew they would only have to contribute inexpensive things as a dowry. Her husband, for example, had provided the living room furniture, but she already had the bedroom furniture and the apartment. (Given the severe shortage of housing, the exorbitant "key money" that must be paid to get a rental unit, and the expenses of furnishing the apartment, considered the responsibility of the groom, many young men find it difficult to marry.) When I asked what would then happen, she explained, "Then they'll take a second wife. Once they have the apartment and money."

If we ask, as the anthropologists Ruth Behar and Laurel Kendall have, about the narrative qualities of life stories, we see that if Behar's Mexican in-

formant's life story was shaped by the Christian model of suffering and redemption, Amira's conforms more closely to the model of melodrama.[47]
Like the television dramas, the themes of her story are money, with the
villain trying to cheat her out of hers, and the secret, with the truth about
her sinister husband discovered too late. The melodramatic heroine, innocent and good, is wronged and victimized. Seeking a better life, symbolized by her sisters' good clothes and gold, she leaves the village and home
to find herself overworked, underpaid, and hungry in a house where the
food is locked up. Seeking love, companionship, or respectability—whatever it is that marriage is supposed to bring—she finds herself betrayed and
beaten.[48]

What I think is most significant about this way of telling her life story,
however, is that through it Amira makes herself the subject, the melodramatic heroine, in fact, of her own life. Perhaps in part by her love of television melodrama, she has been encouraged to see herself as the subject of the
emotions that sweep her and thus as more of an individual. This individuality puts her in a better position to be a modern citizen, subject to the state
rather than family or community, something nationalist and middle-class
television producers want from their melodramas. For Amira, this position
is reinforced by the structures of her life: her migrant status and separation
from her family, her reliance on her own labor for survival, her private
apartment with its own electricity and water bills, and her subjection to the
law and to taxation as an individual.

POSTCOLONIAL DIFFERENCES

Yet Amira's story and her life present certain complications for a straightforward narrative of coming to modern individual subjecthood as we might
tell it along familiar Western lines. First, Amira's tragic story is marked by
critical absences and failures. The most specific is the failure of her brother-
in-law to have taken seriously his family responsibility of protecting her
from a bad marriage. More generally, she suggests that her vulnerability is
caused by the absence of a strong family that could have supported her and
kept her from having to work as a maid. Her emptiness is related to the failure to have married and, as most women do, had a family of her own. As I've
noted before, in all the life stories of domestic servants I have recorded, it is
always a rupture to the ideal of women's embeddedness in family and mar-

riage that accounts for their positions doing work that is both hard and not respectable, and for their not being, in a sense, full persons. Amira's story, while told mostly in terms of herself as an individual moving through life, evokes the ideal she cannot have—the ideal of being a fulfilled person defined by kinship and family.

To note that kinship remains crucial for Amira is not to say that television melodrama is not producing its effects. After all, as I noted earlier, even while the genre conventions encourage individuality and the political messages include citizenship and wider social belonging, television melodramas do not overtly challenge the ideal of family so taken for granted in Egypt. In keeping with urban middle-class ideals, the nuclear family gets more play than the extended, but women and most men characters are still placed within families.

However, there is something else of great importance in Amira's day-to-day life that does not derive from television melodrama and that in some, but not all, ways undermines the processes television encourages. In part because she is cut out of family life and cannot rely on kin to provide community, purpose, and social respectability, Amira is attracted to the new path to individual expression and respectability opened up to women in the last two decades by the movement to make Islam more central to everyday life and politics. Recognizing this further complication, along with acknowledging the continuing centrality of kinship and the ways that Egyptian melodramas embed morality in the social, reminds us of the difference it makes that a modern form of drama and the forms of selfhood it encourages are being produced in a postcolonial nation with its own specific history and, as Dipesh Chakrabarty has argued for Bengal, its own form of modernity.[49]

As much as work and watching television, religious practice organizes Amira's schedule, informs her sense of self, and colors her understanding of her world. Because mosques flourished in the 1980s and 1990s, and because it became much more accepted in that period that women should pray in them and attend religious lessons, Amira's regular attendance is not uncommon for lower-class and middle-class urban women. However, the same structural features that make her more dependent on television and free to follow it—living alone, being unmarried and without children—enable her to pray more regularly, go to mosque on Fridays and sometimes even after work, and to participate in the special mosque prayers of Ramadan, the month of special devotion and fasting as well as heavy television watching.[50] Similarly, that she wears the *hijab,* the modest head covering that has become a fashionable sign of piety and middle-class respectability in the towns and cities, is not unusual. But Amira's regular participation in lessons at the mosque has intensified her identity as a Muslim and given meaning to the wearing of this item of clothing. As a result of her involvement in these religious practices and identifications, Amira is pulled very much into a community, and it is not the national community to which individual citizens are, according to television writers, supposed to relate themselves.[51]

Yet many of Amira's religious observances are self-oriented and thus might be thought of as running along the same tracks as the individualizing and interiorizing of television melodrama (even though many religious authorities preach against television). This is especially the case with the discipline of fasting, which she takes very seriously. She fasts all the days of Ramadan, like most Egyptian Muslims, making up later the days lost because of menstruation.[52] But she also fasts all the other possible and recommended days of the Muslim calendar. One can also see this concern with the self in the way she constantly asks others to forgive her for the smallest things— like angering someone or even helping herself to a piece of cake from an employer's larder. Her references to her sinfulness and the need to cleanse it with fasting, prayer, and asking forgiveness were especially striking to me because her life was so moral and proper. This obsessive concern with the self is, it seems, strongly encouraged by the rhetoric of the lessons at the mosque.[53]

In a sense, television itself seems to be changing to accommodate (not to mention appropriate for its own legitimacy) this new intensity of religious practice and identity. There have long been religious television serials—historical costume dramas about the early history of Islam. These were often aired late at night and were not particularly popular. They, like all religious programming, were segregated from the popular evening serials, as if to compartmentalize religion. But in the second half of the 1990s, major actors participated in the big budget religious/historical serials broadcast during Ramadan, and major writers and directors were suddenly called upon to produce them. These serials were, it turned out, so popular that the newly appointed head of television production announced in 1997 that they planned to do many more serials about "our Arab Islamic heritage," as he gingerly put it, over the next few years.

The serialization of the Hilali epic broadcast during Ramadan in the early slot that children are sure to be watching is part of this effort. Although not, strictly speaking, a religious serial, it gives a prominent place to discourse about God, as does the oral performed epic, since that is recited by and for people for whom being Muslims is an important identity. Yet there is a striking difference in the forms religiosity takes in the television version and the oral epic as performed by traditional poets. This suggests how television religion, much like Amira's, may be part of a new individualizing of religion.

In the epic, as performed in Egypt, God's power is a constant theme. All great deeds and miraculous happenings, like the birth of the hero Abu Zayd, are attributed to it. Poets always open their performances with a praise poem to the Prophet. This praise poetry introduces the themes of the segments to be recited but also, as Slyomovics argues, has the rhetorical effect of praising the poet himself by linking his poetic abilities and his status to that of the Prophet, whose divine words were miraculous, as well as praising the audience for being part of the community of Muslims.[54]

The television serial also represents God's miraculous power—in computer-generated special effects like the strong bird whose likeness Khadra prays for in a son. But mostly religion figures as the emotionalized attitudes of characters—their supplication, their awe, and their gratitude. We see this clearly when Rizq, the hero's father, waits anxiously while his wife is in labor. There is a cut to a scene (perhaps at sunrise of the same day) where he is standing by his horse, watching the sun, his hands held up in the position of prayer. Back home, his hands are clasped and he asks God to keep his wife safe. When he is told the news that he has a son, he repeats again and again, "A thousand praises and thanks to you O Lord." He faces different parts of the room, arms up toward heaven, thanking Bountiful God for having generously given him a son after all these years, and for ending his sorrows and enabling him to face the men and know that his name would remain. He then drops to his knees, thanking God again. Later, his wife will say she accepts her son as a gift from God. In these scenes, it is the personal faith, rather than the power of God, that is stressed. Piety has been made into a characteristic of the self.

In the late 1960s, the noted anthropologist James Peacock wrote a book about a form of proletarian drama in Indonesia that he argued was a "rite of modernization": it helped its participants desire and feel comfortable with modern actions (linear, coming to a climax) and goals (individual achievement and nuclear families). Although his analysis was sophisticated, he shared the confident assumptions of modernization theorists of the time. Indonesia, like every other country, was on a path to modernity; modernity was a singular condition whose features could be easily outlined (rationalization, universalization, bureaucratization, centralization, specialization, monetization, conjugalization); and finally, modernity was an unalloyed good, its individualism, for example, being a mark of increasing freedom, with no element of subjection (as Foucault later cautioned).[55]

My argument is different. In the early '90s, in a popular Egyptian women's magazine, Muna Hilmi, daughter of Nawal El-Saadawi, the Egyptian feminist writer so well known in the West, wrote a paean to the American daytime soap opera *The Bold and the Beautiful*, then being broadcast on Egyptian television.[56] In an unusually sympathetic review of a serial widely condemned by the intelligentsia, she contrasted it with Egyptian serials, which she disparaged for their remorseless attention to social and political problems. She lauded the American soap opera for its feminism (in that it has strong women characters who are determined to achieve what they want in their careers and their lives) but most of all for its subtle exploration of the human psyche. She could have, but did not, mention the elite disdain for the emotional hyperbole of Egyptian melodrama—the disdain so clearly reflected in the satire I described at the start of this essay.

What I have tried to show here, though, is that the emotionality of Egyptian melodramas and the way they thus construct individuals in terms of vivid interior lives is the result of a local effort, developed in the context of Egyptian genres and social circumstances, that is part of the process of trying to produce those individual human psyches that this educated cosmopolitan writer extols. But there is a difference. Instead of constructing these human psyches in a generalized content-less context, as does an American soap opera like *The Bold and the Beautiful* (a lack of political context that rendered the serial harmless in the eyes of the Egyptian censors),[57] producers working in a government-controlled medium and imbued with an ideology of national development and the legacy of Arab socialist ideals insist on placing them squarely within the social and moral national nexus. And because of the increasing hegemony of an assertive religious identity in a society in which most people had never accepted the principle that religious practice and morality are not part of modern everyday life—something Muna Hilmi and the class faction she represents most likely disapprove of—the vectors of modernity crisscross. Melodrama, and to some extent what I would argue to be a new focus on the self in religious practice, may be encouraging the kinds of individuated subjectivities a sophisticated modernist secularist like Hilmi wants. But the enduring ties of kinship and the appealing—and modern—identity politics of Islam pull such selves in a different direction: into communities and subject to other authorities and disciplines.

Cover of *October Magazine* showing the stars of the Ramadan serials,
contemporary and historical. 1997.

[6]

The Ambivalence of Authenticity
National Culture in a Global World

FOR EGYPTIANS, the last two decades of the twentieth century brought radical transformations of everyday life. The *infitah,* or "open-door policies," begun in the 1970s reversed the processes of nationalization and state production and the policies of restricting imports so central to Nasser's programs of the 1950s and 1960s. With so-called economic liberalization, the ideological appeals to Arab unity and socialism also ended. Egypt was opened to foreign investment, returning landowners and businessmen, a huge American government presence, and multinational companies, making especially visible in the world of consumption what goes under the name *globalization.* Escalating in the last decade, these processes have put McDonald's arches, Pizza Hut's roofs, and Jeep Cherokees in and around the fancy neighborhoods of Cairo. They have filled new exclusive shopping centers and tourist resorts with clothing boutiques that are branches of French and Italian companies. More recently, they have dramatically improved the production values of television commercials, which now use rap music to sell Coca-Cola and local film stars to capture female consumers for competing brands of laundry detergent manufactured by Unilever and Proctor and Gamble.

Coinciding with these political-economic processes that have benefited the families and classes able to take advantage of the business opportunities (but have meant serious economic and social decline for the growing majority of the poor) has been another transformation, as noticeable on the streets of Cairo as the new BMWs but reaching far more widely into the everyday lives of people across Egypt.[1] This is the growing hegemony, as the life of Amira sketched in chapter 5 demonstrated, of a self-conscious Islamic identity and the practices (prayer, religious lessons, meetings, and anti-Christian rhetoric) and paraphernalia (clothing, mosques, books, and cassettes) that enact, embody, and inculcate it. Alongside this has been the strengthening of Islamic organizations, some militant, and the shift in leadership of the professional syndicates (for lawyers and medical doctors, for example) to those with strong convictions about religious identity.[2]

The relationship between these apparently contradictory trends is complex and tangled. Analysts have focused on a wide variety of political, economic, social, and cultural events and processes. Although I will explore in the next two chapters media correlates of each, all I will note here is that there is a dialectical relationship between these processes but that each also has had its own logic and compulsions, internal and external.

For anyone analyzing public culture, however, one of the most interesting aspects of such contradictory national developments is how they have positioned Egypt's intelligentsia—its writers, its artists, and its producers of television drama. These are educated people who usually take on for themselves the role of social commentators and architects of understanding and for whom the last decades have been a time of great concern. One powerful response has been, as I will explain, to try to negotiate for their public a cultural identity that is particularly Egyptian, somewhere between the pan-Islamic (and anti-Western) identity implied by the Islamists and charismatic religious authorities who have a wide and mass-mediated audience and the (Western-oriented) cosmopolitanism embraced by the elites, old and new. This effort can be seen especially clearly in some television serials of the 1990s, two of which I discuss in this chapter.

In seeking to articulate, as did intellectuals in an earlier period of anti-colonial nationalism, an Egyptian cultural essence or authenticity, the producers of such serials (with the official approval implied by their ability to speak through state-run television) are trying to shape popular consciousness about Egypt's contemporary situation. They are, in Appadurai's words, engaged in producing the cultural—constituting in their serials "the diacritics of group identity."[3] This is not, as in so many culturalist movements around the world today, a process of creating identities to counter the national but rather the rearguard action of an identity politics meant to shore up the nation-state. What these intellectuals—by and large secular, by and large products of education under a strongly nationalist regime with great claims to revolutionary social reform—are seeking to undermine are, on the one hand, the postnational identities of a cosmopolitan business elite who work within the framework of economic liberalization and, on the other, the Islamists. Islamism can be considered postnational in its "pre-national" religious definition of community (the *umma*) and in its divisiveness for the nation-state, producing as it does both communal strife (divisions between Muslims and Christians) and threats to the integrity and legitimacy of the state apparatus. Although these television producers may draw on a stock of images from Egyptian literature, print media, and film, the current contexts and audiences, and their own views of the current situation, give these television dramas a particular cast.[4]

What happens when the discourses produced by such intellectuals in the extraordinarily popular medium of the television serial enter the social field that is contemporary Egyptian life? In particular, I explore the ambivalences created by their strategies of locating cultural authenticity in the popular (sha'bi) classes in a context in which the state and elites, as I have discussed in previous chapters, have long promoted a developmentalist ideology. Even more problematic is the way this cultural identity is made insistently national, severed from other affiliations and "diacritics" that have had, and still have, great resonance.

The specific case of these rocky attempts to make cultural identity through television drama in Egypt in the 1990s holds some larger lessons for those of us who would like to think about such broad matters as the relationship between the global and the local. If indeed this case supports the increasingly common recognition of culture as something consciously fashioned and disseminated and something linked to mobilizing identities in a complex world of nations and transnations, it also reminds us of the impossibilities of closure for such cultural projects which inevitably work upon shifting sociopolitical landscapes, against competing constructions, and within history. In the conclusion, I consider why such efforts have developed in this period in Egypt and what this might tell us about the relationship between nations, states, and globalization.

SERIALIZING IDENTITY IN THE 1990S

Two major television serials of the mid-1990s starring popular actors crystallized the concern with Egyptian identity and authenticity. Both were brought to my attention by the strong responses they generated among the two kinds of communities for which television is produced—"ordinary viewers" and other members of the intelligentsia, epitomized by critics. I was made aware of the first serial, *Arabesque*, because a friend from Cairo sent me a fat packet of press clippings about it. It was the most discussed Ramadan serial of 1994, written by Egypt's best television writer, Usama Anwar

'Ukasha, whose popularity had just peaked with the brilliant multipart historical drama (*Hilmiyya Nights*) that had filled the coveted Ramadan slot for four years. The articles in major newspapers and periodicals focused on the central character, Hasan (played by the popular actor Salah al-Sa'dani), an artisan who carries on from his grandfathers the art of woodcarving—arabesque—in one of Cairo's traditional or popular neighborhoods.

This is the story of his struggle with himself and for his country. The plot involves the theft of a valuable old chair carved by his grandfather, his service to his country in the 1973 war, the trauma of the 1992 earthquake, the dangers of fundamentalism, the brain drain, and the importance of commitment to community. The protagonist is meant to be an updated version of the prototypical *ibn al-balad* (literally, "son of the country")—the local guy, the salt of the earth, the poor but authentic Egyptian—who has long stood for a set of admired behavioral traits and values in drama, literature, film, and everyday life.

The other serial is called *Lan a'ish fi gilbab abi* (I won't live my father's life), whose literal translation would be "I won't live in my father's robe."[5] It is the rags-to-riches story of 'Abd al-Ghafur al-Bur'i (played by veteran star Nur al-Sharif), who comes to Cairo looking for work (even though the short story on which it is based and whose title it took has 'Abd al-Ghafur's son as the central character).[6] He is taken under the wing of a big merchant of scrap metal in the popular quarter of Bulaq (*wikalat al-balah*), for whom he initially works as a porter. Through his sincerity, hard work, and cleverness (as well as the generosity of his employer and guardian), 'Abd al-Ghafur eventually becomes one of the richest and most powerful scrap metal merchants in the market, going on to develop factories and other enterprises.

As important to the serial as this rise to wealth is his family life. He falls in love with and marries a young woman (played by 'Abla Kamil), who, with her brother, has a food cart selling a quintessentially Egyptian poor person's food (*kushari*). They have a loving—and very touching—relationship into old age. Many of the subplots of the serial revolve around the experiences of their four daughters in different types of marriages and their son who confusedly struggles to find an independent life, through religiosity, study abroad, and a short-lived marriage to an American.

Both serials are about roots, authenticity, and the values of the true Egyptian. Both, in other words, are about cultural identity, using the figure of the *ibn al-balad*—someone of modest or poor background and rooted in what are known as the popular neighborhoods, the crowded urban "traditional" neighborhoods, in older parts of the city where the rich do not live.[7] This figure, as Armbrust has elaborated, is both a sociological type and the embodiment of valued characteristics such as honor, with a history in modernist film, as contrasted with the *ibn al-zawat* (the son of nobility)—the aristocracy—portrayed especially in films made during the '50s and '60s, as in progressive television serials like 'Ukasha's *Al-shahd wa al-dumu'* (Honey and tears), as corrupt and inauthentic, because Westernized. Yet the strategies by which the serials sought to construct Egyptian cultural identity through this figure of the ibn al-balad differed.

THE NOSTALGIC REGISTER

I Won't Live My Father's Life is in a nostalgic register. It plays out, through its subplots and characters, central themes about cultural identity and authenticity. For example, the protagonist 'Abdu (as his wife calls him) is a man of many virtues meant to exemplify the best of Egypt. He is honest, dedicated, and willing to work hard at anything, no matter how menial, to earn a living and work his way up. Once he is wealthy, he does not renounce his origins or community but gives them dignity. He is not, however, humorless or heavy-handed. Along with guts, he has a twinkle in his eye and a clever intelligence. But he is, above all, a man guided by old-fashioned principles (*usul*). In this, he fits the positive stereotype of the ibn al-balad.

The scriptwriter Mustafa Muharram described to me the protagonists of the serial as people who held on to their traditions and customs. Money didn't change their essences. His fear is that those who have gotten rich too fast are "in danger of forgetting their values: fraternity, honesty, and family values." He chose a "simple" man as his main character in order to teach people how to behave, how to live, and how to remember important values, which "still exist in the popular environment (*al-bi'a al-sha'biyya*)." 'Abd al-Ghafur was meant to stand for the authentic Egyptian who is finding the right way to live in the present age of radical economic and political transformation.[8] He is deliberately positioned between the excesses of Islamism in the popular classes and the rootlessness of the westernized cosmopolitan upper classes.

'Abdu's simple religiosity is a component of his authenticity. Unlike the Islamists who befriend his son in the mosque and end up trying to kill him for his refusal to join them, his piety is genuine. As a young man he is humble and grateful for his daily bread. He respects and listens to the advice of his religious shaykh; he and his wife go on the pilgrimage to Mecca as soon as he has "made it"; he deals honorably and honestly with others; and he is scrupulous and generous in giving alms. When a bearded, white-robed member of an Islamist group pressures him for a large donation, he bristles with anger. He says he does not need reminding to give alms (*zakat*); he gives every month. Then he lectures the young man about how it is God, not he, who will judge him and explains that he gives charity the proper way, so that his left hand does not know what his right hand is doing. He suggests that these young men would do better to go out and find jobs instead of begging.

'Abdu's traditionalism also emerges in his role as wise paterfamilias. He is represented as a benign patriarch, a little tough but only because he loves his family. Many viewers likened 'Abdu to "Si Sayyid," as they called him, the more troubling patriarch of Naguib Mahfouz's Cairo trilogy. (The connection they made was, it should be noted, not to the novel but to the popular television serial based on it or the film.)[9] Immediately after mentioning this character, however, people would deny the similarities. Clearly, the figure of 'Abdu evokes the memory of this early patriarch while, and no doubt because, he differs from him in significant ways. One of the most obvious points of contrast—and comparison—is their strictness toward the women in their families. The most telling example of Al-Sayyid Ahmad's stern insistence on retaining traditional standards for women is his severe punishment of his wife when she sneaks out to visit a major saint's shrine.[10]

The television protagonist 'Abdu is different. He is not stern; he is merely firm in his principles and values. Although he objects to many "modern" ways—the ways of people of other classes or of those who have renounced their roots—he is shown not to be harsh and authoritarian but correct. His strictness with his son, though it causes the boy unhappiness and a long road to self-discovery and reconciliation, was intended to make him a man, able to stand on his own. Like Al-Sayyid Ahmad, the protagonist of the Naguib Mahfouz novel, 'Abdu also punishes his wife once for an infraction—allowing her daughters, against his wishes and without his permission, to attend a mixed-sex birthday party at their upper-class neighbors'. But he does not cruelly banish her from the house, as did Mahfouz's character. The trouble with Al-Sayyid's patriarchy is that it is so unfair, his wife's breaking of seclusion being so innocent (to visit a holy place), while he himself leads a double life (frequenting prostitutes and dancers). In contrast, 'Abdu's adherence to old-fashioned principles regarding women is shown to be consistent and wise. He is right, it turns out in the end, to suspect the neighbor's son of bad intentions toward his daughter (discussed further below). He is right in thinking that his family has no business mixing with theirs; it eventuates in grief and humiliation for his naïve daughter. His strictness with his daughters, who are not allowed to go out or join clubs (as others of their level of wealth did), is shown to be for their protection and honor (another value he cherishes).

More interesting is 'Abdu's marriage, presented as extraordinarily loving and, for many viewers including myself, the heart of the serial. This marital relationship can be classified as neotraditional in the way it combines stereotypical "traditional" elements, like a sexual division of labor, with ones that are, I would argue, quite "modern" and middle class—companionate marriage and the nuclear family—but here displaced by the serial onto and confused with "traditional values." The portrayal of this marriage thus represents exquisitely the problems educated professionals like television writers face when they attempt to depict authenticity through the more "traditional"—lower—classes. In particular, we see how they must impose their own values on, or at least mix them with, those of the group they are depicting to make them actually palatable to a broad middle class that makes up an important segment of the audience. In the marriage of Fatma and 'Abdu is a nostalgia for something that never was and a compression of contemporary romantic middle-class ideals for marriage (choice, true love, mutuality) and fatherhood (loving concern) with some older ideals and elements that might also not necessarily have been practices of the lower classes (women's confinement to the domestic sphere).

The idealization of an image of "traditional" roles for women and men begins with the marriage. 'Abd al-Ghafur tells his new bride that she need not fear anything now, for he will be her lover, father, brother, and husband. On their wedding night, when both are unspeakably happy and she sweetly shy, he sits her down on the bed and says he wants to tell her three things so that their marriage will start off on the right footing. It is a hokey, sentimental scene, but in it, very significantly, he gently (and by all accounts wisely) sets the terms. His three requests are that he always find a bite to eat when he comes home from work; that she not look at others and compare herself and what she has to them; and that she never reveal family secrets to outsiders. He adds, however, that she is free to run the household as she wishes. The next morning, he finds her up early, preparing the food to sell from the cart with her brother. He suggests that she not work anymore.

Fatma is thus to be protected from the harshness of life by being supported by her husband. She spends her life in a domestic sphere as the emotional center of her family, which is all she cares about. Although as a woman from a poor family she had had to work and had had the opportunity to get to know her future husband (it had been love at first sight), now she can live out the traditional family ideal of being the wife/mother in charge of caring for everyone in the home.

The assertion of a "traditional" division of labor, with the woman in the home and the man out in the business world, is of course an ideal that was always class based. It may have applied to the wealthy merchant family of Al-Sayyid Ahmad in the Mahfouz novel, but it has been more difficult to achieve among the lower classes, where women have long had to be involved in family enterprises or informal work of all sorts.[11] Furthermore, if we look more closely at the meanings ascribed to feminine domesticity, we see the critical ambivalence of educated middle-class producers themselves toward Egyptian authenticity.

As historians have suggested, notions of motherhood and wifehood underwent shifts in meaning in the early twentieth century among the emerging middle classes in different parts of the Middle East.[12] These roles in fact became occupations for women that required training. Correspondingly, Fatma is shown, somewhat endearingly, as being deficient as a modern housewife and mother. She barely understands what her children are going through in their educations (she stumbles over and mispronounces Economics and Political Science, the college subject her son will study); she treats her children indulgently and emotionally, rather than trying to train them morally; and she does not know much about home decorating. Her traditionalism is manifested by her failure to achieve middle-class ideals.

The good side of her traditionalism is her utter devotion to husband and children and her lack of guile. The rewards of her trust, obedience, and unselfishness are displayed in a scene early in their marriage when 'Abdu asks for her gold bracelets (a woman's personal wealth) because he needs the money for a business deal. She gives them right away and when he asks if she isn't upset she says, "I'd give you my eyes if you asked." She is rewarded some time later with some gorgeous replacements of the bracelets and, by the end of the serial, with a ridiculously huge number of gold bangles that are the envy of her sister-in-law but make her a laughingstock for more-sophisticated people, who express their wealth through other means than the weight of their gold bracelets.

More interesting is 'Abd al-Ghafur's masculinity. As the scriptwriter told me, "He is the husband so many want." He protects and loves his wife. He constantly asks her to pray for him. They both ask God not to part them. He not only makes her financially comfortable and emotionally happy (and there are hints of sexual attraction) but is totally faithful, sharing with her all important matters in their bedroom chats. He is, despite his commitment to his business, a family man. Here we need to think what kind of "traditional" man this is. As Kandiyoti has argued for Turkey, ideals of masculinity in the Middle East shifted with the modernist reforms in the early part of the twentieth century. The authoritarian patriarch was denounced and associated with a devalued rural life. The urban middle-class ideal became the monogamous husband and the caring father involved with his children. These are the qualities of 'Abd al-Ghafur, despite his traditional clothing and pious language. What *I Won't Live My Father's Life* offers for its audiences is, thus, a nostalgic look at something new—a new form of patriarch who is monogamous, involved in a marriage of mutual love and companionship, loving, caring, and concerned deeply about the lives and happiness of his children. Had it depicted Si Sayyid, the old form of authentic Cairene patriarch, it would have moved people less and would have made the authentic Egyptian a little harder to admire.

THE MEANINGS OF CLASS

Despite this romantic vision of a selectively modernized ibn al-balad with an amalgam of appealing qualities, *I Won't Live My Father's Life* ran into some difficulties of reception. These, I will show, arose from the problem of associating the authentic Egyptian of traditions and values with those who are uneducated and from poor backgrounds.

The most compelling and dramatic subplot of the serial concerns the government minister (*wazir*) who rents an apartment in the fancy new building the protagonist bought and moved into in Zamalek, an old, elite neighborhood of Cairo across the river from the scrap metal market. Many viewers spontaneously mentioned the *wazir* when I raised the topic of this serial, recounting one or another aspect of his relationship with the protagonist: either his son's greedy and immoral pursuit of and marriage to 'Abdu's oldest daughter or the fundamental differences in lifestyle and values between his family and 'Abdu's. The relationship between the two men occasions some of the most powerful moments in the serial, moments in which the protagonist's attachment to traditional principles is exonerated and his moral superiority over a supposed social superior grandly revealed.

For Fatma, the Cairo widow who worked as a house cleaner and had raised five children on her own, the negative depiction of the minister happened to fit perfectly with one of her pet obsessions. Besides complaining about the behavior of nurses and white-collar workers, as I described in chapter 4, she was ready to attack the government's negligence of the poor and the unfair concentration of wealth in the hands of politicians. When I asked her about the serial, her first response, like that of so many other viewers, was to name the main actor (Nur al-Sharif) and actress ('Abla Kamil) and sigh affectionately. But then she immediately brought up the government minister. She said, "If anyone's eaten the country's wealth, it is the politicians. There was the earthquake [in 1992] that knocked down some buildings. I don't know who it was, whether it was the American government or what that sent us lots of things, mattresses and things. I swear to God they kept saying they were going to distribute them, but no one saw any of it. The ministers are the ones who take it. They divide it amongst themselves. They say, let's give some to one or two families and then enjoy the rest. It is incredible. But what really makes me mad is the Parliament."

Earlier, when complaining about her children's difficulties finding work or being paid enough to live, she had also brought up the topic of Parliament: "In Parliament each day they talk and talk, and I'm there, watching the ministers. I watch on television. Every minister in Parliament gets a fat salary. Why do they need to meet this way every day? How about meeting once a month instead of every day?" She assumes that these ministers work for a daily wage as she does. Rather than taking this money for themselves, she believes that they should create projects in poor neighborhoods to employ people. She described her own neighborhood this way: "It is crowded and full of children. There is flooding, noise, garbage, and filth. But the government doesn't go in. It doesn't care. . . . If they had any principles, they would bring in projects for people to work on. Instead of the Parliament, spend it on the poor people so they can work. These women, my neighbors, they could work at anything. . . . If they gave them work, they wouldn't just sit on doorsteps dirtying the neighborhood and having babies."

The reactions to this character from others who worked in domestic service were more ambiguous, suggesting clearly the ambivalence at the heart of serials' depictions of *baladi* people and the lingering respect for the more educated discussed in previous chapters. Samira, the woman who had fallen on hard times after her foreign husband abandoned her and now supported herself through home daycare for European expatriates, surprised me by sympathizing with the government minister's family position, despite the patently negative portrayal. She recounted, "The minister's son wanted to marry the daughter of the man who owned the building. His father was a minister but didn't have much money because he was retired. The boy divorced her. He didn't love her. Yes, how could he, the son of a minister, marry the daughter of someone from this [poor] section of town? The father wore a *gallabiyya*. And you saw how they ate, the day of the invitation. They were tearing the chicken with their hands. There is a big difference between a government minister and someone like this."

The disgust she expressed over these baladi people who had money but were boors revealed her identification with the minister's family, despite the intention of *I Won't Live My Father's Life*. There is no ambiguity in the serial's depiction of the self-interested greed of the son, the contemptuous superiority of the pretentious and manipulative mother, and the weakness of the initially arrogant minister who is ultimately brought down. But the woman's own personal sense of superiority derived from her education and former marriage—and the ideas encouraged by her formation, like most Egyptians, by the strong narrative conventions that shaped so many other films and serials, in which the baladi or lower-class person needs cultivation through education and modernization to realize his social and national potential—made her reject the romantic depiction of 'Abdu.

Their keen awareness of their mixed status as baladi made many of the domestics I knew draw lessons the serial had not intended. The reactions of one semieducated mother of four, who worked as a cleaner because her husband was too old, are indicative of the power of this awareness to shape interpretation. She talked about 'Abdu's daughters and how all are good except the one who looks above her station. As she put it, "This wasn't good. She should have married someone from her own level; that would have been better. All she cared about was that he was the son of a government minister. This was wrong. They didn't know the family and hadn't shared a life. She is the one who lost out because he married her out of greed. And his mother's greed. Oh, they looked down on them. That wasn't nice." This woman concluded that the serial is useful because it teaches girls not to look above their social level.

Her concerns with issues of social class also came out in other thoughts she had about what the serial teaches parents. Discussing the key incidents in 'Abdu's son's boyhood that create a rift between father and son—the humiliations of being in a private school and yet not having the spending money or privileges of his peers, with his father refusing to drive him and

refusing to contribute a requested donation to the school, on principle—
this woman said, "If his father had been educated, he wouldn't have misun-
derstood in this way. He would have realized that the school was like that
and that all the children's parents contributed. If you send your son to a private school, you have to pay what's needed. We should treat our kids at the
level of those around them. Send your children to the school you can afford
so they will be like their peers. Every person should be at his own rank."

When I asked if 'Abdu's son is right to feel that his father didn't love him
(because of these deprivations), she said yes. "But," she added, "I think the
father made a mistake. What you should do is to make the boy understand
why you are doing things. I teach my older children. If I refuse one of them
something, I explain why. I say, 'I'm disappointing you not because I'm
stingy or think you don't deserve it. No, my darling, because of this and this
and this.' Even my married daughter, I try to tell her not to take too many
things from home. Not because I want to deprive her. No, it's so she will
live at her husband's level. Today I'm alive, tomorrow I won't be. After that,
where will she get it? If she can't live within her husband's means? But it
is hard."

Naima, the domestic servant who had come from the countryside to
Cairo as a young girl, had described how she had watched the serial with her
employer, a woman of Syrian origins who was from an important family.
She laughed and repeated what her employer had said: "She used to sit there
laughing at them and telling me, 'Baladi people. Look at them eating that
way with their hands. Disgusting. What is this? There is no proper order and
they talk in a baladi way.'" Naima likened her employer to the government
minister's wife, who had "sat there saying to her son, 'Baladi! What are these
people you have gotten to know? I don't know how you can stand them!'"
Her employer would sit there complaining about the things the baladi family did: "She didn't like the way they ate. She didn't like the way they talked.
She didn't like the serial, she didn't like the things they did in it, these baladi
things. She preferred the things she was used to, the ways of the aristocrats
of long ago. She used to tell me, 'I don't know why you like to watch this.'"

When I asked Naima how she herself had felt about *I Won't Live My Father's Life*, she said ruefully, "I really liked it, to tell you the truth." Yet there
are signs that she felt a certain shame or discomfort, given her own position
as a similarly uneducated and ordinary person, far closer in her manners
and dress to the protagonists of the serial than to her aristocratic employer.
This emerged in her ambivalence toward such people, and thus herself,

which was revealed in her reflections on the gender roles of 'Abdu's family. She viewed this family as "the family of long ago. When the father came home, everyone would gather and eat together." When I asked if it was really meant to represent the family of the past, she corrected herself and said it was meant to be between past and present. Then she, like so many others I interviewed, brought up Si Sayyid, the protagonist of the Mahfouz novel, as an example of what happened long ago. She contrasted 'Abdu with him, the latter being a little more "moderne." 'Abdu she described as both baladi and "moderne."

What does "moderne" mean to her? She had first described the past as a time before there was television or radio. The main difference seemed to be in the behavior of girls and women. As she said, "In the days of Si Sayyid, there was no looking out of windows. Girls wouldn't go out by themselves, and women wouldn't go out at all." When I confronted her with the fact that Fatma, 'Abdu's wife, also does not go out, she made an important point about choice. "No, she didn't go out. But he didn't tell her, 'Don't go out.' She's the one who preferred to be a housewife." Yet she did not agree with me that the emotional and indulgent Fatma is a model mother and wife. She admired Fatma's devotion to husband and family but felt that her lack of education and her seclusion are faults. She explained, "Women are supposed to go out. Because when a person goes out, she learns a lot of things. The more one goes out, the more one learns. I see things and learn. But she just stayed at home with her housework and the kitchen and food, wondering what to cook today. There are a lot of things one can learn about besides food. For example, organizing the house. Knowing how to rearrange the house. And how to arrange flowers. She didn't have any idea. The house had been set up and that was that. It was like a house in the old days. You put something in one place and it never moves from its place until the owner dies."

I was intrigued by her citing redecorating as a sign of modernity and pursued it. In response, the domestic servant gave examples of employers whose houses she had returned to, finding that they had rearranged furniture and remodeled kitchens, changing appliances, colors, and cabinets. For women who live in poor neighborhoods, this simply was not done. Some of the women did not even have full stoves in their houses. Many lived without refrigerators. Some did not having running water in their apartments. They might cover shelves and small tables, if they had them, with newspaper. Their furniture was often acquired at marriage and lasted for life.

Yet to this woman, being "moderne" encompassed more than redecorating. It also meant being educated and leading a complex life. The negative contrast she drew between Fatma and her own former employer highlighted the busy life and worldliness of the latter. Although educated, the employer was described as enjoying housework and always busy at home; yet she also went to the club and parties and met with her friends and her daughter. As the servant put it, "Fatma ['Abdu's wife] was nice. And she understood some things. But she didn't know as much as an educated woman would know." And she, too, brought up the government minister's wife as a positive example. "Look at the government minister's wife. She talked in a more highfalutin way and didn't use words like *kidda* [a low speech form meaning 'like this']. Isn't this the way it should be? A woman living in Zamalek [an elite neighborhood] who talks like Fatma? It isn't right. It is too baladi. She should have learned some Western [*afrangi*] things. It is better to be more a part of society. Otherwise a woman will just be sitting in the house with the door shut, not knowing how to talk with anyone or meet people. Sitting in the kitchen wondering what to cook."

For her, being a little "moderne" is a positive thing. Yet becoming educated, knowing how to negotiate a social life independently, going out, and being westernized are all qualities of upper-class women. The only part of this complex she can identify with, as a woman who has worked most of her life and who lives independently, is going out and learning from it. So she seems to look down on Fatma without herself being able to live up to the standards she has internalized or criticize the minister's wife. Her feelings about herself were echoed in the remark a friend of hers, a fellow domestic worker, made. When I was discussing with her a television serial we were watching in which the protagonists are educators, she said, "Yes, they are good people, educated people." When I protested, "But you're a good person even though you're not educated," she responded, "Sure, but it's better if you're educated. You know things."

It is impossible now to use a baladi person to represent all that is good in Egypt. The discourses of development and enlightenment through education are too hegemonic, having more than a century of work behind them. In the discourse of modernism, as Armbrust has noted for film, the baladi person has always been denigrated for his or her ignorance, even while being valued for his or her authenticity. Indeed, the serial cannot resist the discourse of progress in the final episodes, bringing it into line with the kinds of developmentalist treatments of the peasant that I analyzed in chapter 3. If 'Abdu and his wife Fatma are absolutely lovable characters, fulfilling some nostalgic wish about how good Egyptians were and are, they are, in the end, representatives of the past.

The concluding episodes about the resolution of the son's and youngest daughter's careers and marriages show the correct path for the current generation. The future includes higher education (the son has gained his abroad; the youngest daughter, at the American University in Cairo) and a modern way to work hard and be productive without, of course, losing one's values and culture. The son follows, eventually, in his father's footsteps. But he will be more successful, because he knows the ways of the world and he can read and write. The son also sees the light and marries his well-behaved cousin, someone therefore of his own station who shares his values. But she, too, has become educated. The youngest of 'Abdu's daughters, on the other hand, chooses her brother's best friend for a husband. She does what an earlier generation could not: she meets him without benefit of chaperones. But she has an internal chaperone—her principles—that prevents her from doing anything she should not in these encounters. And it is she who convinces him to become a productive citizen before he can win her hand. Theirs promises to be a loving and companionate marriage between knowledgeable, educated professionals. As the writer described it, theirs would be a model marriage, built on love and mutual understanding.

It cannot be forgotten that one of the reiterated messages of *I Won't Live My Father's Life* is the piece of advice 'Abdu's patron had given him: "Educate them [your children] so they'll be better than you are." This raises the specter of the intractable problem that has, as Armbrust has documented, served as a theme for so much Egyptian mass culture: how to become modern without losing one's values and traditions, and, it might be added, authenticity.[13] The problem can best be captured by the subtle shifts in connotations between the positively valued notions of the ibn al-balad, the common people (*sha'b*), and even the adjective *popular* (*sha'bi*) when applied to neighborhoods and expressive culture, which, as Diane Singerman puts it, carry ideas of indigenousness, and the more negative descriptor baladi, which carries meanings of provincialism and lower-class identity.[14] Based on working in a popular neighborhood in Cairo, she observes, "As reservoirs of national identity and the Egyptian character, then, the *sha'b* have a sense of their authenticity and believe that they embody the values and beliefs of the nation."[15] This view is shared by the writers who romanticize them in television drama. But the reactions of many lower-class viewers of *I Won't Live My Father's Life* suggest that it is as easy for them as for the educated middle classes to slip from valuing members of this kind of community as repositories of the authenticity of the nation to disdaining their lack of sophistication and modernity as something that contributes to the "backwardness" of Egypt.[16]

ARABESQUE: A RETURN TO CONSCIOUSNESS?

On a superficial level, *Arabesque,* the second popular serial I will discuss, seems to be about many of the same issues. As a housekeeper summed up the serial for me, it is about a popular (baladi) neighborhood and its authenticity and about a kind of craft that no longer exists. The other theme she mentioned is the threat foreigners pose to Egypt. In the serial, foreigners want to steal a treasure that is part of the national heritage (the carved arabesque chair made by our hero's grandfather), and they want to kidnap an American-trained Egyptian scientist who returns to his homeland to contribute his knowledge.

However, a closer look at the serial, written by a major television writer explicitly to address the question of cultural identity, reveals fundamental differences. Some of the ambivalence toward the ibn al-balad figure I analyzed above is built into the central character. And though the theme is authenticity, the serial is resolutely non-nostalgic. It is not simply about the importance of holding on to values. Rather, it asks what values can sustain people confronted with the present—a present that is national and tied to the contemporary political scene.

The writer, Usama Anwar 'Ukasha, more articulate and political than many of his colleagues in television, was explicit in recognizing that to claim as representing Egyptians such classes as artisans who live and work in popular neighborhoods is not unproblematic. His protagonist, Hasan, is a confused and contradictory character. It is under the influence of drugs that he carelessly reveals the secret of the carved chair, the treasure that symbolizes his cultural and familial heritage. This revelation leads to the theft of the chair. As Amal Bakir, interviewing the actor (Salah al-Sa'dani) who played the central role, describes the character of Hasan, he is "the simple Egyptian citizen who gave to the nation and participated in the war, this informed citizen, artistic, authentic, intelligent, courageous, and giving, who loves his country and protects its authenticity; but on the other hand who is depressed, a hoodlum, lazy, lost, and enmeshed in the world of drugs and other things, as well as having other negative qualities."[17] The actor explained that he was attracted to the character because of the way he is full of contradictions and mood swings but is an ibn al-balad. Both critic and actor recognize that this character represents the ibn al-balad who must find his way in the contemporary period, where significant dangers lurk: "a period in which there was a danger that the citizen [would] be transformed into a profiteer at the expense of his art, authenticity, and culture."

Although one journalistic piece drew out the resemblances between this fictional character and a real artisan now working in Khan el-Khalili, painting a glowing portrait of the latter as the true ibn al-balad (generous, brave, reasonable, manly, standing by his community, helping anyone in need, and fairly resolving disputes), others found fault with the writer of the serial for his ambivalent depiction of the lower-middle-class artisan who is supposed to represent authentic Egypt.[18] Whereas several writers complimented him on the mixed depiction of the Egyptian mother, who (unlike the indulgent Fatma in *I Won't Live My Father's Life*) is harsh with her children but out of love and fear for them, a journalist complained that it was pessimistic to make Hasan the essence of Egypt, because "Hasan Arabesque is an example of a misguided Egyptian, someone with incredible talents and abilities but circumstances that hinder him; who is creative in his art but too weak to deal with his weaknesses; who is capable of acting but doesn't; and who finally expresses a crisis that Egypt is undergoing."[19]

'Ukasha's response to this interlocutor was telling. He defended his depiction of the central character as someone in crisis. First, he said, it was a means to highlight the very issue of a crisis in Egyptian identity. Second, it was "to confront the strands of fundamentalism in which you will not find 'the nation' but only religion; in which no one should say 'I'm Egyptian,' but rather, 'I'm Muslim.'"[20] In 'Ukasha's work, in other words, the political and the cultural are fused. A sense of nationhood is knotted to a cultural essence, again the Egyptian character or personality best embodied by the urban ibn al balad living in the traditional neighborhood.[21]

Arabesque, like all of 'Ukasha's serials, links everyday lives with national politics. In a glowing review in the official newspaper, *Al-Ahram,* Ahmad 'Abd al-Mu'ati Hijazi, a prominent poet and intellectual, credited *Arabesque* with awakening Egyptians from their slumber, restoring their memory, and creating a national consciousness.[22] The aim of the serial, he continued, was "to put the issue of a national existence once again into our collective consciousness. . . . We were not merely viewers but a national mass envisioning its essence . . . and thinking of its future, putting forth the questions it had been quiet about for years and confronting facts it had not confronted before. . . . Our memory was returned to us after months or years of amnesia."[23]

Instead of the apolitical nostalgia of *I Won't Live My Father's Life,* with *Arabesque* we have a politicized opening to the future. The writer of this newspaper article also remarked that the alley/neighborhood (*hara*) stands for Egypt and that like Egypt, its history began happily but then began to decline "until it came to the miserable present in which events unfolded and in which the future advanced, carrying on its waves the stars of the present—evil doers, the ignorant, thieves, and hypocrites. In response, some of the good turn their dreams and feelings toward the past and become nostalgic."[24] But, he added, "Those who have been crushed by disasters are the very ones who will defend us against the approaching dangers, not because they want to protect their personal interests but because of principles." So the serial invokes a national consciousness and presents hope for the future in the authentic class of Egyptians, those who are neither riding the corrupting wave of the new capitalism that liberalization and the opening to the West have brought to Egypt nor succumbing to the rhetoric of an Islamist xenophobia.

Here 'Ukasha draws on a rich tradition of representing the Egyptian nation by the figure of the ibn al-balad. If, as Laila El-Hamamsy notes, the term was used in the nineteenth century to designate the indigenous Muslim population as distinct from foreign rulers and elites (be they Ottoman, French, or other Europeans), the minority religious groups (Copts and Jews) associated with the foreign rulers, or groups from other Arab regions like North Africa,[25] by at least 1941, when the cartoon figure used by a major periodical to represent the average Egyptian was changed from the more educated "al-Misri Effendi" to ibn al-balad because he "represented a more independent and emancipated personality,"[26] the figure had come to be associated more exclusively with "traditional" or unwesternized folk, be they rural or urban.

One small indication of the enduring power of this image, promoted in literature, films, and now television, is apparent in the continuities between the characteristics Sawsan El-Messiri's wide study sample in the early 1970s attributed to the ibn al-balad (they follow old ways, don't use foreign words, are religious, less educated, gallant, generous, funny, loyal to kin and neighbors, and ready to help) and contemporary discussions in the pages of the *Radio and Television Magazine* and other periodicals. In a variety of responses to the question of how realistic were screen representations of the ibn al-balad and the Egyptian alley, the idealization of this figure is clear. One actor who had played the role of an ibn al-balad noted not only that this character is not affected by social and economic changes, but also that "ibn al-balad holds on to principles and values, heritage, and religious upbringing." A set designer likewise argued that what is so distinctive about the people of these popular quarters is that, like the protagonist 'Abd al-Ghafur of *I Won't Live My Father's Life,* the times don't change them. Dr. Ahmad Al-Majdub, the director of the National Center for Sociological and Criminological Research, went so far as to berate television drama for misrepresenting the popular neighborhood when it portrays it negatively. Using the language of sociology, he argued that in fact the people of these areas "preserve old Egyptian customs" like friendship, solidarity, and sacrifice, due to constant face-to-face relations.[27]

What 'Ukasha has done in *Arabesque* is to make this ambiguous figure of authentic and old-fashioned Egyptian culture (now in crisis) stand for the nation. As the scriptwriter explained in response to an interviewer who compared his earlier serial, *Hilmiyya Nights,* to Naguib Mahfouz's trilogy, "Perhaps every writer of my generation graduated from Mahfouz's trilogy, as did a generation of Russian writers from Gogol. Mahfouz's imprint is on all our choices: in the atmosphere we prefer; in the popular alley/ neighborhood where the Egyptian personality/character is to be found, especially in the search for authenticity; and in the fear that Egyptian identity will dissipate."[28]

WE HAVE ALWAYS BEEN TRANSNATIONAL

The writer of the serial explicitly links political hope with a commitment to an Egyptian cultural identity. He explained that although he had been, in the past, an Arab nationalist, he now believes that the solution to national despair and disintegration lies in the answer to the question of identity: "Who are we?" In *Arabesque* and in interviews, he explored a series of possible answers. "Are we Pharaonic?" Here he cited Arnold Toynbee and then quoted Jamal Hamdan, the author of a major tome on Egyptian civilization, to the effect that "there are remains and material remnants that continue in the fabric of contemporary Egyptian civilization."[29] In this he invokes an earlier nationalist discourse, described in the context of our discussion of *Dreams of the Southerner,* that in the 1920s and '30s sought in ancient Egypt a source of modern unity.[30] To the next question, "Are we Copts?" he answered inclusively that though Copts have been a minority, their art is the only true Egyptian art. To the next question, "Are we Mediterranean?" he rejected earlier intellectuals' assertions of Mediterranean unity, seeing such discourse as serving European cultural power and interests.[31] Finally, to the question "Are we Arab Muslims?" he answered, not really. He admitted a continuous interaction and influence, and a hybridization. But he asserted finally that the Arab Bedouin "were only an igniting force in the pre-existing essence of Egyptian civilization; they did not alter the essence itself."[32]

'Ukasha denied the viability of Islamic or Arab nationalism, saying, "There is only an Egyptian nationalism." But what this consists in is the power of assimilation and hybridization. He insisted, in this 1994 interview by Mahmud al-Kardusi, that "the only identity—if we must have one—is related to how we absorb or appropriate other cultures, whether brought in by occupation, colonization, or the new open door policies. There is always a process of Egyptianization . . . which derives from the Egyptian's pride and respect for his Egyptianness."[33]

'Ukasha's conclusion is that Egyptianness lies in the ability to Egyptianize "the other." This is the subject he was exploring in the major three-part serial he was writing when I interviewed him in 1997, and whose first installment aired during Ramadan, January 1998. Called *Zizinya*, it is set in a couple of neighborhoods in Alexandria, including Zizinya, during the decades of the 1940s and 1950s, before the exodus of foreigners following Nasser's nationalization of the Suez Canal. As he said, it was a time when "the other" lived side by side with the Egyptian and shared his/her everyday life. There were Greeks, Armenians, and Italians. The serial even included a Jewish family. To 'Ukasha, the questions for this serial are, Who affected whom? Which culture dominated? And again, in a 1997 interview, he reiterated his admiration for Jamal Hamdan's theories about Egypt being a large stomach whose enzymes digest foreign cultures, creating the unique hybrid, "the Egyptian personality/character."[34]

Both *I Won't Live My Father's Life* and *Arabesque* traffic in images of foreigners, as have many television serials of the 1990s, to make their points about cultural identity. *I Won't Live My Father's Life*, appealing to the sensibilities of many ordinary people, presents the American Rosalind as utterly different and in the end "not one of us." Her improbable character is an excuse to praise Egypt; she wants to live in Egypt where, she says, families are close and there is no fear on the streets; she also converts to Islam to marry 'Abdu's son, a young man whose stay in Europe has made him want to "marry someone who has the attributes of a European woman—her power, her education, her acceptance of responsibility"—but who also is Egyptian and pious, because, he adds, "piety [*iman*] is the foundation of a good character/personality." Rosalind has some admirable qualities, despite her atrocious Arabic. She works hard and takes charge of life, unlike the more passive daughters of 'Abdu. But she puts money first and does not bring happiness to her husband. Their marriage fails, much to the relief of her mother-in-law, Fatma.

Arabesque is more complex. Foreigners figure in the serial as villains, but the real question regarding transnational exchange is whether or not there is an Egyptian essence that can emerge victorious despite would-be conquerors. *Arabesque*'s answer is that indeed the real victory of Egyptians will come with their loyalty to the community along with some preservation of past values. If some of the villains are foreigners, the problematic local characters are two who had attended university and are trying to distance themselves from the community and emulate another class. When questioned by an interviewer about whether his lesson in this is that education destroyed values, the director, Gamal 'Abd al-Hamid, explained that it is not learning but ambition that ruins people. The lower-class woman had seen at the university the lifestyles of the wealthy and had become infected. She then wants to escape the community.[35]

What kind of response does this sort of construction of "the Egyptian character" produce in the public? I would argue again that, like the figure of the ibn al-balad who shades into the uneducated baladi person, it can only produce ambivalence for viewers. This is for two reasons: first, because of the complicated class assumptions of the association of authenticity with the "simple" class already noted and explored more fully below; second, because of its denial of the importance of Islam and even Arabness to identity.

The issue of class can be drawn out through an examination of the key symbol of Egyptian authenticity in the serial—the form of intricate wood carving called arabesque. For one actress interviewed, the highly respected Huda Sultan, who will be discussed further in the conclusion, the symbol of handmade arabesque is linked to lasting value—the authentic is priceless.[36] But what kind of authenticity is arabesque? First, for many viewers, the term itself might have been puzzling. Not an Arabic word, they would have been more comfortable describing the form of wood carving as *mashrabiyya* instead. And instead of being part of the present, it is a craft of the past, as the working woman who told me about the serial described it. Mashrabiyya is found in the grand old houses of the old city, many now museums; it is found in the Islamic Museum. Not insignificantly, arabesque is today sold

to two kinds of buyers: tourists and antique connoisseurs wanting a dis-
tinctly Middle Eastern look, and Egyptian and Arab elites seeking to express
their Arab heritage against Western styles. The appreciation of arabesque is
thus an elite and expensive taste, not shared by the poor or lower-middle-
class in Egypt who want the mass-produced signs of modernity, even if the
distinctive product is manufactured in their alleys.[37] In fact, the largest factory for the revival of the production of high-quality mashrabiyya was
started by As'ad Nadim, an Indiana University–trained folklorist hoping to
keep the craft alive. It now sells to wealthy customers all over the Arab
world. Thus arabesque is an ironic symbol of authenticity, one that excludes the very classes that are supposed to symbolize this authentic Egyptian essence.

Second, as one journalist pointed out in his questions to 'Ukasha, why
use an Arabo-Islamic art form to symbolize Egyptian identity? 'Ukasha's response shows how problematic, from the very angle of identity, his position
is. Saying that "there is nothing more expressive of a people's identity than
their art," he simply denied conventional understandings of arabesque as
Arabo-Islamic, either Mamluk or Fatimid (two periods of medieval Egyptian history). Instead, he opined, woodworking resembling arabesque was
found in the Coptic churches present when the Arabs entered Egypt (in the
seventh century).[38] This downplaying of the Arab and Islamic character of
Egyptian authenticity is a tricky strategy for someone who cares so much
about moving his public. *Arabesque* was watched by people whose family
members had died in wars with Israel and who still express great sympathy
for Palestinians, a sentiment given support, even now, by official government rhetoric despite widespread disillusionment with the notion of Arab
nationalism. Long decades of education since the 1952 revolution have
stressed the Arab character of Egyptian identity, with Arabic language, literature, and folklore being given pride of place, the heroes of Arab-Islamic
history being glorified, and, as El-Hamamsy notes, mass media "helping to
diffuse ideas and to standardize taste" such that a great degree of "cultural
consanguinity" has been created.[39] This general sense of Egyptian culture as
Arab (despite increasing hostility and distance from the wealthy Gulf Arabs
and the policies of reviving the Pharaonic heritage of Egypt pursued by President Sadat from the 1970s), alongside pride among many segments of the
rural population from Upper Egypt to the northwest coast about being of
Arab stock (with origins in the Arabian peninsula), make it awkward for a
serial to return to the ideas of a prerevolution cultural elite who argued for
a purely (even if digestive) Egyptian national identity.

More problematic is that the majority of those who watched *Arabesque* feel rather strongly that being Muslim is quite central to who they are and how to be a good and moral person. The newly appointed head of the Production Sector in national television noted to me in the late 1990s the growing popularity of religious serials and those about medieval Arab history.[40] Even 'Ukasha grants that "the Egyptian people are the most pious of all Muslim peoples" while condemning "extremism."[41] Yet he has expressed his concern over television officials' strategies over the last decade of "waving Qur'ans," eagerly claiming to be good Muslims by programming religious shows, proudly interrupting programs for the call to prayer, and submitting more and more scripts to the censorship of Al-Azhar, the major religious establishment.[42] He declares that he is "anti-theocratic" and believes in the civil nation, citing the importance of the fall of the church to the development of European civilization.[43] But this strong secularism is a minority position in Egypt, linked with an increasingly small part of the intelligentsia who defend the "enlightenment" values of modernist reform, or some version of leftism. If during the Nasser era Egyptian patriotism and Arabism eclipsed religious identity in rhetoric and policy, the current government does not even endorse secularism, despite its negative treatment of "extremists."[44] How can millions of viewers of a range of classes who are themselves pious and for whom being Muslim is increasingly vocalized as a key part of their social identity accept the absence of religion as a major diacritic of identity, or accept "the Egyptian character" as secular or as religiously observant in a quiet and private way?

The response to the first segment of *Zizinya,* aired during Ramadan 1998, seems to have been lukewarm, even though it was reported to have been the biggest production of the year, costing six million Egyptian pounds and involving most of Egypt's favorite actors. The serial's explicit treatment of identity through the main protagonist, who moves between the worlds of his patriarchal and traditional Egyptian Muslim father and his elegant Italian mother and uncle, received less attention in the press than the general matter of the value of historical serials (which glutted that Ramadan season) and the specific politics of the serial. In particular, those sympathetic to the Wafd party (the "liberal" party that was active at the time) were incensed that the party is portrayed as less than militant in its opposition to the British, attacking 'Ukasha as they had when his *Hilmiyya Nights* had seemed too Nasserist. The tone of this criticism can be seen in one columnist's charge that in the thirty-fourth episode 'Ukasha "devalues the role of the Wafd as a popular party that led the struggle against the English. Every nationalist in

Egypt has been educated and inspired by the nationalist school of the Wafd. This is a truism for every historian and observer, except for the author of *Zizinya*."[45]

Again, it is not clear how a serial that treats explicitly the theme of Egyptians, linked to soil and location, able to absorb all others, can be received unambivalently by people whose prerevolution (1952) memories of foreigners (*khawagas*) are tied to class difference and whose current sensibilities have been forged during a long period of nationalistic antiforeign politics, bolstered by the construction of an Egyptian history that tells the story of the territorial nation-state throwing off the yoke of foreign rule.[46] This nationalism recently has been revived and glorified for the benefit of the younger generation in the wildly popular made-for-television film (that was shown in movie theaters instead) about the nationalization of the Suez Canal (*Nasser '56*).[47] This is a film intended, according to its director, Mohammad Fadil (who had often collaborated with 'Ukasha in the past), to combat what he saw as a collective depression in Egypt. He wanted to give hope by showing that "as Egyptians we are capable of accomplishing things, in contrast to the current portrayal of us as economically impoverished and insecure, faced with the sole option of submitting to the New World Order."[48]

But even without that nostalgic throwback, the general rhetoric of the Islamism that has appealed to more and more people since the 1967 defeat— even while Sadat and Mubarak have pursued "globalization" through the "open-door" policies—has pushed anti-Western sentiment. Could viewers really embrace the protagonist of *Zizinya*, who shifts back and forth between heavy drinking, flirting, and European clothing and the fez and robes of his father and half-brothers or friendship with a religious cleric who has been anointed head of a religious brotherhood? Even more problematic, how are they to respond to the Greek grocer with accented Arabic who not only defends his decision to keep his shop in the popular alley because the people there are good people, people with *shahama* (the attributes stereotypically associated with the ibn al-balad of nobility, gallantry, friendship, and generosity), but declares that he is an Egyptian Greek and this is his country, too, a country whose occupation (by the British) he must help fight? Because I was not in Egypt when *Zizinya* was screened, I do not have answers. I suspect, however, on the basis of other portrayals of foreigners and colonial occupation in the media, and people's long experiences with rich foreigners, that for lower-class and even middle-class viewers, the effort to rehabilitate Europeans would have been difficult to accept.

CONCLUSION

In Egypt, the culture industry seems to be in the business of producing not just art or entertainment but national pedagogy. If earlier chapters described the developmentalism that infused serials, this chapter has considered how, especially in the 1990s, cultural identity itself has been the subject and object of some key serials. Such works that appear on state-controlled television are inevitably tied up with the nation-state, which, despite pronouncements in the Western academy about its demise and the very real economic and political forces threatening its sovereignty, integrity, and legitimacy in Egypt as elsewhere, is still a dominant matrix of social and political life for most individuals and communities. Mass media by definition reach large audiences, often crossing national and regional boundaries, a fact that has some impact on what is produced, since it affects representations of the nation abroad.[49] In this chapter, however, I have been concerned with another less obvious way that local and global dynamics work themselves out in media, as they do in other arenas where political and cultural life are ordered. Rather than looking at the impact of the "global" circulation of media (such as Hollywood films), I have been tracking the impact of political-economic processes and cultural movements that might be glossed as global or transnational on the content and intents of nationally produced television drama. As the power and appeal of the transnational grows, as the open-door policies come to fruition, the cultural products of state media in Egypt seem to be seeking more and more to assert a local authenticity. The case of the television serial in Egypt also illustrates crucial features of the dynamics of globalization: the way that cultural identity and national identity get linked, and the way that both are mobilized by certain groups in response to processes of transnationalization.[50] As Saskia Sassen has noted, "global processes materialize in national territories," and it is the nation that is still the crucial frame for the workings of, and imaginative responses to, all sorts of processes.[51]

What I have also argued is that a close examination of the strategies writers and others have pursued in the 1990s to affirm national identities through constructing cultural essences reveals that because their efforts are tied so closely to contemporary national debates and dilemmas, they are likely to be undermined by conflicting ideologies and the actual social experiences of the people to whom they are directed. If writers represent the

Egyptian cultural essence as lying in the "simple" classes, those of modest means who live in the old neighborhoods and preserve old values, these constructions, even when doctored to suit newer tastes, encounter ambivalence. The backwardness and ignorance associated with such classes, imprinted by the hegemonic rhetoric of developmentalism, where modernity and education are the keys to national and individual advancement, haunt their value. To represent the nation by one local segment and lifestyle is always tricky, too, because of all the other territorial "locals" it excludes—localities of region, ethnicity, rural areas, and even the middle and upper classes.[52]

And if, as in *Arabesque,* television writers represent the Egyptian cultural essence as being in crisis but present the resolution as lying in an appreciation of national heritage and an assimilative identity rooted in the ancient soil of Egypt, they may well provoke unease at the silences on other crucial "diacritics of group identity" that link people imaginatively to wider worlds: Islam and Arabness, in this case. Also, they may not be able to shake some common ways of marking such identity—as in opposition to Europeans as "other" and as colonizers.

A close look at the case of Egypt suggests the sorts of political situations that inspire efforts—however problematic—of national culturing. The urgency with which television serials are trying to shore up a national identity is surely related to the weakening of that strong sense of the nation that had been produced a few decades ago by wars and the rhetoric and policies of nation building. If Egypt is one of the places where, as Hannerz puts it, "the national may have become more hollow than it was," it is also the place where the political regime in power and the mass media instruments at its disposal are working quite hard to fill in that hollowness.[53]

What seems confusing is that television writers like 'Ukasha and other members of the intelligentsia who work through mass media perceive themselves as critics of the system or the regime in power. They counter accusations of toeing government lines (such as those leveled against 'Ukasha when he wrote *And the Nile Flows On,* the serial with a family-planning message) with arguments like "I do not support the government, because the government does not sympathize with the people." 'Ukasha is also particularly outspoken against censorship. He cynically interprets the considerable freedom he has recently been given in presenting his socially critical work as a product of the current regime's belief that "no television drama can incite people to speak up about their problems or make their demands in demonstrations."[54]

The strong point of contact and common cause, however, in this cultural support of the nation is the opposition to Islamism. 'Ukasha describes himself as a secularist and antitheocratic. This means that despite his tough criticisms of economic liberalization policies and his message that individualism and profit seeking are leading Egypt astray, he is in the end less fearful of the state's close involvement with transnational corporations and foreigners than of militant Islamist demands for purity. 'Ukasha, perhaps the first to explore the character of an extremist in his *Hilmiyya Nights,* joined in willingly once the Minister of Information declared (as I describe in the next chapter) the new policy in 1993 of combating extremism with media. He integrated, as have so many television writers now, a succession of violent Islamic terrorists into his plots.[55] His reassuring message in *Zizinya,* following thinkers from the 1920s, is that Egyptians need not fear contact with Europeans or the West more generally. The genius of Egypt is that it can absorb and make its own all these outside influences. The current flirtation with global capital, he thus implies, is no more dangerous than were earlier contacts with foreigners or the West. This is a message that is sure to sit well with a state regime whose fortunes now depend so intimately on intercourse with Western- and especially American-dominated global actors, the interlocutors who speak the language of privatization, capitalism, and free markets. Yet the ambivalent responses of many Egyptians to such constructions of Egyptian cultural identity as found in *Arabesque* and *I Won't Live My Father's Life,* not to mention *Zizinya,* suggest the uncertainties of any straightforward success of this national media effort—even if ambivalence does not dampen the pleasures of watching such television serials and may even keep "the Egyptian character" in emotional focus.

Cover of the book *Repentant Artists,* about the actors and belly dancers
who took on the veil and renounced their sinful careers. 1991.

[7]

Managing Religion in the
Name of National Community

IT SEEMED TO MANY in Egypt in the 1980s and '90s that the nation was in danger of being torn apart from within. The state was faced with a political-cultural crisis that it dealt with mostly by force—through arrests, executions, and the arbitrary powers of a continually renewed state of emergency. The problem was represented as religious extremism; the most obvious villains, the members of Islamic groups. Increasingly, there had also been concern about sectarian conflicts between Muslims and Copts (the Egyptian Christian community), linked to a growing religious "extremism" since the 1970s on both sides. For intellectuals, the crisis tended to be understood more broadly as a social issue with economic roots and wide cultural ramifications, but there was a surprising consensus among the political and intellectual elite about the threat posed by zealous religious identification.

Television drama in the 1990s reflected, if unevenly and with certain lags, these concerns just as it sought, in keeping with its self-consciously pedagogical mission, to condemn, preach, and offer up alternative models for the future. It followed three strategies for treating religious extremism. Two of these—discrediting terrorists and modeling forms of Coptic-Muslim unity —were pursued deliberately, with government sanction. The third, which involved recuperating "traditional" rural cultural values, appears to have been somewhat more serendipitous but was very important, because it offered up "authentic" positive alternatives to Islamic identity from and for Upper Egypt, the very region most associated in the minds of the northern urban elite with Islamic militancy.

The obvious question is whether these strategies were effective in smoothing over the divisions that threatened the Egyptian national body. Can media management of religion help create national community? A more complex and important question, I would suggest, is how mass media may be participating in the configuration and reconfiguration of "religion" in Egypt. Can religion be understood without reference to the nation-state? The historical transformations of religious life over the past two centuries—including the meanings of secularism, and the impact of various institutions of the modern state from law to mass media on the structure and significance of religion in public and private life—have been explored by some fine scholars of Egypt, including those like Armando Salvatore, concerned with the public sphere, and like Gregory Starrett, concerned with education and what he calls the functionalization of religion.[1] Some work in Egypt and beyond has been inspired by Talal Asad's critique of the naturalization, and perhaps universalization, of a modern Christian notion of religion as a separate realm of belief and his interrogation of secularism as both ontology and political doctrine. Islam, like other "religions"—as is clear from this work and that of scholars whose areas are colonial and postcolonial South Asia, where a nation-state founded on secularism has been foundering on communalism—must be understood in specific historical, political, and cultural terms.[2] I will build on these ideas, exploring how television in the 1990s was used to try to counter religious extremism, reflecting and establishing a certain nation-based understanding of the place and nature of religion. To reverse the title of Eickelman and Anderson's edited volume, I will be exploring something like "new Islam in a national media world."[3]

I will analyze the public reception of these television serials mostly through debates in the press in an attempt to illuminate something of the public sphere in Egypt. Only in the case of the recuperative strategy toward Upper Egypt will I consider the responses of other kinds of viewers—in particular Upper Egyptian villagers, the alleged models for these dramas. I will argue that the airing of these serials variously ends up revealing and exacerbating social cleavages, thus seemingly undermining the government's and some secular intellectuals' intentions of creating national community. Television's enthusiasm for circumscribing religious sensibilities in its serials rubs up against widespread convictions. However, I will suggest that one cannot infer from these failures that television does not foster national community through its treatments of religious extremism. It does so indirectly, I will show, by appropriating for itself the role of a charged and popular arena for public discussion of and debate about Islam. The arena is national and in this way contributes to an ongoing sense of the nation as the critical frame for all aspects of life, including the religious.

GOOD AND BAD ISLAM

Writers of Egyptian television drama often get their ideas from life around them. It is remarkable, then, that until 1993 there was no treatment in television drama of the phenomenon that was noticeable to everyone and troubling to some: the rising visibility on the streets of Cairo and provincial cities and towns of a self-conscious Islamic identity and move toward piety, especially among educated youth—not to mention the more sensational acts of violence committed by militant Islamic groups. The first phase of this violence is epitomized for many in Egypt and abroad by the assassination of Egypt's second president, Anwar Sadat, in 1981. The second phase began in the early 1990s in the form of a campaign to weaken the regime by hitting Egypt's tourist industry. It involved attacks on tourist buses, especially in Upper Egypt, and was followed by skirmishes—some call it a feud, as I will discuss below—with the government security forces in the major cities of Upper Egypt, such as Asyut and Sohaj. The third phase, dramatized by the World Trade Center attack of 2001, seems to have taken the form of an exported violence, some of which has been directed at the United States. This phase owes much to the suppression of these groups at home and their exclusion from political power or participation.[4]

In the late 1980s and early 1990s, as I have argued elsewhere, the most talked-about Ramadan serials like *Ra'fat al-Haggan, The Journey of Abu 'Ela al-Bishri, The White Flag,* and the first few installments of *Hilmiyya Nights* were silent on the issue of Islamism.[5] Instead, they were concerned with issues of patriotism, citizenship and the law, culture, and Egyptian history. *Ra'fat al-Haggan* is an especially interesting example of the revival of interest in Nasser's days, related both to the growing disaffections with the social and economic changes being brought about by the neoliberal policies and the political choices accompanying the regimes of his successors. Its first two installments aired in 1989 and 1990 and might not be unconnected to efforts to present Egypt in a certain light to the rest of the Arab world, which had just accepted it back into the Arab League (from which it was excluded after signing accords with Israel that left Palestinians under occupation). The serial tells the story of an Egyptian spy successfully planted in Israel for twenty years beginning in the 1950s.[6] Its hero is a handsome James Bond character backed by a team of dedicated and patriotic intelligence officers.

Offering the simple message of identity politics, *Ra'fat al-Haggan's* treatment of religion is instructive for understanding one of the strategies the government has taken toward religion. The opening scene sets the terms. Shown writhing in pain, the protagonist is dying of cancer in his home in Germany. He confesses to his German wife (played by Yusra): "I'm not an Israeli, I'm an Egyptian. I'm not a Jew. I'm a Muslim." His widow then goes to Egypt in search of the truth about her husband. The rest of the serial unfolds the story of his life through flashbacks accompanying the narrative his handler recounts to her. What matters in this opening scene and another in the same episode is that Ra'fat al-Haggan, initially a small-time crook, is a patriotic Egyptian who has sacrificed himself for his homeland by giving up his identity and living outside his own country—among the enemy.

What is fascinating is how the serial asserts Islam as an essential part of our hero's Egyptian identity, even though he is not living a religious life, or even a moral one. In Israel he is regularly shown drinking wine with his meals and gambling (to obtain secrets). He is surrounded by attractive women trying to seduce him. Moreover, since he is passing himself off as an Egyptian Jew, he even attends a synagogue. Yet two moving scenes claim for him his Muslim identity. The first occurs in the opening episode, right after his death. His body has been prepared for burial and lies in a casket. The Egyptian intelligence officer who had special charge of him cannot bear the thought that he will have a Jewish burial and that no Egyptians will be in attendance to honor him. So he flies to Europe and, disguised as a rabbi, manages to get into the house while everyone is away. As he stands before the casket he slips off his shoes, as one would do to pray in a mosque, and pulls out from his pocket a copy of the Qur'an. With tears in his eyes, he recites over Ra'fat al-Haggan's corpse the proper verses for praying over the dead.

We see this officer cry in another episode as well, the one in which he first discovers the file of Ra'fat al-Haggan. When he opens the folder, he finds an envelope marked "To be opened after my death." It begins (and we hear Ra'fat's broken voice repeating after him), "In the Name of God the Merciful the Compassionate. Truly we are God's and to Him we return." This is our hero's will, to be executed if he does not return alive to his beloved Egypt. After listing who should get what, he ends, practically sobbing, with the Muslim profession of faith: "Thus I will have cleared myself of all guilt in front of God, after I sacrificed everything in the service of the cherished homeland. God is Great, and for the glory of Egypt, I testify that there is no god but God and that Muhammad is his prophet."

The protagonist has, in this document, neatly linked Egyptian patriotism with Muslim identity. The serial can be interpreted as asserting that those in the more militant Muslim movements today—and by implication

perhaps their brethren jailed during the Nasser era, when a serious crackdown on the Muslim Brotherhood left many jailed and some executed—
have no grounds for accusing their secular government of being less than
fully identified with Islam. And yet these groups, and anyone from the
growing group of Egyptians of many classes who began to call, in the 1980s
and 1990s, for Egyptian society be more fully Islamic in its mores, found no
place in the serials of the 1980s and even early 1990s.[7] All viewers could see
in the regular evening serials were characters for whom faith was a taken-
for-granted part of their identity and morality that sometimes offered sol-
ace in times of personal trouble.

That the avoidance of any representation of Islamists or religious youth
on television was partly due to the censorship to which television drama is
subjected, both from the censor's office of the Egyptian Radio and Television Union (ERTU) and "higher up," became clear when official policy suddenly shifted.[8] In 1993, newspapers trumpeted the new policy announced by
the Minister of Information, Safwat al-Sharif, of "confronting terrorism
with media." As with most political moves, the policy was cleverly satirized
by Egypt's best cartoonists in popular periodicals. One cartoon (fig. 1) shows
a gun-toting terrorist looking at a television set with the Minister of Information's face on the screen. He imagines the antennae sitting on top of the
television to be guns. Another (fig. 2) shows two men chatting in a café.
One says to the other, "Those terrorists have really gone too far. But they're
not up to Safwat al-Sharif. He could hit 'em with two serials that'd knock
'em flat!"

It suddenly became acceptable for a writer like Usama Anwar 'Ukasha,
who had earlier battled with censors over the inclusion of a mosque scene
(to show the early development of the Islamist movement) in the third installment of his celebrated serial, *Hilmiyya Nights,* to feature as a key character a young man who had joined an extremist Islamic group and to show
how two characters who had collaborated with the British become suddenly
"pious" and then swindle people through their Islamic investment company.[9] More telling, in 1994 a serial whose screenplay had been allegedly held
up for three years (given only the excuse "We are unable to present a serial
on terrorism") was produced to great fanfare and some controversy.[10]
Called *Al-'a'ila* (The family), it was written by Wahid Hamid, better known
for his film scenarios. It features some popular actors, including Layla 'Ilwi,
an attractive star who has played racy parts in the past but in this serial portrays a troubled college graduate who, after having family problems and being raped, searches for meaning first in materialism and then in an Islamist

Figure 1. Minister of Information, Safwat al-Sharif, on the television screen.
Drawn by Gomaa, *Ruz al-Yusuf*, April 26, 1993.

group. This character takes on the *niqab,* the more severe form of the new veiling in which all but eyes are covered, causing quite a stir for viewers used to the long hair and makeup of even the most modest women characters.

A close look at the discussion of this serial in the Egyptian press reveals not just the strategies pursued in this new media campaign but something the public reception makes very clear: that multiple positions have been taken regarding the campaign itself. Most of the articles, especially in the official press, were positive. Some reported on reactions of people on the streets, especially in the poorer neighborhoods that had a strong Islamist presence. The citizens quoted praised the serial with comments like the following: "The serial 'The Family' shook all the families of Egypt and helped parents become aware of the nascent danger by warning them and enabling them to protect their children from these groups." "Many of us in 'Ayn Shams and Matariyya [poor neighborhoods] live in fear for our children. . . .

The danger that 'The Family' illustrated was quite realistic and showed us what goes on at the moment amidst Islamic groups. To be honest, the serial enabled my two sons [recently recruited to Islamic groups] to argue with the leaders of the group, as did Layla 'Ilwi (the actress) in the serial. It also helped us convince our children of the importance of home and family." [11] These responses corresponded to the critics' assessment of the serial as showing how educated youth from disadvantaged backgrounds were drawn into terrorism, and how corruption is rife in these groups.[12] Even the actors who starred in *The Family* stressed its pedagogical value. Mahmud Mursi, who played the lead character, explained, "The path to religion can never be through blood . . . I think we need to admit there is a 'lack of awareness' among people that left an empty field to be filled by words said in the name of religion. This is what facilitates irrational terrorism. It is also precisely

Figure 2. "Those terrorists have really gone too far. But they're not up to Safwat al-Sharif [Minister of Information]. He could hit 'em with two serials that'd knock 'em flat." Drawn by Bahgat, *Ruz al-Yusuf,* April 26, 1993.
Courtesy of the Bahgat heirs.

why we need strong attempts at raising awareness—to clarify for people the weak logic of terrorism. I think—I am sure—that this serial provides one such means of consciousness-raising."

The public opposition, not surprisingly, came from well-established moderate Islamist thinkers like Muhammad Ibrahim Mabruk, who wrote a long piece criticizing the serial for not distinguishing between extremism and religiosity. As he laid it out in the Labor Party opposition newspaper *Al-Shaʿb* (which had become a forum for Islamists, including the Muslim Brotherhood), there is a basic struggle in Egypt between secularists, who "wish to cantonize religion in places of worship and refuse to allow it to enter into all aspects of life," and Islamists, who "wish to follow the understanding and principles of Islam in all aspects of their life." The latter, he added, differ little from the average Muslim. His analysis was that the ongoing struggle between the ruling factions of the government and a small extremist faction of Islamists had enabled secularists (like Wahid Hamid, the writer of this serial) to get away with vilifying Islam and ridiculing all forms of piety.[13] Another Islamist writer in the same newspaper shared this position. He accused *The Family* of mocking millions of viewers by ridiculing their religion. He was particularly incensed that the serial misrepresented Islam as the religion of the poor and powerless. The effusive response in the press was, for him, part of "a brain-washing campaign" initiated by the Minister of the Interior to attack the Islamist movement.[14] These Islamist writers were not persuaded by the arguments of Hamid, who said that he was presenting terrorism not from a political point of view but as a social issue linked to social and economic conditions following Egypt's defeat by Israel in 1967.[15] A book published on *The Family* the year it came out offered similar views.[16] Subtitled *Artistic Terrorism and the Attack on Islam,* it argued that the serial attacked piety, not terrorism, and destroyed values and doubted religious doctrines, including torture in the grave and the presence of angels in Muslim battles. The book offered "corrective" religious interpretations and texts.

In their jockeying in the press, both the moderate Islamist thinkers and government and television officials tried to align themselves with the religious authorities of Al-Azhar, the major religious establishment of Egypt and the wider Muslim world. A mosque and university that has been the seat of Islamic learning since the eleventh century, Al-Azhar also has become one of the important voices of official Islam, with a tangled relationship to the state. The desire of the intellectuals and officials to align themselves with Al-Azhar stemmed from its popular image as representing the orthodox authority of religion, even though in recent decades it has been criticized by Islamists for being under the state's thumb and has been regarded with some anxiety by the state for harboring scholars with strong Islamist sympathies.[17] The Islamists stressed the number of letters and phone calls Al-Azhar had received, urging it to take action to get *The Family* off the air. They demanded to know why the script had not been sent to Al-Azhar for approval.[18] Others contended that comments by Al-Azhar on the script (submitted not by the television sector but "another sector") had been disregarded. Controversy over a scene in which the enlightened modernist challenges the extremist on the doctrinal basis of beliefs about torture in the grave led to calls to halt broadcast of the serial and even responses in the press by the Mufti, the leading government religious authority, clarifying doctrine and offering a set of phone numbers for the public to use if it had questions about religious matters.

By attempting to align themselves with Al-Azhar, the government and television officials constructed themselves as the preservers of proper, as opposed to excessive or incorrect, Islam. The Minister of Information and the head of television production were compelled by the controversy to meet with officials at Al-Azhar to go over scenes in *The Family* that had religious content. Although the head of television production claimed before the meeting that he had been "hoping to receive a thank you note from Al-Azhar for the role television had played in guiding the people to proper aspects of their religion, in a manner far removed from the extremists who take on the outward appearances of religion in order to cover their crimes," he assured them that the points they had "clarified" about torture in the grave, Islamic banks, the sanctity of mosques, and the role of religious scholars would be corrected in the final episode.[19]

The government's strategy to align itself with proper Islam and Al-Azhar became even clearer in the following months. In late March of 1994, just as *The Family* had come to an end, television broadcast the videotaped confessions of a repentant Islamist, 'Adel 'Abd al-Baqi.[20] In these he told of how he had been initiated into the movement and had led his own extremist group after being released from prison. He admitted that they had condoned robbery and engaged in a form of wife swapping.[21] A few months later, another series of three television broadcasts "uncovered" the terrible practices of the Islamists through discussions between repentant militants and religious scholars from Al-Azhar on the lawn of a maximum-security prison. Viewers were told that the repentant militants "wished to share their experiences with others to save them from falling into the 'spider's web' of terrorist groups." The prisoners talked about how the Islamist groups deliberately misinterpreted Islam to serve their lust for power (since violence, they reiterated, runs counter to Islam), misused funds, engaged in shady practices to satisfy sexual urges, and were obsessed with superficial matters such as veiling and makeup in women and beards for men.[22]

When accused of failing to truly dialogue with Islamists in such staged events, the Minister of Information responded with a statement that takes us to the heart of the official construction of religion. He said, "[T]here are repenters who speak with remorse and provide an essential critique of their errors in understanding Islamic doctrine and participating in terrorist crimes. They discuss how it was that they came to understand the truth and lost their faith in those erroneous ideas that had led them to commit deviant terrorist activities. As such, they demonstrate, through their experiences, what constitutes false and sound thought."[23] Making the distinction is key: serials like *The Family* contrast the good, correct, and reasonable Islam of the people, the cultured and educated, Al-Azhar, the state, and television with the bad, violent, misinformed, twisted Islam of the extremists. The big film *The Terrorist,* released on the feast immediately following the Ramadan screening of *The Family,* sends a similar message. As Armbrust notes, it draws a stark opposition between modern enlightenment and Islamist backwardness, making the brainwashed fundamentalist character ignorant and barely literate, reading religious pamphlets about hellfire out loud, rocking back and forth "in an old-fashioned Qur'an-school style."[24] The policy paper of this media campaign asserts that combating terrorism and defending true religion are not contradictory. As the Minister of Information put it, "We are deepening the authentic religion and promoting higher values to form a valid society capable of taking responsibility."[25]

Some TV writers have criticized what they see as television's attempts to appease Al-Azhar, and by extension Islamists (a policy that began to shift in 1992).[26] Hamid, the writer of *The Family,* was wary of contemporary religious figures and the way they influenced people. "There must be a separation," he insisted, "between religion and politics. Among the reasons for the chaos and extremism we're living through these days is that men of religion have converged on politics and abandoned religion. The sermons in the mosques have been political. They've forgotten that people need to be taught about their religion. . . . They've all been transformed into Ministers of Foreign Affairs, even though Islam knows no such thing as a religious state." Yet in the end, he made use of the dichotomy between proper and bad

Islam. When asked whether, if he were in charge, he would combat terrorism by means of serials like his own, he said, "No." He then argued that "television could solve the problem of terrorism by choosing who gets to speak about religion. People who do not have any ulterior motive and speak for the sake of God, and no one else." [27]

Usama Anwar 'Ukasha, the writer who defended *The Family* on grounds that it provoked discussion and was, after all, just a media product geared to fighting "backwardness and closed mindedness," has generally been the most outspoken in his criticism of state television's attempt to appease Islamists. [28] A year earlier, in 1993, responding to the general increase in religious programs over the past couple of decades and the growing deference of the ERTU to Al-Azhar, he had written, "The policy of media confrontation of extremism will not succeed simply by encouraging works that deal with extremism. It will succeed only if it ceases to attempt to demonstrate its religiosity . . . which has led . . . television to abdicate some of its basic rights, like the right to choose programs." Discussing a program that was submitted to Al-Azhar and then censored, he asked, "Why are you placing a religious institution in a position of power and judgment in a matter that does not concern it?" [29]

In the same year, the well-known director Muhammad Fadil actually blamed television's compromises for the spread of extremism. He said in an interview, "Egyptians have always been a religious people, without any outside interference, and without the excessive religiosity that is now present in the mass media. It is as if those responsible feel guilty, and thus the mass media feel the need to assert their religiosity. Why? We have always been religious individuals. We should resist this [apologetic] impulse and . . . limit the amount of religious programming on television." [30] When I asked whether he thought extremism should be confronted through media, he responded harshly, and with support for government policy that was uncharacteristic of this social critic who was known for targeting the government's neoliberal economic policies in his serials like *The White Flag*. It was too late, he argued. "Today as a citizen I don't feel safe walking in the street. I'm even afraid to go to the theater or cinema. The situation has degenerated so much that it can no longer be confronted by art . . . [I]t is beyond being dealt with by words; it has to be dealt with forcefully with repressive security."

These television personnel are part of a minority who claim to be secularists—that is, they believe in a separation between personal piety and the state, a legacy of their intellectual and political formation in the Nasserist

1950s and 1960s that pushed secular ideals. Yet, despite the objections of such prominent television personnel and their own relative silence on religion in their serials, Egyptian television continued to increase religious programming in the 1990s, adding to the popular shows featuring Qur'anic exegeses by religious authorities like the late Shaykh al-Sha'rawi or commentaries by lay authorities like Mustafa Mahmud in his program *Al-'ilm wa al-iman* (Science and faith), and big-budget serials about the history of the Arabo-Islamic world such as the 1997 Ramadan serial, *Harun al-Rashid,* starring Nur al-Sharif and 'Abla Kamil (the same pair that earlier won hearts for *I Won't Live My Father's Life*).[31] These were broadcast alongside serials like *Dream of the Southerner,* with subplots about violent militants, and serials explicitly about terrorism, such as *Al-wahm wa al-silah* (Illusion and arms), written by the conservative writer Tharwat Abaza, whose religious sensibilities, as expressed in the adaptation of the Qur'anic (and biblical) story of Joseph, were discussed in chapter 5, in the context of the differing political/moral ideologies of melodrama. The director of *Illusion and Arms* defended this serial in nationalist social terms as "a means to mobilize public opinion against terrorism."[32]

Moreover, the moral authority of the religious establishment and pressure from below, including from professionals such as doctors and lawyers sympathetic to the Islamist project in its more peaceful forms, have made it impossible for television, or the state, to stand either against religion or for secularism. The broad piety movement and the widespread feeling against cordoning off religion as a private matter of faith have indeed led Egyptian television to capitulate to the desire for more religious programming and to try to appropriate for itself the role of supporter of a legitimate Islam. Egyptian state television respects the call to prayer and the religious calendar and offers Qur'anic exegesis and somber religious songs on the proper holidays even while entertaining viewers with the wild and attractive dancers of the traditional Ramadan riddle shows (*fawazir*); sexual innuendo in the classic black and white films of an earlier era; a growing industry of music videos; and, as I explore in chapter 8, flashy consumption in the increasingly slick advertisements for products promising the good life.[33] These contradictions open the medium to criticism from various quarters, since those who believe it would be a good thing to live in a society with Islamic mores are suspicious of certain forms of entertainment, while many viewers (some the same) and sponsors seem to want the rest of what is transmitted.[34]

The more serious problem for Egyptian television, when it is mobilized to fight terrorism or religious extremism, is that it risks offending large portions of the national community who may be against terrorism but are happy enough with other aspects of religiosity and Islamism. Not everyone accepts the television story that Islamists are "the other" within the nation. Many people are pious—not just the poor working women like Amira and Naima who attend mosque lessons, but middle-class professionals and even, as we will see in the conclusion, movie stars. Certainly almost everyone now has associates, friends, or relatives who have become insistently Islamic in their identities. Private Islamic schools preparing elite students have sprung up in Cairo and Alexandria. Teachers in state schools in Upper Egypt train their students not to use greetings common in the local dialect and to use instead the proper Islamic salutations. Many see greater adherence to Islamic law and morality as leading to the reform and restoration of the good society and nation, not its downfall. Serials like *The Family* ironically provided the occasion for the expression of such differences between those who see religious zeal as "extremism" and those who do not. Thus, rather than healing wounds in the national body, unifying everyone against extremists, such didactic serials may actually work to expose them, the heated debate in the press indicating that such serials may lead to the public articulation of differences concerning the place of religion in society and the nation.

However, it can still be argued that the serials and the debates about them do work to create national community in a more subliminal way, even if the specific messages about extremists are resisted. The serials and the controversy they provoke may contribute to a shared construction in Egypt of religion as a sphere of beliefs and practices that can be wrong or right and whose holders can act excessively or moderately, in the right or wrong social spheres. There is good Islam and bad Islam and these judgments are made, ultimately, on the basis of how Islam relates to the nation and social responsibility. They are not, as they might have been in the past, part of the struggle among religious authorities. This is reflected in the Minister of Information's statement about his new policy of using media to confront terrorism, in which he called on intellectuals to participate by "disseminating enlightenment and modernity, treating social problems in a balanced way, and encouraging people to remember the nation."[35] The media campaign surely reinforced a construction of religion as something distinct that pertains to the nation, a somewhat peculiar and historically specific vision of religion that gives body to the nation as the basic ground of experience and the measure of truth.

ONE NATION: MUSLIMS AND COPTS

The second strategy television has been following since the 1990s for the management of religion is to work toward a recognition of Egypt's two religious communities, Copts and Muslims. In the year 2000, Hamid, the writer of *The Family,* found himself again at the center of a controversy spawned by what must have been another decision by officials to use media to resolve a perceived threat to the national body. After years of occasional sectarian clashes, with incidents like church burnings and lootings, and growing Muslim and then Coptic extremism and separatism that culminated in early 2000 in a terrible incident in the Upper Egyptian town of Al-Khosheh, in which 21 were killed and 50 houses, shops, and warehouses were burned and looted when an argument between a Muslim and a Copt got out of hand, a couple of serials incorporated Coptic characters; one tackled the volatile subject of relations between Muslims and Copts. It was *Awan al-ward* (Time of roses), the 2000–2001 Ramadan serial about Coptic-Muslim relations written by Hamid, that received the most attention, both positive and negative.

Again, the sensitivity of the topic and some of the sides involved can be gleaned from the press coverage. For example, in December 2000, two articles appeared on the same page of the weekly *Akhbar al-Adab* (Literary news) about his serial. One was billed as the perspective of an emigrant. Written by a Copt living in New York, it stressed the originality of the serial, commending it for its frank discussion of everyday realities and, more important, for the astonishing way it represented Egyptian Copts in all their "Coptness"—that is, with their distinctive customs and language, making, for instance, the sign of the cross. The writer credited the serial with revealing just how absent Copts had been from all previous television serials, which included hundreds and thousands of characters whose names and prayers identified them as Muslim. He was impressed with the serial's clear presentation of the issues of national unity and Muslim-Coptic relations, excusing the inclusion of documentary footage of sectarian clashes because of the novelty of the subject.[36] The second article was a news item about a Coptic lawyer's attempt in a Cairo court to halt broadcast of the serial on grounds that it would destroy Christianity, harm national sentiment, and foment sectarian strife. The reason? The serial's topic is a Christian girl who marries a Muslim man. This, according to the lawyer, is contrary to the teachings of Christianity, which forbids this kind of marriage. He asked how people would feel if the serial showed a Muslim girl marrying a Christian man who had not converted. Were not all religions equal before the state?

The press had been full of articles on this serial, and this was not the only court case to be raised against it. The consensus was that the scriptwriter, Wahid Hamid, had "broken taboos." And just as had been the case with his serial tackling Islamic fundamentalism, the production of *Time of Roses* was understood as a sign that the government wished to address, rather than censor, discussion of this troubling national issue that goes under the code word *national unity*. Hamid expressed surprise at the furor it generated and felt betrayed by the negative reaction of Copts. "We are partners in this nation," he explained.

This was not the first time relations between Christians and Muslims in Egypt had been broached in a dramatic serial. In 1996 a lawsuit was filed against the Minister of Information, the head of the television sector, and the director of Channel Two for airing two serials, *I Won't Live my Father's Life* (discussed in chapter 6) and *Wa man alladhi la yuhibb Fatima* (And who doesn't love Fatima), that allegedly "looked down on Christianity and contained offensive scenes" depicting celebrations of the conversion to Islam of the female protagonists.[37] In both cases, the conversion was by European women, so even though Egyptian Copts took offense and accused television officials of flirting with (Islamic) fundamentalists, they were not directly affected. These two serials also provoked the response of those who commended censors for allowing television drama finally to touch "taboo" topics of religion. Scriptwriter Fayiz Ghali, for example, noted that religious issues were sensitive and engendered defensive reactions, but he urged television officials to move forward in addressing "objectively and courageously" sensitive issues and social problems in the hope of nurturing "maturity and awareness" in Egyptian society. The alternative was to shrink back to insipid dramas that didn't tackle sensitive issues, no matter how pressing or realistic.[38]

The airing of *Time of Roses* during the prestigious month of Ramadan was a sign that officials did indeed desire that this sensitive issue be tackled and that they wanted a serial that could foster national community. The production deliberately evokes a nationalist past, secular in character, presumably before Islamic (and Coptic) extremism and during which there was greater harmony between Copt and Muslim. The nostalgia is created through the credits, which include clips from old film favorites and the portraits of past presidents, feminists, and writers.[39] Issues of community arise through explicit discussions of problems such as the mutual stereotyping that takes place between the Coptic and Muslim families joined through marriage and united through their search for a kidnapped baby—a symbol, perhaps, of Egypt itself. Although in the end the Coptic woman who had married a Muslim man says she regrets the decision, "shocking" lines such as "Love is a third religion that has no prophets" pronounced along the way suggest more unconventional, and apparently intolerable, possibilities.

When critics proclaimed *Time of Roses* a first in tackling taboo topics, they were referring more to the sexual issues than to Coptic-Muslim relations. The theme of Coptic-Muslim unity is an old one, well illustrated by the television serial four years earlier adapted from Bahaa' Taher's novel, *Khalti Safiyya wa al-dayr* (Aunt Safiyya and the monastery), which had successfully depicted positive relations in the past between Copts and Muslims.[40] A tragic story of love and revenge in Upper Egypt, the serial (and novel) shows peaceful relations between Muslim villagers and Copts in a nearby monastery, with the hero released from prison being sheltered and generously taken care of by the monks. It also shows ongoing exchanges and trust between the head of the village and the head of the monastery. According to a long article in *Ruz al-Yusuf,* Taher, who wrote the novel in 1990 when he was living at various times in Cairo, Geneva, and Sierra Leone, was disturbed by the events of what was known as "communal strife" and wanted to refer "to a world where love, forgiveness, and amity prevailed between Muslims and Christians in the heart of Luxor and Upper Egypt." Although the novel is far richer in themes, and Taher himself insists that it is primarily about tragic fate and traditional customs, the scriptwriter, Yusr Al-Siwi, said that she was enthusiastic about adapting the novel, because "it deals in a splendid and different, humane, way with a significant concept—namely, national unity."[41] Any lingering doubts about the centrality of the religious issue to the story are removed by Taher's objections to the censors when they suggested that for the serial, the word *monastery* be eliminated from the title.

Although some critics objected to the serial's relentless tragedies and the absence of a happy ending, others praised it for reviving ancient tragedy through grand heroes and fateful events. The reason the positive depiction of Muslim-Coptic relations was not so controversial was that the serial does not raise the specter of intermarriage. What we have are two amicable but separate and self-contained communities. This conforms to the more conventional nationalist vision, a vision Taher referred to when defending his novel as "about intermingling, not about disassociation, about bridging the ties, not about separation. This kind of bridging goes back to the persistent idea, since the revolution of 1919, of union between 'both elements of the nation.'"[42]

Just like the serial *Time of Roses,* the intentions of the novel and serial are didactic. The novelist saw the earlier union of the "two elements" of the nation as disintegrating from social, economic, and political crisis. He said of the television production, "As long as the nation is composed of two elements and not 'just one' we will continue to need works which remind us that we should understand and love one another. . . . We will need works that offend 'the extremists' who were annoyed when television presented a positive image of a Christian monk. . . . However, we will dream of something greater than this. We will dream of dispensing with works about national unity . . . and of a future in which we forget that we constitute two elements of the nation and remember that we are one."[43] As if in confirmation, Pope Shanuda, the head of the Coptic Church, was reported to have approved of works linking Muslims and Copts.

Again, one must ask, What are the effects of this media strategy for managing religion? Although Copts and Muslims in Egypt have long been conscious of their distinctions, television drama's responses to the more spectacular antagonisms of recent years in this form of moralistic representation could actually contribute to fixing the communities as indeed quite separate. The contentious responses to these serials, like the public responses to the serials on terrorism, are evidence that the dramas may expose divisions more than they smooth them over. Yet I think there is more. By drawing attention to the religious identities of characters in their relations to each other, such serials help objectify the communities. And in symbolizing the religions in terms of forms of dress (like the Coptic monk's) and actions such as making the sign of the cross, they may contribute to the objectification of religion itself as a kind of cultural element. Thus, they may rewrite distinctions as cultural differences, which leads the way for conceptions of religions as national subcultures, not opposing truths or political antagonists.[44] If the nation is presented as the framework within which religiocultural difference occurs, then one has, despite loud differences in responses, state-supported pedagogic television reinforcing a kind of national unity.

RESTORING THE HONOR OF UPPER EGYPT

The classic association in the powerful urban centers of the north of religious strife with Upper Egypt, like the condensation of the Islamist threat into that same disadvantaged region, is deliberately confronted by serials like *Aunt Safiyya and the Monastery.* One exchange about this serial reveals another element in the configuration of region and religion that brings us to the third media strategy for managing religion and community. One critic, Dr. Nasar 'Abd Allah, offered an idiosyncratic interpretation of one of the main characters, the dashing young man called Harbi. He suggested that Harbi is a Jesus figure, with the same good looks and voice, the same honesty, and the same absence of a father. He is similarly loved by the people but then betrayed. He is crucified on a palm tree by order of "the consul," which is a Roman title. The critic even suggested that Safiyya's inability to exorcise Harbi supports this analogy.[45]

When taken to task by readers for bias, false inferences, and the insult of likening a murderer to Jesus (because murder was not in the spirit of Christianity), 'Abd Allah defended himself, saying that this character is a modern messiah who suffers for others. As for the charge of murder, in fact Harbi had killed only to defend himself. Unlike others in Upper Egypt, he did not kill as part of a vendetta. The telling point comes out clearly in 'Abd Allah's final remark, where he suddenly finds in religion a tamer of the feud: "Would not Harbi's sufferings compel us—Upper Egyptians at least—to start questioning the logic and value of the vendetta?"[46]

In the national imagination, revenge or the vendetta (*tha'r*) has been the cultural trait most associated with Upper Egypt. The obsession of northern, urban, educated people with the horrors of the feud and their condemnation of Upper Egyptians as backward and unenlightened have been longstanding, as we saw in chapter 3. Without denying the existence or importance of this practice to communities in the region, one must still be suspicious whenever a cultural trait is singled out and made to stand for a whole region or community.[47] And there is no doubt that literature, social science, film, and now television have reinforced this image, playing generously with the theme of revenge.

What is new since the 1990s, when the Islamists began their campaign to target tourists, is that the clashes between security forces and Islamic groups—especially in Upper Egypt, where some of the major Pharaonic sites lie—have fallen under the label of the vendetta. Serials like *Aunt Safiyya and the Monastery,* alongside other serials such as Fathiyya al-'Assal's *Harvest of Love* (discussed in chapter 2) and television films with titles like *Revenge,* show how destructive of human life and of community, and in the latter case, of economic and social progress, feuding is. In this, television echoes themes long treated in cinema, where numerous famous films of the 1950s and '60s, from Youssef Chahine's *Nile Boy* and *Struggle in the Valley* to *Bahiya,* have turned on (and against) the backwardness and destructiveness of the vendetta.[48]

When Islamic groups are understood as taking revenge on government forces, not engaging in an insurrection that is being repressed or constituting a social movement intent on changing the fundamental structures of governance and society to bring them in line with a vision of an Islamic society, their sociopolitical motivation is collapsed into a backward tradition with which no one should sympathize. The further implication is that the Islamists are destroying the life and body of the nation, as is regularly said of feuding.

But it seems to me that something shifted in the second half of the 1990s. Just as *Aunt Safiyya and the Monastery* revolves around revenge, so have other recent serials set in Upper Egypt. But the most popular of these have balanced the theme of revenge with that of authentic values such as honor and integrity. The recent spate of serials set in Upper Egypt that depict positive qualities in that region are the work of one writer, himself originally from that region. Although based in Alexandria, Muhammad Safa' 'Amir makes much of the fact that he was born near Qina, a large town in Upper Egypt not far from Luxor. The first and still most popular of his serials was *Dhi'ab al-jabal* (Mountain wolves), which I first heard about because of a reported lawsuit against it (before it was aired) for defamation of the character of a powerful clan known as the Hawwara.[49] Years later, as noted in chapter 3, the writer said that the lawsuit was dropped when people watched the serial. *Mountain Wolves* was followed by *Hilm al-janubi* (Dream of the southerner) in 1997 (discussed in chapter 3), *Al-daw' al-sharid* (Diffuse/refracted light) in 1999, and *Farar min al-hubb* (Fugitive from love) in 2000.

My impression of a shift in representations of Upper Egyptians in these highly visible serials is consistent with the results of a study reported on in 1996 in the official newspaper *Al-Ahram.* Conducted by a college professor in Sohaj, Dr. Sahar Wahbi, the survey showed that 78% of a sample of Upper Egyptians said they did not identify with their image on television and in films, faulting these for portraying them as intimidating and for generalizing "abnormal" qualities (presumably revenge) to the whole population of the region. They feared that the effect of these portrayals was to intensify social (read: urban or northern Egyptian) attitudes of wariness or sarcasm toward Upper Egyptians. Significantly, the only exception they mentioned was *Mountain Wolves,* the only one of Safa' 'Amir's serials to have been completed at the time. They deemed it realistic because it focused on the true aspects of the Sa'idi character: generosity, courage, honesty, and valor.[50]

Although the sudden popularity of a television writer and his capitalization on a successful product through spin-offs surely explain part of this phenomenon of positive serials about Upper Egyptians, the timing in the wider context of the state's enlistment of media in its struggle against Islamists places the serials in a particular light. We might see them as trying to work rhetorically on audiences in two ways. For northerners, such as the millions of viewers in Cairo who loved them, these serials function as propaganda, enhancing the image of Upper Egyptians by disaggregating the population. Some groups and families are shown to have admirable qualities of valor, loyalty, and honor. They are struggling, as in *Diffuse Light,* with upstarts who resort to violence, driven by material greed or hunger for power, or with Islamists masking the same motivations through religious zeal. Moreover, some of the serials reassuringly show that Upper Egyptians have links to the north (historically true); they travel back and forth and mix with northerners. That is, Sa'idis are part of the nation; they do not live in a closed society and do not constitute a backward or frightening "other." The most important message is that they are by no means all religious extremists.

Upper Egyptians, on the other hand, are being told that they have within their own traditions important values worth preserving and nurturing, values that are social, cultural, and regional, not particularly tied to religion. In other words, their true identities are not as Islamists but rather as people with an indigenous regional nobility and code of honor.

From my fieldwork in Upper Egypt I would say that this message was widely appreciated by locals. Although many people told me how hilarious they found the TV dialects and expressions, they were quite forgiving, explaining readily that dialects vary enormously in Upper Egypt, even from village to village. Their dedication to these serials was apparent when I watched one evening in 2001 the final episode of *Diffuse Light* being rerun on Channel 8, the local channel broadcast from Aswan. It was on quite late, and yet the family I was with stayed up to watch. Suddenly, during the climactic events of the episode, something went wrong with the transmission. People took turns adjusting the aerial and playing with the television to get the snowy static to stop, but to no avail. It was difficult to follow either picture or sound, but they watched until the romantic end, excited that police capture the terrorists and outlaws, the evil upstart family is exposed for what it is, and the noble lord and the honest and humble widow of his beloved brother confess their mutual affection. Everyone in the family was certain (wrongly, it turned out) that the channel would rebroadcast the episode the next evening, because viewers would have been so frustrated otherwise.

This appreciation of the positive image of Upper Egyptians was clearly duplicated in the public's response to *Fugitive from Love,* the fourth of these serials set in Upper Egypt, broadcast during Ramadan in 2000–2001. People I knew were thrilled that it was filmed in recognizable locales on the east and west banks of the Nile around Luxor. The key to its popularity came out when one young woman said, "This serial really enhanced the reputation of Upper Egyptians." She claimed that the message the serial was conveying is that Sa'idis are tough and honorable, "real men," as she said. The government shouldn't interfere in their affairs; things will work better if they are left to sort out their own problems. She described how the government officials in the serial are shocked that the Sa'idis stand up to them. When the government minister's son wants them to sell him some land that they don't have the rights to, the mayor (*'umda*) challenges him, saying, "You can remove me if you want, but I won't go along with your scheme." Another young woman I spoke with about the serial described another episode with a similar message. She was impressed with how the mayor's son responds when the young professional woman (with ancestry in the region) who had been brought up in Alexandria accuses him of stealing the deed to her land. His reply: "I wouldn't do something like that. I'm a Sa'idi!"

This serial, like *Diffuse Light* and *Mountain Wolves,* was organized around the honor of the big families or clans, something considered authentic and familiar, if vanishing. Many viewers described the serials in terms of the clans pitted against each other. As one young woman commented, "We have these customs. Only if they are actually from Upper Egypt can the police understand." For many girls and women, though, it was not just the affirmation of local values that made the serials popular but the condemnation of some customs related to family. Both *Mountain Wolves* and *Dream of the Southerner* celebrate love, challenging the patriarchal values of arranged marriage and endogamy. In this regard, although attempting to restore the honor of Upper Egypt by linking Upper Egyptians to Egyptians from the rest of the country and by offering rural Upper Egyptian traditional values as an alternative to Islamism, these prominent serials nevertheless rely on the difference between north and south for their meaning. They sustain stereotypes of clannishness, patriarchal custom, and codes of revenge in that region. And by associating a certain enlightenment with educated northerners and those from the south who have redeemed themselves through education (as in *Dream of the Southerner*), they reaffirm, in the conventional language of social progress, the inferiority of underprivileged Upper Egypt and give support to the younger educated generation in making invidious distinctions among communities, even within their own region. Among young people I talked with, for example, it was common to hear comments like "In Qina they are more rigid and clannish, not giving their women to outsiders" or "I don't like going to Village X; they are less civilized there."

The serials thus confirm, even in their more positive depiction of the south, the distance Upper Egyptians experience regularly between themselves and those from the north, especially in direct encounters. The children face this in schools, where some of the teachers or inspectors come from the north. The adults confront this in their encounters with government bureaucrats, engineers, and Antiquities Service personnel. The locals, even the educated ones, know that they are considered inferior. But they also sometimes resist this positioning, asserting a moral superiority, as described in chapter 3. I witnessed this resistance in some of the encounters so common in this tourist region. When women who wear black overdresses, cloaks, or, in the case of the younger and more sophisticated, a long black coat known as the Saudi *'abaya,* watch overweight older women in sunglasses, pants, and large overblouses, or young university students in tight bell-bottom jeans, climb out of tour buses to stand around sucking sugarcane, shouting to each other loudly or talking on their mobile phones, they cannot help thinking these people are not very respectable. Of the young people in the latest fashions, people say contemptuously, "They're just imitating Europeans." They see them as deracinated, not sophisticated.

One day in spring 2001 when I was visiting someone in the local hamlet, a large group of older women from Cairo, on a trip to see the Pharaonic sites, seated themselves at a local makeshift café usually frequented only by local men, avoiding the tourist cafés around the corner that catered to foreign tourists. They had persuaded an old musician who occasionally entertained foreign tourists at a nearby café to recite portions of the Hilali heroic poem, the classic "traditional" epic discussed earlier in this book. The women urged him on loudly and two even got up to dance, incongruously wearing baseball caps over their Islamic headscarves. This spectacle attracted the young men of the hamlet, who surrounded the group, watching and exchanging among themselves raised eyebrows and knowing winks. When I asked some local women who these people were, they said the group was from an old-age home. Old-age homes, they explained, were where people whose families rejected them were sent. Consequently, they both pitied these women and were shocked by their immodest behavior. Several women whispered seriously that older women should act more decorously. In other words, they seemed to feel superior in their morality and respectability—even though they knew, from the way they were patronized or ignored by the domestic tourists, that "They just see me as a woman from Upper Egypt," as one local woman put it.

Indeed, when one of these visiting women came into a nearby house to use the toilet, she carried herself with the assurance of a social superior, stepping daintily away from the animal pen and exclaiming with wonder as she looked around, "This is just like the houses we see on television serials or in old films!" She bragged about her police officer sons and her own profession as a lawyer. Although she did admit that she was a widow and that she didn't live with her sons, she insisted that she was on a trip with her social club. She obviously felt no embarrassment at her companions' "inappropriate" public behavior and could never have suspected that these uneducated rural people might be looking down on her and her associates, or even pitying them.

The serials on Egyptian television feed into such uneasy relations with those from the powerful north and urban centers. They do not weaken the strength of a local regional identity, an identity especially apparent among those who have not been through the nationalistic school system. Two incidents that depend on the ambiguity of *Misr*,—a word that can mean the country of Egypt, or the capital, Cairo (and by extension the heavily populated north of Egypt), depending on its application—illustrate this continuing local identification. When I was telling one family the story of how we had asked permission from our children's school principal in the United States to take them to Egypt (I used the word *Misr*), the smart but uneducated mother laughed sharply. "Are we *Misr*? This isn't *Misr*!" She seemed genuinely surprised when her educated son then patiently explained, "Yes,

mother. This is *Misr,* too—from Aswan to Alexandria." Another uneducated man who ran a local restaurant had been invited to France by the or-
ganizer of a traditional music festival. As he told the story, in Paris he ran
into a major Egyptian actor, Jamil Ratib, who plays many refined and cultured roles in television—for example, the retired ambassador in *The White
Flag* or the Italian uncle in *Zizinya.* In a friendly overture, the actor had said
to him, "So, you're from *Misr?*" He had replied proudly, "No, I'm from
Luxor." The actor had presumed their bond was a shared national identity,
defined by that word meaning both nation and northern capital; the Upper
Egyptian had instead invoked his distinct regional identity, even when in
France.

Although the serials about Upper Egypt do not undermine regional differences, they are meant to perform the important function of affirming
Sa'idi values, not the newer ones that have swept the region, inspiring
mosque building and intolerance. Here again, there is certainly some fit between the serials and the experiences of locals, especially in a part of Upper
Egypt that depends heavily on tourism for economic survival. The community in which I worked was shaken badly by the massacre of tourists in 1997
at the Pharaonic temple of Queen Hatchepsut, in the nearby valley. Members of a small splinter group of Islamists broke the general agreement of the
Islamic groups in Egypt to renounce violence.[51] When I returned to the village a year after this event, people were still anxious to talk about their experiences. Some friends, who lived in one household at the edge of the
desert, just off from the main hamlet, had first heard about what had happened when a man came running by, shouting, "Terrorism! Terrorism!"
One young woman from this household told me, "We couldn't believe it
could happen here." She and her family had heard only the shots fired at a
nearby police checkpoint, where a local policeman was killed. She then described how her uncles, along with many other local men, had run up into
the mountains (the Theban hills) to give chase to the terrorists, well before
the police came. Many people in the village recounted with pride the brav-
ery of the local men and their superior knowledge of the mountains. The
terrorists, disguised as police, had hidden themselves in a cave and eventually killed themselves. One young woman said she still couldn't get the image out of her mind of the bloody feet she saw as the bodies of the militants
were carried away on stretchers.

The rage and horror the villagers felt were expressed perfectly by her insistence that these terrorists were "not Muslims, not Christians, not of any

religion. They were not even human if they could do such a thing." She reported that people had thrown stones at them after they were dead. Others talked about how people spat at the corpses in disgust and contempt. If the government hadn't been there, one woman claimed, people would have set the bodies on fire; they certainly didn't deserve a burial!

The trauma to the community in the aftermath of the incident was widespread. Everyone had a story to tell about where he or she had been and what had happened. There was no sympathy anywhere for these men and some lingering worries about the supernatural consequences of the violent events. It was rumored that the Coptic priests from the monastery nearby had come to recite from the Bible in the place where the militants had been killed. The location of the deaths, explained one young woman who told me this rumor, was right on the path to the monastery, and the priests would have to travel through this area at night as would pilgrims during the religious holidays. When I looked puzzled, she then clarified that she thought the priests must have done this to make sure that the terrorists would not turn into ghosts who would haunt the area.

Alongside this heartfelt condemnation of the incident and the militants who perpetrated it, people in this region are also sympathetic to many forms of strong Islamic identity, from popular to reformist.[52] Some examples give a sense of the variety of forms this takes. There has long been a major religious figure in the area, Shaykh al-Tayyib, with a wide following and enormous local respect as a mediator and leader.[53] In addition, during an international music festival celebrating Muslim religious music, locals thronged the venue when certain religious singers performed, not sitting quietly like the foreigners but doing *dhikr,* the ritual practice of the Sufi orders. Similarly, the *moulids* (saint's day celebrations) of major and minor figures are well attended, with the Sufi brotherhoods organizing *dhikrs* as well. Observers have also noted that more orthodox religious observance (Ramadan fasting, mosque attendance, and criticism of alcohol) has been steadily increasing over the last twenty years. Religious education is considered useful, a good proportion of the local children going, for varied reasons, to the parallel school system run by Al-Azhar. Many children are sent to a Qur'anic teacher (*kuttab*) in the afternoons and summer holidays. All Muslim girls at the intermediate and secondary school wear the *hijab* (the head covering associated since the late 1970s with modest Islamic dress), and the strict young men who teach in their schools are serious about religious matters.

There was, among all those I knew, a keen consciousness of religious identity. Although many Muslims have cordial relations with their Coptic neighbors (some who live in separate hamlets), mix with them freely in the state schools, and sometimes defend them (as did one who criticized the serial *Time of Roses* for reflecting badly on Copts by showing a Coptic woman dressed immodestly), stereotyping is common. For example, one young man gave a disquisition on Copts' careers from his experience in Upper Egypt, noting that they seemed to go into all the complex trades that require training, like medicine, hairdressing, tailoring, and carpentry, whereas Muslims were just farmers or butchers. Those who attend the Azhar schools, especially at the college level, can be far more prejudiced and hostile, convinced that only Muslims will go to heaven. They are quick to condemn the immorality of Westerners, some of whom they see close up in this area, and extend some of their hostility to Copts on religious grounds, justifying their greater virtue by noting that Christians had the opportunity to realize the truth of Muhammad's prophecy but refused.

Thus not just in terms of its reinforcement of the differences between north and south but also in its elision of a positive Islamic identity for the region, television drama's third strategy, that of recuperating some sort of Upper Egyptian culture as a way to unite the nation, forge community, and fight terrorism, is seemingly not without problems. The audiences for such television programs, even if encouraged to be proud of their Upper Egyptian heritage, would be loath to see themselves as only Upper Egyptians and not also as good Muslims—or Copts, for that matter, since observers have noted that Coptic chauvinism and "extremism" have also been growing over the past couple of decades.[54] Media's attempts to promote a culture stripped of religion, as I noted earlier in the context of a discussion of 'Ukasha's serial on identity in pre-Nasser cosmopolitan Alexandria, may be even less healing of the torn body than its attempts to turn religion into a cultural system linked to the nation. This is because it bears little resemblance to local experiences.

RELIGION IN THE NATIONAL PUBLIC SPHERE

The diverse contents of and contentious responses to the serials mobilized against terrorism and religious extremism should not distract us from the commonalities that underlie them and the commonplaces they reinforce. In this chapter, I have presented the serials as vehicles for carrying messages and the press as a sphere in which political debate about such messages occurs. Recent work on Islamism and the history of Muslim reform in Egypt reminds us that we should treat mass media, from the press that flourished in the late nineteenth century to the television of the late twentieth century, as part of a distinct public sphere in which intellectuals could debate and discuss norms, policies, and the future of the community and civilization. Scholars have been concerned about what the outlines of this public sphere are and how the changing terms of debate and discussion are set.

I have argued throughout this book that the intelligentsia, who produce television, film, theatre, and literature, must be understood as having a certain independence from the state and laboring to a large extent in their own cultural fields. That some writers used praise for the serial *The Family* as a way to attack censorship is one index of the oppositional nature of the relationship between intellectuals and the state. For example, 'Adil Hamuda, then deputy chief editor of the adversarial and sometimes muckraking political and cultural journal, *Ruz al-Yusuf,* asserted, "The serial dealt with many issues which had been forbidden in television drama—terrorism, Islamic banks, the brutality of the security police, the development and hegemony of the corrupt classes, the nature of extremism in Saudi Arabia, dictatorship, hypocrisy, social mixing, poverty, deprivation, the traffic in religion, oppression, addiction."[55] He thus drew a picture of the state as repressive.

Yet as the various chapters have shown, there are significant points of collaboration and convergence between intellectuals and the state. The last chapter analyzed the efforts of television writers to shore up a cultural-national identity based on "native sons" as a response to two countervailing forces: globalization and Islamism. The debates in the public sphere about religious extremism make even clearer that the basis of this collaboration is the national interest. This would seem to represent a significant departure from the initial formation of the public sphere in the nineteenth century. Arguing persuasively that there has been a history of the public sphere in Egypt that is different from that of Europe, Salvatore has suggested that Islam and religious norms were not initially considered distinct from other norms or antithetical to the development of the state and nation. The nineteenth-century public sphere was, in fact, the locus of Muslim reform. Whether the history of the late nineteenth and early twentieth centuries is the history of the abstraction and codification of religious norms into *shari'a,* now understood as religious law, which laid the groundwork for the current representation of Islamic virtue, law, and social order as somehow distinct from and opposed to what could then be considered the secular state, as Salvatore argues—or whether, as Asad argues, in becoming circumscribed and made equivalent to other kinds of law *shari'a* came to be intertwined with the modern secular state—the point is that religious matters were gradually made to seem separate.[56] Following Jakob Skovgaard-Petersen, Salvatore argues that nationalist discourse eclipsed Islamic reform as the ideological hub of the public sphere in the 1920s.[57] Nasserism in the 1950s and '60s would contribute even more definitively to the doctrine of a demarcation of separate spheres of religion and state, even if Islamic ideals were never purged from morality, pious practices continued in all classes, and various accommodations were made between state and religious institutions. What we seem to be seeing now in the debates in which television programs of the 1990s participated is that religion has become again an ideological hub of the public sphere, but with a certain form of the nation-state so entrenched and established that "the nation," and what is good for the nation, now forms the only legitimate ground for debates about religion.

Thus, Islam has come to be debatable in the public sphere because it is a matter of national concern. Whether through vilifying Islamic extremists, modeling Coptic-Muslim relations, or recuperating Upper Egyptian traditional values, treatments of religion in television drama reaffirm the primacy of the nation. Defining good and bad versions of Islam depends on and upholds a value: national integrity. Even when contentious disagreements occur, they occur within a public sphere defined largely by the parameters of the nation. When television serials construct religious communities as national subcultures, they imply that the nation is the encompassing culture, the container for these religious subcultures. And finally, when regional values are offered as cultural ideals, this lends support to the national frame, since regions are defined by national territory. Upper Egypt only has meaning as a distinct region if understood as part of a larger Egyptian nation. This does not mean that challenges to the nation-state in Egypt will not come in the name of Islam or from those who want to live their lives and see society guided by what they define as religious values. It is only that at this point, those positions will have already been developed within the frame of the nation-state. And in the last decades of the twentieth century and into the next, those positions are also taken in relation to a different trajectory that the regime is encouraging, one that differs from either the modern developmentalism of the Nasser era or the programs the Islamic groups and their sympathizers want to institute. The next chapter will consider the erosion of the hegemony of developmentalism in the face of the consumerism associated with the neoliberal economic policies of globalization.

Customers at a local shop, a one-room structure put up near the woman owner's home, Upper Egypt, 2001. Lila Abu-Lughod/Anthro-Photo.

[8]

Consumption and the Eroding Hegemony
of Developmentalism

GLOBALIZATION AND the capitalist marketing for which it is, in a way, a euphemism are regarded by many critics as undermining nations and national sovereignty. It is often said now that people are no longer addressed as citizens but as consumers. Television in most countries today, having never had or since abandoned its public-service ideology, has also become a commercial medium, the conduit for the advertising which Michael Schudson has characterized as governed by "the aesthetic of capitalist realism," which, "without a masterplan of purpose—glorifies the pleasures and freedoms of consumer choices in defense of the virtues of private life and material ambitions."[1] Cynics argue that television is merely a means of delivering consumers to the doorsteps of marketers. The words of a chief executive of TV Globo, the major Brazilian network, confirm this. He told an interviewer in the mid-1980s, "This is the basic importance of communication [media] for a productive system: to transform the population into an active consumer market, generating the disposition to consume, by relating each consumer good, product, or service to the social group to which it is appropriate, reaching all the social strata, simultaneously, and making markets more dynamic and agile."[2]

In Egypt, as I have been arguing, new forms of globalization have been gaining force over the last couple of decades, the way paved by the economic liberalization of the 1970s and Egypt's entry into the American orbit. In a reversal of Nasser's policies of the preceding two decades, consumption is being celebrated and promoted. Television has been affected by, and is in turn helping to shape, this transformation. The organization of the industry has been changing, especially in the late 1990s with the spread of satellite. Television programming has also changed, among other ways in terms of the number and quality of the commercials and the content of the dramatic serials themselves. One can detect in the serials the erosion of the hegemony of developmentalism, the ideology and aesthetic that governed political discourses and some of the best television into the 1990s.

Have these transformations meant the demise of the national as a frame of reference and a node of identity? Are these processes smooth and linear? What does consuming this kind of television do to people? These are questions an ethnography of the Egyptian nation at the turn of the twenty-first century cannot avoid. In this chapter, I will seek answers to them through a careful look at the relationship between television and consumption in the lives and discourses of some Egyptians, arguing that the juggernaut of mass consumption bumps up against some serious challenges and that the nation is far from superseded.

In other parts of the world where developmentalism as political ideology and state practice is being undermined by structural adjustment and economic reforms, analysts have suggested that citizens are being more regularly addressed as consumers. A number of those who have studied television and advertising in India, however, challenge the utility of the dichotomy between national citizen and consuming subject. Leela Fernandez's study of the advertising industry in India suggests that the neoliberal reforms and globalization of the late 1990s have resulted in the promotion of the urban middle class, the targets of most advertising, as representatives of the nation, the new modern India.[3] "The markers of the progress of the Indian nation," she explains, "no longer rest on the mass-based factories of the Nehruvian vision or the physical labor of grassroots self-reliance which marked Gandhi's conception of village development" but on middle-class consumerism.[4] Moreover, she argues that the aesthetics of the commodity have come to inform politics such that the nation itself has become something of a commodity. Arvind Rajagopal's reflections on the "sentimental education of the Indian consumer" suggest that Indian television commercials that follow motor scooters or cigarettes across varied urban landscapes are attempting to bring fragmented social groups into (a Hinduized) national unity.[5] The same continuing power of the national frame is evident in Purnima Mankekar's observation that even transnational products like MTV had to be Indianized to capture local markets.[6]

Writing on Papua New Guinea, Robert Foster makes an even stronger case for the conjunction between citizenship and consumption, arguing that in this relatively new nation-state, mass consumption and the advertising campaigns promoting it have fostered a sense of nationhood among the disparate populations brought together rather arbitrarily.[7] He looks at the "instrumental role of commodity consumption in nation-making" in a variety of settings and historical periods.[8] Although he acknowledges that a sense of national affinity may not be the same as positive national or civic feeling, he nevertheless finds in Papua New Guinea evidence for both, facilitated by national consumption.

These examples alert us to the fact that capitalist marketing and mass commodity consumption, two elements of globalization, are not necessarily antithetical to national identity formation. One must tease out the complex relations between these processes at particular historical moments if one wants to understand what globalization means in the countries that are now subsumed by the designation of the global South. Analyzing the specific relationships between television and consumption in one nation-state and at one historical moment leads one to acknowledge that messy configurations, full of tensions, disjunctures, and lags, seem more likely to exist than neat situations of either hegemony, as the Frankfurt school argued (whether direct or understood more subtly in terms of preferred readings and models of coding and decoding, as does cultural theorist Stuart Hall), or counter-hegemony, represented variously as resistance, appropriation, or creative redeployments. I explore in this chapter the contradictions and cross-currents evident within the ideological or cultural sphere: in inconsistencies in the messages of various programs even within the same genre; in contrasts between what is conveyed in the most powerful genre of drama and in the advertising that increasingly frames it; and in struggles between the cultural productions of television and other popular cultural discourses (including the religious) on the one hand and even between television and everyday lives on the other. The complex results are felt in the disjunctions between people's social situations and their desires, whether inculcated by television or other forms of mass culture. Again it is the lives of the socially marginal that reveal the starkest contrasts.

THE BUSINESS OF TELEVISION

The answers to questions about the relationship between television and consumption, capitalism and the nation, and the citizen and consumer lie not just in the images and spectacles of television but also in its organization as an industry. In the last decade, the television industry in Egypt has become an unstable and hybrid mix of public and commercial. There is an increasing reliance on advertising revenue, generated by the government-supported reforms encouraging privatization of public-sector enterprises and "free markets" for goods, as well as opening Egypt to the products of multinationals and local businesses. Major new initiatives, linked to satellite television as well as the film industry, have been undertaken, with state television a major shareholder. Although privatization is a buzzword in Egypt these days, the crucial political role of television is still so unquestioned that the Egyptian Radio and Television Union (ERTU) remains in the hands of the state and controls the terrestrial airwaves. Yet the 1990s saw major shifts in the television industry that foreshadowed the changes in this domain, marked in 2001 by the surprising entry into the mediascape of the first privately owned Egyptian satellite channel.[9]

The state industry had already long lost its monopoly on television serial production in Egypt because of the massive demands from the wealthy Arab Gulf states for televisual material. A large private sector in television production had developed to take advantage of this opportunity; according to Diase, the first privately produced serial was broadcast on state television in 1975.[10] This sector flourished during the 1970s and even 1980s, with some filming occurring outside Egypt where color television studio facilities were cheaper. The flip side of this, as Basim Mahfuz, a young director who has only worked in this sector, put it, is that he and his colleagues used to talk about producing "secret serials."[11] By this he meant that such serials might never be seen on Egyptian television, a prospect that accounted for the continued attraction of directors, writers, and actors to public-sector national television, despite the much lower pay scale and the bureaucratic headaches.

This parallel production system, using private studios and funded by private investors, with scripts vetted by a different censorship bureau from that of the official ERTU, was by no means completely separate. It used the same actors and professionals who also worked in state television. Actors made more of their money from participating in these productions than their work in state television. If a beginning actress in the mid-1990s was paid 175 L.E. per episode in an ERTU Production Sector serial, she might make 800 L.E. per episode acting in a privately produced serial. The big stars signed contracts for as much as 15,000 L.E. per episode. Despite the much higher rates of pay for directors, writers, and actors, the quality of the serials in many cases was poorer, as were production values, because of pressures to make quick profits for the investors. Some of the better productions, however, returned to be broadcast on Egyptian state television.

In the midnineties, a further shift occurred to confuse the boundaries between public and private production. The head of the Production Sector of the ERTU, Mamduh al-Laythi, actually began farming out work to private producers. He introduced the concept of an executive producer, someone who is given a budget and then takes responsibility for organizing the production and delivering the final tapes to be shown on state television. Some industry professionals cynically assumed that this new strategy was meant to give the Production Sector more control over the private sector; others believed it was a way to offload the responsibility of micromanaging the production process. Reactions to this development have been mixed, with critics complaining that this new approach has led to a decline in quality and opened up possibilities for corruption in the awarding of contracts. Mahfuz noted that the policy certainly had an enormous impact on the industry: serials made by private producers dropped from fifty or sixty serials a year to five in 1996.

The biggest changes in the Egyptian television industry came about because of satellite television. When introduced to Egypt in the early 1990s, satellite was prohibitively expensive and attractive to a minuscule elite. As Sakr and others have noted, it has not been as popular in Egypt as in many other places, and the number of subscribers has grown relatively slowly (although more quickly than the cable Pay TV station CNE, which never took off, in part because it was introduced in 1991, just before satellite became available). Analysts point to the expense and the ready availability of fairly good programming on state television as the reason.[12] But as satellite was becoming standard for the elite, state television began to get nervous about competition. The major theme of the first Arab Television Festival in the summer of 1995, echoed in many subsequent symposia, was what to do about satellite television. Besides the political answer—that agreements about standards, moral and otherwise, for Arabic-language satellite broadcasting to Egypt and the Arab world would have to be made—the official public answer to satellite was that Egyptian state television had to create works that could compete with what was available on satellite.[13] This would take money.

The explosion of advertising has been the most obvious correlate of these budgetary requirements. As it turned out, with more private companies providing goods and services and the return to the Egyptian market of multinational corporations, the advertising industry had been changing at the same time as television. Whereas in 1991 much of television advertising was still being handled by the major public-sector firms, Al-Ahram and Al-Akhbar, an increasing number of private advertising agencies sprang up in the 1990s, and a range of big international agencies like Saatchi and Saatchi began working directly or through Middle East–based agencies in Egypt.[14]

State television finances benefited tremendously from this boom in private advertising.[15] One can still see the lingering ideology of public service in television in the discounts given for advertisements for educational materials, for the Ministry of Culture, or in support of family planning. Furthermore, commercials for major cultural events like the Cairo Film Festival and for the Ministry of Health immunization programs are free. However, for a thirty-second commercial on prime time (for example, after 6 p.m. or during the month of Ramadan) on one of the two major channels (1 and 2), the basic charge in 1997 was 2500 L.E. (approx. $750 US) for local and almost double that for imported brand-name goods.[16] This does not include the hefty stamp tax and other surcharges, such as those imposed if a particular time slot is requested, if the commercial is to be repeated, or if it is to be aired before a soccer match.[17] Moreover, advertising breaks are stretched to accommodate clients, subjecting viewers to intolerable (to judge by complaints) numbers of commercials.

Yet one can track the impact of globalization on the television industry not just in advertising but in the other means of financing national television and the changing status of the Egyptian Radio and Television Union. The next frontier seems to be the blurring of distinctions between public and private and terrestrial and satellite. The government invested in NILE-SAT, a satellite station that carries Egyptian television broadcasts. In addition, the state-owned ERTU is the biggest shareholder in an ambitious venture, Egypt's Media Production City, initially envisioned as a "Hollywood of the East" to house twenty-nine studios, editing facilities, hotels, and an amusement park. To shore up this white elephant, a scheme was put in place in 2000 to develop a Media Free Zone adjacent to it, an area in which tax exemptions as well as the resources and facilities of the Media Production City could be offered to private satellite TV stations.[18]

The most dramatic new development was the launch in 2001 of Dream TV, the first privately owned Egyptian television station, followed by several others in 2002, all on satellite. Although the ERTU owns a small share of Dream TV, which some put at 10%, the station is owned by Ahmad Bahgat, a businessman close to the regime whose empire extends from appliances to amusement parks.[19] Although satellite still reached only about 10% of Egyptian households, concentrated in urban areas and among the affluent, this new satellite station has caused a stir. With its sexy music videos and frank political discussions, it has tested some of the limits of the freedom from interference promised by the government for those who produced in the Media Free Zone[20] and has quickly gone from one to two channels, with plans for a third. Media entrepreneurs still hope that soon Egypt will allow private terrestrial transmission as well.

If, as I have just argued, the television industry has changed with the times, transforming itself more blatantly into a commercial venture, the worlds that television brings to viewers have also become infused with the ethos of consumption. The links to consumerism are especially apparent in two aspects of television that are contiguous to the melodramas that rivet viewers. First, the glitter can be seen in the star system on which television serials rely for their popularity. The stars of the serials people are supposed to admire, in real life and on the screen, live lives that only a wealthy minority could dream of having. They wear clothes most could not afford, attend well-publicized parties, drive fancy cars, and are known to have business investments. Taxi drivers gossip with awe about the number of Mercedes-Benzes the star Shirihan has in the parking garage of her five-million-pound apartment in the elite neighborhood of Zamalek, or the fifty million pounds 'Adil Imam is supposed to have paid for his apartment. Every major actor used a mobile phone at a time when telephone service was still not taken for granted. Stars are the most visible and accessible of the wealthy, with television interview shows bringing them into people's homes in ways that the magazines, which have built stars' reputations since the early days of cinema in Egypt, could not. Revealing "intimate" details about their lives on *Night of a Lifetime,* for example, they describe their marriages and show video clips from their weddings. They are celebrities who turn heads wherever they go and are often rumored to be involved in scandals. People are encouraged to think they know a lot about these celebrities—who is married to whom, who has just died. If they read magazines, they will think they know how much these stars command in salaries.[21] Although, as I will explore in more depth in the next chapter, many criticize performers and "artists" for their immoral lifestyles, and the veiling of born-again stars made waves in the early 1990s, there is little doubt that actors are popular.

The stars' links with money and consumption are assumed by the television industry, too. They are blamed for such major infrastructural changes as the separation in the 1980s of what was to be called the Production Sector (*qita' al-intaj*) from the other two basic units of the Radio and Television Union. Their salaries, it was said, created special budgetary needs that had to be addressed separately. The extravagant displays associated with the stars and the serials appeared not just on-screen but in Maspero, television head-quarters. When I first went to meet Mamduh al-Laythi, the head of this unit, in 1990, I was overwhelmed by the difference between his office and the rest of the building I had just been taken through. While the other offices had simple wooden desks and bare floors and the stairwells were shabby and crowded with employees, his capacious office was guarded by three attractive secretaries in makeup and fancy clothing. It was air conditioned, its windows graced with curtains, its furniture consisting of a seating area of chintz couches and a huge desk facing several velvet and chrome chairs. On a wall in view of the desk was a video screen showing the filming going on in each of the studios in the building. On the desk were piles of silver business cards and no less than five pushbutton phones that rang continuously in some sort of parody. As he answered the phones and dealt with the people coming in and out of his office he kept muttering "Dirty work, dirty work." He complained to the senior television officer who had brought me that working with people was so difficult. He explained, "You know these stars. You'd be surprised to know they are terrible, very temperamental in their work. All they are interested in is money."

The star system is not the only sign of television's escape from the sobriety of the values of developmentalism. The aesthetic of development realism and the values of social welfare and national progress are being edged out most explicitly in a second domain connected to the serials: television commercials. Introduced in the 1970s with the encouragement of private enterprises and competition between brands, these advertisements had by the 1990s increasingly hemmed in the serials, gained on them in production values, and taken up more airtime. They helped provide funds to pay for the salaries of the big stars, the extravagant sets, the new props such as the Mercedes-Benzes and Jeeps, and the location shoots in exotic places from Luxor to London. The fifteen, twenty, and even forty minutes that precede the broadcast of the most popular programs are a persistent insertion of capitalist realism (the fantasy counterpart to the nuts and bolts of commercial television described above) into the television flow. The commercials, mostly selling fast-moving consumer goods, trumpet the joys of comfort, pleasure, consumption, and modernity.

Although people can ignore commercials as they wait for the evening serials or soccer broadcasts, they often do not. Even in 1990, when I began my study, it was fairly standard to have forty commercials preceding the start of a serial, with a few immediately following the program credits just before the program proper began. During Ramadan, when viewing is highest, the commercials preceding the main evening serials can last up to half an hour. Over the years, the ads have multiplied and advanced in sophistication. Their prominence as programming is such that one critic assessing the 1999–2000 Ramadan television season thought to comment on the commercials as well as the serials. He noted, at the end of his discussion of the serials and before discussing the commercialized Ramadan riddle shows (that Armbrust has characterized as "rituals of mass consumption"), "The two mobile phone companies dominated Ramadan's equally anticipated ad scene, and even produced several programmes each." [22]

The commercials to which viewers are treated range from the old-fashioned low-budget animations with jingles or lip-synched songs and dances that were so popular in the late 1980s to ads that rival American or European ones in production values. Over the 1990s, the number of inexpensive advertisements for local shops and cinemas, consisting of either handwritten boards or film clips with voice-overs, declined in favor of advertisements for the products of transnational companies shot on location or adapted from international commercials. Fierce competition was waged among firms that produce ceramic tiles, laundry detergent, potato chips, and candies, although ads for processed foods from stock cubes to cooking oils, cheese, and meats as well as appliances from water heaters to television sets were common. By the late 1990s, commercials for large items like automobiles and a variety of personal care products from soaps and shampoos to disposable diapers had appeared. These same years were notable for the "soap wars" between Ariel (Proctor and Gamble) and Persil (Unilever) laundry detergents. Probably the most noted and memorable commercial, aired during Ramadan in 1997, was one for Jawhara ceramics. It appeared regularly in the most expensive slot, just before the main evening serial during the month with the most expensive airtime. It featured the glamorous actress Yusra discussing tiles (on her mobile phone, of course) with none other than the debonair actor Omar Sharif, whose return to his homeland was well publicized. The magnificent clothing of these cosmopolitan celebrities was matched by the elegant interiors, conjuring an extravagant, if tasteful, romance with consumption. The commercial was directed by Sharif 'Arafa, a major cinema director who, like many colleagues, has set up his own advertising production house in response to the decline of support for the film industry.

Most advertisements for household products feature attractive, light-skinned, modern professional women with glossy straight hair, some wearing glasses to show that they must know what they are doing when they bake a cake or buy a dishwasher. Small, happy families sit around well-stocked dining room tables with lovely serving dishes, eating food that has been cooked in vegetable oils or with processed tomato sauce. Well-scrubbed and neatly dressed children come home from school to well-appointed kitchens and mothers offering them chocolate milk. An extreme example of a rare lifestyle can be found in recent advertisements for soft drinks set in bars where handsome young men in tuxedos ogle attractive women with bouncy hair and satin dresses, or in ads for coffee where blond women in soft focus sip fragrant coffee from porcelain cups. A 1999 commercial for an exclusive new housing development outside Cairo boasted that Dreamland was to be the first electronic village. The amusement park next to it was described as "something we only dreamed of" by a beloved older actor, Sana' Gamil, who urges viewers, "Take your kids there." The amusement park, she doesn't mention, costs more in entry fees than many people in Egypt earn in a week, and the electronic village must seem very dreamy to the majority who live with unreliable electricity.[23] These lifestyle ads are complemented by those which draw on scientific authority to prove the effectiveness of unfamiliar products like toilet bowl cleaners and disposable diapers.

Only a handful of commercials play on national themes. An Egyptian identity was constructed for Ideal, local manufacturer of washing machines and refrigerators, in a 1990 commercial. The jingle that accompanied shots of the Pyramids was "Famous among us, as famous as the Pyramids." Nearly ten years later, ads for imported items also featured national themes. A 1999 advertisement for Chevrolet showed pickup trucks in Egyptian rural and urban settings, including weddings, accompanied by the slogan "Our Egypt." Ads for detergents by multinational companies like Ariel cleverly draw the whole population in by showing village women washing or Nubians (an ethnic minority) with folkloric blankets hung on the walls of their houses carrying their laundry up to the roof to dry. Even more compelling, perhaps, are their ads that show the surprise and gratitude on ordinary people's faces when they open the door to find they have won a prize or been granted a wish by Ariel. A national inclusiveness is also covertly promoted by ads for locally produced cooking oils that feature folkloric stereotypes of village women or Bedouins. They may exist because of a segmented market, but their effect is to suggest that all of this variety is part of Egypt.

Although these advertisements would repay careful analysis, I will simply note that they promote the pleasures of consumption, defining the good life in terms of an upper-middle-class lifestyle, even if they gesture occasionally toward a pluralistic nation through a folklorized regionalism. The capitalist realism of commercials and the real capitalism infiltrating the industry do not go unchallenged, however. The rest of the chapter will examine these challenges, beginning with the serials that have an uneasy relationship to these processes.

MELODRAMATIC TENSIONS

One can detect in the television dramas of the 1990s the tentative emergence of a new aesthetic as development realism began to be infiltrated by capitalist realism. But the process is not straightforward. The 1990s actually saw a great investment in powerful messages about the immorality of money and the dangerous seductiveness of consumption. These messages pose one kind of challenge to the forward march of capitalist consumption. The contrast between rich and poor, often portrayed as corrupt versus noble, is an old formula in cinema and television drama, Egyptian and otherwise. Greed and its moral consequences are not new themes, either. But what has characterized serials of the 1980s and the 1990s in Egypt is the association of greed with an entrepreneurial class of nouveau riche businessmen and women associated with the *infitah* (open door policy). In some serials of the early '90s, like the brilliant 'Ukasha/Fadil collaboration, *The White Flag*, or Wafiyya Khayri's *Akhir 'awda* (The final return), the first serial to deal critically with the big money Egyptians made in the Gulf, issues of taste and class are problematized; the nouveau riche are condemned for their lack of taste, their failure to appreciate genuine beauty and the virtues of education, and even their national heritage—in short, all the values of an old, modernist, educated middle class.[24] But most of the serials are more concerned about how the desire for money at any cost leads to illegalities such as bribery, embezzlement, drug dealing, and various other contemporary corrupt business practices. Financial dishonesty and its associated moral turpitude are portrayed as damaging to society, the younger generation, and the nation.

These stories about financial corruption certainly resonated among domestic workers in Cairo that I knew. A good example is *Ahalina* (Our folks), 'Ukasha's Ramadan 1997 serial. It is a story about the difficult life circumstances beleaguered middle-class families face. One new theme is the hopeful message for the younger generation that they should work hard to make something productive—in this case, the suggestion is to make the desert bloom.[25] The major theme of *Our Folks*, however, is the more familiar one of economic crisis: unemployment, low salaries, and the temptations to which these lead, from bribery to embezzlement.

Talking about this serial launched Amira, the woman whose melodramatic life stories were the subject of chapter 5, into long disquisitions on the problems she was having trying to hook up electricity to the small house she was building in an informal neighborhood. (Much of Cairo's expansion has been in the form of unregulated neighborhoods in which people build their own housing and city services are not available.) In the process of doing the paperwork for this utility, she had been forced to bribe every single functionary in the chain. Only one man refused her payoff, she told me. She recalled with approval, "'Don't you dare,' he said, when I started to pull out some money." Her most recent aggravation was with a fixer who had already taken 300 L.E. from her and now wanted 200 L.E. more. She was stuck because he had her papers—the deed to her land and her identity card. At least during Ramadan, she complained, people shouldn't behave this way.

Fatma, another domestic worker, thought that *Our Folks* reflected reality. She said as we discussed it,

Yes, people get degrees, and [yet] there's no work here. This is true. In the serial and in life. Here my sons face this. . . . And to make something happen, you have to put money down. Bribes, many bribes. I, as a woman, if I want to get something done, I put money down. I won't lie. My daughter tells me this is wrong. But I say no, it isn't wrong. I won't be able to make anything work otherwise. And so when my daughter began to try to get her papers as a doctor and had a hard time, she came to me. She couldn't give a bribe because she's a doctor. It would be shameful. . . . So I had to get her papers from Ministry of Health. I swear to God. They sent her this way and that. The papers haven't arrived; the papers have arrived, they'd tell her. If she'd paid, she would have got them right away.

Samira, the downwardly mobile educated childcare provider, was more incensed by the corruptions of an educational system she believed was based on money and bribes. Talking about this serial led her into a sad story about how much her son's private lessons for his engineering course had cost her. Like many parents who feel coerced into this vast system of private lessons, she is suspicious.

The boy was good, very good. He could pass without private lessons. But one teacher told him, "You should take private lessons with me." He said he didn't need to, because he was good in this subject. The man flunked him. All the teachers are like that. So he had to have lessons.

More troubling to her was her impression that people could buy their way into professions like law and medicine. She told me,

I used to have a [rich] neighbor whose kid got leukemia. So they took him to the U.S. for treatment. His father is a doctor. When the kid came back from America, the exam period was over. Yet he got his degree with distinction! I was going to go crazy. How did he pass when he was in America? They told me, his father is a doctor. So what, I said, if his father is a doctor! Can he do what his father does? Maybe he'll kill people. How can he treat people if he hasn't learned properly? He'll forget a piece of cotton inside, a scissors, a bandage!

Many serials include storylines about youth, warning about the special vulnerability of these young people whose dreams cannot be realized. Whether it is marrying for financial security, doing work that is illegal or demeaning to make money, or turning to drugs for profit and (addictive) consumption, these serials try to hold these lost youth up as object lessons. These themes reflect general worries about youth in Egypt and in real life can take the form of the strategies of a concerned mother like Salwa. In line with her pious view of the world, Salwa ultimately recognizes that God sometimes sends the Devil to tempt people to sell drugs, steal, or kill. But she grants that family and friends, the general environment, are also important. "The most important thing is the family. . . . The most important problem is too much spending money." Her philosophy is not to give her children too much. She explains, "For example, my son eats breakfast at home. I give him a little money for transportation and for a cold drink if he wants one. I make sure he has good clothes and I get him everything he needs for school. This is good. But not more than that, otherwise he might go to the cinema or go to watch videos at a café or a video club." Her fear is that these films will corrupt his morals.

Such worries about today's youth can also take the more general form of the hysterical arrest in 1997 of a large group of youth, many reputed to be wearing earrings and black shirts, that was hanging out in front of the chic restaurant, McDonald's. Initially accused of being Satanists, with lurid stories circulating about their bizarre practices, they were released without charges, many of them the children of a shocked elite. The message in this incident is clear: morality is at risk among today's youth, especially those in the cosmopolitan world, where money is too free. Three astute cartoons printed around that time in the weekly magazine *Sabah al-Khayr* capture the issues nicely. The first shows a young man wearing hip Western clothes and sporting the type of haircut that symbolizes for Egyptians rebellious youth: long on top and shaved below. Behind him stand two horned devils. One says to the other, "Here's an easy customer. A teenager, his mother and father are not here . . . and he's loaded!" The second shows a man bowing down on his prayer carpet in front of a stack of money. "Shhh [don't disturb]," his wife says to their daughter, "your father really 'worships' money." The third cartoon is perhaps most interesting, because it flags the pedagogic role of media in the countryside. A small peasant family sits around their low table, eating supper. Their TV in the background broadcasts news of Satan worship. The wife says to her husband, "Be careful man, don't let the devil trick you the way he did those city people!"

Satan-worshipping, drug-taking young people made their way two years later into an earnest Ramadan serial called *Woman from the Time of Love* (another 'Ukasha product), which addresses youth issues. Here the specific danger being pointed to was the dissolution of Egypt's youth. An upright woman who holds on to good old-fashioned values is brought in to help rescue her rebellious nieces and nephews, children who have grown up without a mother, with far too much money, and with an avaricious father too busy for them. One son takes drugs and hangs out with Satanist heavy-metal fans; one daughter sneaks out to see her boyfriend; all of them stay up all night watching foreign videos and spend hours listening to their Sony Walkmans. As Geir Sakseid points out, it is significant that in the final episode, when this noble woman is interviewed by Egyptian television about a search for her grandson, probably in the hands of the Israelis, the television hostess declares, "Egypt does not forget her children." [26]

Despite the inclusion of themes such as the danger money poses to national values, many of the Ramadan serials of the mid- to late 1990s differ from the standard developmentalist serial format. Whether to appeal to a wider pan-Arab satellite market, to compete with it, or to show off the new resources available for Egyptian television serial production, the most memorable features of these new, slightly racy serials are the magnificent clothes, the immaculate and lavishly furnished villas (always with swimming pools no one ever swims in), and the glamorous actors, many coming from the decimated film industry. These features, I would argue, are evidence of the beginnings of an aesthetic counterpart to the new political-economic realities of post-*infitah* Egypt. Although serials continued to promote the moralism of developmentalist serials, with the exoneration of the good, law-abiding, educated middle class, as I have argued previously, or even making an authentic lower-middle class the repository of Egypt's values, as I argued in chapter 6, there is little doubt that the alluring spectacles of consumption the serials purport to condemn vie for viewers' attention.

Nusf Rabi' al-akhar (The other half of Rabi'), directed by top director Yahya al-'Alami (who in 1997 replaced the scandal-ridden Mamduh al-Laythi as head of the Production Sector of the ERTU), is a perfect example of the uneasy mix of morality and consumption that came to dominate the latter half of the 1990s. It is a story about a respected lawyer and citizen torn between his wife, a socially concerned and dedicated school principal, and his first love, who returns, twenty years after running off with his best friend, as an incredibly wealthy businesswoman still longing for him and wanting him back. Gorgeous, her jewelry glinting and her lipstick glistening, she offers him love and extravagant consumption, giving him the keys to a new car and furnishing a villa for him that makes his comfortable but very ordinary apartment, shared with his longtime wife and teenage children struggling to pass exams, seem shabby. The story is complicated, because his former lover lures him simultaneously with money and love. She seems to believe in him and reminds him of his youthful aspirations. She pushes him to realize his dream of running for Parliament (although her presence by his side makes him as unpopular with the local neighborhood crowds as with his own family).

Much of the heated debate over *The Other Half of Rabi'* in the columns of the newspapers revolved around the emotional and interpersonal dilemmas—the exquisiteness of first loves, the rights of wives, the feelings of men, the problems of keeping husbands, and the evils of polygamy, thus ignoring the main political and moral messages hammered home in the serial's final episode.[27] The conclusion indicates that *The Other Half of Rabi'* is supposed to be a story about the importance of honor, the corrupting temptations of money, and the moral victory of honesty and concern for the wronged. There is an earthquake in which school buildings collapse, killing innocent children. It turns out that the multimillionaire first love, who has all along painted herself as a victim of her unscrupulous ex-husband, knowingly imported the defective cement that led to these collapses. She and her ex-husband then beg the protagonist to help cover things up. His former friend and the woman's ex-husband taunt him: you won't be able to give up the cars, the villa, and the apartment on the Nile (gifts/payments he has re-

ceived for working for his former love)! But he does. He returns to his wife
and family at the same time that he finally prosecutes in the name of the
people his sweetheart, who has betrayed her country and people. And yet
along the way, people have seen what money can buy.

The next year, in 1997, other Ramadan serials like *Hayat al-Gawhari* and
Didd al-tayyar (Against the current) similarly dealt with the corruptions of
illegally gained money. That some of these serials come a little too close to
threatening powerful interests is suggested by reports that *Against the Current* was almost blocked. According to a young actress who participated in
it, it was Samira Ahmad, the star of the serial and a major star of black-and-
white film who was acting in her first television serial in ten years, who prevailed upon the television authorities to allow the serial to be broadcast.[28]
Interestingly, in a televised conference about the serial, its respected director, Isma'il 'Abd al-Hafiz denied that it is about corruption (*fasad*). He insisted that its main point is the nature of marriage: what the relationship between a faithful wife and a corrupt husband should be.[29] Like *The Other Half
of Rabi'*, *Against the Current* is carried along mostly by these interpersonal
relations, which may well be the focus of viewers' attention. But there is little
doubt that a message about dishonesty and financial greed runs through the
plotline. The director's denial of this theme may have been done to protect
his project. Criticizing too harshly the new entrepreneurs who are taking
advantage of neoliberal reforms, which is government policy after all, may
be dangerous.[30]

Hayat al-Gawhari, a serial featuring the return to the small screen of another female film star, Yusra, deals even more explicitly with the temptations of money. In one crucial scene the honest wife, a lawyer like her husband, confronts him about succumbing to some crooks to forge papers so
that he can suddenly acquire a fancy apartment on the Nile. She reminds
him how they met in the state youth organization in the 1960s, how they fell
in love, and how devastated they were when Nasser and Egypt were defeated
in 1967. They had always lived honorably and by the law. Her husband defends his actions by saying he didn't want to eat meat only once a week or
see his wife want a dress she couldn't afford, living off the crumbs of the rich.
She argues back that he used to be patriotic. Remember, she says, how we
worked in literacy classes because we had become educated and were so excited about it? "Screw honor," he retorts. He doesn't want to work and serve
people all his life and end up leaving nothing for his kids. He lectures her:
"This is not the same age—now I want to give my kids everything." His wife

responds that it isn't the age that has changed but people: "Now everyone is out for himself."

All these dramatic stories are framed morally, with characters' desires for money and luxury leading them to compromise their principles and to go astray, only to be found out and confronted, if not condemned, in the end. And yet one has to wonder about the seductions for viewers of the clothing, the furnishings, the cars, the restaurants, and the general lifestyles these serials portray. The contradiction has not escaped critics. One columnist in the English-language *Al-Ahram Weekly,* concluded his roundup of the Ramadan 2000 serials by saying, "The thematic unity of most of the Ramadan dramas this year is reminiscent of a few years ago, when the central theme of most series was historical. . . . This year, it is are they corrupt or not? Have they repented for their sins? Regardless, look how nicely they're living as a result."[31]

After having imported such famous American soap operas of the '80s and '90s as *Dallas, Falcon Crest,* and *The Bold and the Beautiful,* Egypt thus seems to have begun to produce serials that flirt boldly with the same aesthetic.[32] One can even detect a loosening of the clear moralism in some glitzy serials of the late 1990s in which the message about the immorality of money is totally overwhelmed by the tempting displays of consumption and undermined by the fact that the bad characters are never truly punished.[33] In *'Ali 'Alewa,* a serial broadcast in 1996, the man who betrays his family and threatens its heritage by wanting to sell off the books from the family publishing house and going into drug dealing and other commercial ventures, dies before being punished. That this outcome violated viewers' expectations was clear when a village man complained to me that he had expected the law to intervene and arrest the man and his accomplices, an ending predicted to me by several other village women who had understood the serial to be about greed (*tumu'*). He did not think the final episode was morally satisfying, apparently finding too ambiguous an ending that glorifies community solidarity to save precious books that are part of their Arab heritage.

Al-Hawi (The magician), broadcast in the best slot in 1997, the first half of Ramadan, is an even better example. It was directed by the same person who produced *The Other Half of Rabi'* the previous year and stars the same glamorous superstar, Ilham Shahin. It contains scenes that are unusually risqué, including heavy whiskey consumption and an implied extramarital sex scene, in contrast with the self-conscious chastity of *The Other Half of Rabi'.*[34] (The presence of these uncensored scenes might be understood in the context of the director's elevation to head of television's drama production unit.) Moreover, the sets are lavish. In one villa the bridal couple lies on a satin-covered round bed that revolves at the touch of a button. In the morning after they are married, she appears in satin lingerie. The villa has two swimming pools, and scenes are set in a club on the Nile, in restaurants with views of the Pyramids, in modern offices with plate-glass windows, and in apartments with wet bars and glass coffee tables.

Although the director described the story as twenty years in the life of Egypt—suggesting some allegorical significance to the victimized woman who was betrayed by at least three men, her Egyptian hustler sweetheart (who married a rich foreigner to set himself up, and who eventually dealt in arms with Americans and Israelis), the wealthy Gulf Arab she married first, and an Islamic fundamentalist (who colluded with this ex-husband to steal her son)—many viewers found *The Magician*'s characters hard to identify with and the moral message confusing. Amira, for example, who lost interest in it early on, commented to me the day after the final episode that she thought the serial was just beginning to get a little better. She had not even realized that it was over, perhaps because its plotline broke so strongly with the usual conventions and morality. Her alienation may also have had another source—the spectacular wealth and consumption that dominated the serial—which leads us to other dimensions of the challenges to television's, and Egypt's, infatuation with consumption.

ALTERNATIVE IDEOLOGIES AND UNEVEN CONSUMPTION

The uneasy mixture of private and public that characterizes television in Egypt is mirrored in the ambivalent ideological messages about consumption found in the serials and in the juxtaposition of moral melodramas and advertisements. Globalization and neoliberal economic reforms have produced these disjunctures, which might be considered internal contradictions. Yet there are other tensions in the relationship between television and consumption that pose greater challenges to any smooth transition in Egypt to the neoliberal ideal of the consuming citizen. The first of these is ideological opposition, not only from the Left, as in the condemnation of the immorality of capitalism found in the serials of developmentalists, but also from those seeking a more Islamic life and society.

From some quarters inhabited by the middle and lower-middle classes and even others comes a confident excoriation of consumption and a compelling alternative vision of the good life in Egypt. Although one could point to many public statements by new religious authorities, it might be best to look on the ground at some ordinary women who are among the many who attend mosque lessons all over Cairo and other towns and cities of Egypt. Saba Mahmood, whose research on pious women I discussed in chapter 4, argues that her informants thought that "with greater displays of wealth and imported consumer goods on the streets, increased inflation, and a greater incitement to adopt expensive life styles promoted by the foreign and local media . . . Egyptians [were] becoming more ambitious, competitive and selfish, with less regard for their family, friends and the larger community." Many of Mahmood's informants blamed media, "facilitated by the neo-liberal economic policies of the Egyptian state," for the corruption of "values and desires central to an entire way of life." They saw themselves as trying to counter this trend through the cultivation of Muslim virtues, which participation in the mosque movement would help them achieve, and through seeking to encourage the development of a public Islamic sociality in Egypt,[35] even if Linda Herrera's research among teenagers shows that mosque lessons combine easily with pop music and clubs.[36]

This vision of the ideal life and national identity sets itself in opposition to the current state-sponsored Western-style consumerism. It also jostles with the earlier state-sponsored secular developmentalism, still lingering in television dramas, as I have described above. The promotion of these ideals does not signify their achievement. And it does not preclude Islamists from becoming filthy rich or being caught up in scandals such as those that rocked the country when Islamic investment companies defrauded many. But it does allow many well-educated professionals with Islamist sympathies to regularly raise morals charges against the media industry. (Actresses including Yusra and Ma'ali Zayd have fallen afoul of such people for appearing in the new glitzy serials or films serving whiskey, engaging in adultery, or wearing lingerie.) And it does allow religious authorities to denounce consumption and television in their Friday sermons, as Naima's characterizations of these sermons, quoted in chapter 4, reveal.

The second and strongest challenge to the encroachment of the market and the values of mass consumption is to be found in the everyday lives of Egypt's poor, whether urban or rural. They give the lie to the democratic and inclusive promises of consumption that justify the state's claims to be providing citizens with the good life, despite the removal of subsidies and the abandonment of the earlier values of national development and the welfare policies that supported them. On the one hand, as I will show through some ethnographic vignettes, their lives are organized around economic practices that are quite different from those associated with the market and consumerism, even if they partake of some of the latter.[37] On the other hand, their encounters with television's "capitalist realism" are entangled with experiences of exclusion. They have a keen sense of the unevenness of participation in a nation riven by inequalities.

To illustrate the ways in which their experiences are at odds with the incitements of the globalized consumer world represented in television advertisements and the glitzy serials discussed above, I first want to tell a story about a water buffalo. I returned to the Upper Egyptian village from Cairo one time to the big news that Zaynab's water buffalo had given birth. The whole family was anxious to talk about their trauma. The animal had been fine immediately after. On the second day they found her lying on the ground, burning up with fever. The children had wailed in fear. After all the work of feeding and caring for her, to lose her now? Zaynab had gone to get the veterinarian. He gave the water buffalo some injections and sewed up her "womb." He instructed the family not to let her fall asleep. They stayed awake all night, the boys beating the animal to keep her awake, Zaynab and her eldest daughter nervously keeping vigil. A close neighbor kept them company. They appreciated what she had said when Zaynab insisted she go home to bed: "How could I when you are going through this!" Zaynab's daughter told me, "We endured the worst days and nights of our lives."

Losing the water buffalo would have been calamitous, not just for the 3,000 L.E. (approximately $950 US at that time) she had cost them but for all those months of hard work caring for and feeding her. To plant the fields of clover (*barsim*) or to rent a field to harvest; to follow the sugarcane harvest, stripping the stalks of their leaves and bringing them home on donkey carts; or to purchase the hay and fodder to fill the animals' bellies is not easy. Many women complain about the work they do for their water buffalos, not just feeding them but bringing them water, taking them into the sun in the winter and to the canals in summer, and milking them.

In Zaynab's household they had all been desperately looking forward to the birth of the calf. The children had been dreaming of fresh, foamy milk and plentiful cheese. Zaynab had debts to pay off and wanted to make some major purchases. There were so many things everyone wanted to buy. The little calf was to help provide this, a calf that several months earlier Zaynab had confided might bring in 500 L.E. Now, Zaynab was ministering to this calf, firmly holding his mouth open to dispense medicine from an old Coke

Boy leading the family water buffalo to be milked, Upper Egypt, 2001.
Lila Abu-Lughod/Anthro-Photo.

bottle. Talking about him as if he were a child, the family said that he would
have run about in the pen if he had been healthy.

All the next week, Zaynab's friends paid her visits as if there were a sick
family member. Soon there was another crisis. Zaynab panicked when the
water buffalo suddenly began walking round and round in crazy circles. The
stitches must have been bothering her. The veterinarian was fetched again,
at great expense. Dressed in a white pressed *gallabiyya,* he was clean-shaven
and educated, only recently returned from many years in Cairo. He surprised them when he repeated the diagnosis he had given them the first
time, a diagnosis they would have come up with themselves but did not expect from someone so educated. Their water buffalo was a victim of the evil
eye (*manzura*). "Envy (*hasad*)," clarified Zaynab for my benefit, using the
more classical term found in the Qur'an.

In the next weeks, Zaynab worked frantically to help the calf grow strong
and healthy. Several times a day she wrestled him to the ground. Sitting on
him and using her legs to keep his own down, she would reach around and
force his mouth open, revealing his pink gums and wide teeth. Then she
would take handfuls of soft beans from a bowl she had prepared and would

push these into the calf's mouth. She had to force his mouth shut to make him chew. Her hands were wet with his saliva and her legs bruised from wrestling the calf down. He would look at her with big brown eyes, his dark hide with its soft hair an odd contrast to her disheveled dress and disarranged black head cloth.

Although mother and calf were to recover, Zaynab was devastated. She knew she would have to sell off the water buffalo for meat now, losing money, since a reproducing female was much more valuable. Although the vet had urged her to keep quiet about the stitches, she knew there was no way to keep such a secret. She didn't want to be accused of cheating if things went wrong in the buffalo's next pregnancy. She and the rest of the family watched anxiously to see how well the calf would grow.

Three lessons can be drawn from this family crisis over a water buffalo. First is a lesson about the nature of the goods that dominate the everyday lives of villagers in Egypt. A water buffalo is the biggest purchase an ordinary family might make, desired especially if there are children. The relationship of owners and their water buffaloes, especially owners of one or at most two, is quite different from their relationships to other kinds of commodities, like the consumer goods they see advertised on television. Besides being an investment, the water buffalo provides milk, cheese, and butter, gives birth to calves that can be sold, and becomes something of a family member, demanding food and spending its days nearby and its nights in a pen behind the house, safe from rustlers.

The intimacy of families with their water buffaloes and the vulnerability created by their dependency on a valuable commodity that is at the same time a live and productive being are striking to those of us who live more completely in the world of mass-produced goods.[38] The intimacy is of two kinds: the physical intimacy of Zaynab's concerned force-feeding of the calf and the emotional intimacy of her whole family with these animals who lived within their walls. Everyone knows that each water buffalo has her own personality; some are docile, while others will not let anyone near them except the person who usually milks them. Children imitate water buffalos, tying scarves around each other's necks and leading them along. And people even empathize with them. Two years after this incident when I returned to the village after an absence, Zaynab told me she had finally sold the old water buffalo for 1,800 L.E, cheap because she was just old meat (*kunduz*). She had purchased another one for 2,300 L.E., pregnant at the time. The new water buffalo had since had two offspring, one of which Zaynab had sold just a few weeks ago. Sympathetically, Zaynab said the mother buffalo was only now beginning to recover from the loss. She had been so angry for the first four days she wouldn't let anyone come near her to milk her. Zaynab's children clarified, "She was upset about her little one (za'lana 'ala 'ayyilha)." Later that week I saw a scrawny water buffalo tied up outside another house, moaning. The old man caring for her explained that she was crying because she wanted her calf, which they had just sold but that she believed was still in the pen opposite. It is difficult to imagine this kind of feeling for other kinds of goods people own or desire, such as television sets or nonstick frying pans.

The ready acceptance of the veterinarian's diagnosis of the water buffalo's problems as due to "evil eye" or "envy" holds the second lesson about villagers' relationship to consumption. It reminds us that people in many small communities still feel a certain discomfort owning more than others. There is no need to rehearse the many arguments in the literature on the evil eye in circum-Mediterranean (and even South Asian) societies. Fears of the evil eye are related to social pressures—knowing that others in your community are noticing what you have, consume, purchase, build, or make. And some will not be happy to see your material success or good fortune.

The undercurrent of ambivalence about goods and wealth this explanation of misfortune both reflects and keeps alive is also clear in a story someone told me about selling a sheep in the market. Many village families raise sheep and goats, grazing them in the stubble of fields and in barren areas at the outskirts of the cultivated fields. Although they do not develop the individual relationships with these small animals that they do with the water buffalo, a sheep or goat is a big enough item a small household might own that its sale is a big moment. The woman who owned the sheep was visibly shaken when she returned from the market. She had taken it to sell and described the way prospective buyers had tried to grab the animal, tugging it this way and that, each claiming to have got it first. They had offered her too low a price, but the fodder merchant who had helped her get the sheep to market said she could not go home again with the sheep because it would die. Because of the evil eye. So she was forced to agree to the sale. When they got back home, she discovered she'd been cheated, and the fodder merchant had had to go back to confront the man who had bought the sheep. The sale was fraught, not a simple financial transaction.

The third lesson the water buffalo story holds is about the complex situation in which villagers now live, straddling different kinds of economies. For many in the village, sheep and water buffalo remain the dominant form of commodity, along with land, making villagers quite different from the ideal consumers—the urban middle classes—targeted by television advertising. Nevertheless, these animals are sold for cash that people want in order to pay for other services and commodities. They may have use value (milk and wool) and, unlike ceramic tiles for bathrooms and kitchens or automobiles, only very secondarily are seen as markers of wealth or status, especially the sort that depend on indicating one's sophistication or modernity. But they do have exchange value as well. For Zaynab, the water buffalo and her progeny were seen as the only means for acquiring cash for consumer goods. If Zaynab wanted to pay debts for fodder or fertilizer, she also wanted to buy dentures. Her children entertained other fantasies. Her daughter wanted stainless-steel pots and pans, her sons wanted clothes and running shoes, her younger children wanted toys and candy. These are the consumer items they have all seen advertised on television and that some other wealthier local families have actually bought. Their most eager and persistent dream at the time, however, was for a color television set, the first item several other young people mentioned when they talked about what they wanted to buy if only they could have afforded to sell off family land.

In short, Zaynab and her family, like other struggling Egyptians, were not immune to the lures of consumption emanating from television. But they lived in a community where the persistence of one set of negative social attitudes toward consumption was revealed in the explanation of "evil eye" for the misfortunes of Zaynab's water buffalo. This popular cultural construction could be denigrated as backward and superstitious, but it could also be lauded as authentic and traditional. For many more than would like to admit it, it subconsciously counters appeals to the pleasures of consumption and the type of good life to which they are integral. An even more radical challenge to the ideals of consumerism lies in these kinds of families' financial vulnerability and lack of purchasing power, with consequences for the potential of consumerism to form the basis of national belonging.

URBAN CARTOGRAPHIES

Debates about mass consumption, like television, tend to have a moral cast, Daniel Miller has pointed out. He is critical of the easy condemnation of consumption and has done a good deal to show how mass-produced goods and foreign media images can be positively appropriated as a means of self-fashioning, how objectification is not such a bad thing, and how shopping can be a part of love and nurturance.[39] But he has also pointed out the crux of the problem with consumption, and one reason to take a critical moral stance. In the Third World, if we can still use this term, the relationship to goods and the dynamics of consumption seem to differ from what we know of them in the First World because of uneven access. He argues in his essay, "Consumption as the Vanguard of History,"

For the First World consumer, capitalism has in many respects "delivered the goods," with vast increases in real wealth for all but a substantial minority. . . . The rich of previous centuries might well look enviously at the possessions and mobility of the lower-middle class of today. . . . It is not just, as some suggest, a case of home commodities and appliances replacing the servants, since today it is the households of those who would once have been servants that also have the basic appliances and associated mass commodities.[40]

Miller's assessment of the generality of affluence points to rising expectations about ownership of mass-produced consumer goods. However, he underestimates wealth disparities in places like the United States. He also ignores here the way that consumption is stratified such that the affluent buy top-of-the-line brand-name goods and luxury items and those with less shop at discount stores, buy on credit, and cannot always buy branded goods. But with large middle classes in much of the First World, it is only a minority who consider built-in kitchens luxuries, even if some kitchens have peeling Formica countertops while others have granite. Everyone but the homeless and most destitute of the sheltered expects to have the basics, from refrigerators and shampoos to showers and televisions. In France, Bourdieu used the stratification of consumption goods and the tastes they index to analyze the reproduction of class.[41] But this presumes access to a range of such goods. The distinctions are far more radical in places like Egypt, India, Indonesia, Nigeria, and many other places where "servants," the lower middle classes, and even the middle classes have far less access to rich worlds of consumer goods that are available to the cosmopolitan class of the wealthy few in their countries.

One way this gap between Egyptians having access to the world of consumption and those who do not is represented is through the cartography of the capital city, Cairo. This is drawn on as shorthand in television dramas and invoked in everyday conversations about class. For example, four elite neighborhoods figure here as sites of consumption and comfort: Zamalek,

Heliopolis, Ma'adi, and Garden City. Zamalek, to which 'Abd al-Ghafur moved in *I Won't Live My Father's Life* and which provides the setting for many an aristocratic family in television dramas, is where you can spot the stars you see on television. Heliopolis is the setting for the television film *Nuna Al-Sha'nuna*, in which the village girl learning to be a servant must negotiate the unfamiliar terrain of supermarkets and dry cleaners. In *Our Folks* it is the location of the brother who has made good, where his psychologically troubled teenaged daughter calls him "Daddy" and sprinkles her conversation with English while his wife goes off to do aerobics at her club. Garden City, on the other hand, is a favorite setting for aristocrats in historical dramas about the early twentieth century, whether the dazzling femme fatale Nazik Hanim of the early 1990s classic *Hilmiyya Nights* or the dysfunctional group portrayed in the late 1990s serial, *Hawanim gardin siti* (The ladies of Garden City). As a woman who worked as a domestic once explained to me, a propos of Nazik Hanim, "Hilmiyya used to be a place of palaces and rich people, not the poor (*masakin*); later, when poor people moved into the neighborhood, Nazik wanted to move out. She went to the villas of Garden City."

At the other extreme are the popular neighborhoods with their homey, authentic alleys that provide the settings for so many novels, short stories, films, and television serials about the *ibn al-balad*. These include Mgharbalin, Bulaq, and Hilmiyya, which are contrasted with the wealthy neighborhoods by their street life, the intimacy of social relations (including arguments), and their more austerely furnished rooms. Rarely portrayed are the neighborhoods in which most of Cairo's poor live, including some of the women domestics I knew: the newest areas in the urban sprawl or even older but tougher areas like Imbaba and Wara' al-'Arab. These are neighborhoods whose residents complain bitterly. Amira, for example, hated her home and neighborhood in Imbaba. As indicated earlier, by 1996 she had saved enough to buy herself a piece of land way out in a new working-class neighborhood on the outskirts of Cairo. She had built a one-story structure, which, as described above, was causing her enormous headaches and costing her a great deal in bribes to get hooked up to electricity. Not only did she have trouble with water and landlords in her old neighborhood, but she also described what had happened to her married sister nearby. One day two bearded Islamists had come to the door and asked where her husband was. If they had found him there, she said, they would have forced him to go and pray in the mosque. "That's what they do in our neighborhoods," she explained. "They'll beat people up for not praying in the mosques." [42]

Another domestic worker spoke with horror about her neighborhood in Wara':

It's no good at all. Crowded and full of children! And there is water in the streets, and noise and garbage and filth. And the government doesn't go in. It doesn't care. The president orders them to go in and clean the streets. He gives orders but they don't come at all. Not at all. They go to the clean neighborhoods where the streets are clean.

When I interrupted to explain that it was a private company that cleaned the streets in Zamalek, where she worked, she retorted,

Well, maybe here in Zamalek, yes, but not in the popular neighborhoods. If the government went in or tried to carry out these orders, they would be afraid, despite themselves. The Egyptian people have been poor—the British colonized them. They are afraid, but they are shameless. Since there is no government presence or anyone in charge, they throw things in the street. . . . When I go home I sweep the top of the stairs and the alley in front, and I turn around and find they've thrown more garbage and filth. I try to clean and talk with my neighbors. I tell them this will breed mosquitoes and make your kids ill. They say, "Yes, dear," but it goes out the other ear.

For her the contrast between neighborhoods was obvious. When she expressed interest in the government setting up factories and workshops to employ people in all the popular neighborhoods, she explained, "We have problems and bad people and needy people. How many neighborhoods don't? Just Ma'adi and Zamalek and Heliopolis; these are the nice neighborhoods. But the rest of the city is full—Cairo and Giza are full of popular neighborhoods that are disgusting. The government should pay a little attention to them!"

Naima, the sickly working woman whose complaints about her unhappy marriage to an old man we heard in chapter 4, now lived in a small room among several others on the roof of a building in the elite neighborhood of Zamalek. She explained why she had given up her apartment in Imbaba. Her current place was tiny and expensive, but it was both closer to possibilities for work and far less of a headache than the other one. Transport had been time consuming and expensive, but the more aggravating part was the trouble she had with her landlords in that kind of neighborhood. They had kept asking for money, even when she was not using her apartment because she was sleeping at her job. The last straw was when they had demanded the key to her ground-floor apartment in case the water was cut off, they said. She had refused, fearing they would use her bathroom to do their washing, ruining it. Water shortages in such neighborhoods are notorious.

Newspapers, those instruments of national belonging, according to Anderson,[43] provide a poignant index of the differences between neighborhoods and their participation in worlds of consumption. Whereas the well-off consume the news in the newspapers, the poor are interested in the paper on which it is printed. Naima and other domestic servants always ask for the discarded newspapers and magazines of their employers in the wealthy neighborhoods. They used to sell them to food vendors to make a little extra cash. Now that the government has banned newsprint for food wrapping (because the ink is toxic), they give the newspapers to poor people in other neighborhoods. As Naima explains, they can always use them to line kitchen shelves and tables.

COUNTRY STYLES

In the countryside, the gap between rich and poor is less obvious because neighborhoods are not segregated and the people live where they do as a result of family histories. The rich and poor are also more similar in their common distance from the shiny middle-class worlds of consumption envisioned by advertising, although this has been changing over the last decade. When I first arrived in the village in 1990, the wealthier families were well known, their assets in land or tourist enterprises recognized. One obvious way they could be distinguished was that they were the only ones to have color television sets, to the envy of other people in the village. By 1999, many more families had color TV sets, with only some bought on installment. These sets, though, sat in houses that were radically more diverse than they had been ten years earlier—a sign of the enormous changes in consumption patterns in the last decades of the twentieth century, in which everyone wanted and expected more varied mass-produced goods, but stratification was on the rise. Building in concrete and brick instead of mud brick is now considered de rigueur for the well off, and even aspired to by those without the resources. Whereas in the past, the wealthy families who owned land had houses distinguishable from those of the less fortunate only by size— there being minimal furnishing, little decoration in the mud walls, bare light bulbs for illumination, and a kitchen that was multipurpose, containing a stove on bottled gas and a fridge whose motor was usually blown from the electricity surges—now the distinctions money allows are more extreme. In fact, people in the village, like those in the cities, are coming to distinguish themselves through their differential consumption of mass-produced and "modern" goods.[44]

For example, in 1996 the wealthiest landowner in the village built a large house for his youngest son. It had flowers in the garden, granite floor tiles through the main part of the house, ceramic tiles in the bathroom and kitchen, gold ceiling moldings, couches and velvet chairs, and curtains everywhere—on the walls, on the TV, on the bed. The youth's mother bragged that the steel rebars alone had cost 20,000 L.E., though she stumbled over the brand name of the ceramic tiles used in the bathroom. The older brother showed off this house to me. He had married in an earlier time when moving out of the family home was unthinkable. His own earlier fantasies of a modern lifestyle were tangible in the upstairs rooms of the large family house, where dust covers hid his unused suite of cheap velour couch and chairs and where crude hand-painted designs on the wall vied for attention with sheets of newspaper and election posters, a decor that his sister disdained as "old fashioned."

Similarly, as described in chapter 2, the youngest son in the family of wealthy wholesalers in the next hamlet, in anticipation of his marriage, had built for himself a two-story concrete house, complete with blue-tiled bathroom with bathtub, bamboo furniture, ornate beds and wardrobes, and a small custom-made kitchen. Balconies upstairs remained shuttered and the whole thing unused as his brother and sister-in-law continued to live in the original mud-brick family home with cement floors to which this new structure had been attached.

Ordinary homes, on the other hand, were and continue to be decorated with the detritus of a world that is far from the lives of ordinary villagers. Their occupants recycle and give new value to these bits and pieces.[45] Stuck to the mud walls in the entryway that usually serves as the sitting room, or the room in which the television set is kept, might be not just framed photographs of family members and small posters of soccer and movie stars, including the Indian film star Amitav Bachan, but also bits of colorful gift wrap with kittens or chicks on it (for a community where gifts are more likely to arrive in baskets), sheets of newspaper (rarely read), and homemade hangings created by sewing together in clever designs the shiny wrappers of a popular chocolate wafer regularly advertised on television. Young teens are especially excited by posters and save their piasters to purchase them from town. In one freshly decorated room, nearly the whole wall was lined with these small posters, with a religious poster of a Qur'anic saying tucked in among them, in no particular place of honor. Other items that might be picked up to add to the collection are pages from old calendars, especially those showing provocatively posed female screen stars or singers.

If the chocolate wafer wrappers sewn into shiny displays indicate that such "fast-moving consumer items" are purchased by even poor villagers, along with Coca-Colas (mostly during the promotion that advertised that a bicycle could be won if you got the right bottle cap) and competing brands of potato chips, these are still considered something of a treat. Most families eat fresh food, either grown themselves or bought at the weekly market. Even in the wealthy households, bread must be baked at home from wheat grown and milled locally, or flour bought through government rations and on the open market. The resistance to junk food and processed food is not just financial. Unlike her children, Zaynab remains fairly unmoved by advertisements. One promoting a national brand of meat products suggests the complicated reasons why. This commercial, which aired regularly for years, shows the large factory where the meat is processed.[46] From displays of carcasses hung from butcher hooks we are taken to the workers, technicians in lab coats busy at gleaming stainless-steel machines. The advertisement is selling modernity—with its scientific procedures and hygiene. To gain consumers beyond those already attracted by convenience foods, it would have to overcome the aversions of women like Zaynab (who raise chickens, ducks, and pigeons at home) to eating anything "from outside." In any case, these products are expensive and mostly unavailable locally, except in a few up-market grocery stores across the river in Luxor—stores that Zaynab only occasionally visits when her children beg her to buy something they have seen on television.

Not having enough money to realize the lifestyles associated with certain products does not stop children from whining for potato chips or clothes they see in commercials. It does not stop young women from talking dreamily about stainless-steel pots and pans and imagining themselves in kitchens with cabinets while they scour their flame-blackened traditional aluminum pots. Nor does it prevent them from hoping to be able to purchase a certain kind of stove when they become brides, since it is the bride who is responsible for contributing the stove and refrigerator to the new household. Blankets and televisions, too, are items all newlywed couples will buy. Yet even when people buy things advertised on television, it is often not quite for the reasons marketers expect. For example, virtually all the brands of hair cream featured in commercials were on the list one set of children gave their father when he went into Luxor to buy them things for the major religious holiday. This was not because they wanted to sample them all, or that each child had a favorite brand, or even that any of them wished to show taste or express an identity through a brand. Rather, they explained, it was because they wanted to avoid arguments about who was using more. The brands made individual ownership clearer.

Television may be both an index and an instrument of participation in the larger world of mass consumption, disseminating images that people, as audiences, consume. However, the glimpses I have given into the everyday lives of the urban and rural poor reveal how television offers goods and evokes dream worlds that, even if they have become part of a familiar cognitive or imaginative landscape, are unevenly realizable. In chapter 2 I talked about some village women in terms of cosmopolitanism, noting their exposure to different aspects of Egyptian and transnational modernity. I also noted the different ways, depending on wealth and generation, that such women were able to appropriate for themselves parts of these worlds and express their status through them. But given economic realities and local markets, for many in Upper Egypt these images are so far from local realities that they must either be ignored or taken as painful signs of disenfranchisement from the nation, not participation in it. When one cannot purchase the lifestyles and goods locally, or when they are way beyond one's means, one is reminded of one's marginality. Water heaters for people who have only recently installed running water and still bathe in a metal washbasin, or whose water flow is unreliable? BMWs and Jeeps in a region where almost all vehicles are share-taxis, usually pickup trucks, with only the occasional private-car license plate in evidence, or where streets are unpaved? Ceramic tiles advertised by cosmopolitan celebrities with cell phones to families who are only now beginning to get ordinary telephone service and who live with dirt or cement floors in rooms that are sometimes so small and cluttered that the floors don't show? [47]

CONCLUSION

The specific historicopolitical question that this consideration of consumption and television in Egypt raises is whether an emerging aesthetic of capitalist realism, supported by the restructuring of the television industry but ambivalently confronted by some powerful dramas, by Islamist ideology, and by the everyday circumstances of the lives of many, can capture the imaginations of Egypt's poorer citizens, like urban domestic servants or villagers in the disadvantaged regions. Can it win their loyalty to a state that no longer tries to justify itself in terms of giving its citizens a helping hand unmediated by "the market"? Can citizenship be made a function of consumption in a country of deep inequalities in access to "the good life"?

Living their lives in and among the competing discourses and visions this chapter has outlined are the various people of Egypt. For many of them, the promises of education of an earlier era, still lingering in the development aesthetic on state television, may have seemed more accessible once but are now in doubt because of the diminution of state support and the abandonment of the ideals of social welfare and national uplift that were associated with the Nasser regime. But consumerism and middle-class (not to mention glittering) lifestyles are well out of the reach of the majority. There is a keen sense among the poor that they are excluded from this new Egypt. As Amira put it, in explaining to me the meaning of the title of a popular serial of the 1980s, *Al-shahd wa al-dumu'* (Honey and tears), "There is sweetness, the rich family living in comfort and luxury, and there are tears, the poor family with its struggles." She described the wealthy as money-hungry. They want money, she explained, and are trying to save so they can have more: thousands, millions. People like herself, she said, people who live in the popular neighborhoods and who are poor/downtrodden (*ghalaba*), don't bother to save. What's the point? At most they'll save a few hundred pounds that won't be worth anything. But the rich, like those here in Zamalek, can turn their thousands into millions. Just then a Porsche drove by. I commented that this was an expensive car. She said, "There are lots of people in this country who have not just millions but billions."

This reminded me of a comment made by an older village woman when I had asked her what she thought of the enormous house in which a serial was set. It was modern and tacky, featuring a grand staircase with plants trailing down to the marble center hall. We were sitting on a hard bench in the small center room of the old family mud-brick compound, watching a television perched on a shelf. When I asked, "Do people really live in places like that?" she was quick to say, "Oh, yes! Villas, villas—lots of people live in them." I asked, "In Egypt?" She answered, "In Egypt and other countries." Grossly underestimating their worth, she added, "These cost thousands of pounds!" This was the same old woman who had confessed to me that she watched the serials but never understood what was going on in them; her daughter interpreted this for me by explaining that these serials represented worlds that her mother had not grown up with.

Both these women at the margins of a country that is itself, as part of the "developing" world, at the margins are conscious of the fact that lots of luxury and consumption are available to others in Egypt and elsewhere, but not to themselves. They are mostly on the outside looking in, whether it is when they venture forth from their poor urban neighborhoods into the elite areas or when they glimpse, in their mud houses, the scenes television brings to them. For a long time they were used to watching affluent worlds, given the middle-class and even upper-class biases of serials. But now these televised worlds that they are sure reflect realities somewhere out there, beyond the village, are more fantastically so.[48] They watch television at war with itself, and they cope with the circumstances on the ground of removed subsidies, dwindling public services, and richly varied consumer goods with prohibitive price tags. They will certainly not be swept along in the inexorable march of triumphant globalizing capitalism, with television at the helm, going from backwardness to modernity, from colonized subjects to citizens trading loyalty for welfare and now to consumers of the good life. When I asked Zaynab's daughter what happens when people see things on television that they can't have, she was quick to defend her village, saying there had been lots of progress. She listed the homes with ceramic bathrooms. "Little by little," she said. Yet it could be that the alternative visions that challenge this path, whether the old developmentalism that is still validated by the stalwarts of television or the newer Islamic alternative that is excluded from television serials but finds some support in other programming, will dovetail more closely with many people's immediate experiences of exclusion to give the lie to any optimistic pronouncements.

Ironically, this does not mean that the nation has been made superfluous. On the contrary. Because it is so widely shared, television makes available a set of conversations about where the nation is going, what government responsibilities should be, and who should have access to all these goods that appear to be available to at least some Egyptians. Television reinforces the nation as the setting in which such conversations should occur; just as I have argued in chapter 7, it set itself up, through the media campaign against terrorism, as the public forum for debating the place of religion in national life. As the stories of the economically and socially marginal individuals I have recounted reveal, when people make comparisons among themselves or try to determine whether or not they are included in the visions of television, the relevant frame is that of the nation. It is the nation, they have been taught, both through the institutions of the state and the culture of television, that is the ground on which they stand and the relevant frame for identity.

Photograph of an Upper Egyptian woman that inspired the comment that she resembled Tahiyya Carioca, dancer and film star who often played a tough and independent lower-class woman who is also an entertainer (see p. 229). Photograph courtesy of Mary Cross.

[Conclusion]

Star Magic and the Forms of National Affinity

ON A HIGH FLOOR in Maspero, the iconic and well-guarded state television building along the Nile, the metal-framed windows have been pushed wide open to let the cigarette smoke out into the night air. Around a large table, presided over by the scriptwriter and director, sit many of the actors I have been watching on television for years. I cannot keep my eyes off them, recognizing with delight one after another of the stars. The women are well-dressed and their makeup as perfect as on television. Some of the senior male actors around the table look more rumpled than they do on-screen, but some are dapper. Leaning against the back wall, eating potato chips and whispering, are the young actors, usually called "new faces" in the credits of the serials. Their parts are much smaller and they don't have to say much. I am embarrassed to be as thrilled as any fan to meet the characters from serials I have been writing about, even though I am supposed to be observing as a scholar. The actors are familiar because they appear and reappear in the serials I have been studying; and yet they are magically glamorous, transposed from screen to life. There is only one thing that brings them down to earth: many are wearing reading glasses.

My feelings that evening are a reminder that a book on mass culture cannot conclude without at least some attention directed to one of the most crucial extra-textual elements of the television serials: the stars. If I, an outsider who had not grown up with Egyptian television and who followed it in order to analyze rather than for pleasure (although I could not help deriving some pleasure from it), could find myself so captivated by these actors, imagine how much more they mean to most viewers who have spent their lives with them, who know them all by name, who have seen them in hundreds of roles, and who, as I have described, know, or think they know, a lot about their lives.

In this final chapter, I want to suggest that of all the ways in which tele-vision is bound up with and helps produce the nation in Egypt, the public's affection for stars may be the most personally meaningful, even as the am-bivalence in this relationship mirrors the tensions of national pedagogy that I have been describing in previous chapters. The moral confusion the stars elicit is tied to the social differences that exist in Egypt, differences that make for blockages in the acceptance of the messages of television. Moreover, the stars' lifestyles exquisitely embody the transformations of the Egyptian na-tion in the last couple of decades, with all the inequalities and exclusions these have entailed.

NATURALIZING THE NATION

There are multiple ways that a more thickly textured sense of national be-longing in Egypt is spun from the magic of television and film stars. Just as I have suggested that a good reason to take television as a salient national in-stitution is that people in Egypt are proud that their country produces so much television drama that other countries want, so one could argue that a national sense, mingled with some pride, is supported by the stars—living national treasures whose faces adorn magazines and walls and are known re-gionally. Not all stars of Egyptian television and film are themselves Egyp-tians—a few are Lebanese, Syrian, and Palestinian, for example. And not all the celebrities who fascinate people are Arab, as viewers' involvement with the characters in the imported American prime-time soap operas like *The Bold and the Beautiful* and posters of American pop stars and Indian movie idols pasted to village walls make clear.[1] But because most of the stars are na-tive sons and daughters, because Egypt has been a major cultural center of the Arab world throughout the twentieth century, and because everyone takes pride in the excellence and regional fame of its film and television in-dustries, to be involved with the stars is to be part of a national romance.

National life is naturalized as much by the stars as the serials in which they appear. If the rhythms of daily life are organized by the television sched-ule (as the emptying of the parking lot indicated in the opening pages of the book) and the serials take up ongoing events of national concern—the same scandals of Islamic investment companies, dissolute youth allegedly involved in Satanism, business corruption, and militant Islamic violence appearing first in the news and later in the plots of television serials—so the familiarity of a stable of actors makes for a taken-for-granted universe defined, for the most part, nationally.

Even when distant and recognized as not part of one's life, as I will describe below, the stars provide common reference points. The photograph taken by a friend that opens this chapter is a good example. I gave it as a gift to the woman who posed for it. Several days later, as we looked at it together, she laughed and said her sister-in-law had commented that she looked like Tahiyya Carioca. When I pressed her on why, it turned out that it was because this famous film star and dancer, known to a younger generation through old black-and-white films shown on television, had played many roles of the *mu'allima*, a tough lower-class businesswoman or entertainer. The bold stance of the beautiful woman in the photograph, her head thrown back, her arms gesturing, and her neck immodestly revealed, had inspired the comparison. Such widely shared reference points contribute to something of a national culture.

In fact, a special brand of community is fostered through common and mediated knowledge about the nation's television stars. This is perhaps not so surprising in Cairo, the capital, where many of the actors live and work and from which television is broadcast. But from my first conversation about television in 1990 with Upper Egyptian villagers, in which someone eagerly educated me about which stars were successful and which not, to an occasion more than a decade later when the same older woman who had not thought of herself as living in Egypt/*Misr* quizzed me about the names of actors (rattling them off while I stumbled), it was clear that people shared a keen interest in the actors who appeared and reappeared on their screens. Younger people, both male and female, were full of information about the lives and loves of the stars, their knowledge gleaned, as I have described, from fanzines, special programs commemorating deaths of actors or singers, celebrity game shows, and programs such as *A Star in Your Home* or the latest interview show, *Very Frank Talk*.[2] Because films and serials are very often rebroadcast and the number of actors is not that great, the public is very familiar with these figures. It was clear from my conversations with people across Egypt that they have been drawn into a national imaginary in which these actors are as prominent symbols of Egypt as its president, and more loved.

The actors' national fame can be put to use for various purposes. As in many parts of the world, celebrities in Egypt market goods on television. In the late 1990s, for example, Yusra, hard up for cash, advertised Jawhara ceramic tiles; Hisham Salim, hero of many serials including *And the Nile Flows On,* in which he played the sensible religious authority with an enlightened attitude toward family planning, rode a tourist boat in Upper Egypt advertising "Chipsy" potato chips; 'Abla Kamil, who played the beloved wife of 'Abdu in *I Won't Live My Father's Life,* confided in us the virtues of Persil laundry detergent; and Sana' Gamil, who breathed life into the role of the marvelous villainess of *The White Flag,* told people to trust her—taking their children to Dreamland's amusement park would make them happy.

Although there is not as much crossover between media and politics in Egypt as in Bombay or Tamil Nadu, and no actor has become president, as happened in the United States with Ronald Reagan, some of those involved in television have also tried to work in politics, making use of their connections to the world of film and television. The writer Fathiyya al-'Assal (whose serial *Mothers in the House of Love* was the subject of chapter 2) ran in the 1995 elections for Parliament as a candidate of the leftist Tagammu' Party. Her platform was secular nationalist, antiterrorist, and in support of the rights of women and the downtrodden, especially workers and artisans. In an interesting analysis of her campaign in Imbaba, a poor neighborhood where some of the domestic servants I have written about live, she denied exploiting her television connections, saying that all the "artists" who supported her publicly were members of her party and did so in that capacity. And yet a distinctive aspect of her campaign was that she was accompanied in the neighborhood by famous television actors like Jamil Ratib and 'Abla Kamil, and her posters and newspaper ads highlighted the support of other actors and writers. Among the ways she was described in the newspaper that supported her was "Fathiyya al-'Assal, a Fighter who Conquered the Impossible," a reference to her award-winning feminist serial about literacy and independence, *She and the Impossible.*[3] Although al-'Assal's campaign was not successful, others involved in television have become public figures. Safiyya Al-'Umari, for example, who played the outrageous femme fatale of *Hilmiyya Nights,* was appointed the Egyptian representative to Habitat's second U.N. Conference on Human Settlements, in 1996.

What is most important to the sense of national affinity is the affection people feel for these stars who have become familiar figures, known intimately through the many roles they play in the serials. Because the stable of actors who play television roles is so small, even someone like myself who has only watched for a decade comes to have strong feelings about these figures. The power of intertextuality is apparent in viewers' "readings" of characters and the actors who play them. Memories of their other roles infuse interpretations of and feelings toward new characters, carrying the affection or rage one might have felt toward one character into views of the next. This works particularly strongly because many writers and directors prefer to use the same actors, writers imagining as they write their scripts certain actors in the lead roles. The dense associations and level of intimacy felt toward certain long-lived stars like Nur al-Sharif and Fatin Hamama (whose television serial debut was as the principled school principal determined to improve schooling) are immeasurable.

These actors are also instrumental in perpetuating the generic conventions of emotionalized acting that I argued in chapter 5 may play a role in the sentimental education of the modern citizen. They animate the individualization encouraged by the focus on the emotional states of the characters they portray. Their locations in domestic settings, usually consisting of small nuclear families, often middle or upper class, are partly due to budgetary and logistical issues not unrelated to the hiring of actors. Both features of the serials—the emotionalization and the domestication—communicate certain values subliminally, whatever the plot or overt messages; they construct naturalized models of personhood, which actors bring to life.

The overt developmentalist or nationalist pedagogy of the serials is also carried into audiences' homes and hearts by the actors. It is they who make compelling, through clever interpretation, a range of national cultural stereotypes, including the salt-of-the-earth traditional *ibn al-balad* or his female equivalent *bint al-balad,* or the cultured, educated, patriotic modernist who has not lost his or her authentic values.

As chapter 7 showed, many stars indeed share the ideology that television is pedagogical, which they claim is patriotic. Like everywhere, stars and characters intermingle in Egypt, with the help of fan magazines, newspapers, and television itself. The actors are asked to comment on the roles they play and the serials in which they act. They regularly appear in seminars and grant interviews where they talk about the importance of the serials' treatments of national issues. They often justify their work in terms of social and national responsibility, as did Layla 'Ilwi, when she explained her acceptance of the role of a lost soul who joined a militant Islamist group in *The Family,* donning the face veil (*niqab*). She said, "My feelings as an artist and a citizen are inseparable and naturally I'm repulsed by what is happening around me in my own society as a result of terrorism and corruption. Working in television is extremely difficult but it is worth it if our message reaches people."[4] This is a film star who has played racy and glamorous roles. In collapsing her art into her nationalism, she affirms the location of television drama in the nation. This quote also provides further evidence for the argument I made in chapter 7 about the serials that were pushed as part of the state's confrontation with religious extremism. Even if perceived as heavy-handed or propagandistic and sparking public debate that exposed rather than healed national differences, serials like *The Family,* in which this actor starred, may well have naturalized the nation as the all-important context for people's lives by setting it as the ground for judging religious behavior.

That actors are recognized as citizens is also apparent in the way they are often held accountable for the roles they play. The furor over the much-watched 2001 Ramadan serial called *'A'ilat al-Haj Mitwalli* (The family of Haj Mitwalli) illustrates this point. (This serial was written by the same man who gave us the benign patriarch 'Abdu of *I Won't Live My Father's Life* and starred the same actor.) *The Family of Haj Mitwalli* outraged feminists because it showed a rich merchant with three wives, all living happily together in luxury. Scathing articles renamed the serial "The Harem of Haj Mitwalli"[5] and criticized it for suggesting that polygamy was the solution to a marriage crisis in the Arab world, where single women abound. Comparisons were made between the protagonist and Si Sayyid, Naguib Mahfouz's character to whom so many had likened 'Abdu, as discussed in chapter 6.[6] Feminist television writer Fathiyya al-'Assal blamed the scriptwriter, Mustafa Muharram. But she was more furious with the star, Nur al-Sharif, for agreeing to act in a reactionary serial that would set back women's rights across the Arab world.[7] She considered him especially responsible, she said, because the warm support he had as such a beloved actor made him particularly influential.

Viewers' deep and regular involvement with actors whose relationships and experiences bring to life the melodramatic serials makes for strong cathexis that some television personnel believe is essential to the pedagogical mission of the industry. In the acting world, film is considered superior to television, with the common justification that people pay attention to film because they have paid to go to the cinema. Yet in an article in which the writer Usama Anwar 'Ukasha details his admiration for the actor Yahya al-Fakharani, who plays the lead role in so many of his productions, he notes that this actor aspires to be a film star and that "so talented an actor as he deserves to be a movie star." But he reminds the actor, "Your true audience is that of television, not cinema. That is the broadest, most responsive, and most deeply influenced audience."[8]

In this quote 'Ukasha, like so many of his peers and like those who write about mass communication, whether in Egypt or elsewhere, uses a language of influence, believing in the effectiveness of television drama in changing lives. As we have seen, in Egypt many hoped that television would bring viewers into the national fold, uplifting them and inculcating in them the values of the good modern citizen, values that tend to be those of an educated middle class, as I have shown throughout this book. This faith in media's, particularly television's, effectiveness in this regard also underlies the increasing involvement of development organizations and the US Agency for International Development in funding what is known in the business as "enter-educate" (entertainment-education) health and family-planning spots and serials. Actors are involved in myriad ways in the larger pedagogical efforts that are themselves buttressed to a certain extent by bureaucratic state institutions that individualize, examine, license, and school Egypt's citizens.

NATIONAL INTIMACY AND MORAL AMBIVALENCE

To say that viewers cathect to the stars, the serials in which they act, and perhaps ultimately to the nation that is imbricated with these serials is not to deny that people in Egypt are ambivalent about actors, just as they are about the nation. There is, in fact, a strong moral cast to their evaluation of actors and the world of "art" that blocks identification, attachment notwithstanding. This can be seen as paralleling the relationship of marginal social groups to the nation itself as a site of inequality and power that regularly places them in positions of inferiority or excludes them. I want in this conclusion to use Egyptians' ambivalence about the stars as a metaphor for a larger ambivalence, not just about television drama but about the nation it supposedly upholds. This requires an appraisal of how it is that television serials, even while contributing to the naturalization of the nation, fail to meet their goal of properly educating citizens and run into interference when they try to bring the viewing public into either the dominant developmentalist national ideals or the emerging visions of a consumer society.

There are obvious reasons why the messages of television serials might go awry. First, of course, serials are only part of what Raymond Williams has called "the flow" of television, coming between children's cartoons, parliamentary debates, cooking shows, confrontations with criminals, celebrity game shows, and advertisements, which may dissipate or offset their messages. Moreover, the genre of the Arabic serial, as it is known in the television guide, is itself a complex genre with many producers, directors, and scriptwriters, not all of whom share the same political perspectives or ideas about "art." As we saw in chapter 5, conservatives like Tharwat Abaza write very different scripts, more sympathetic to landowners and an old regime, from progressives like Usama Anwar 'Ukasha, who glorifies the alliance between the working class and the middle class, sometimes even the elite.

The internal differences among television personnel are often related to wider political struggles but surely also have something to do with class, experience, or aspirations. The distinctively psychological and upper-class feminine dramas like *Love in a Diplomatic Pouch* (to be discussed below) or *Hawanim gardin siti* (Ladies of Garden City) of Muna Nur al-Din are infused with different sensibilities and politics from those of feminist leftist Fathiyya al-'Assal, who began writing for radio and then television because like many idealistic youth in the '60s, she had taught literacy classes in the countryside. As a result of these differences, the messages of the serials are actually quite mixed, despite the shared generic conventions of emotionality, family size, and modern middle-class values.

Furthermore, the messages are not consistent because what viewers are watching are serials whose themes change with the times. The 1990s, I have been arguing throughout this book, represented a moment of major transition involving the erosion of the hegemony of developmentalist ideologies associated with quasi-socialist institutions. Since the mid-1990s, serials increasingly have treated both religious extremism, one of the forces challenging the regime, and fantastic consumption with transnational reach, a result of some of the regime's policies. There are lags as the directors and writers of an earlier era maintain their developmentalist outlook, valorizing modernity, education, and the law, while others, both of an older and a new generation, flirt with the amorality of a glitzy world in which business tycoons linked to Europe are never quite punished for lifestyles that earlier would have been disapproved of as treasonous.

But the most basic reason why the national pedagogy of television may not be as straightforward and successful as its promoters, including the state, might hope is that television serials are fundamentally entertainment. There is a difference between schooling and entertaining people, claims for the educational value of drama notwithstanding. Some television producers are invested in constructing their own serials as serious art that is socially or politically uplifting and whose effects last, in contrast with what they call commercial entertainment. In the words of director Muhammad Fadil, the latter are "pumpkin seed serials"—serials that are fun to watch, like munching on snacks, but give no real nourishment.[9] The discourse of "art" to describe serials such as 'Ukasha's *Hilmiyya Nights* likened it to high-quality foreign imports such as *Roots* and *Upstairs Downstairs,* and distinguished it from American prime-time serials like *Dallas, Falcon Crest,* and *The Bold and the Beautiful.*[10] In the early '90s even *Oshin,* the first Japanese serial to be broadcast in Egypt (a high-quality production that valorized honesty and simplicity and "symbolized the triumph of the Japanese character over the tyranny of nature . . . the character that built a civilization and achieved a high standard of technology and economy"), was contrasted favorably to the American soap operas "exported to poor Third World countries as part of American aid."[11]

Yet even art must be entertaining if it is to draw audiences. Over the course of fifteen to thirty hours' worth of episodes, serials have time to develop plots and characters, dress actors in costumes and put them in sets, create moods with music, and captivate the viewers with complex dialogue. In the best serials, the stars carry off their role with great talent, bringing the worlds of the serials alive and sometimes contributing to the undermining of intended messages. Whether "art" or "commercial" entertainment, the serials burst with an excess of meaning whose interpretations are made all the more uncontrollable by the acting that gives them substance. The producers can guide but in the end cannot determine audiences' readings.

This is well illustrated by 'Ukasha's "nourishing" serial *Hilmiyya Nights,* acclaimed by many viewers and critics as the best serial ever made, and a national drama of epic proportions. *Hilmiyya Nights* has numerous important women characters, most sympathetically portrayed and shown to be facing dilemmas shared by different generations of women. Morally good older women put up with mistreatment by husbands, including secret marriages and deceptions. Younger women struggle with the tensions between career and marriage. The serial glorifies education, showing most of the daughters of working-class men going on to university, the daughter of a coffee shop owner and a singer becoming a university professor and the daughter of factory worker and a dancer becoming a physician. In general the women are independent and able to make decisions on their own. The state feminism of Nasser's era is commended: one tough-minded wife of a factory worker counsels a friend to stand up for the rights "Gamal" had given her.[12]

However, when asked what they liked about the serial, several of the poor working women I knew in Cairo volunteered not the serious political or social messages but the character of Nazik Hanim, the aristocratic, conniving, blond, magnificently dressed *femme fatale* (played by Safiyya al-'Umari) who has the leading female role. One young woman, whose husband had abandoned her with two children to raise on her own, suggested, "Nazik is the reason everyone watches *Hilmiyya Nights*. She's tough; she married four men. She wouldn't let anyone tell her what to do." An older woman who was working because her husband was disabled explained why Nazik was so great: "She's fickle, not satisfied with one type. She married many times. She represents what? What's it called? The aristocracy? She was strong-willed. And stubborn. Because of her desires she lost her fortune." After a short silence she added, "And Hamdiyya, the dancer, did you see her?" She laughed as she imitated a characteristic arrogant gesture of this belly dancer turned cabaret owner, played by Lucy, a gorgeous real-life belly dancer.

These two glamorous women are the characters in *Hilmiyya Nights* with little nationalist sympathy who wrap men around their fingers and will not act like respectable ladies, despite the pleas of their children, their ex-husbands, and their other relatives. These are also the two who take dramatic falls. The dancer becomes addicted to heroin after being strung along by a man she hoped to marry. By the time she is cured she has lost everything and has nowhere to go. Nazik Hanim's end is more complex but brilliantly played. She is someone who cannot accept her age, even after being swindled out of her fortune by her fourth husband, a younger man who throws her aside. She becomes increasingly temperamental and then begins dressing up like someone half her age, with a wig covering her gray hair, to flirt with a twenty-year-old student. When scolded for this behavior, she has a nervous breakdown.

None of the poor women who admired Nazik or the dancer ever mentioned the moral lesson of the fall; rather, they seemed to take vicarious pleasure in these women's defiance of the moral system that keeps good women quiet. As I have shown, these domestic workers were women whose respectability was threatened by their need to work outside the home and as servants. They struggled daily to claim and proclaim their respectability. They hid from their neighbors and sometimes even their relatives the actual sort of work they did, and they had all adopted the *hijab*, the head covering of the new modest Islamic dress that in Egypt has come to signify Islamic piety and middle-class respectability.

'Ukasha might have himself to blame for this lack of attention to his nationalist feminism and morality, although I would argue that the quality of the acting was probably as much a factor in the subversions of pedagogy as the writing and directing. For popular appeal and clarity in creating the righteous, modern, patriotic character, talented television drama producers often reach out to popular images, such as those purveyed in American soap operas, or introduce the debased "other," usually parodied, for contrast. This can backfire when outrageous characters like Nazik Hanim or Hagga Fadda, the corrupt ignorant villainess of *The White Flag,* the other success-ful serial in the early '90s by the same writer, steal the show from tiresomely earnest protagonists.[13] Martha Diase offers another wonderful example of misguided identifications in her analysis of *The Family House,* the 1994 se-rial discussed earlier that was funded by USAID and foreign NGOs to pro-mote public health messages. She reports that viewers liked and identified most with the character of Amina, a former dancer who had moved to the city and was supporting five children by making handicrafts, even though she and her family had been written into the script to model the negative consequences of failure to practice family planning. The too-good Dr. Omar, a man of generous social conscience and ideal behavior, like the earnest pro-tagonist in *The White Flag* (played by the same cultured actor, Jamil Ratib), seems not to have captured their affection.

Viewers, as most media studies today confirm, are selective in their read-ings and appreciation of the messages of television dramas. They can dis-agree with the politics; they can marvel at and take pleasure in the defiant characters who live as they cannot. In Egypt, they accept the moral stances presented only when these resonate with their worlds. This was clear again in the poor urban women's positive responses to the moral conservatism about family and a mother's role promoted by Egyptian serials generally and *Hilmiyya Nights* in particular. As one admirer of Nazik Hanem noted, to ex-plain why Nazik's daughter Zuhra never found happiness: "The poor thing. It was because her mother didn't take care of her. She abandoned her as a baby with her father. When the girl got sick and had a bad fever, his new wife brought her to Nazik, saying, 'Here, take your daughter and hold her close.' But she refused. So Zuhra never knew the love of a mother. She had to depend on herself. So that man [her boss] duped her [tricking her into a shameful secret marriage and a pregnancy]. Poor thing."

Selective readings are not just a result of star magic or the excess essen-tial to making entertaining television drama. One of the arguments of this book is that viewers' responses are dictated by the often vast distance be-tween the "realities" dramatized in the serials and people's everyday lives and experiences. If the fashionable blond stars of American soap operas, working in plush offices and grand mansions, are most obviously distant from local realities, the characters portrayed in the Egyptian programs are hardly closer. Most Egyptian serials are set in urban locations and deal with urban, often upper-class problems that, even when "realistic," present something of a challenge to believability for both rural villagers and the urban poor.[14]

I was alerted very early on to this challenge and the selective readings through which people met it. On an evening during one of my first visits to the village where I was to spend so much time, I was sitting with Yamna, the vivacious but exhausted mother of one family while she was preparing dinner with the help of her sister. *Love in a Diplomatic Pouch,* the serial by Muna Nur al-Din, came on the air.[15] Yamna's sister had been there all day helping this overworked woman, who had bread to bake and children to be watched when she went off to get fodder for the animals. Moreover, between the fever of the eldest son, the measles that had struck all four of the little girls, the three boys' end-of-year exams, the expenses and fatigue of a recent trip to a hospital in Asyut in search of a cure for the chain-smoking father's asthmatic cough, and the government's announcement the previous day that the price of flour was to be doubled, the family was particularly miserable that night. They wondered how they would cope. Yet the serial they watched centered on a wealthy diplomat's family and included characters like ballet teachers, woman doctors, journalists, and radio personalities with career problems.

As Yamna cooked, her sister, wrapped in the black cloak women wear when they go visiting, shouted out a summary of the plot for her. She focused on the family dynamics that are the regular stuff of their own forms of telling life stories in the village: divorces, arguments, absences, thwarted matches. She also picked up the moral message about women and family—the importance of the mother's role in raising her children and the ill consequences for them if she were to abandon them or put herself, her marriage, or her career first—just as the Delhi women whose engagement with television serials Purnima Mankekar studied selectively relate their dilemmas to those they watch.[16] However, many of the "women's issues" in this serial were constructed in psychosocial terms that were foreign to Yamna and her sister: "psychological" problems like psychosomatic paralysis that love could heal; men unable to commit themselves to marry for fear of losing their freedom; mothers who cried because their children were not emotionally open with them; and psychiatrists treating drug addiction among the wealthy and educated. The women simply ignored in their discussions these aspects of the serial that were not part of their experience.

It cannot be forgotten, however, that even more than through selective readings of a genre characterized by excess and a certain lack of realism, at least about certain lives, viewers are shielded from the didactic messages of television programs by the very status of television as entertainment. The world of the serials mimics and intensifies life but is, like the stars who people it, constructed fantasy. Like any place where audiences are sophisticated and experienced television viewers, in Egypt audiences do not really confuse actors and the characters they play. They also know that they are watching television—they compartmentalize television dramas as worlds unto themselves, even as they take them into their homes and imaginations.

The best way to characterize the relationship of the world of television drama and its associated stars to people I knew in the village in Upper Egypt and the poor neighborhoods of Cairo, and most likely many others, is as a mix of intimacy and distance.[17] Again, *Hilmiyya Nights* can give us a good sense of this. Although by definition serials differ from soap operas in having resolutions, this serial was unusual in deferring its resolution for so long. Drawn out over five years and far more episodes than any previous Egyptian serial, it allowed for the development of the kind of attachment to characters that soap opera audiences relish. Following the tribulations and successes of some of the characters from childhood to adulthood and others through marriages, divorces, losses, imprisonments, and careers well into old age, audiences were treated to the pleasurable experience common to American soap opera viewers: of finding meaning in scenes because they had knowledge of the characters' histories.[18] An intimacy was created by the deep familiarity viewers came to have over time of characters' personal pasts and tangled relationships, especially since old episodes of the serial were rerun each year before the new installment was aired, and the whole serial was rerun one episode per week after it was over.[19]

This intimacy was balanced not just by viewers' knowledge that these were only characters in a drama but that the stars who played them were part of a world of which they would never be part or fully approve. Moral reserve about stars and the world of entertainment may be quite widespread, but in Egypt and the Arab world it takes a particular form, as remarked by many who have written about other kinds of performers, including dancers, singers, and even epic poets.[20] The moral disapproval mostly comes from the lifestyles associated with actors and other entertainers as well as some publicized concerns about their religious propriety. There are some public efforts to temper negative assessments of actors, even from outside the industry. The former Rector of Al-Azhar, Jad al-Haq Jad al-Haq, a religious authority looked to for guidance, condemned most "art" but offered the qualification that "acting could be used as a tool to educate society through discussing issues that threaten the harmony of a successful society. Issues like families and how they are weakening. Or how selfishness, betrayal, and dishonesty are widespread in modern societies."[21] And for fifty years the Egyptian Catholic Center Film Festival has celebrated Egyptian films, awarding them prizes on the basis not just of artistic merit, but of ethics, morality, and humanistic values. All those awarding or receiving prizes are careful to stress how special the prizes are because of the criteria on which they are based. What such festivals do, run as they are by priests, is suggest that entertainment for the screen can be moral, and that actors participate in media that have the capacity to promote good values.

And yet this is not enough to overcome widespread feelings that the world of acting is immoral. One young actor, Muna Zaki, took great pains in her interview with me to distance herself from other actors and the world of stars. She expressed disdain for the current generation of superstars and idolized the classic film stars instead. She lived at home with her parents, who insisted that she finish college. Her mother fielded all calls for her. And she said that those she worked with were colleagues but not friends. In explaining the need to distance herself from their world, she said she had her brother and family to think of.[22]

Such views are even more pronounced among the kinds of ordinary people whose relationships to television and the nation I have been describing in this book. As I have argued elsewhere, there is a long-standing view in the Muslim world that performers, especially women performers, are disreputable.[23] They mix with strangers, appear in public, and have been associated, justifiably or not, with "the oldest profession." However much they try to present themselves as nationalists, as Armbrust shows Farid Shauqi did by making patriotic films and publicizing himself as a good husband, or as upstanding citizens, as did the diva Umm Kulthum more or less successfully, it is hard to shake off the moral questions.[24] In the 1990s, media stars were associated with risqué "westernized" and wealthy lifestyles, from non-family-oriented activities to drugs, divorces and affairs, fancy clothes and makeup, and European travel. For many ordinary women and men, there is felt to be a vast moral gulf between themselves and these stars. The actors, like so many of the serials they participate in, are thus compartmentalized, considered to belong to a different world, interesting if sometimes scandalous.

This compartmentalization allows for a certain generosity of spirit. Knowing the moral standards by which villagers judged each other and by which domestic servants felt themselves to be judged, I was initially rather shocked by what people took for granted on television. No one turned off the television when the latest beauty to star in the annual Ramadan riddle shows (*fawazir*) appeared in tight clothing and gyrated wildly. That was what that holiday had come to be about, as Armbrust has so vividly shown in his work on the commercialization of Ramadan.[25] And despite the urban and sophisticated personas of these stars that became apparent when they played themselves in celebrity charades or other game shows, village children were perfectly happy to imitate the games in local fields. It was touching to see teenagers even seeking ways to sympathize with the plights of these stars. Some village girls were anxious, in the early 1990s, to tell me that Yusra, the westernized film star who played the German wife of our Egyptian spy in Israel, *Ra'fat al-Haggan,* and was later to sell Jawhara ceramic tiles, married very late. There was pathos in what they added: "She says she loves children and has photos of children on her walls."

There was, in fact, a certain tolerance and suspension of judgment in effect because it was understood that these stars lived in a world of their own, outside the bounds of people's face-to-face moral communities. The affection viewers directed toward them came from their familiarity and the magic they wove into the serials as well as the spectacles they created to entertain people and enrich their ordinary lives. This did not completely erase the tensions their "immorality" created for those in whose daily worlds these stars were enmeshed, as we will see, but their confinement to the special world of television and film kept them within the pale. Television, in other words, is considered a world unto itself, with its own rhythms, standards, and conventions. It need not bleed fully into daily life, even if it is an intimate part of it.

SOCIAL DIFFERENCES AND NATIONAL TRAJECTORIES

A crucial argument of this book has been that the nationalist messages of pedagogical serials are broadcast into a complex social space where not only the very local but the transnational exert powerful pulls. On the one hand, people live in the local worlds of their daily experiences in Cairo, Upper Egypt, or even the Western Desert, of which television is only a small part. On the other hand, as I explored in detail in the third section of this book, as multinational companies bombard the Egyptian market with their products and advertising flourishes, as Islamic political groups with broader-than-national identifications vie for loyalty, and as elites look to the West, television's nationalists have much to compete with.

Most important, serials enter social worlds whose realities do not correspond to the promises of national television. Among many groups of Egyptians—with poverty intense, the dreams of social mobility through education no longer viable, social services desperately inadequate, government bureaucracies vast and unfeeling, the gap between the wealthy and the majority of the population widening, and the nation-state experienced as much through institutions of surveillance, discipline, and gross inequity as patriotic songs and the technologies of civic pride—there is little corroboration for uplifting visions.

The serials also enter discursive spaces filled with competing and sometimes incompatible stories and ideals, some of which are barely represented in the television shows people watch. These include not just Islamism and the discourses and practices of piety or global consumerism and pop culture, with the dreams of capitalism that are associated with them, but whatever local subcultural discourses with which people have grown up. The latter are not authentic or pure cultures of the peasantry or the urban poor but more like the "common sense" Gramsci ascribed to the subaltern, a jumble of values and ideas that have resulted from local histories and social relations combined with the experiences of having been subjected to centuries of larger state projects, colonial and postcolonial, to integrate and transform them. As the Awlad 'Ali parents' disapproval of radio soap operas reminds us, all the discourses are connected to particular social and political groups and thus are part of the larger field of power that is, in large measure, national.

The reactions I witnessed to one film and television star, Huda Sultan, tell an important story about the intersection of discourses in Egypt in the 1990s. It is a tale that can serve as a conclusion to this ethnography of a nation because it suggests why the resolution of the moral ambivalence toward stars, and the nation, that Islamism might offer still fails to address the fundamental problem I have been uncovering in my assessment of television and social fragments in the "national space": the problem of social inequality.

I have argued that one must look beyond explicit media messages, even of the most popular genres and programs, and beyond strategies of media policy, to understand television's place in everyday lives and its relationship to historical process. If the emotionality and domesticity of television serials help produce modern subjectivities, then a new extratextual interfacing of television and religion may be nurturing national affiliations where direct state efforts to manage religion have only produced conversation. The most dramatic phenomenon in the world of stars in the early 1990s was the highly publicized retirement from acting, and in the case of women, the taking on of the hijab (head covering), of a number of "artists." Their new roles stirred controversy, including accusations of taking money from Saudi sources for doing this. The religious authorities associated with their "repentance" were very visible figures, like the late Shaykh al-Sha'rawi and Dr. 'Umar 'Abd al-Kafi, well known through television appearances and sermons on audiocassette. The mosque and charitable associations most associated with their "conversions" were those of the lay religious authority Mustafa Mahmud, best known for his television program, *Faith and Science.*[26]

Books with titles like *Repentant Artists and the Sex Stars* and *Artists behind the Veil* and dedications such as "To every retired artist who had faith that what is of God is better and more lasting" carried glowing interviews with these stars, as well as with the religious figures who mentored them.[27] Dr. 'Umar 'Abd al-Kafi, for example, explained his support of these actresses by reporting what he tells them: "I wouldn't want my sister—and you are a sister to me—or my daughter or my wife, to embrace a man in the name of art . . . or to sleep with him in the same bed, surrounded by cameras and to call this art!!, or to strip to a swimsuit on the beach with him and we say this is art!! This is not the art that God wants."[28] The publications also reported the opinions of other actors, who disagree with their colleagues' verdicts that acting and dancing, or entertainment in general, are sinful, though they carefully defend their colleagues' personal freedom of choice.

At least one of these stars (Sawsan Badr) eventually removed the veil and went back to acting, but the most interesting case is Huda Sultan. An older actor who was an extremely successful singer and film star even in the 1950s,[29] Sultan now says she prefers to work in television and wears the hijab on-screen and off. So unlike her younger "born-again" colleagues, she has not given up acting. She explained in an interview in 1994 regarding her role in *Arabesque,* the 'Ukasha production discussed in chapter 6, "I respect my audience very much and am quite careful to appear respectable in front of them. . . . Hijab is a duty that is not inimical to artistic performance. I am veiled and therefore I choose roles that are suitably modest, like the role of the mother." She admitted that when she began her career as an "artist," her brother, ironically himself a singer, was not happy with her choice because of the poor image artists had in those days. But now, she explained, "Artists are fairly well respected at all levels. The artist has become a sort of ambassador for his country, the carrier of a social message who has a political stance and a role in enlightenment."

Taking the middle road of wearing the veil but continuing to act seems to have made Sultan universally admired. Those who direct her or have written scripts for shows in which she appears praise her talent. As Usama Anwar 'Ukasha said of her role as the sincere Egyptian mother in his *Arabesque*, "I was personally astounded by her and thought the role I had written of Umm Hasan was smaller than her talent deserves. Yet any scene in which she appeared raised the caliber of the episode."[30] When she was given a prize at the Forty-Fifth Annual Catholic Center Film Festival, the announcer said she was being rewarded for integrity, honesty, and her love of people. Sultan thanked the festival organizers graciously, letting it be known what an honor this was after her recent return from the *'umra* (the "lesser" pilgrimage to Mecca, undertaken at a different time of year than the annual pilgrimage). I witnessed the extraordinary respect and affection directed toward her by her colleagues when I sat in on the final script reading in 1997 for 'Ukasha's production, *Zizinya*, described in the opening of this chapter. When she entered the meeting late, there was shuffling and interest and immediately a senior male actor got up from the head of the table to give her his seat. Everyone else greeted her warmly. When the reading was over, a large cake from a good patisserie was brought in to celebrate the end of this stage of production and the commencement of shooting in a few weeks. Deferentially, the group asked her to cut the cake.

I suspect that only a small elite that is not that fond of Egyptian serials in any case might be offended by the appearance of Huda Sultan in hijab. For the rest of the public, including a large middle and lower middle class, the majority of whom now accept veiling, and rural communities in which women had never gone without some sort of head covering, she represents the perfect compromise. They can identify with, or at least respect, her moderate piety. Yet because her piety, unlike that of the younger born-again stars, does not seem to entail the condemnation of the popular entertainment of television drama, she gives people license to continue to be captivated by the magic of stars and to partake in the nationwide affective community of those drawn to them.

The affection for Huda Sultan illustrates how if there is today in Egypt a way that media fosters a sense of belonging to a national community, it may be less because of an educated elite's desire to create the good citizen, the state's attempts to use television to manage religious extremism and create harmony, or capitalist projects to create national consumers than because of people's common attachments to such actors who are familiar figures on screens in homes, shops, and cafés across the nation. But it also symbolizes the illusory nature of the equality and shared national vision that available discourses on or off television promise. Huda Sultan's piety may make her seem now closer to the worlds of those who watch television, but presumably she has retained the wealth and privilege she won as a prominent star many decades ago. And ultimately, she remains part of a system that claims affection for the public but can only make those who do not share its elite or middle-class lifestyles and values feel inferior and excluded, with nothing to defend themselves with but their discourse of moral superiority. Huda Sultan, in her modest Islamic dress, offers no more revolutionary commentary on the inequalities and power differences that characterize the nation than the most progressive of television serials that may criticize lapses and corruptions in state institutions but not the inherent inequalities of the nation-state.

Fostering attachment to stars, including ones like Huda Sultan who seem to bring together national and religious identities, must finally be seen as one of the many ways that television participates in the nation-state's attempts at hegemony. Intellectuals participate in a different way by deploying pedagogical discourses and bringing television serials into a public sphere where national political, social, and economic issues from modernity and authenticity to religious extremism and consumerism can be debated. Neither television serials nor the stars who make them vivid upset the divide between the educated and the uneducated, the privileged and the marginal, and those struggling for power and those excluded from it. Without denying the importance of the large middle class in Egypt who are both consumers and producers of television, I have wanted in this book to highlight the special relationships to television serials and the nation of the more marginal communities that I've tapped into through my fieldwork—communities that represent a not unsizeable proportion of the citizens of Egypt. The serials entertain these communities and seek to draw them into the nation, but do not suggest how they might transform their nation-state to make it a more equitable or just place.

Appendix

What follows is a rough guide to major serials and TV films discussed in the book. Plots are far more complex than can be indicated here. I offer only the bare outlines to jog readers' memories.

Abu-Zayd al-Hilali: The Hilali Epic (Abu-Zayd al-Hilali: al-sira al-hilaliyya), 1997: Yusri al-Jindi; dir. Magdi Abu-'Umayra. Costume drama of the Arab epic of Abu-Zayd al-Hilali.

Against the Current (didd al-tayyar), 1997: Muhammad Safa' 'Amir; dir. Isma'il 'Abd al-Hafiz. Business corruption and the temptations of money for someone from the former aristocracy.

And the Nile Flows On (wa ma zala al-nil yajri), 1991: Usama Anwar 'Ukasha; dir. Muhammad Fadil. Population problems and family planning. Funded by USAID.

Arabesque (arabisk), 1994: Usama Anwar 'Ukasha; dir. Jamal 'Abd al-Hamid. Authenticity and national risk faced by the ibn al balad, this one an artisan who makes mashrabiyya woodwork.

Aunt Safiyya and the Monastery (khalti Safiyya wa al-dayr), 1996: Yusr al-Siwi; based on novel by Bahaa' Tahir. Love and revenge in Upper Egypt, with Muslims and Copts living in harmony.

The Conscience of Headmistress Hikmat (damir abla Hikmat), 1990: Usama Anwar 'Ukasha; dir. In'am Muhammad 'Ali. Moral head of school tries to maintain values and standards in the face of corruption. Headmistress played by the legendary film star Fatin Hamama.

Diffuse Light (al-daw' al-sharid), 1999: Muhammad Safa' 'Amir; dir. Isma'il 'Abd al-Hafiz. Big clans, upstarts, love, and terrorism in Upper Egypt.

Dream of the Southerner (hilm al-janubi), 1997: Muhammad Safa' 'Amir; dir. Jamal 'Abd al-Hamid. Antiquities, nationalism, and Upper Egypt.

The Family (al-'a'ila), 1994: Wahid Hamid; dir. Isma'il 'Abd al-Hafiz. Dangers of Islamic militant groups.

The Family of Haj Mitwalli ('a'ilat al-haj Mitwalli), 2001: Mustafa Muharram. Polygamist merchant keeps wives happy.

Final Return (akhir 'awda), 1993: Wafiyya Khayri; dir. Fu'ad 'Abd al-Jalil. Values of the middle class threatened by nouveau riche and those returning from working in the Gulf.

Forgiveness (ghufran), 1990: Tharwat Abaza and Fathi Salama; dir. 'Adil Sadiq. Modern tale of greed and betrayal based loosely on the Qur'anic (and biblical) story of Joseph.

Fugitive from Love (farar min al-hubb), 2000: Muhammad Safa' 'Amir; dir. Majdi Abu-'Umayra. Land and honor of Upper Egyptians, set around Luxor.

Harvest of Love (hasad al-hubb), 1993: Fathiyya al-'Assal. Modern-day Romeo and Juliet in rural Upper Egypt trying to overcome the bad tradition of the vendetta.

Hayat al-Gawhari (Hayat al-Gawhari), 1997: Muhammad Jalal 'Abd al-Qawi; dir. Wa'il 'Abd-allah. Woman lawyer who tries to maintain ethical standards while husband succumbs to business corruption and adultery. Starring Yusra.

Hilmiyya Nights (layali al-hilmiyya), 1988, 1989, 1990, 1992, 1995: Usama Anwar 'Ukasha; dir. Isma'il 'Abd al-Hafiz. Epic of modern Egyptian history following rich and poor of the neighborhood of Hilmiyya from the days of anticolonial activities against the British to the present. In five installments.

Honey and Tears (al-shahd wa al-dumu'), 1980s: Usama Anwar 'Ukasha. Family drama of strong widow who raises children well despite the greed of her brother-in-law, pushed by aristocratic and selfish wife, who cheats them out of their inheritance.

Illusion and Arms (al-wahm wa al-silah), 1995: Tharwat Abaza; dir. Hasan Bashir. The violence of Islamic militants.

I Won't Live My Father's Life (lan a'ish fi gilbab abi), 1996: Mustafa Muharram; dir. Ahmad Tawfiq. Based on a short story by Ihsan 'Abd al-Quddus. Rags-to-riches story of man who doesn't give up his roots and principles, has adorable relationship with traditional wife, and watches children face complex situations in changing times.

The Journey of Abu 'Ila al-Bishri (rihlat abu 'ila al-bishri), 1980s: Usama Anwar 'Ukasha; dir. Muhammad Fadil. Trials of the middle class trying to maintain morality and honesty in tough times as children are tempted by drugs, pop music, and unrespectable work.

The Ladies of Garden City (hawanim gardin siti), 1998: Muna Nur al-Din; dir. Ahmad Sakr? Historical psychodrama about aristocratic women.

Love in a Diplomatic Pouch (hubb fi haqiba diblumasiyya), 1990: Muna Nur al-Din. Psychological problems among the wealthy, mothers who fear their children won't talk to them, men afraid of commitment, ballerinas, drug addiction.

The Magician (al-hawi), 1997: Muhsin Zayid; dir. Yahya al-'Alami. Hustler gets wealthy by marrying foreigner and engaging in shady business deals; his first love, also from poor origins, marries Gulf Arab who mistreats her and later kidnaps her son; she in turn marries first love, who tries to betray her in business, but she outwits him.

Mothers in the House of Love (ummahat fi bayt al-hubb), 1996: Fathiyya al-'Assal. Women in old-age home band together to fight developer intent on razing their building to make an apartment complex.

Mountain Wolves (dhi'ab al-jabal), 1993/94: Muhammad Safa' 'Amir; dir. Majdi Abu 'Umayra. With songs by Upper Egyptian poet 'Abd al-Rahman al-Abnudi. Revenge, honor, and patriarchy in Upper Egypt, pitted against enlightened modernity.

Nasser 56, 1995: Mahfuz 'Abd al-Rahman; dir. Muhammad Fadil. Black and white biopic about President Nasser, chronicling the decision to nationalize the Suez Canal.

The New Street (al-Shari' al-jadid), 1998: 'Abd al-Hamid Juda al-Sahhar; dir. Muhammad Fadil. Historical drama about an extended family during the time of British colonial occupation.

Nutty Nuna (Nuna al-sha'nuna), 1996: Lamis Jabir; dir. In'am Muhammad 'Ali. Domestic servant from rural area discovers school from kitchen window. Based on short story by Salwa Bakr.

The Other Half of Rabi' (nusf Rabi' al-akhar), 1996: Muhammad Jalal 'Abd al-Qawi; dir. Yahya al-'Alami. Socially responsible lawyer and good husband is tempted by wealthy first love and narrowly escapes corruption and divorce.

Our Folks (ahalina), 1997: Usama Anwar 'Ukasha; dir. Isma'il 'Abd al-Hafiz. Struggling middle-class families deal with low wages, unemployment, temptations to embezzle and bribe.

Ra'fat al-Haggan, 1989, 1990: Salih Mursi; dir. Yahya al-'Alami. Egyptian spy in Israel.

She and the Impossible (hiyya wa al-mustahil), 1980s: Fathiyya al-'Assal; dir. In'am Muhammad 'Ali. Divorced woman gets educated, becomes a writer, and has a career.

Time of Roses (awan al-ward), 2000–2001: Wahid Hamid; dir. Samir Sayf. Muslim and Coptic intermarriage and the search for a kidnapped baby.

The White Flag (al-raya al-bayda), 1989: Usama Anwar 'Ukasha; dir. Muhammad Fadil. Art, beauty, and social values in danger from crass nouveau riche.

Woman in the Time of Love (imra'a fi zaman al-hubb), 1999: Usama Anwar 'Ukasha; dir. Isma'il 'Abd al-Hafiz. Upright aunt with morals saves rich spoiled nieces and nephews about to sink into drugs and immorality, corrupted by money, westernization, and paternal neglect.

Zizinya (Zizinya), 1998, 1999: Usama Anwar 'Ukasha; dir. Jamal 'Abd al-Hamid. Historical drama of multicultural Alexandria before Nasser's nationalization of the Suez Canal in 1956 and the exodus of foreigners from Egypt.

Notes

1. For a fuller discussion of these trends:, see Lila Abu-Lughod, *Writing Women's Worlds: Bedouin Stories* (Berkeley and Los Angeles: University of California Press, 1993), especially 225–26 and "The Romance of Resistance: Tracing Transformations of Power through Bedouin Women," *American Ethnologist* 17 (1990): 41–55.

2. Naomi Sakr, *Satellite Realms: Transnational Television, Globalization and the Middle East* (London: I. B. Tauris, 2001), 19.

3. Naomi Sakr notes that access to satellite "remained substantially lower in Egypt than in any other Arab country," with only 1% of households with television sets in 1996 having satellite and less than 10% two years later, compared with figures like 40% for Lebanon by 1998, 33% for Algerians by the mid-1990s, and one-quarter of Moroccans. Ibid., 19–20.

4. Nadia Abu El-Haj, *Facts on the Ground: Archaeological Practice and Territorial Self-Fashioning in Israeli Society* (Chicago: University of Chicago Press, 2002), 48; emphasis in the original.

5. Catherine Lutz, *Homefront: A Military City and the American Twentieth Century* (Boston: Beacon Books, 2001).

6. Katherine Verdery, *Nationalist Ideology under Socialism: Identity and Cultural Politics in Ceausescu's Romania* (Berkeley and Los Angeles: University of California Press, 1991).

7. Liisa Malkki, *Purity and Exile: Violence, Memory, and National Cosmology among Hutu Refugees in Tanzania* (Chicago: University of Chicago Press, 1995).

8. Benedict Anderson, *Imagined Communities* (London: Verso, 1991). Debra Spitulnik, for example, has analyzed the ways that radio helped create the postcolonial nation in Zambia by creating language hierarchies in a multilingual state, influencing speech styles, signifying modernity itself, and even embodying the state. Debra Spitulnik, *Producing National Publics* (Durham, NC: Duke University Press, 1999). Arvind Rajagopal, *Politics after Television: Hindu Nationalism and the Reshaping of the Public in India* (Cambridge: Cambridge University Press, 2001) and Purnima Mankekar, *Screening Culture, Viewing Politics: An Ethnography of Television, Womanhood, and Nation in Postcolonial India* (Durham, NC: Duke University Press, 1999), among others, have asked how certain popular mythological television serials in India might have participated in the strengthening of Hindu nationalism. Arlene Davila, on the other hand, has studied the intersection of commercial imperatives with the cultural production of nationalities in cases like the US Hispanic advertising industry's construction of "Latinidad," a nation within the nation. See Arlene Davila, *Latino Inc.: The Marketing and Making of a People* (Berkeley and Los Angeles: University of California Press, 2001).

9. Doris Sommer, *Foundational Fictions: The National Romances of Latin America* (Berkeley and Los Angeles: University of California Press, 1991); Robert Foster, *Materializing the Nation: Commodities, Consumption and Media in Papua New Guinea* (Bloomington: Indiana University Press, 2002); and Richard Handler, *Nationalism and the Politics of Culture in Québec* (Madison: University of Wisconsin Press, 1988). Similarly, Karl Heider has examined Indonesian film as "a vehicle for the development, shaping, and diffusion of a national Indonesian culture." Karl Heider, *Indonesian Cinema: National Culture on Screen* (Honolulu: University of Hawaii Press, 1991), 134.

10. Lila Abu-Lughod, "Editorial Comment: On Screening Politics in a World of Nations," *Public Culture* 5 (1993): 465–69.

11. Richard Fox, ed., *Nationalist Ideologies and the Production of National Cultures* (Washington, DC: American Anthropological Association, 1990).

12. Following on a wartime applied anthropology tied to problems of morale at home and understanding one's allies and enemies, some of it conducted under the auspices of the U.S. Office of Naval Research, 120 scholars took part in a huge project nominally under Ruth Benedict's direction and called Columbia University Research in Contemporary Cultures. One of its publications was a manual called *Studying Culture at a Distance*, edited by Margaret Mead and Rhoda Metraux in 1953. This was recently reissued with an introduction by William Beeman, who claims parallels for this project with contemporary cultural studies. *The Study of Culture at a Distance*, ed. Margaret Mead and Rhoda Metraux (New York: Berghahn Books, 2000). Unable to do fieldwork in the nations they wished to understand, they used feature films, novels, and other media, alongside interviews with immigrant or exiled nationals, to analyze what they understood as "the national character" of China, Russia, France, Romania, England, Poland, and others. During the war Japan had been subjected to the same scrutiny. For a more critical assessment, see Federico Neiburg and Marcio Goldman, "Anthropology and Politics in Studies of National Character," *Cultural Anthropology* 13 (1998): 56–81.

13. For a discussion of this concept and references to key works, see Jessica Winegar, "Claiming Egypt: The Cultural Politics of Artistic Practice in a Postcolonial Society" (Ph.D. diss., New York University, 2003).

14. Theodor Adorno, *The Culture Industry: Selected Essays on Mass Culture*, ed. J. M. Bernstein (London: Routledge, 1991).

15. A good recent example is John Kelly and Martha Kaplan, *Represented Communities: Fiji and World Decolonization* (Chicago: University of Chicago Press, 2001).

16. Partha Chatterjee, *The Nation and Its Fragments* (Princeton, NJ: Princeton University Press, 1993); Claudio Lomnitz-Adler, *Exits from the Labyrinth: Culture and Ideology in the Mexican National Space* (Stanford, CA: Stanford University Press, 1992).

17. Cited in Kate Crehan, *Gramsci, Culture and Anthropology* (Berkeley and Los Angeles: University of California Press, 2002), 157.

18. Ibid., 143.

19. Etienne Balibar, *Race, Nation, Class: Ambiguous Identities* (London: Verso, 1991).

20. For a comprehensive study of Umm Kulthum, see Virginia Danielson, *The Voice of Egypt: Umm Kulthum, Arabic Song, and Egyptian Society in the Twentieth Century* (Chicago: University of Chicago Press, 1997).

21. I take these words from a study done by my father in the late 1950s in rural Egypt. Ibrahim Abu-Lughod, "The Mass Media and Egyptian Village Life," *Social Forces* 42 (1963): 97–104. For more on the history of mass media in Egypt, see Douglas Boyd, *Broadcasting in the Arab World* (Ames: Iowa State University Press, 1999); CEDEJ, "Anciens et Nouveaux médias in Egypte: Radio, Télévision, Cinéma, Vidéo." *Bulletine de CEDEJ* 21, Premiere semestre (1987);

and Martha Diase, "Egyptian Television Serials, Audiences, and *The Family House,* a Public Health Enter-Educate Serial" (Ph.D. diss., University of Texas at Austin, 1996). See also chapter 8 for more detailed discussion of the industry.

22. Boyd, *Broadcasting in the Arab World,* 39.

23. Omnia El Shakry, "The Great Social Laboratory: Reformers and Utopians in Twentieth Century Egypt" (Ph.D. diss., Princeton University, 2002).

24. Boyd has argued that entertainment was central to its mission, but this book suggests a more complex relationship between entertainment and education. Boyd, *Broadcasting in the Arab World,* 37–49.

25. Interview with the author, April 15, 1990.

26. Interview with the author, July 22, 1990.

27. Shahinaz M. Talaat, *Mass Media and Rural Development in Egypt* (Cairo: Anglo-Egyptian Bookshop, 1987). From her charts of educational programs, one could calculate that in 1986 approximately 31 hours, out of about 175 weekly broadcast hours on the three channels available at the time, were filled with such "developmental" programs.

28. Interview with the author, April 29, 1990.

29. Homi Bhabha, "DissemiNation: Time, Narrative, and the Margins of the Modern Nation," in *Nation and Narration,* ed. Homi Bhabha (London: Routledge, 1990), 297–99.

30. For a rich example of the consequences of such lags, see Ruth Mandel's "A Marshall Plan of the Mind: The Political Economy of a Kazakh Soap Opera," in *Media Worlds: Anthropology on New Terrain,* ed. Faye Ginsburg, Lila Abu-Lughod, and Brian Larkin (Berkeley and Los Angeles: University of California Press, 2002), 211–28.

31. See Terence Turner, "Representation, Politics, and Cultural Imagination in Indigenous Video: General Points and Kayapo Examples," in *Media Worlds: Anthropology on New Terrain,* ed. Faye Ginsburg, Lila Abu-Lughod, and Brian Larkin (Berkeley and Los Angeles: University of California Press, 2002), 75–89; and Annabelle Sreberny-Mohammadi and Ali Mohammadi, *Small Media, Big Revolution: Communication, Culture, and the Iranian Revolution* (Minneapolis: University of Minnesota Press, 1994).

32. For an explication of what this distinction does and does not mean and intellectuals' role in social hegemony, see Crehan, *Gramsci, Culture and Anthropology.* The distinction is cited on p. 139. Another good source on the concept of hegemony as a process of contest is William Roseberry, "Hegemony and the Language of Contention," in *Everyday Forms of State Formation,* ed. Gilbert Joseph and Daniel Nugent (Durham, NC: Duke University Press, 1994), 170–209.

33. E. Valentine Daniel, *Charred Lullabies: Chapters in an Anthropography of Violence* (Princeton, NJ: Princeton University Press, 1996), 154–93.

34. Sayed Yassin, "Cultural Papers: 'Hilmiyya Nights' and Political Activity," *Al-Ahram al-iqtisadi,* September 7, 1990, pp. 96–97.

35. Hanan Abu al-Dia', "Hal min haq mu'allaf layali al-hilmiyya kitabat al-tarikh min wijhat nazar al-nasiriyyin?" {Does the author of *Hilmiyya Nights* have the right to write history from the Nasserites' perspective?) *Al-Wafd,* June 10, 1990, p. 10.

36. 'Abd al-'Azim Ramadan, "Al-ta'thir al-siyasi li-layali al-hilmiyya" [The political impact of *Hilmiyya Nights*], *Al-Wafd,* May 14, 1990; and "Haqa'iq al-tarikh wa musalsal layali al-hilmiyya" [Historical facts and *Hilmiyya Nights*], *Al-Wafd,* May 21, 1990.

37. See Eberhard Kienle, *A Grand Delusion: Democracy and Economic Reform in Egypt* (London: I. B. Tauris, 2001), 89–115 for a discussion of how limited the new freedoms from censorship actually were under President Mubarak.

38. Mamduh al-Laythi, then head of the Production Sector at the Union of Radio and

Television, kindly gave my research assistant Maha Mahfuz 'Abd al-Rahman (who happened to be the daughter of a respected television writer) access to the files for *Hilmiyya Nights* in 1990.

39. Interview with Usama Anwar 'Ukasha by Aynas Ibrahim, *Sabah al-Khayr,* May 24, 1990, p. 56.

40. For good analyses of film and mass culture in general, see Walter Armbrust, *Mass Culture and Modernism in Egypt* (Cambridge: Cambridge University Press, 1996); and Viola Shafik, *Arab Cinema: History and Cultural Identity* (Cairo: American University in Cairo Press, 1998). See Robert Vitalis, "American Ambassador in Technicolor and Cinemascope: Hollywood and Revolution on the Nile," for an analysis of the political economy of the early film industry. In *Mass Mediations: New Approaches to Popular Culture in the Middle East and Beyond,* ed. Walter Armbrust (Berkeley and Los Angeles: University of California Press, 2000), 269–91.

41. As Yang notes for post-Mao reform China, although eager to keep control over media, the state's cautious embrace of capitalism and encouragement of links (for investment) to overseas Chinese have led to the development of transnational subjectivities and desires that threaten to shake its authority. See Mayfair Yang, "Mass Media and Transnational Subjectivity in Shanghai: Notes on (Re)Cosmopolitanism in a Chinese Metropolis," in *Media Worlds: Anthropology on New Terrain,* ed. Faye Ginsburg, Lila Abu-Lughod, and Brian Larkin (Berkeley and Los Angeles: University of California Press, 2002), 189–210. Also see James Lull, *Media, Communication, Culture: A Global Approach* (New York: Columbia University Press, 1995), 122–23, where he explains,

> Several factors interact to destroy the omnipotence of any presumed official ideology in China: the diversity of perspectives held by influential workers in the nation's media industries; the inability of the state to manage and control its cultural policy in any consistent or uniform way; contradictory values expressed within the totality of domestic and foreign programs and advertisements; a desire on the part of TV station managers to attract and please large audiences; and the rapidly increasing number of television stations, each with its own requirements to fill airtime.

42. He argued that the findings of "macrocosmic" methods such as those of political science or sociology, with their demographics and statistics, were useful only to place these microcosms in perspective and in relation to each other. Lloyd A. Fallers, *The Social Anthropology of the Nation-State* (Chicago: Aldine Publishing Co., 1974).

43. Ibid., 12–13.

44. George Marcus, *Ethnography through Thick and Thin* (Princeton, NJ: Princeton University Press, 1998), 79.

45. These are the kinds of general issues taken up in studies like John Tomlinson, *Globalization and Culture* (Chicago: University of Chicago Press, 1999); and John B. Thompson, *The Media and Modernity* (Stanford, CA: Stanford University Press, 1995).

46. Mankekar, *Screening Culture, Viewing Politics.*

47. Rajagopal, *Politics after Television,* 28.

48. Adorno, *The Culture Industry.*

49. David Morley and Charlotte Brunsdon, *The Nationwide Television Studies* (London: Routledge, 1999); Lull, *Media, Communication, Culture;* and Roger Silverstone, *Television and Everyday Life* (London: Routledge, 1994).

50. Ien Ang, *Desperately Seeking the Audience* (London: Routledge, 1991), 162. Also see Ien Ang, *Living Room Wars: Rethinking Media Audiences for a Postmodern World* (London: Routledge, 1996).

51. Marie Gillespie, *Television, Ethnicity, and Cultural Change* (London: Routledge, 1995).

52. Ang, *Desperately Seeking the Audience,* 184n11.

53. The focus group is the most common instrument for market and communications research. For the value of "ethnographic focus groups" consisting of groups of friends, a bit less artificial, see Andrea Press and Elizabeth R. Cole, *Speaking of Abortion: Television and Authority in the Lives of Women* (Chicago: University of Chicago Press, 1999).

54. George Marcus, "Ethnography in/of the World System: The Emergence of Multi-Sited Ethnography," in *Ethnography through Thick and Thin,* 90; Emily Martin, *Flexible Bodies: Tracking Immunity in American Culture from the Days of Polio to the Age of AIDS* (Boston: Beacon Press, 1994); and Rayna Rapp, *Testing Women, Testing the Fetus: The Social Impact of Amniocentesis in America* (New York: Routledge, 1999).

55. I have contributed elsewhere to a major review of the anthropology of media and will not repeat most of the arguments here. See Faye Ginsburg, Lila Abu-Lughod, and Brian Larkin, introduction to *Media Worlds: Anthropology on New Terrain* (Berkeley and Los Angeles: University of California Press, 2002), 1–36.

56. Richard Fox, ed., *Recapturing Anthropology: Working in the Present* (Santa Fe: School of American Research Press, 1991).

57. George Marcus, "On the Unbearable Slowness of Being an Anthropologist Now: Notes on a Contemporary Anxiety in the Making of Ethnography," *Xcp: Cross-Cultural Poetics* 12 (April 2003): 7–20.

58. Among the key works are James Clifford, *The Predicament of Culture: Twentieth-Century Ethnography, Literature, and Art* (Cambridge, MA: Harvard University Press, 1988); Edward Said, *Orientalism* (New York: Pantheon Books, 1978); Eric Wolf, *Europe and the People without History* (Berkeley and Los Angeles: University of California Press, 1982); Arjun Appadurai, "Putting Hierarchy in Its Place," *Cultural Anthropology* 3 (1988): 36–49; Lila Abu-Lughod, "Writing against Culture," in *Recapturing Anthropology,* ed. Richard Fox (Santa Fe: School of American Research Press, 1991), 137–62; and Akhil Gupta and James Ferguson, eds., *Culture, Power, Place: Explorations in Critical Anthropology* (Durham, NC: Duke University Press, 1997). For an attempt to defend the culture concept, see Christoph Brumann, "Writing for Culture," *Current Anthropology* 40, Special Supplement: "Culture—A Second Chance?" (February 1999), S1–S13); for critical responses, including my own, see S13–S15. For excellent critiques that link the culture concept to nationalist thought and the legacy of national character studies, see among others Neiburg and Goldman, "Anthropology and Politics in Studies of National Character"; and Brackette Williams, "The Impact of the Precepts of Nationalism on the Concept of Culture: Making Grasshoppers of Naked Apes" *Cultural Critique* 24 (1993): 143–91.

59. Arjun Appadurai, "Global Ethnoscapes: Notes and Queries for a Transnational Anthropology," in *Modernity at Large: Cultural Dimensions of Globalization* (Minneapolis: University of Minnesota Press, 1996), 48–65.

60. Most mass communication research on Egyptian television drama has been concerned with effects. The titles of the studies by Egyptian researchers are revealing. See published works such as Ibrahim Abdelwahab Elsheikh's *Mass Media and Ideological Change in Egypt (1950–1973): An Inquiry into the Relation between Media Activities and the Ideological Change Process as Illustrated by the Propagation of Socialism* (Amsterdam: University of Amsterdam, 1977), Marwan Kashak's *Al-Usra al muslima amam al-fidiyu wa al-tilifizyun* [The Muslim family in front of video and television] (Cairo: Dar al-Kalima al-Tayyiba, 1987), and Nadya Radwan's *Dawr al-drama al-tilifizyuniyya fi tashkil wa'i al-mar'a: dirasa ijtima'iyya maydaniyya* [The role of television drama in forming women's consciousness/awareness: A field-based social study] (Cairo: Al-Hay'a al-misriyya al-'amma l-il-kitab, 1997). Numerous

unpublished M.A. and Ph.D. theses produced out of Cairo University's Faculty of Mass Communication follow a similar pattern, seeking to determine, mostly through content analysis and some questionnaire-based fieldwork, the effects of television drama on such matters as the professions, psychological problems, rural social development and cultural change, rural women's consciousness, provision of news, dissemination of agricultural information, and changing family mores.

61. This seems to have been the case with a popular television show in Puerto Rico that was a vehicle to promote Budweiser beer (see Arlene Davila, "El Kiosko Budweiser," *American Ethnologist* 25 [1999]: 452–70) or with the hookup to satellite that brought U.S. television directly to Belize (see Richard Wilk, "Television, Time, and the National Imaginary in Belize," in *Media Worlds: Anthropology on New Terrain*, ed. Faye Ginsburg, Lila Abu-Lughod, and Brian Larkin (Berkeley and Los Angeles: University of California Press, 2002), 171–86.

62. In Syria the debate focused on who has the right to control public representations of history. See Christa Salamandra, "Moustache Hairs Lost: Ramadan Television Serials and the Construction of Identity in Damascus, Syria," *Visual Anthropology* 10 (1999): 227–46. In China the dissent revolved around state repression of intellectuals' challenges to state power. See Lisa Rofel, "Yearnings: Televisual Love and Melodramatic Politics in Contemporary China," *American Ethnologist* 21 (1994): 700–22.

63. Appadurai, *Modernity at Large;* Ulf Hannerz, *Transnational Connections* (New York: Routledge, 1996), 89.

CHAPTER TWO

1. Clifford Geertz, "Deep Play: Notes on the Balinese Cockfight," in *The Interpretation of Cultures* (New York: Basic Books, 1973), 412–14.

2. Timothy Mitchell, "The Invention and Reinvention of the Egyptian Peasant," *International Journal of Middle East Studies* 28 (1990): 129–50. For an update on the sordid story, see Timothy Mitchell, *Rule of Experts: Egypt, Technopolitics, Economy* (Berkeley and Los Angeles: University of California Press, 2002).

3. I use pseudonyms here to preserve some anonymity for the village women. The folklorist in question, however, is Elizabeth Wickett, whose dissertation is entitled "'For Our Destinies': The Funerary Laments of Upper Egypt" (Ph.D. diss., University of Pennsylvania, 1993).

4. Clifford Geertz, "Thick Description: Toward an Interpretive Theory of Culture," in *Interpretation of Cultures*, 3–30.

5. Clifford Geertz, *Works and Lives* (Stanford, CA: Stanford University Press, 1988).

6. Jean Baudrillard, *Selected Writings*, ed. Mark Poster (Stanford: Stanford University Press, 1988).

7. Sherry Ortner, "Resistance and the Problem of Ethnographic Refusal," *Comparative Studies in Society and History* 37 (1995): 173–93. For a classic celebration of television viewers' resistance, see John Fiske, *Television Culture* (London: Methuen, 1987).

8. Janice Radway, *Reading the Romance: Women, Patriarchy, and Popular Literature* (Chapel Hill: University of North Carolina Press, 1984).

9. Silverstone, *Television and Everyday Life*, 133.

10. Ang, *Living Room Wars*, 182.

11. Debra Spitulnik, "Anthropology and Mass Media," *Annual Review of Anthropology* 22 (1993): 293–315; quotation is from p. 307.

12. Faye Ginsburg, "Culture/Media: A (Mild) Polemic," *Anthropology Today* 10 (1994): 5–15; quotation is from p. 13.

13. Brian Larkin, "The Social Space of Media" (panel organized for the Annual Meeting of the American Anthropological Association, San Francisco, 1996).

14. Rofel, "Yearnings," 703.

15. Purnima Mankekar, "National Texts and Gendered Lives: An Ethnography of Television Viewers in a North Indian City," *American Ethnologist* 20 (1993): 543–63; quotation is from p. 553.

16. I am certainly not alone in exploring this question. For a comprehensive look at the work of anthropologists engaged in the ethnography of media, see Ginsburg, Abu-Lughod, and Larkin, eds., *Media Worlds.*

17. Important audience studies include James Lull, *Inside Family Viewing: Ethnographic Research on Television's Audience* (London: Routledge, 1990); David Morley, *Family Television* (London: Comedia, 1986); and the collection edited by Ellen Seiter, Hans Borchers, Gabrielle Kreutzner, and Eva-Maria Warth, *Remote Control: Television, Audiences, and Cultural Power* (London: Routledge, 1989). Cross-cultural studies include Robert C. Allen, ed., *To Be Continued . . . : Soap Operas around the World* (New York: Routledge, 1995); and Tamar Liebes and Elihu Katz, *The Export of Meaning: Cross-Cultural Readings of "Dallas"* (New York: Oxford University Press, 1990).

18. Debra Spitulnik's suggestion, drawn from functional linguistics, that one examine the way "forms both presuppose and create the contexts for their interpretation" would make this notion of the framing of television messages more subtle. See Spitulnik, "Anthropology and Mass Media," 297.

19. Silverstone, *Television and Everyday Life,* 132.

20. I am grateful to Brian Larkin for this phrase (personal communication).

21. Geertz, "Thick Description," 16.

22. Ibid., 23.

23. Ibid., 21.

24. Michel Foucault, "Afterword: The Subject and Power," in *Michel Foucault: Beyond Structuralism and Hermeneutics,* ed. Hubert Dreyfus and Paul Rabinow (Chicago: University of Chicago Press, 1982), 208–26; quotation is from p. 210.

25. I have borrowed this felicitous concept from Marcus, "Ethnography in/of the World System," 79–104.

26. Ibid., 91–92.

27. All quotations from Al-'Assal are from an interview with the author on June 26, 1993.

28. For more on feminist views of marriage, see Lila Abu-Lughod, "The Marriage of Feminism and Islamism in Egypt: Selective Repudiation as a Dynamic of Postcolonial Cultural Politics," in *Remaking Women: Feminism and Modernity in the Middle East,* ed. Lila Abu-Lughod (Princeton, NJ: Princeton University Press, 1998), 243–69; and Beth Baron, "The Making and Breaking of Marital Bonds in Modern Egypt," in *Women in Middle Eastern History,* ed. Nikki Keddie and Beth Baron (New Haven, CT: Yale University Press, 1991), 275–91.

29. Interview with the author, June 26, 1993.

30. See L. Abu-Lughod, ed., *Remaking Women;* Margot Badran, *Feminists, Islam, and Nation: Gender and the Making of Modern Egypt* (Princeton: Princeton University Press, 1995); Beth Baron, *The Women's Awakening in Egypt: Culture, Society, and the Press* (New Haven, CT: Yale University Press, 1994); Marilyn Booth, *May Her Likes Be Multiplied: Biography and Gender Politics in Egypt* (Berkeley and Los Angeles: University of California Press, 2001); and

Mervat Hatem, "Economic and Political Libera(liza)tion in Egypt and the Demise of State Feminism," *International Journal of Middle East Studies* 24 (1992): 231–51.

31. Interview with the author, June 26, 1993.

32. As it turned out, Umm Ahmad was able to arrange for literacy classes to be offered in the clan reception center next to her house and began studying in 2000.

33. This conventional depiction of the backward peasants of Upper Egypt has many literary and cinematic antecedents, some of which are discussed in chapters 3 and 7. Martina Reiker, "The Sa'id and the City: The Politics of Space in the Making of Modern Egypt" (Ph.D. diss., Temple University, 1996), also provides examples of this depiction.

34. For India, see Veena Das, "On Soap Opera: What Kind of Anthropological Object Is It?" In *Worlds Apart: Modernity through the Prism of the Local*, ed. Daniel Miller (London: Routledge, 1995), 169–89; and Mankekar, *Screening Culture, Viewing Politics*.

35. This point is made in materialist critiques of the culture concept. For good examples, see Talal Asad, *Genealogies of Religion* (Baltimore: Johns Hopkins University Press, 1993); and Pierre Bourdieu, *Outline of a Theory of Practice*, trans. Richard Nice (Cambridge: Cambridge University Press, 1977).

36. Ulf Hannerz, *Cultural Complexity* (New York: Columbia University Press, 1992).

37. Appadurai, "Putting Hierarchy in Its Place"; Clifford, *The Predicament of Culture*; Nicholas Dirks, Sherry Ortner, and Geoffrey Eley, eds., *Culture/Power/History: A Reader in Contemporary Social Theory* (Princeton, NJ: Princeton University Press, 1993); and Gupta and Ferguson, *Culture, Power, Place*.

38. Wolf, *Europe and the People without History*.

39. L. Abu-Lughod, "Writing against Culture" and *Writing Women's Worlds*. See also my "Comments on 'Writing for Culture,'" *Cultural Anthropology* (1999): 40:S13–S15.

40. Sloppy misreadings have interpreted this as implying that there are no cultural differences. See, for example, Sylvia Yanagisako and Carol Delaney's introduction to *Naturalizing Power: Essays in Feminist Cultural Analysis* (New York: Routledge, 1995).

41. Marshall Sahlins, *How "Natives" Think: About Captain Cook, for Example* (Chicago: University of Chicago Press, 1995), 12–13.

42. Arjun Appadurai, *Modernity at Large: Cultural Dimensions of Globalization* (Minneapolis: University of Minnesota Press, 1996), 16, 146–47.

43. See Mitchell, *Rule of Experts*.

44. Hussein Amin, "Egypt and the Arab World in the Satellite Age," in *New Patterns in Global Television: Peripheral Vision*, ed. John Sinclair, Elizabeth Jacka, and Stuart Cunningham (Oxford: Oxford University Press, 1996), 101–25; statistic is from p. 104.

45. The notion of a "national habitus" comes from Orvar Löfgren, cited in Robert Foster, "Making National Cultures in the Global Ecumene," *Annual Review of Anthropology* 20 (1991): 235–60; quotation is from p. 237. See especially the concluding chapter of the present text for arguments about how viewing television might create a sense of national affiliation despite the failures of nationalist messages to reach socially peripheral viewers.

46. The discussion of cosmopolitanism has become wide-ranging. In anthropology, Paul Rabinow's "Representations Are Social Facts" (in *Writing Culture*, ed. James Clifford and George Marcus [Berkeley and Los Angeles: University of California Press, 1986]) was a starting point. Key texts are Appadurai, *Modernity at Large*; James Clifford, "Travelling Cultures," in *Cultural Studies*, ed. Lawrence Grossberg, Cary Nelson, and Paula Treichler (New York: Routledge, 1992); and Hannerz, *Cultural Complexity*.

47. I describe the extravagantly "modern" villa he built for this son in chapter 8. This may

have been to mollify the youth, whom he had forced into an arranged marriage, leaving behind a trail of gossip and the brokenhearted girl his son had promised to wed.

48. See L. Abu-Lughod, "The Romance of Resistance" and "Movie Stars and Islamic Moralism in Egypt," *Social Text* 42 (spring 1995): 53–67; and more generally on the new veiling, Leila Ahmed, *Women and Gender in Islam: Historical Roots of a Modern Debate* (New Haven, CT: Yale University Press, 1992).

49. A particularly eloquent theorist of the processes of hybridization and translation is Homi Bhabha, *The Location of Culture* (London: Routledge, 1994).

50. Bruce Robbins, in *Secular Vocations: Intellectuals, Professionalism, Culture* (London: Verso, 1993), 194–95, argues persuasively that the efforts of James Clifford and Arjun Appadurai to make us recognize cosmopolitanism as a feature of people and communities previously thought of as resolutely local and particular (cultures, in the old sense) enable us now to use the term more inclusively and to look for "discrepant cosmopolitanisms."

51. Appadurai, *Modernity at Large.*

52. Max Weber, "Objectivity in Social Science and Social Policy," in *The Methodology of the Social Sciences* (New York: Free Press, 1949).

53. Ang, *Living Room Wars,* 66–81.

54. Geertz, "Thick Description," 30.

55. Ang draws on the work of James Clifford, Donna Haraway, and myself to support this argument. See her *Living Room Wars,* 79–80.

56. Lila Abu-Lughod, *Veiled Sentiments: Honor and Poetry in a Bedouin Society* (Berkeley: University of California Press, 1986/2000).

57. This worldliness is what Ang says distinguishes "critical" cultural studies; Ang, *Living Room Wars,* 45–46, 79.

58. L. Abu-Lughod, *Writing Women's Worlds.*

59. Anna Tsing, *In the Realm of the Diamond Queen: Marginality in an Out-of-the-Way Place* (Princeton, NJ: Princeton University Press, 1993).

60. Clifford Geertz, *After the Fact: Two Countries, Four Decades, One Anthropologist* (Cambridge, MA: Harvard University Press, 1995), 43.

CHAPTER THREE

1. Faris Khidr, "Hilm al-Janubi: Qasida tilifizyuniyya fi 'ishq al-watan" [*Dream of the Southerner:* A television ode to the love of the nation], *Al-Idha'a wa al-tilifizyun,* January 18, 1997, p. 20.

2. Interestingly, these themes also figured in another serial about Egyptian life that was being broadcast at the same time, called *Ahalina* [Our folks] and written by Usama Anwar 'Ukasha. It is particularly striking for the contrast between the broad sympathy and subtlety with which ordinary urban Cairenes are represented and the crudeness of the portrayal of rural people. These rural characters include a psychotic nouveau-riche Bedouin from Sallum (accused of being "ignorant" despite his education) and a closed-minded elder brother of the protagonist family. This elder brother, still living in the countryside, refuses to sell the land and share out the family inheritance, despite the desperate financial needs of his brothers, and he attempts to force his educated niece to marry her cousin. He had previously cut off ties with his sister (until her death) when she had insisted on a love marriage.

3. For a nuanced critical analysis of *The Mummy* in the context of the importance of what

he describes as cultivating relations between modern Egyptians and the objects of ancient Egypt in "the nationalist project of forming ethical, aesthetic citizen-subjects," see Elliott Colla's wonderful piece, "Shadi Abd al-Salam's *al-Mumiya:* Ambivalence and the Egyptian Nation-State," in *Beyond Colonialism and Nationalism in the Maghreb,* ed. Ali Ahmida (New York: Palgrave, 2000), 109–43; quotation is from p. 25. For an analysis of how "the socialist work ethic continued to collide with the fundamental mistrust of peasant world view" in the film *The Mountain,* see Joel Gordon, *Revolutionary Melodrama: Popular Film and Civic Identity in Nasser's Egypt* (Chicago: Chicago Studies on the Middle East, Center for Middle Eastern Studies, University of Chicago, 2002), 178–83.

4. Seminar sponsored by *Al-Idha'a wa al-tilifizyun* [Radio and television magazine], May 16, 1997. Partial transcription in *Al-Idha'a wa al-tilifizyun,* May 24, 1997, pp. 8–15. Unfortunately, the west bank across from Luxor became the scene of a horrific terrorist incident in 1997 when a militant Islamist splinter group attacked tourists in Hatchepsut's Temple. For some local reactions to the incident, see chapter 7. For more on tourism, archaeology, and violence, see Lynn Meskell, "The Practice and Politics of Archaeology in Egypt," in *Ethics and Anthropology: Facing Future Issues in Human Biology, Globalism, and Cultural Property,* ed. A.-M. Cantwell, E. Friedlander, and M. L. Tram (New York: Annals of the New York Academy of Sciences, 2001), 146–69.

5. For a detailed examination of the tropes by which the Sa'id is represented in the literature and political discourse of the north, see Rieker, "The Sa'id and the City." Also see Elliott Colla, "The Stuff of Egypt: The Nation, the State and Their Proper Objects," *New Formations* 45 (winter 2001–2): 72–90.

6. For more on this, see Lila Abu-Lughod, "Finding a Place for Islam: Egyptian Television Serials and the National Interest," *Public Culture* 5 (1993): 493–513 and "The Objects of Soap Operas," in *Worlds Apart: Modernity through the Prism of the Local,* ed. Daniel Miller (London: Routledge 1995), 191–210.

7. Khidr, "Hilm al-Janubi," p. 21. The concept of the Egyptian character was discussed in chapter 1.

8. Seminar sponsored by *Al-Idha'a wa al-tilifizyun,* May 16, 1997.

9. I am grateful to Amahl Bishara for asking about this point.

10. For more on this program, see chapters 2 and 4.

11. Diase, "Egyptian Television Serials, Audiences, and *The Family House,* a Public Health Enter-Educate Serial."

12. See chapter 4 for further examples, feminist in this case, of the expectation that television should raise awareness or consciousness.

13. Khidr, "Hilm al-Janubi," p. 21.

14. See Kamran Asdar Ali, *Planning the Family in Egypt: New Bodies, New Selves* (Austin: University of Texas Press, 2002). He explores in much more detail the history and politics of family planning, looking less at the media interventions than the actual training of doctors and running of clinics.

15. See L. Abu-Lughod, "Finding a Place for Islam," for more on their television works such as *The White Flag* and *Rihlat Abu-'Ila al-Bishri* [The journey of Abu-'Ila al-Bishri] that promote such themes.

16. Diase's dissertation, "Egyptian Television Serials, Audiences, and *The Family House,* a Public Health Enter-Educate Serial," provides a detailed analysis of the rocky production process (in particular, the power of commercial and generic constraints in undermining the incorporation of the research findings and wishes of the foreign funders into the serial) and the

causes of the fairly negative reception of this serial, called *Bayt al-'a'ila* [The family house], which finally aired in 1994.

17. Sandra Lane, "Television Minidramas: Social Marketing and Evaluation in Egypt," *Medical Anthropological Quarterly* 11, no. 2 (1997): 164–82, p. 168.

18. Seminar sponsored by the Association of Women in Film, Cairo, March 24, 1997.

19. Private lessons provided the moral theme for a serial called *Damir abla Hikmat* [The conscience of Headmistress Hikmat], in which the silver-screen star Fatin Hamama made her television serial debut. As we will see in the next chapter, this was the serial playing in the background in a scene from the film about a girl's desire for literacy.

20. This is an important point made by Walter Armbrust regarding the gap between media messages and actual lives. Armbrust, Mass *Culture and Modernism in Egypt*, 133–36.

21. This and the names of other villagers are pseudonyms.

22. See chapter 2. For more on the concept of discrepant cosmopolitanisms, see Appadurai, *Modernity at Large*.

23. Iman Mansur, "Yu'akkad annahu yuqaddam al-Sa'id min al-dakhil Muhammad Safa' 'Amir: Al-Sa'id mughlaq raghm al-samawat al-maftuha" [Muhammad Safa' 'Amir confirms that he presents Upper Egypt from the inside: Upper Egypt is closed despite open skies], *Al-Idha'a wa al-tilifizyun* [Radio and television magazine], February 3, 2001, pp. 22–23.

24. Armbrust, *Mass Culture and Modernism in Egypt*.

25. A series of ten television spots entitled *Egypt's Heroines* was reported as in production in 1997 as part of a literacy campaign targeting women in Upper Egypt and jointly sponsored by the Egyptian government and the British Council. Made by the filmmaker Attiyat al-Abnoudy, the series "spotlights Egyptian women talking about how learning to read has enriched their lives." Dalia Abbas, "Upper Egypt's Ongoing War Against Illiteracy," *Middle East Times,* May 16–22, 1997, p. 14.

26. This somewhat reactive and romantic valorization of the local knowledges of the countryside's poor, presented as criticism of fellow cultured and educated peers who identify too closely with power, provides the gist of an article by Khalid Isma'il, "Sayyidna al-muthaqqaf" [Sir Intellectual], *Akhbar al-Adab,* March 12, 2000, p. 11. I am grateful to Jessica Winegar and Hamdi Attia for bringing this article to my attention. Reem Saad (personal communication) also notes a growing Sa'idi public voice in the early years of the twenty-first century through publications like *Al-Usbu'* and *Al-Dawwar.*

27. Personal communication.

28. Ghada 'Abd al-Min'im, "Qal ayh . . . fallaha min 'qaryat' al-tilifizyun" [He said what? . . . A peasant woman from television village], *Al-Idha'a wa al-tilifizyun,* March 22, 1997, pp. 90–91.

29. Martha Diase also was surprised at the absence of criticism of the fancy clothing and comfortable settings of the television serial she studied, an absence she attributed to the conventionality of upper- and middle-class settings for television serials. See Diase, "Egyptian Television Serials, Audiences, and *The Family House*, a Public Health Enter-Educate Serial," 235.

30. For another persuasive argument that images of the peasant are put into service to justify policies detrimental to their lives and livelihoods, see the discussion of the role of media representations of tenant farmers in the debate on the change in tenancy laws. Reem Saad, "State, Landlord, Parliament and Peasant: The Story of the 1992 Tenancy Law in Egypt," in *Agriculture in Egypt from Pharaonic to Modern Times,* ed. Alan Bowman and Eugene Rogan, *Proceedings of the British Academy* (Oxford: Oxford University Press, 1999), 96:387–404.

31. Michael Gasper, "'Abdallah al-Nadim, Islamic Reform, and 'Ignorant' Peasants: State-Building in Egypt?" in *Muslim Traditions and Modern Techniques of Power*, ed. Armando Salvatore, *Yearbook of the Sociology of Islam*, ed. Helmut Buchholt and Georg Stauth (Munster: Lit, 2001), 3:75–92.

32. Nathan Brown, *Peasant Politics in Modern Egypt: The Struggle against the State* (New Haven, CT: Yale University Press, 1990).

33. El Shakry, "The Great Social Laboratory," 150.

34. Colla, "The Stuff of Egypt," 75.

35. One dissenter is Nawal Hassan, who in 1997 began a campaign to save Gurna, using the argument of preserving vernacular architecture. In addition, Caroline Simpson, an English-woman who has set up a small museum depicting the long history of Gurna in hopes of persuading officials and the people themselves of their historical rights to remain there, has been very active, even succeeding in having the Chief Inspector of Antiquities give a speech at the museum opening that recognized the importance of historical presence. For more on this project, see her Web site, http://www.sepcom.demon.co.uk/Hay/main.html.

36. Colla, "The Stuff of Egypt," 85.

37. See Siona Jenkins, "Lifting Roots and Moving Home," *El-Wekalah*, March 1996, pp. 36–37; and Siona Jenkins, "Letter from Egypt," *Guardian Weekly*, September 15, 1996, p. 25.

38. See Timothy Mitchell, "Worlds Apart: An Egyptian Village and the International Tourism Industry," *Middle East Report* 196 (September-October 1995): 8–11, 23.

39. For more on this project, as well as its precedents in Hassan Fathy's building of New Gurna, see Timothy Mitchell, "Heritage and Violence," in *Rule of Experts*, 179–205.

40. Christopher Larter, "Tourism Has a Bright Future after a Boom Year: Interview with Tourism Minister Mamdouh Al Beltagui," *Middle East Times*, January 19–25, 1997, p. 2.

41. See Reem Saad, "Shame, Reputation and Egypt's Lovers: A Controversy over the Nation's Image," *Visual Anthropology* 10 (1998): 401–12, for an insightful discussion of the way in which Egyptian intellectuals try to censor work that represents their nation's poor because it is a "shame." Hania Al-Sholkamy has also written eloquently on the problems caused by this defensiveness about Egypt's image for those trying to do social research there. See her "Why Is Anthropology So Hard in Egypt?" *Cairo Papers in Social Science*, ed. Seteny Shami and Linda Herrera, 22 (1999) 119–38.

CHAPTER FOUR

1. Michael Schudson, *Advertising, the Uneasy Persuasion: Its Dubious Impact on American Society* (New York: Basic Books, 1984), 210–18.

2. See also Akhil Gupta, *Postcolonial Developments: Agriculture in the Making of Modern India* (Durham, NC: Duke University Press, 1998).

3. Feminism is a contentious issue in Egypt and in the scholarly community concerned with Middle East feminism. I have made a number of contributions to these discussions, which I will not repeat here. See Lila Abu-Lughod, "*Orientalism* and Middle East Feminist Studies," *Feminist Studies* 27 (spring 2001): 101–13, and "Introduction: Feminist Longings and Postcolonial Conditions," in *Remaking Women*, ed. L. Abu-Lughod, 3–31. That many in Egypt deny the feminist label is clear from Margot Badran's interviews. See her "Gender Activism: Feminists and Islamists in Egypt," in *Identity Politics and Women: Cultural Reassertions and Feminism in International Perspective*, ed. Valentine Moghadam (Denver: Westview Press, 1993), 202–27.

4. L. Abu-Lughod, "Feminist Longings and Postcolonial Conditions" and "The Marriage of Feminism and Islamism in Egypt," 243–69.

5. The voluminous literature on the subject of feminism in Egypt can be approached through some key works: Ahmed, *Women and Gender in Islam;* Nadje Al-Ali, *Secularism, Gender and the State in the Middle East: The Egyptian Women's Movement* (Cambridge: Cambridge University Press, 2000); Badran, *Feminists, Islam and Nation;* Baron, *The Women's Awakening in Egypt;* Booth, *May Her Likes Be Multiplied;* and Cynthia Nelson, *Doria Shafik, Egyptian Feminist: A Woman Apart* (Gainesville: University Press of Florida, 1996). Mervat Hatem has some important articles; two of the best are "Economic and Political Libera(liza)tion in Egypt and the Demise of State Feminism" and "Secularist and Islamist Discourses on Modernity in Egypt and the Evolution of the Post-Colonial Nation-State," the latter in *Islam, Gender and Social Change,* ed. Yvonne Haddad and John Esposito (New York: Oxford University Press, 1998), 85–99.

6. It happens that the scriptwriter is married to one of Egypt's favorite television actors, Yahya al-Fakharani, someone with whom this actress had worked.

7. Salwa Bakr, *Such a Beautiful Voice,* trans. Hoda El-Sadda (Cairo: General Egyptian Book Organization, 1992), 14.

8. The story has been translated into English in two collections of Salwa Bakr's short stories: *The Wiles of Men,* trans. Denys Johnson-Davies (Cairo: American University in Cairo Press, 1997) and *Such a Beautiful Voice,* trans. Hoda El-Sadda.

9. Salwa Bakr, "Loony Nuna," in *Such a Beautiful Voice,* 56–57.

10. Ferial Ghazoul, "Balaghat al-ghalaba (The Rhetoric/Eloquence of the Downtrodden)" (paper presented at "Women and Contemporary Arab Thought," Second International Conference of the Arab Women's Solidarity Association, November 3–5, 1988, Cairo).

11. Interview with the author, 27 May 1997.

12. Bakr, "Loony Nuna," 53.

13. Interview with the author, May 27, 1997.

14. Caroline Seymour-Jorn has argued that this view of the poor characterizes all her work. In a discussion of Bakr's use of language, based on interviews with the writer, she notes, "She argues that poor women, whose horizons, social contacts and daily activities are limited by harsh economic and social realities, experience time in a cyclical manner. These women, she feels, spend the vast majority of their time performing mundane household tasks or working at menial jobs, and experience their lives as a series of repeated, mundane and unfulfilling activities." Caroline Seymour-Jorn, "A New Language: Salwa Bakr on Depicting Egyptian Women's Worlds," *Critique: Critical Middle Eastern Studies* 12, no. 2 (2002): 151–76.

15. L. Abu-Lughod, "The Marriage of Feminism and Islamism."

16. Bakr, *The Wiles of Men,* 97–104.

17. Discussed in Elsheikh, *Mass Media and Ideological Change in Egypt (1950–1973).* This study, based on questionnaires administered in 1972–73, concluded that television, which at the time did not reach the majority of the population living outside Cairo, had little effect in promoting understandings of socialism among the illiterate or "the lower echelons of literates."

18. Safi Naz Kazim, "Nuna al-sha'nuna: bayn 'al-fann' wa 'al-fijj'!" [Nutty Nuna: Between "art" and "crudeness"], *Al-Hilal,* June 1996, pp. 144–149. I am grateful to Reem Saad for sharing this article with me.

19. I am grateful to Walter Armbrust for pointing out the conventions of this narrative trope in film; many serials discussed in this book also associate morality with the educated middle and even upper classes, especially those written by progressives inspired by the ideals of the 1950s and 1960s, as my discussions of *The White Flag* and *Hilmiyya Nights* should have

made clear. See Armbrust, *Mass Culture and Modernism in Egypt;* and Gordon, *Revolutionary Melodrama,* for excellent discussions of class, education, and morality in Egyptian film.

20. Gayatri Chakravorty Spivak, "Cultural Talks in the Hot Peace: Revisiting the 'Global Village,'" in *Cosmopolitics,* ed. Pheng Cheah and Bruce Robbins (Minneapolis: University of Minnesota Press, 1998), 329–48.

21. The Public Information Agency Center for Media, Education and Communication, "Mu'shirat sari'a awwaliyya nahw musalsal 'wa ma zala al-nil yajri'" [Quick initial findings about the serial *And the Nile Flows On*] (Cairo: Al-hay'a al-'amma li-l-isti'lamat, markaz al-i'lam wa al-ta'lim wa al-ittisal [The Public Information Agency Center for Media, Education and Communication], 1992). Unpublished report.

22. Ibid., 8.

23. Carol Underwood, Louise F. Kemprecos, Bushra Jabre, and Muhamed Wafai, "*And the Nile Flows On:* The Impact of a Serial Drama in Egypt," Johns Hopkins Center for Communication Programs Project Report (May 1994), 14. Two other useful sources on media and family planning are Sawsan El-Bakly and Ronald Hess, "Mass Media Makes a Difference," *Integration* 41 (September 1994), 13–15; and Ali, *Planning the Family in Egypt.*

24. Interview with In'am Muhammad 'Ali by Khalid Hanafi, "Nuna al-sha'nuna: Majnuna bi-al-ma'rifa" [Nutty Nuna: crazy about knowledge], *Al-Idha'a wa al-tilifizyun* [Radio and television magazine], July 15, 1995, pp. 42–43.

25. L. Abu-Lughod, "The Marriage of Feminism and Islamism."

26. Interview with the author, June 25, 1993. See also my discussion of women television writers, including Khayri, in chapter 5 and in "The Marriage of Feminism and Islamism in Egypt." For a discussion of this serial, directed by In'am Muhammad 'Ali and written by a number of progressive men and women, including Wafiyya Khayri, see Ivlin Riyad, "Mashakil al-mar'a al-'amila wa sitt al-bayt wa muhawalat li-halliha" [Problems of the working woman and the housewife and attempts to solve them], *Akhar Sa'a,* January 7, 1970, p. 27.

27. Interview with the author, 27 May 1997.

28. Because of the complex nature of researching national media and my decision to concentrate on village ethnography, I have had to rely on interviews and conversations with the domestic servants. I was unable to do proper fieldwork in the communities in which they lived, though I am familiar with such neighborhoods. I hope from their own words to have conveyed a great deal about such neighborhoods and lives, but readers who want a richer sense of the various types of communities such women came from should consult accounts by other anthropologists who have worked with poor and working women in various Cairo neighborhoods. A sample would include Evelyn Early, *Baladi Women of Cairo: Playing with an Egg and a Stone* (Boulder, CO: Lynne Reinner Publishers, 1993); Homa Hoodfar, *Between Marriage and the Market: Intimate Politics and Survival in Cairo* (Berkeley and Los Angeles: University of California Press, 1997); Farha Ghannam, *Remaking the Modern: Space, Relocation, and the Politics of Identity in a Global Cairo* (Berkeley and Los Angeles: University of California Press, 2002); Heba Aziz El-Kholy, *Defiance and Compliance: Negotiating Gender in Low-Income Cairo* (New York: Berghahn Books, 2002); Petra Kuppinger, "Cracks in the Cityscape: Traditional Spatial Practices and the Official Discourse on 'Informality' and Irhab (Islamic Terrorism)," in *Muslim Traditions and Modern Techniques of Power,* ed. Armando Salvatore, *Yearbook of the Sociology of Islam,* ed. Helmut Buchholt and Georg Stauth (Munster: Lit, 2001), 3:185–207; Sawsan El-Messiri, *Ibn al-Balad: A Concept of Egyptian Identity* (Leiden: Brill, 1978); Helen Watson, *Women in the City of the Dead* (London: Hurst & Company, 1992); and Unni Wikan, *Life among the Poor in Cairo* (London: Tavistock Publications, 1980). Unfortunately, I also interviewed or watched television with such women mostly in the homes of their employers, in-

cluding my own. This admittedly less-than-ideal method no doubt colored their responses, making them perhaps less critical of authorities and more oriented toward trying to generate sympathy. It is hard, however, to gauge this, and the consistency of some of their attitudes makes me more confident than I would otherwise be that I have captured some more general trends.

29. For an amusing account of his impromptu appearance on this show, see Joel Gordon, "Becoming the Image: *Words of Gold,* Talk Television, and Ramadan Nights on the Little Screen," *Visual Anthropology* 10 (1998): 247–63. For more on Tariq 'Allam and the program discussed in this chapter, see Joel Gordon, "Golden Boy Turns Bête Noire: Crossing Boundaries of Unscripted Television in Egypt," *Journal of Middle East and North African Intellectual and Cultural Studies* 1 (2001): 1–18.

30. Gordon, "Golden Boy," reports that the show's host believed that it was this criticism that was behind the show's cancellation after only nine episodes.

31. For an analysis that links Oprah's popularity to suffering, see Eva Illouz, *Oprah Winfrey and the Glamour of Misery: An Essay on Popular Culture* (New York: Columbia University Press, 2003).

32. It is interesting that Tariq 'Allam went on to try his luck as a film actor and was prevented from continuing this program. *Who Is to Blame?* can be compared to the 1990s Bolivian show *The Open Tribunal,* described by Jeff Himpele in "Arrival Scenes: Complicity and Media Ethnography in the Bolivian Public Sphere," in *Media Worlds: Anthropology on New Terrain,* ed. Faye Ginsburg, Lila Abu-Lughod, and Brian Larkin (Berkeley and Los Angeles: University of California Press, 2002), 301–16. That show's host, Carlos Palenque, went on to found an oppositional political party. The same sort of authoritative moral commentary on family situations seems to have been part of the first Indian television serial, *Hum Log,* which Das describes in "On Soap Opera."

33. According to Gordon, "Golden Boy," the show's host said her program was taken off the air because she refused to include authorities as commentators. This confirms my argument that the role of educated authorities is considered extremely important in television.

34. Bouthayna Kamel, "Night Confessions: Social Boundaries of Talk Radio" (paper presented at the Middle East Studies Association Annual Meeting, Washington, DC, 1999). *Confrontation* was discussed in chapters 2 and 3. According to one young woman in Upper Egypt, it went off the air because one of the anchors was beaten up by a criminal's associate. I have not been able to confirm this.

35. I am grateful to Faye Ginsburg for the connection to "compassion spectacles."

36. My own position as the listener to their stories might have affected these women's tendency to resort to complaint, as they might also have hoped to elicit sympathy and resources from me.

37. It is especially interesting to consider her expectations and experience in light of the promotional video on proper counseling in family planning clinics described by Kamran Asdar Ali, an advertisement he sees as linked to the individualization of women clients and the confirmation of the authority of counselors. "Faulty Deployments: Persuading Women and Constructing Choice in Egypt," *Comparative Studies in Society and History* 44, no. 2 (2002), 370–92; quotation is from pp. 375–76.

38. Hoodfar, *Between Marriage and the Market,* has good examples. Armbrust, *Mass Culture and Modernism in Egypt,* has statistics and believes this failure of the educational system has led to disillusionment and the embrace of new commercial cinema that scoffs at developmentalist ideals.

39. Armbrust, *Mass Culture and Modernism in Egypt.*

40. As I discuss in chapter 8, this incident of the so-called Satan worshippers was incorporated into the plot of a serial.

41. For more on women and Islamism from an anthropological perspective, see Fadwa El Guindi, *Veil: Modesty, Privacy, and Resistance* (Oxford: Berg, 1999); Saba Mahmood, *Politics and Piety: The Islamic Revival and the Feminist Subject* (Princeton, NJ: Princeton University Press, 2004); Saba Mahmood, "Feminist Theory, Embodiment, and the Docile Agent: Some Reflections on the Egyptian Islamic Revival," *Cultural Anthropology* 16 (2001): 202–36; Saba Mahmood, "Rehearsing Spontaneity and the Conventionality of Ritual: Disciplines of Salat," *American Anthropologist* 8 (2001): 827–53; and Al-Ali, *Secularism, Gender and the State in the Middle East*. See also Sherifa Zuhur, *Revealing Reveiling: Islamist Gender Ideology in Contemporary Egypt* (Albany: State University of New York Press, 1992); Elizabeth Fernea, *In Search of Islamic Feminism: One Woman's Global Journey* (New York: Doubleday, 1998); Arlene MacLeod, *Accommodating Protest: Working Women, the New Veiling, and Change in Cairo* (New York: Columbia University Press, 1991); and Ghada Talhami, *The Mobilization of Muslim Women in Egypt* (Gainesville: University Press of Florida, 1996). Also useful for an articulation of an independent Islamic feminist's position is Heba Raouf, "The Silent Ayesha: An Egyptian Narrative," in *Globalization, Gender and Religion: The Politics of Women's Rights in Catholic and Muslim Contexts,* eds. Jane H. Bayes and Nayereh Tohidi (New York: Palgrave, 2001), 231–57; and Karim El-Gawhary, "An Interview with Heba Ra'uf Ezzat," in *Women and Power in the Middle East,* ed. Suad Joseph and Susan Slyomovics (Philadelphia: University of Pennsylvania Press 2001), 99–102.

42. Mahmood, "Feminist Theory, Embodiment, and the Docile Agent" and "Rehearsing Spontaneity and the Conventionality of Ritual."

43. Mahmud Fawzi, *'Umar 'Abd al-Kafi . . . wa fatawa sakhina . . . fi al-din wa al-siyasa wa al-fann!* ['Umar 'Abd al-Kafi and hot fatwas on religion, politics, and art!] (Cairo: Al-jadawi li-l-nashr, 1993), 57. I want to thank Farha Ghannam for bringing this text to my attention.

44. Ali, "Faulty Deployments," 388.

45. Radwan, *Dawr al-drama al-tilifizyuniyya fi tashkil wa'i al-mar'a* [The role of television drama in forming women's consciousness/awareness].

46. Ibid., 241.

47. Ibid., 163.

48. Ibid., 253–56.

49. Ibid., 322–27.

CHAPTER FIVE

1. I am grateful to Reem Saad for sharing with me an audiocassette of the performance. The participants included Khaled Montasser, Akmal Safwat, and Khaled Fahmy.

2. Peter Brooks, *The Melodramatic Imagination: Balzac, Henry James, Melodrama, and the Mode of Excess* (New Haven, CT: Yale University Press, 1976).

3. Ibid., 15.

4. Ibid., 21.

5. Das, "On Soap Opera"; Ranggasamy Karthigesu, "Television as a Tool for Nation-Building in the Third World," in *Television and Its Audience,* ed. Phillip Drummond and Richard Paterson (London: British Film Institute, 1988), 306–26; Mankekar, "National Texts and Gendered Lives"; and Purnima Mankekar, "Television Tales and a Woman's Rage," *Public Culture* 5 (1993): 469–92 and her later book, *Screening Culture, Viewing Politics.*

6. Russell Merritt, "Melodrama: Postmortem for a Phantom Genre," *Wide Angle* 5 (1983): 25–31. See also Christine Gledhill, ed. *Melodrama: Stage, Picture, Screen* (London: British Film Institute, 1994).

7. Allen, *To Be Continued . . .* , 21.

8. Ana Lopez, in "Our Welcomed Guests: Telenovelas in Latin America," in *To Be Continued . . . Soap Operas around the World,* ed. Robert C. Allen (New York: Routledge, 1995), 261, notes that the Mexican *telenovelas* are stereotypically more weepy. Clearly the Egyptian serials are less sophisticated, glossy, and sexually charged than the Brazilian *telenovelas,* but even these have something in common: in Egypt, as in Brazil, many television writers are serious and progressive. For Brazil see Alma Guillermoprieto, "Letter from Brazil: Obsessed in Rio," *New Yorker,* August 16, 1993, 44–55. As this book was going to press, a new study of Brazilian telenovelas came to my attention. See Thaïs Machado-Borges, *Only for You! Brazilians and Telenovela Flow* (Stockholm: Stockholm Studies in Social Anthropology, 2003).

9. See Asad, *Genealogies of Religion,* for a discussion of the idea that secularism, and the notion of religion it implies, is a concept that developed as part of the history of Christianity in the West. For his later examination of secularism, including work on Egypt, see Talal Asad, *Formations of the Secular: Christianity, Islam, Modernity* (Stanford, CA: Stanford University Press, 2003).

10. Michel Foucault, "Technologies of the Self," in *Technologies of the Self,* ed. L. Martin, H. Gutman, and P. Hutton (Amherst: University of Massachusetts Press, 1988), 16–49, and "About the Beginning of the Hermeneutics of the Self," *Political Theory* 21 (1993): 198–227.

11. See Toby Miller, *The Well-Tempered Self* (Baltimore: Johns Hopkins University Press, 1993), for an analysis that links modern forms of subjectivity—the individual as consumer and as citizen—to mass-mediated cultural forms.

12. Veena Das, "The Making of Modernity: Gender and Time in Indian Cinema," in *Questions of Modernity,* ed. Timothy Mitchell (Minneapolis: University of Minnesota Press, 2000), 166–88.

13. Sheila Petty, "*Miseria:* The Evolution of a Unique Melodramatic Form," *Passages: A Chronicle of the Humanities* 8 (1994): 19–20; and Paul Willemen, "Negotiating the Transition to Capitalism: The Case of Andaz," in *Melodrama and Asian Cinema,* ed. Wimal Dissanayake (Cambridge: Cambridge University Press, 1993), 179–88.

14. While no television serial can simply be attributed to the writer as author, since it involves so many stages and so many personnel—from those in the television administration, including the censors, to those directly involved in production, including the director, other scriptwriters, and the actors—there is in Egypt a certain integrity to the texts of well-known writers. When they feel excessive censorship or radical changes endanger their text, they protest publicly and sometimes even withdraw their texts. The most respected writers, like 'Ukasha, are closely involved in all aspects of production. Writers with less clout and standing lose control to the director and others. In most cases, though, the germ of the plot and the themes are retained, and so I will, in the discussion that follows, treat the serials as if they were the works of authors. On a comparative note, Guillermoprieto, "Letter from Brazil," 49, notes that in Brazil authors are believed to be "the soul and essence of a telenovela," and Lopez, "Our Welcomed Guests," 60–61, extends this to all Latin American contexts. Esther Hamburger, however, makes a much more complex argument that recognizes the importance of scriptwriters, especially leftists, in creating telenovelas but also appreciates the interplay between them and the producers, who rely on audience research to affect the course of a storyline as it is being produced. However, Egypt is different because its television is not commercial and its serials are neither long running nor affected by audience research. See Esther

Hamburger, "Politics and Intimacy in Brazilian Telenovelas" (Ph.D. diss., University of Chicago, 1999).

15. Interview with the author, June 25, 1993.

16. See Armbrust, *Mass Culture and Modernism in Egypt.*

17. Interview with the author, June 17, 1993. This film, although produced by the Egyptian Radio and Television Union, was eventually released in theaters rather than broadcast on television. It was enthusiastically received, especially by youth, who had never experienced Nasser. For a good analysis of *Nasser 56,* see Joel Gordon, "Nasser 56/Cairo 96: Reimaging Egypt's Lost Community," in *Mass Mediations: New Approaches to the Middle East in Popular Culture and Beyond,* ed. Walter Armbrust (Berkeley and Los Angeles: University of California Press, 2000), 161–81.

18. The differences are reflected even in the aesthetics or styles of the melodramas. 'Ukasha's serials, like those of Khayri and many other progressive writers, strive for realism, a style associated with socialism or the socially concerned. The moral universe, they suggest, lies within the lives of ordinary people. Some of Abaza's serials are striking for their exaggerated tones and lack of naturalism.

19. The secularity of the state is a complex question, of course. I say "ambivalently secular," because Islam and Christianity are still considered valid and important aspects of personal life and identity, even of public officials, and even beyond. Although the relevance of religion to state policy and law may have been minimized in the twentieth century, especially during the Nasser period, it is still given a role to play—one that, as I will argue in chapter 7, is increasing. For example, part of the religious establishment ratifies government policies, and others can make trouble; and family law continues to be Islamic. See Partha Chatterjee, "Religious Minorities and the Secular State: Reflections on an Indian Impasse," *Public Culture* 8 (1995): 11–39, for an argument that secularism is a Western concept that sits uneasily in other places, like India. On the exclusion of Islamists from Egyptian television, see L. Abu-Lughod, "Finding a Place for Islam" and "Dramatic Reversals," the latter in *Political Islam: Essays from Middle East Report,* ed. Joel Beinin and Joe Stork (Berkeley and Los Angeles: University of California Press, 1997), 269–82.

20. Jane Feuer, "Melodrama, Serial Form and Television Today," *Screen* 25 (1984): 4–16.

21. Brooks, *The Melodramatic Imagination.*

22. Ien Ang, "Melodramatic Identifications: Television Fiction and Women's Fantasy," in *Television and Women's Culture: The Politics of the Popular,* ed. Mary Ellen Brown (London: Sage, 1990), 75–88; quotation is from p. 81.

23. My own hunch is that they do offer alternative models of the acceptability of emotional expression—especially of sadness or misery—to women and men like those I knew in the Awlad 'Ali community, where public expression of these was culturally restricted. See L. Abu-Lughod, *Veiled Sentiments.*

24. Feminist critics have done for television soap opera what Brooks did for literary melodrama—forced a reevaluation of a genre dismissed as pap—as well as developed some critical ideas about female pleasure through its serious analysis. The feminist literature on soap opera is extensive, and much of it quite good. Some key texts are Robert C. Allen, *Speaking of Soap Opera* (Chapel Hill: University of North Carolina Press, 1985); Ien Ang, *Watching "Dallas": Soap Opera and the Melodramatic Imagination* (London: Methuen, 1985); Ang, "Melodramatic Identifications"; Charlotte Brunsdon, "The Role of Soap Opera in the Development of Feminist Television Scholarship," in *To Be Continued,* ed. Allen, 49–55; Charlotte Brunsdon, *Screen Tastes: Soap Opera to Satellite Dishes* (London: Routledge, 1997); Feuer, "Melodrama, Serial Form and Television Today"; Christine Geraghty, *Women and Soap Opera: A*

Study of Prime-Time Soaps (Cambridge: Polity Press, 1991); Lynne Joyrich, "All That Television Allows: TV Melodrama, Postmodernism, and Consumer Culture," in *Private Screenings: Television and the Female Consumer,* ed. Lynne Spigel and Denise Mann (Minneapolis: University of Minnesota Press, 1992), 227–51; Tanya Modleski, *Loving With a Vengeance: Mass Produced Fantasies for Women* (Hamden, CT: Archon Books, 1982); Laura Mulvey, "Melodrama in and out of the Home," in *High Theory/Low Culture,* ed. Colin McCabe (Manchester: Manchester University Press, 1986), 80–100; Laura Stempel Mumford, *Love and Ideology in the Afternoon* (Bloomington: Indiana University Press, 1995); and Seiter et al., *Remote Control.* Allen's edited collection on the global reception of soap opera, *To Be Continued . . . ,* is also an excellent resource.

25. See Catherine Lutz, "Emotion, Thought, and Estrangement: Emotion as a Cultural Category," *Cultural Anthropology* 1 (1986): 405–36.

26. Tanya Modleski, "The Rhythms of Reception: Daytime Television and Women's Work," in *Regarding Television,* ed. E. Ann Kaplan, American Film Institute Monograph (Frederick, MD: University Publications of America, 1983), 67–75.

27. Raymond Williams, "Drama in a Dramatised Society," in *Raymond Williams and Television,* ed. A. O'Connor (London and New York: Routledge, 1989), 2–13.

28. For critiques along these lines, see Lila Abu-Lughod, "Shifting Politics in Bedouin Love Poetry," in *Language and the Politics of Emotion,* ed. Lila Abu-Lughod and Catherine Lutz (Cambridge: Cambridge University Press, 1990), 24–45; and Lila Abu-Lughod and Catherine Lutz, "Introduction: Emotion, Discourse, and the Politics of Everyday Life," in *Language and the Politics of Emotion,* 1–23.

29. For a nice elaboration, using the example of the portrayal of the widow in the Bengali novel, see Dipesh Chakrabarty, "Witness to Suffering: Domestic Cruelty and the Birth of the Modern Subject in Bengal," in *Questions of Modernity,* ed. Timothy Mitchell (Minneapolis: University of Minnesota Press, 2000), 49–86.

30. Michel Foucault, *The History of Sexuality,* vol. 2, trans. R. Hurley (New York: Random House, 1985), "Technologies of the Self," and "About the Beginning of the Hermeneutics of the Self."

31. L. Abu-Lughod, "Shifting Politics in Bedouin Love Poetry."

32. Ann Cvetkovich, *Mixed Feelings: Feminism, Mass Culture, and Victorian Sensationalism* (New Brunswick, NJ: Rutgers University Press, 1992), 6.

33. Serious contributions to our understanding of modernist cinema in Egypt include Armbrust, *Mass Culture and Modernism in Egypt;* Gordon, *Revolutionary Melodrama;* and Viola Shafik, *Arab Cinema: History and Cultural Identity* (Cairo: American University in Cairo Press, 1998). Lizbeth Malkmus and Roy Armes, in *Arab and African Film Making* (London: Zed Books, 1991), also give some background. The background of Muhammad Fadil, Egypt's preeminent television director, hints at the kinds of influences on those in mass media. He describes having been exposed to theatre in university and having pursued his interests through extensive reading not only at the public library in Alexandria but at the United States Information Library (interview with the author, June 17, 1993). Many television writers have backgrounds in literature. For general background on radio and television in Egypt, see CEDEJ, "Anciens et nouveaux médias en Egypte."

34. Dwight Reynolds, *Heroic Poets, Poetic Heroes: The Ethnography of Performance in an Arabic Oral Epic Tradition* (Ithaca, NY: Cornell University Press, 1995); Susan Slyomovics, *The Merchant of Art* (Berkeley and Los Angeles: University of California Press, 1986). My experience has been that many men and women in their sixties, at least in the Awlad 'Ali Bedouin community in Egypt's Western Desert, where I have spent the most time, can recite verses.

Men of the next generation who grew up in cities around the Arab world have boyhood memories of listening to traveling poets reciting the tale in the coffee shops.

35. Susan Slyomovics, "Praise of God, Praise of Self, Praise of the Islamic People: Arab Epic Narrative in Performance," in *Classical and Popular Medieval Arabic Literature: A Marriage of Convenience,* ed. Jareer Abu-Haidar and Farida Abu-Haidar (London: Curzon Press, 2004).

36. Susan Slyomovics, "The Death-Song of 'Amir Khafaji: Puns in an Oral and Printed Episode of Sirat Bani Hilal," *Journal of Arabic Literature* 18 (1987): 62–78. Dwight Reynolds argues that punning is actually quite rare in most Egyptian poets' recitations of the epic (personal communication).

37. See Reynolds, *Heroic Poets, Poetic Heroes,* 180–83.

38. All translations from Susan Slyomovics, "The Epic of the Bani Hilal: The Birth of Abu Zayd. II (Southern Egypt)," in *Oral Epics from Africa: Vibrant Voices from a Vast Continent,* ed. John William Johnson, Thomas A. Hale, and Stephen Belcher (Bloomington: Indiana University Press, 1997), 240–51.

39. *The Epic of the Bani Hilal,* trans. Dwight F. Reynolds (forthcoming).

40. Ibid.

41. As Foucault put it,

The disciplines mark the moment when the reversal of the political axis of individualization—as one might call it—takes place. In certain societies. . . . it may be said that individualization is greatest where sovereignty is exercised and in the highest echelons of power. The more one possesses power or privilege, the more one is marked as an individual, by rituals, written accounts or visual reproductions. The "name" and the genealogy that situate one within a kinship group, the performance of deeds that demonstrate superior strength and which are immortalized in literary accounts. . . . all these are procedures of an "ascending" individualization. In a disciplinary regime, on the other hand, individualization is "descending": as power becomes more anonymous and more functional, those on whom it is exercised tend to be more strongly individualized.

Michel Foucault, *Discipline and Punish,* trans. Alan Sheridan (New York: Random House, 1978), 192–93.

42. It could be argued that the interiority of the domestic scenes of soap opera is a metaphor of the inner life of the persons around which their plots revolve. Thomas Elsaesser, in his classic article on cinematic melodrama, "Tales of Sound and Fury: Observations on the Family Melodrama," has suggested in fact that "the space of the home" does relate "to the inside space of human interiority, emotions, and the unconscious." Cited in Laura Mulvey, "Melodrama in and out of the Home," 95.

43. L. Abu-Lughod, *Veiled Sentiments.*

44. See Lila Abu-Lughod, "Islam and the Gendered Discourses of Death," *International Journal of Middle East Studies* 25 (1993): 187–205 for a discussion of some of the literature on lamentation.

45. Wickett, "'For Our Destinies,'" 166.

46. The televised version of the Hilali epic was preceded by a revival through commercial audiocassettes for mass consumption, thanks to the Upper Egyptian writer 'Abd al-Rahman al-Abnudi. Listened to in Cairo as well as back in the Upper Egyptian villages where people had enjoyed poets' performances at weddings, it has taken on a new and different life, entering a cultural field where it can be deployed as a marker of the Egyptian "heritage" as well as a source

of regional pride. Similarly, in the Western Desert, the Awlad 'Ali *ghinnaawa* has moved out of its context of the wedding and the oral recitation onto the commercial cassette, in the process excluding women reciters and being turned into a nostalgic form that marks regional or ethnic identity and an acceptable medium for the rebellion of young men against their elders. See L. Abu-Lughod, "Shifting Politics of Bedouin Love Poetry."

47. Ruth Behar, "Rage and Redemption: Reading the Life Story of a Mexican Marketing Woman," *Feminist Studies* 16 (1990): 223–58; and Laurel Kendall, *The Life and Hard Times of a Korean Shaman* (Honolulu: University of Hawaii Press, 1988). As this book was going to press, a new study of melodrama and women's lives came to my attention. For an intriguing analysis of soap opera and narratives of class mobility in Korea, see Nancy Abelmann, *The Melodrama of Mobility: Women, Talk, and Class in Contemporary South Korea* (Honolulu: University of Hawaii Press, 2003).

48. One could, of course, ask what the social effects of this discursive self-presentation were intended to be—especially for a poor domestic worker telling the tale to a wealthier foreigner. Certainly Amira wanted sympathy and might have wanted to present herself as wronged and in need of support. The story, as I noted above, flowed easily and sounded well rehearsed, as are many of the stories people tell about themselves and others in cultures where storytelling is so important. And one could also ask about the personal or psychological functions, for the socially marginal Amira, of telling her own story in this melodramatic form—a form that I have suggested owes so much to television and radio, with their stars and glamour. And one could ask whether we are not hearing here some of the language of complaint I described in chapter 4 as the effect of being patronized.

49. See Dipesh Chakrabarty, "Witness to Suffering" and "The Difference-Deferral of a Colonial Modernity: Public Debates on Domesticity in British Bengal," the latter in *Subaltern Studies VIII*, ed. David Arnold and David Hardiman (Delhi: Oxford University Press, 1994), 50–88, reprinted in *Tensions of Empire: Colonial Cultures in a Bourgeois World*, ed. Frederick Cooper and Ann Laura Stoler (Berkeley and Los Angeles: University of California Press, 1997), 373–405. For other ways of thinking about alternative modernities, see Appadurai, *Modernity at Large.* For a critique of some theories of alternative modernities, see Timothy Mitchell, "The Stage of Modernity," in *Questions of Modernity*, ed. Timothy Mitchell (Minneapolis: University of Minnesota Press, 2000), 1–34.

50. Willy Jansen has written about the special vulnerabilities and freedoms of women living without men in her study of the various occupations of such women in Algeria. Willy Jansen, *Women without Men: Gender and Marginality in an Algerian Town* (Leiden: E. J. Brill, 1987).

51. For the opposition between television and religion, see my "Dramatic Reversals" and "Finding a Place for Islam" as well as chapter 7.

52. Women cannot pray or fast while menstruating because they are not in a state of purity.

53. For an excellent analysis of the self-cultivation encouraged in women in the piety movement in Egypt, see Mahmood, *Politics of Piety.*

54. Slyomovics, "Praise of God, Praise of Self, Praise of the Islamic People."

55. James Peacock, *The Rites of Modernization* (Chicago: University of Chicago Press, 1966). The weakest chapter is the one in which he examines *ludruk* (the form of drama) in terms of Marion Levy Jr.'s *Modernization and the Structure of Societies* (Princeton, NJ: Princeton University Press, 1966).

56. Muna Hilmi, "Al-jari' wa al-jamila: musalsal bi-dun 'uqad dhukuriyya" [*The Bold and the Beautiful:* A serial without male complexes], *Sabah al-Khayr,* February 11, 1993, p. 59.

57. The censor defended the serial, saying, "The serial carries general human values and debates that are not place-specific; they are close to many of the problems of Eastern society." Dalal 'Abd al-Fatah, "Hadhafna mashhad al-ightisab" [We cut the rape scene], *Ruz al-Yusuf,* January 18, 1993, p. 10.

CHAPTER SIX

1. Many studies have confirmed this growing gap. For summaries of these findings and references to the political economic literature, see Janet Abu-Lughod, "Cairo: Too Many People, Not Enough Land, Too Few Resources," in *World Cities beyond the West,* ed. Josef Gugler (Cambridge: Cambridge University Press, 2004), 258–313; and Mitchell, *Rule of Experts.*

2. This phenomenon has been the subject of a good deal of scholarly and popular literature. The literature is too huge to reference here, but I can mention a few important works by anthropologists: Gregory Starrett, *Putting Islam to Work: Education, Politics and Religious Transformation in Egypt* (Berkeley and Lost Angeles: University of California Press, 1998) and "Political Economy of Religious Commodities in Cairo," *American Anthropologist* 91 (1995): 8–13; Charles Hirschkind, "Civic Virtue and Religious Reason: An Islamic Counterpublic," *Cultural Anthropology* 16 (2001): 3–34; and Mahmood, "Feminist Theory, Embodiment, and the Docile Agent" and "Rehearsing Spontaneity and the Conventionality of the Ritual."

3. Appadurai, *Modernity at Large,* 14.

4. For excellent discussions of Egyptian cinema, with which television serials have both continuities and differences, see Armbrust, *Mass Culture and Modernism in Egypt;* Gordon, *Revolutionary Melodrama;* and Shafik, *Arab Cinema.* Walter Armbrust demonstrates strong continuities in the issues, especially about leisure and consumption, dealt with by print media and cinema in "Bourgeois Leisure and Egyptian Media Fantasies," in *New Media in the Muslim World,* ed. Dale Eickelman and Jon Anderson (Bloomington: Indiana University Press, 1999), 106–32.

5. Other idiomatic equivalents might be "I won't live my father's way" or "I won't follow in my father's footsteps." In a previously published version of this chapter, I used the translation "I won't live in my father's shadow." Lila Abu-Lughod, "Asserting the Local as National in the Face of the Global: The Ambivalence of Authenticity in Egyptian Soap Opera," in *Localizing Knowledge in a Globalizing World: Recasting the Area Studies Debate,* ed. Ali Mirsepassi, Amrita Basu, and Fred Weaver (Syracuse, NY: Syracuse University Press 2003), 101–27.

6. The scriptwriter, Mustafa Muharram, said that although the serial is based on a short story by the writer Ihsan 'Abd al-Quddus, influential editor of *Ruz al-Yusuf* in the 1950s and writer of many stories turned into films, he had invented the whole rags-to-riches story of 'Abd al-Ghafur, whom he had asked Nur al-Sharif to play. He picked up the short story's actual theme—about a young man and his marriage to a foreigner who converts to Islam— only in episode 21. Telephone interview with the author, May 1997. For more on Ihsan 'Abd al-Quddus, see Gordon, *Revolutionary Melodrama.*

7. There is a good literature on the complex subject of *ibn al-balad.* The classic work is El-Messiri, *Ibn al-Balad.* Walter Armbrust has explored the use of this figure in mass culture, especially cinema, in *Mass Culture and Modernism in Egypt.* A subtle discussion can be found in Marilyn Booth, *Bayram al-Tunisi's Egypt: Social Criticism and Narrative Strategies* (Oxford: Ithaca Press, 1990).

8. Interview with the author, May 1997.

9. Gordon discusses the 1964 film *Palace Walk,* directed by Hasan al-Imam and often

shown on television, and offers some references to studies of Naguib Mahfouz's relationship to cinema and television in *Revolutionary Melodrama*, 81–82, 93–94. Soraya Altorki discusses the patriarchy represented by Al-Sayyid Ahmad in "Patriarchy and Imperialism: Father-Son and British-Egyptian Relations in Najib Mahfuz's Trilogy," in *Intimate Selving in Arab Families*, ed. Suad Joseph (Syracuse, NY: Syracuse University Press, 1999), 214–34.

10. Naguib Mahfouz, *Palace Walk*, trans. William M. Hutchins and Olive E. Kenny (New York: Doubleday, 1989 [1956]).

11. For nineteenth-century Egypt, see Judith Tucker, *Women in Nineteenth Century Egypt* (Cambridge: Cambridge University Press, 1985).

12. See essays in L. Abu-Lughod, ed., *Remaking Women*: Afsaneh Najmabadi, "Crafting an Educated Housewife in Iran," 91–125; Omnia Shakry, "Schooled Mothers and Structured Play: Child Rearing in Turn-of-the-Century Egypt," 126–70; Marilyn Booth, "The Egyptian Lives of Jeanne d'Arc," 171–211; and Lila Abu-Lughod, "The Marriage of Feminism and Islamism in Egypt: Selective Repudiation as a Dynamic of Postcolonial Cultural Politics," 243–69. See also Baron, *The Women's Awakening in Egypt*; and "The Making and Breaking of Marital Bonds in Modern Egypt," in *Women in Middle Eastern History*, ed. Nikki Keddie and Beth Baron, (New Haven, CT: Yale University Press, 1991), 275–91.

13. Armbrust, *Mass Culture and Modernism in Egypt*.

14. Diane Singerman, *Avenues of Participation: Family, Politics, and Networks in Urban Quarters of Cairo* (Princeton, NJ: Princeton University Press, 1995), 11.

15. Ibid., 14.

16. The ambiguities of using "the people" in nationalist fictions are explored for Latin America, and Venezuela in particular, by Julie Skursi, "The Ambiguities of Authenticity in Latin America: Dona Barbara and the Construction of National Identity," in *Becoming National: A Reader*, ed. Geoff Eley and Ronald Grigor Suny (New York: Oxford University Press, 1996), 371–402.

17. Amal Bakir, "Hiwar ma' Salah al-Sa'dani al-shahir bi 'Hasan al-Na'mani'" [Conversation with Salah al-Sa'dani famous as Hasan al-Na'mani], *Al-Ahram*, March 25, 1994, Friday Supplement, p. 2.

18. 'Ali al-Sayyid, "Dunyat al-arabisk" [The World of *Arabesque*], *Nusf al-Dunya*, March 20, 1994, pp. 74–77.

19. Mahmud al-Kardusi, "Al-'ashiq Hasan wa al-'ishq arabisk" [The lover is Hasan and the loved, *Arabesque*], *Nusf al-Dunya*, March 20, 1994, pp. 57–60.

20. Ibid., 58.

21. In contrast, the nostalgic *I Won't Live My Father's Life* scrupulously avoids the political (except to offer the obligatory swipe at Islamic militants; see chapter 7). One of the most amusing subplots is one in which 'Abdu suddenly seems to take an interest in politics—he is very concerned about a hijacked jumbo jet on the ground at Cairo Airport and what the government will do about it. Those around him are surprised at this uncharacteristic concern with national and international politics. But it turns out that behind his interest in the jumbo jet is an amazing business opportunity: he sees the airplane as a potentially profitable hulk of scrap metal for his trade. And when he becomes a national hero for purchasing the plane, he and his wife are only concerned to use the profit to make the pilgrimage to Mecca.

22. Ahmad 'Abd al-Mu'ati Hijazi, "Al-'A'ila wa arabisk" [*The Family* and *Arabesque*], *Al-Ahram*, April 13, 1994, p. 18.

23. For a discussion of this as a common metaphor, see Gabriel Piterberg, "The Tropes of Stagnation and Awakening in Nationalist Historical Consciousness: The Egyptian Case," in *Rethinking Nationalism in the Arab Middle East*, ed. James Jankowski and Israel Gershoni

(New York: Columbia University Press, 1997), 42–62. In using the imagery of a return to consciousness, the writer must also be invoking the famous book of the Sadat era by Tawfiq al-Hakim, '*Awdat al-waʿi* [Return of consciousness], 1st English ed. (New York: New York University Press, 1985), which sought to explain how Egyptians had fallen under the spell of Nasser and the 1952 revolution, a book whose title echoed his own earlier work, '*Awdat al-ruh* [Return of the spirit], 1st English ed. (Washington, DC: Three Continents Press, 1990), which asserted a deeply rooted Egyptian identity dating to the Pharaohs.

24. The alley is a resonant symbol of community and lower-class life in Egypt. To explain his successful depiction of ʿAbd al-Ghafur, the scriptwriter of *I Won't Live My Father's Life* pointed to his own upbringing in the alleys, in the neighborhood of Sayyida Zaynab in Cairo.

25. Laila Shukry El-Hamamsy, "The Assertion of Egyptian Identity," in *Ethnic Identity: Cultural Continuities and Change,* ed. George DeVos and Lola Romanucci-Ross, 2nd ed. (Chicago: University of Chicago Press, 1982), 276–306.

26. El-Messiri, *Ibn al-Balad,* cited in Beth Baron, "Nationalist Iconography: Egypt as a Woman," in *Rethinking Nationalism in the Arab Middle East,* ed. James Jankowski and Israel Gershoni (New York: Columbia University Press, 1997), 105–24; quotation is from pp. 115–16. Being an "effendi" meant being of the educated class and wearing Western clothes, among other things.

27. ʿIsmat Hamdi, "Awlad al-balad mazalim ʿala al-shasha" [The sons of the country are wronged on screen], *Al-Idhaʿa wa al-tilifizyun,* March 15, 1997, pp. 46–47.

28. Interview with Usama Anwar ʿUkasha, *Akhir Saʿa,* April 8, 1992, pp. 27–29; quotation is from p. 29. Naguib Mahfouz himself wrote many scripts for cinema and has had many novels adapted for film.

29. Al-Kardusi, "Al-ʿashiq Hasan wa al-ʿishq arabisk," 59.

30. Colla, "The Stuff of Egypt."

31. Interview with the author, March 10, 1997.

32. Al-Kardusi, "Al-ʿashiq Hasan wa al-ʿishq arabisk," 59.

33. Ibid., 60.

34. Interview with the author, March 10, 1997.

35. ʿAli Al-Sayyid, "Jamal ʿAbd al-Hamid: Hayati baqat arabisk khalis" [Jamal ʿAbd al-Hamid: My life became completely *Arabesque*], *Nusf al-Dunya,* March 20, 1994, p. 69. The dangers of a loss of roots in the embrace of the lifestyles of the decadent and nonpatriotic wealthy class is a very common trope in Egyptian literature, film, and now television, discussed at length in Armbrust, *Mass Culture and Modernism in Egypt.*

36. Akram al-Saʿdani, "Hasan Arabisk: sura 'a'iliyya ʿan qurb" [Hasan Arabesque: A close family portrait], *Sabah al-Khayr,* March 10, 1994, pp. 44–45.

37. I am grateful to Walter Armbrust for reminding me that this is a common pattern.

38. Al-Kardusi, "Al-ʿashiq Hasan wa al-ʿishq arabisk," 59.

39. El-Hamamsy, "The Assertion of Egyptian Identity," 304.

40. Interview with Yahya al-ʿAlami, May 27, 1997.

41. Interview in *Akhir Saʿa,* April 8, 1992, pp. 27–29.

42. Usama Anwar ʿUkasha, "Al-tilifizyun yarfaʿ al-masahif" [Television raises Qur'ans], *Ruz-al-Yusuf,* December 27, 1993, p. 68.

43. Interview with the author, March 10, 1997.

44. On the government position as expressed in the campaign to fight "extremism" with media, see chapter 7.

45. Majdi Muhanna, "Fi al-mamnuʿ" [Out of line], *Al-Wafd,* February 5, 1998, p. 9.

46. See Piterberg, "The Tropes of Stagnation and Awakening in Nationalist Historical Consciousness."

47. For a marvelous discussion of this film and its impact, see Gordon, "Nasser 56/Cairo 96," 161–81.

48. Interview with the author, June 17, 1993.

49. The most commonly known example of the global reach of a local national product is the export of U.S. soap operas and Hollywood films to the rest of the world. However, Mexican soap operas are popular in Russia, Lebanon, and New York City, and Brazil's Globo Television soap operas are watched in many countries around the world, including Cameroon. Egypt has been the major producer of Arabic films in the twentieth century and of Arabic-language television serials for more than thirty years, long exporting its programs to the Arab world and now, via satellite, to London and the United States. For discussions of satellite broadcasting in the Arab world, see Amin, "Egypt and the Arab World in the Satellite Age"; Boyd, *Broadcasting in the Arab World;* and Sakr, *Satellite Realms.* Many articles on contemporary media in Egypt, including satellite, can be found in the online journal *Transnational Broadcasting Studies,* http://www.tbsjournal.com. Anyone considering the significance of media has to assess the impact of this kind of traffic on local mass media industries; on local political, social, and cultural dynamics; and on individual subjectivities. This is apart from general concerns about media's possible roles in such processes as deterritorialization, modernity, and transnational civil society. For good discussions of these debates, see Sandra Braman and Annabelle Sreberny-Mohammadi, eds., *Globalization, Communication and Transnational Civil Society* (Cresskill, NJ: Hampton Press, 1996); and Tomlinson, *Globalization and Culture.*

50. There is a good literature on identity and global processes. Work by Hannerz and Appadurai is cited elsewhere; see also Jonathan Friedman, *Cultural Identity and Global Process* (London: Sage, 1994).

51. Saskia Sassen, "Cracked Casings: Notes toward an Analytics for Studying Transnational Processes," in *Sociology for the Twenty-First Century,* ed. Janet Abu-Lughod (Chicago: University of Chicago Press, 1999), 134–45; quotation is from p. 136.

52. For an example of this problem, television programs in Syria that glorify Old Damascus "exacerbate regional and sectarian tensions, provoking resentment and hostility rather than kinship and fraternity," according to Salamandra, "Moustache Hairs Lost," 227.

53. Hannerz, *Transnational Connections,* 89.

54. Interview with the author, March 10, 1997.

55. Joel Gordon similarly argues that the resuscitation not only of Nasser but also the pre-Nasser aristocracy and royalty in films and historical serials is part of a strategy for countering Islamism. See Gordon, "Nasser 56/Cairo 96."

CHAPTER SEVEN

1. Armando Salvatore, *Islam and the Political Discourse of Modernity* (Reading, UK: Ithaca Press, 1999); Armando Salvatore, ed., *Muslim Traditions and Modern Techniques of Power, Yearbook of the Sociology of Islam,* ed. Helmut Buchholt and Georg Stauth (Munster: Lit, 2001), vol. 3; and Starrett, *Putting Islam to Work.*

2. Asad's *Genealogies of Religion* and *Formations of the Secular* both offer thoughtful and unconventional reflections on secularism. A good source for the debates about secularism in India is Rajeev Bhargava, ed., *Secularism and Its Critics* (Delhi: Oxford University Press, 1998).

See also Chatterjee, "Religious Minorities and the Secular State"; Partha Chatterjee, "Secularism and Tolerance," in *Secularism and Its Critics,* ed. Rajeev Bhargava (Dehli: Oxford University Press, 1998), 345–79; Dipesh Chakrabarty, *Habitations of Modernity: Essays in the Wake of Subaltern Studies* (Chicago: University of Chicago Press, 2002); and Peter van der Veer, *Imperial Encounters: Religion and Modernity in India and Britain* (Princeton, NJ: Princeton University Press, 2001). Feminist writings on the uniform civil code made especially clear the special meanings and politics of secularism in India, quite different from its meanings and politics in Egypt and the Middle East. See Rajeswari Sunder Rajan, "Women Between Community and State: Some Implications of the Uniform Civil Code Debates in India," *Social Text* 65, vol. 18 (4) (winter 2000): 55–82; Kumkum Sangari, "Politics of Diversity: Religious Communities and Multiple Patriarchies" *Economic and Political Weekly,* 30, nos. 51 and 52, December 23 and 30, 1995.

3. Dale Eickelman and Jon Anderson, eds., *New Media in the Muslim World: The Emerging Public Sphere* (Bloomington: Indiana University Press, 1999). I will not be concerned, however, with the Islamic public sphere or the use of print and other media by Muslim organizations, even though this, too, is an important topic.

4. Timothy Mitchell, "McJihad: Islam in the U.S. Global Order," *Social Text* 73 (2002): 1–18.

5. For more on this, see L. Abu-Lughod, "Finding a Place for Islam." A few of the following paragraphs first appeared in that article.

6. For a review of the press concerning this serial, see the dossier in CEDEJ, "Renseignements égyptiens: Le héros, la pécheresse et l'agent double," *Revue de la presse égyptienne* 32/33, 2ème semestre (1988): 109–54.

7. Walter Armbrust similarly notes that none of the Islamist activity so prominent in Egyptian society in the 1980s found its way into cinema until the mid-1990s, with the release of 'Adil Imam's *The Terrorist,* even though scattered films since the 1960s had occasional scenes that mocked Islamists. Walter Armbrust, "Islamists in Egyptian Cinema" *American Anthropologist* 104, no. 3 (2002): 922–31.

8. Another part of the explanation, everyone is quick to add, is the constraints felt by private producers of television serials who must be able to sell dramas to Saudi Arabia and the wealthy Gulf states, where moral and political censorship is more restrictive. Chapter 8 considers the structure of the industry.

9. See L. Abu-Lughod, "Finding a Place for Islam" and "Dramatic Reversals."

10. 'Imad 'Abd al-Rahman, "Waqa'i' muhawalat ightiyal musalsal al-'a'ila" [The facts about the attempt to assassinate the serial *The Family*], *Akhbar al-Adab,* March 20, 1994, pp. 1, 5–7.

11. Sabir Shawkat, "Dajja fi kul bayt . . . wa al-sabab musalsal al-'a'ila" [Uproar in every home . . . and the reason is the serial *The Family*], *Akhbar al-Yawm,* 12 March 1994, p. 16.

12. Salah Mursi, "Al-sinima wa qadiyat al-watan" [Cinema and the case of the nation], *Al-Musawwar,* March 18, 1994, pp. 46–47.

13. Muhammad Ibrahim Mabruk, "Musalsal al-'a'ila . . . wa ish'al nar al-fitna bayn al-muslimin" [The serial *The Family* . . . and inflaming sedition among Muslims], *Al-Sha'b,* March 22, 1994, p. 9.

14. Muhammad al-Qudusi, "Musalsalat 'al-ajhiza' wa akhta' al-kitaba qabl itqan al-qira'a" [State serials and errors of writing before perfecting reading], *Al-Sha'b,* March 22, 1994, p. 9.

15. 'Imad 'Abd al-Rahman, "Waqa'i' muhawalat ightiyal musalsal al-'a'ila."

16. Ashraf bin 'Abd al-Maqsud bin 'Abd al-Rahim, *Musalsal al-'a'ila: Al-irhab al-fanni wa*

al-hujum 'ala al-Islam [The serial *The Family:* Artistic terrorism and the attack on Islam] (Cairo: Maktabat al-turath al-islami, 1994).

17. Eberhard Kienle describes the crackdowns in the 1990s on Islamists from within the religious establishment that paralleled the media campaign: first the 1996 law restricting independent mosques by requiring preachers to be authorized by the Ministry of Religious Affairs and then the 1998 dissolution by the rector of Al-Azhar (after investigation by the Ministry of Social Affairs) of the board of an increasingly conservative and Islamist association of scholars called the Front of the Scholars of al-Azhar (jabhat 'ulama al-Azhar). Kienle, *A Grand Delusion,* 104–5, 113–14.

18. Kienle describes the increasing power, especially in the 1980s, of the Academy of Islamic Research at Al-Azhar, which since 1961 had been legally authorized to "follow" publications concerning "Islam and its heritage." Ibid., 109–10.

19. "Al-'a'ila fi hiwar bayn wazir al-i'lam wa al-imam al-akbar" [*The Family* in a discussion between the Minister of Information and the Grand Imam], *Al-Ahram,* March 11, 1994, p. 22; "Hikayat al-musalsal alladhi haz misr" [The story of the serial that shook Egypt], *Akhbar al-Yawm,* March 12, 1994, pp. 1–2.

20. Armbrust, "Islamists in Egyptian Cinema."

21. Steve Negus, "Militant Repents on TV: Soap or Sincere?" *Civil Society* 3, no. 29 (May 1994): 6–8.

22. Jailan Halawi, "Repentance on the Air," *Ahram Weekly,* June 2–8, 1994, p. 2.

23. 'Abd al-Sattar al-Tawila and Jailan Jabr, "Interview with Safwat al-Sharif," *Ruz al-Yusuf,* June 13, 1994, pp. 12–13.

24. Armbrust, "Islamists in Egyptian Cinema," 924–25.

25. "Sherif Highlights Media Role in Confronting Terrorism," *Egyptian Mail,* May 22, 1993, p. 2.

26. Kienle, *A Grand Delusion,* 110.

27. Ibrahim 'Isa, "Interview with Wahid Hamid," *Ruz al-Yusuf,* March 21, 1994, pp. 16–20.

28. Usama Anwar 'Ukasha, "Wahid Hamid—huqul ilgham al-'a'ila" [Wahid Hamid—The Minefields of *The Family*], *Ruz al-Yusuf,* March 21, 1994, p. 19.

29. Usama Anwar 'Ukasha, "Al-tilifizun yarfa' al-masahif," 70.

30. Interview with the author, June 17, 1993.

31. See Armando Salvatore, "Social Differentiation, Moral Authority and Public Islam in Egypt," *Anthropology Today* 16 (April 2000): 12–15.

32. Hasan Bashir, "Al-irhabiyun yuridun tahqiq al-wahm bi-l-silah" [Terrorists want to realize illusions by force], *Sabah al-Khayr,* July 20, 1995, pp. 48–49. None of these, or the endless subplots about violent and misguided extremists that began to appear in other serials, stirred the same controversy as the explicit *The Family,* though objections continued to be raised from time to time, as when the Rector of Al-Azhar University fired off a memo about the depiction in 'Ukasha's 1999 serial, *Imra'a fi awan al-hubb* [Woman in the time of love], of a depraved religious scholar.

33. The relationship between the state and religious authorities, whether the formal establishment of Al-Azhar or the Muslim Brotherhood and other Muslim organizations, and between the government and the wider piety movement, are far too complex to detail here. There is a huge literature on the subject, but some helpful starting points in the recent literature include Asad, *Formations of the Secular;* Mahmood, "Feminist Theory, Embodiment, and the Docile Agent" and "Rehearsing Spontaneity and the Conventionality of Ritual"; Tamir Moustafa, "Conflict and Cooperation between the State and Religious Institutions in Contemporary

Egypt," *International Journal of Middle East Studies* 32 (2000): 3–22; Salvatore, *Islam and the Political Discourse of Modernity;* Salvatore, ed., *Muslim Traditions and Modern Techniques of Power;* Jakob Skovgaard-Petersen, *Defining Islam for the Egyptian State* (Leiden: Brill, 1997); Starrett, *Putting Islam to Work;* and Malika Zeghal, *Gardiens de l'Islam: Les Oulémas d'Al Azhar dans l'Egypte Contemporaine* (Paris: Presses de la Fondation Nationale des Sciences Politiques, 1996).

34. The anxiety about television is expressed in criticism in the pages of Islamic media and in studies such as Marwan Kashak's, which, in addition to marshaling local anecdotes and authoritative findings of European and North American researchers on the negative effects of television, reports on a study of Egyptian university students' responses to television conducted by Dr. Muhyi al-Din 'Abd al-Halim. This study found that more than 70% of students said that television offered negative values, including the undermining of religious values. Kashak, *Al-Usra al-muslima amam al-fidiyu wa al-tilifizyun,* 177–78. A 1987 master's thesis in mass communication similarly betrayed religious concerns and thanked Al-Azhar University for its cooperation. Sabir Sulayman 'Asran Sulayman, "Al-qiyam al-islamiyya allati yatadamanuha al-musalsal al-'arabi fi-l-tilifizyun" [Islamic values included in Arabic television serials] (master's thesis, Faculty of Mass Communication, Cairo University, 1987).

35. "Al-Usbu' al-i'lami: al-i'lam fi muwajahat al-irhab" [The media week: Media in confronting terrorism], *Al-Idha'a wa al-tilifizyun* [Radio and TV magazine], April 3, 1993.

36. "Kayf yara aqbat al-mahjar musalsal awan al-ward?" [How do emigrant Copts see the serial *The Time of Roses?*], *Akhbar al-Adab,* December 17, 2000, p. 10.

37. Muhammad Hani, "Qadiyya amam al-mahakim: Islam al-masihiyyat fi musalsalat al-tilifizyun" [A lawsuit: Female Christians' conversion to Islam in television serials], *Ruz al-Yusuf,* March 4, 1996, pp. 70–71. In an interesting response, 'Ayda al-Azab Musa counters that the serials have a different message: they show that the solution to the problems Egyptian youth face lies in foreign women, who are portrayed as strong, positive figures compared to their weak, jealous, or ill-tempered Egyptian counterparts. Musa, "Fi hadhihi al-musalsalat ma huwa aswa'?" [In these serials what is worse?], *Ruz al-Yusuf,* March 18, 1996, p. 79.

38. Fayiz Ghali, "La muharramat fi-l-drama" [No taboos in drama], *Ruz al-Yusuf,* April 1, 1996, pp. 68–69.

39. Amira Howeidy, "This Rose Has Thorns," *Ahram Weekly,* December 14–20, 2000, p. 1.

40. For the English translation, see Bahaa' Taher, *Aunt Safiyya and the Monastery,* trans. Barbara Romaine (Berkeley and Los Angeles: University of California Press, 1996).

41. Wa'il 'Abd al-Fatah and Suhayr Jawda, "Ma lam tushahadahu wa ma la ta'rafahu 'an 'khalti Safiyya wa al-dayr'" [What you didn't see and don't know about *Aunt Safiyya and the Monastery*], *Ruz al-Yusuf,* April 15, 1996, pp. 60–62.

42. Ibid.

43. Ibid.

44. It is interesting to compare current representations with an earlier nationalist strategy under the Nasser regime that Talal Asad describes as "inspired by a secular vision that denies the existence of any significant 'cultural' distinction between Christians and Muslims within a unified Egyptian nation." Asad notes the contributions to this effort of folklorists who, in the 1950s and 1960s, helped "create a secular mass 'culture' for Egypt . . . within an evolutionary framework that secures its continuous national personality." Talal Asad, *Formations of the Secular,* 254n101. Much like the "digestive" theories described in chapter 6 that appealed to 'Ukasha, these folklorists tried to uncover a common Egyptian culture, across regions, lifeways, and religions.

45. Dr. Nasar 'Abd Allah, "Al-masih al-sa'idi" [The Upper Egyptian messiah], *Ruz al-Yusuf,* April 15, 1996, p. 63.

46. Dr. Nasar 'Abd Allah, "Al-masih al-sa'idi . . . qatilan!" [The Upper Egyptian messiah . . . A Murderer!], *Ruz al-Yusuf*, April 22, 1996, p. 63.

47. For the problems with making cultural traits metonymic for regions, see Lila Abu-Lughod, "Zones of Theory in the Anthropology of the Arab World," *Annual Review of Anthropology* 18 (1989): 267–306; and Arjun Appadurai, "Is Homo Hierarchicus?" *American Ethnologist* 13 (1986): 745–61 and "Theory in Anthropology: Center and Periphery," *Comparative Studies in Society and History* 28 (1986): 356–61.

48. For summaries, see Gordon, *Revolutionary Melodrama*, pp. 169–72.

49. I have translated the title of the serial as *Mountain Wolves* but must note that the connotations are different in English and Arabic. Mountains, in this Upper Egyptian context, refer to the barren hills that dramatically mark the edge of the fertile Nile valley and the beginning of the desert, such as the Theban Hills that house the burial chambers of the Pharaohs across the river from Luxor. In some parts of the south, the hills at the edge of the cultivation are not that distant. Most probably we are talking about jackals rather than wolves. More accurate renditions might be *Jackals of the Hills* or even *Desert Jackals*.

50. Mahmud Musa, "Al-sura al-namatiyya li-l-sa'idi" [The modal image of the Upper Egyptian], *Al-Ahram*, February 18, 1996, p. 7.

51. For an excellent discussion of the links between archaeology, tourism, and violence, including an analysis of this incident in the Valley of the Queens, see Meskell, "The Practice and Politics of Archaeology in Egypt."

52. For background on Islamism in Upper Egypt, see Patrick Gaffney's work on preaching in this region, based on fieldwork in Minya in the late 1970s and mid-1980s: *The Prophet's Pulpit: Islamic Preaching in Contemporary Egypt* (Berkeley and Los Angeles: University of California Press, 1994).

53. See Rachida Chih, *Le Soufisme au Quotidien: Confréries d'Egypte au XXe Siècle* (Arles: Actes Sud-Sindbad, 2000); and Valerie Hoffman, *Sufism, Mystics, and Saints in Modern Egypt* (Columbia: University of South Carolina Press, 1995).

54. I did not do any fieldwork with any Coptic villagers, although I recount my encounter with the local monastery and the infertility cures that local Muslim women seek there in Lila Abu-Lughod, "A Tale of Two Pregnancies," in *Women Writing Culture*, ed. Ruth Behar and Deborah Gordon (Berkeley and Los Angeles: University of California Press, 1995), 339–49.

55. 'Adil Hamuda, "Al-'a'ila bayn al-qusur wa al-qubur" [*The Family* between the palaces and the graves], *Ruz al-Yusuf*, March 21, 1994, pp. 13–15.

56. Armando Salvatore, "After the State: Islamic Reform and the 'Implosion' of Shari'a," in *Muslim Traditions and Modern Techniques of Power*, ed. Salvatore, *Yearbook of the Sociology of Islam*, ed. Helmut Buchholt and Georg Stauth (Munster: Lit, 2001): 3:123–140; Talal Asad, "Reconfigurations of Law and Ethics in Colonial Egypt," in *Formations of the Secular*, 205–56.

57. Armando Salvatore, "Introduction: The Problem of the Ingraining of Civilizing Traditions into Social Governance," in *Muslim Traditions and Modern Techniques of Power*, ed. Salvatore, 3:9–42; quotation is from p. 19.

CHAPTER EIGHT

1. Schudson, *Advertising, the Uneasy Persuasion*, 218.

2. Vilmar E. Faria and Joseph Potter, "Television, *telenovelas*, and Fertility Change in Northeast Brazil," in *Dynamics of Value in Fertility Change*, ed. Richard Leete (Oxford: Oxford University Press, 1999), 252–72. This cited quotation was translated from A. H. Costa et al., *Um*

Pais no Ar (Sao Paulo: Brasiliende/Funarte, 1986), 103. Brazil is a part of the world where, like the United States, television began as a commercial enterprise, though it went through a period of serious state control, as Caroline Tauxe points out. See Caroline Tauxe, "The Spirit of Christmas: Television and Commodity Hunger in a Brazilian Election," *Public Culture* 5 (1993): 593–604.

3. Leela Fernandez, "Nationalizing 'The Global': Media Images, Cultural Politics and the Middle Class in India," *Media Culture and Society* 22 (2000), 611–28; and "Rethinking Globalization: Gender and the Nation in India," in *Feminist Locations: Global and Local, Theory and Practice in the Twenty-First Century,* ed. Marianne de Koven (New Brunswick, NJ: Rutgers University Press, 2001), 147–67.

4. Fernandez, "Rethinking Globalization," 154.

5. See Arvind Rajagopal, "Advertising, Politics and the Sentimental Education of the Indian Consumer," *Visual Anthropology Review* 14 (fall–winter 1998): 1–18; and "Thinking Through Emerging Markets," *Social Text* 60 (fall 1999): 131–49.

6. Mankekar, *Screening Culture, Viewing Politics,* 346.

7. Robert Foster, "The Commercial Construction of 'New Nations,'" *Journal of Material Culture* 4 (1999): 263–82.

8. Ibid., 264.

9. Some useful articles and interviews related to Dream TV and other new private television stations can be found in *Transnational Broadcasting Studies,* an electronic journal published by the Adham Center for Television Journalism at the American University in Cairo. For a discussion of El Mehwar, see Naila Hamdy, "El Mehwar the Mercurial," *TBS* 9 (fall/winter 2002), http://www.tbsjournal.com/Archives/Fallo2/Mehwar.html. For Dream TV see Naila Hamdy's interview with Hala Sirhan, "A Dream TV Come True," *TBS* 8 (spring/summer 2002), http://www.tbsjournal.com/Archives/Springo2/sirhan.html.

10. Diase, "Egyptian Television Serials, Audiences, and *The Family House,*" 87.

11. Interview by the author with Basim Mahfuz 'Abd al-Rahman, May 6, 1997.

12. Sakr, *Satellite Realms,* 19; Sherin Moody, "Pay-TV in Egypt: Impediments and Developments," *TBS* 2 (spring 1999), http://www.tbsjournal.com/Archives/Spring99/Documents/Sherin/sherin.html.

13. These coordination plans proposed by the Egyptian Minister of Information Safwat al-Sharif, in a speech to the 1998 Annual Radio and Television Festival in Cairo, were reported in Sakr, *Satellite Realms,* 64, 162.

14. The advertising agencies, which make a large part (15% to 20%) of their profits from commissions paid them by the Television and Radio Union or the print media where they place ads, are doing well. Some follow media plans developed through market research and computer software, working in consultation with young, cosmopolitan, European-trained marketers. These professionals are the sort whose children play with Nintendos and own bikes, in contrast with the majority of viewing children, who must make do with cheap plastic toys bought at the saints' festivals and who consider a ball a treat. Private production companies have also sprung up to produce high-quality commercials. The firms flood the airwaves with increasingly sophisticated commercials advertising a wide range of products. I am grateful to Abbas Fahmy, consultant to TEAM advertising and owner of a private production house, for his help in explaining this industry. Another useful source was Aida Nasr, "Selling Time," *Cairo Today,* November 1992, pp. 96–100, 127.

15. In a recent business-oriented analysis of Egyptian and Arab television advertising, Jihad Fakhreddine gives numbers to the hefty increase in advertising in television, even while deploring the near-monopoly of state television on advertising revenue. He reports,

Overall, the size of the Egyptian TV sector grew from 70 million US$ in 1995 to 170 million US$ in 2001. This 142% increase in advertising revenues in a period of six years was, nevertheless, well below the 191% growth rate experienced by the TV sector for all the Arab markets combined during the same period. From a business perspective, there is no reason why the local Egyptian TV sector should lag behind its counterparts at the regional level in overall growth. However, the fact that close to 90% of the advertising revenues are generated by Egypt's Channels 1 and 2 illustrates the seriousness of the bottleneck situation, whereby advertisers are trying to reach a population of about 70 million largely through two TV channels.

Jihad Fakhreddine, "National versus Pan-Arab Reach: Which Way for Egypt's Private Commercial TV Channels?" *TBS* 9 (fall/winter 2002), http://www.tbsjournal.com/Archive/Fall02/Fakhreddine.html.

16. All information on prices comes from the Egyptian Radio and Television Union's Economic Sector's official bulletin on the prices of advertisements on television for 1997.

17. For example, there is a surcharge of 150% for a commercial broadcast during a match between Egypt's two best teams, Zamalek and Ahli.

18. Heba Kandil, "The Media Free Zone: An Egyptian Media Production City Finesse," *TBS* 5 (fall 2000), http://www.tbsjournal.com/Archives/Falloo/Kandil.htm.

19. His associate at that time (2002), Hala Sirhan, explained his interest in the station in terms of advertising markets. She said,

This man owns the biggest development company in Egypt, Dreamland development. He has 28 factories including some that manufacture furniture, TVs, refrigerators, and marble. Which means he spends 40 million pounds [about $10 million] a year on advertising. So he got the idea of owning his own TV station where he could run his own ads. Three quarters of his annual budget for advertising could be used on his own station, with the double benefit of being able to target clients. The people who have a decoder and can watch Dream TV are his potential buyers.

Hamdy, "A Dream TV Come True."

20. Dream TV made a splash with the 2002 Ramadan serial it produced, "Faris bila jawwad" [Horseman without a horse], whose inclusion of reference to the Protocols of Zion caused such a furor in the United States and Israel. See *Al-Ahram Weekly Online*, November 7–13, 2002, p. 611, http://www.ahram.org.eg/weekly/2002/611.

21. Yahya al-Fakharani, for example, is reported to have demanded 35,000 L.E. plus a 10,000 L.E. advance to act in a play that was guaranteed to run for three seasons at the same price; the belly dancer Fifi 'Abdu along with the other eleven most famous belly dancers is reported to have paid the equivalent of $264 million in taxes, a staggering figure that suggests some fairly big incomes. Reported respectively in *Ruz al-Yusuf*, December 29, 1997, p. 75; and *Middle East Times*, January 19–25, 1997, p. 3. For more on the star system and the magazines that supported it in an earlier period, see Walter Armbrust, *Mass Culture and Modernism in Egypt*; and "Manly Men on a National Stage (and the Women Who Make Them Stars)," in *Histories of the Modern Middle East: New Directions*, ed. Israel Gershoni, Hakan Erdem, and Ursula Wokock (Boulder, CO: Lynne Rienner Publishers, 2002), 247–75.

22. Tarek Atia, "Sins and Salvation," *Al-Ahram Weekly*, January 6–12, 2000, Culture Page (http://www.ahram.org.eg/weekly/2000/463). This is not unlike the situation of the high-profile television ads that accompany the U.S. Super Bowl. On the commercialization of Ra-

madan, see Walter Armbrust, "The Riddle of Ramadan: Media, Consumer Culture, and the 'Christmasization' of a Muslim Holiday," in *Everyday life in the Muslim Middle East*, ed. Donna Lee Bowen and Evelyn A. Early (Bloomington: Indiana University Press 2000), 335–48.

23. Ahmad Bahgat, later to become owner of Dream TV, owns the development company behind Dreamland.

24. See L. Abu-Lughod, "Finding a Place for Islam"; and Armbrust, *Mass Culture and Modernism in Egypt.*

25. This is in line with the dream the government has promoted with its desert reclamation schemes; it conforms even more closely to the popular middle-class professional pastime these days of building weekend homes and starting farms on newly reclaimed land.

26. Geir Sakseid, "Values in Conflict: A Study of the Values in the Egyptian Television Serial 'A Woman from the Time of Love'" (unpublished MS, January 2000).

27. See the exchanges in Salah Muntasir's column, "Mujarrad ra'i" [Just an opinion] in *Al-Ahram*, February 27, 1996; March 7, 1996; March 20, 1996; April 17, 1996; and April 18, 1996.

28. Interview by the author with Muna Zaki, March 14, 1997.

29. March 3, 1997.

30. Such television serials cover themselves by validating authority. In this serial, like many others, there are always those in the upper and middle classes, sometimes members of the same family as the corrupt, who remain moral and hold on to their principles. In *Against the Current,* these include authorities like security officers, along with the wife, who is herself a university professor. Her moral credentials are boosted by a scene in which she criticizes a colleague for making the students lazy, selling them the texts of his lectures and not requiring any other reading or research. (He tries to defend himself by pointing out that the difference between himself and Oxford professors is that Egyptians have such low salaries that they are forced to resort to such measures.)

31. Atia, "Sins and Salvation."

32. For a wonderful example of the complex ways foreign serials can influence locally produced ones, see Mandel, "A Marshall Plan of the Mind," 211–28.

33. The breakdown of the old moral codes favored by state television is even clearer, some would argue, in the kinds of new programs, like the controversial *Al-kamira al-khafiyya* [The hidden camera], in which ordinary people are humiliated. See Nader K. Uthman and Leah Ida Harris, "Zii'! (Broadcast It!): Reading the Construction of Cultural Negotiation in the Egyptian TV Show 'Hidden Camera'" (paper presented at the Middle East Studies Association Meetings, Washington, DC, 2002).

34. The chastity and honor of the protagonist is made clear in a scene when the couple goes to Alexandria for a weekend. It is nighttime and they can't sleep. The woman says, "I know why you didn't want to go on a trip to Europe. You couldn't go if you weren't married to me. Now here we are, each in our own room. We can't sleep. We keep coming out onto the balcony as if to show those people across the Mediterranean—'Look, look, we are honorable. We are still fully clothed.'"

35. Mahmood, "Feminist Theory, Embodiment, and the Docile Agent" and "Rehearsing Spontaneity and the Conventionality of Ritual." See also Mahmood, *Politics of Piety.*

36. Linda Herrera, "Accommodating Disco and Quran: Lay Female Pedagogues and the Education of Metropolitan Muslims," in *Muslim Traditions and Modern Techniques of Power,* ed. Armando Salvatore, *Yearbook of the Sociology of Islam* (Munster:Lit, 2001), 3:225–39.

37. For an extended discussion of the impact of structural adjustment policies, the ideology of the market, and the economic practices of the poor, see Mitchell, *Rule of Experts.*

38. I am not the first urban person to find the powerful relationship between people and

their cows worth writing about. Not only do we have the classic ethnographies by E. E. Evans-Pritchard and Francis Mading Deng describing the songs Nuer and Dinka in the southern Sudan sing to their cattle, but John Berger's unforgettable story in *Pig Earth* about the French mountain villager who has lost his cow in the snow, and Darius Mehrjui's 1969 classic Iranian black-and-white film, *Gav* [Cow], that eerily chronicles the descent into insanity of a farmer whose cow disappears. See E. E. Evans-Pritchard, *The Nuer: A Description of the Modes of Livelihood and Political Institutions of a Nilotic People*, rev. ed. (New York: Oxford University Press, 1969); Francis Mading Deng, *The Dinka and Their Songs* (Oxford: Clarendon Press, 1973); and John Berger, *Pig Earth*, rev. ed. (New York: Vintage Books, 1992).

39. See Daniel Miller, ed., *Acknowledging Consumption* (New York: Routledge, 1995); and Daniel Miller, *The Dialectics of Shopping* (Chicago: University of Chicago Press, 2001).

40. Daniel Miller, "Consumption as the Vanguard of History," in *Acknowledging Consumption*, 6.

41. Pierre Bourdieu, *Distinction: A Social Critique of the Judgment of Taste*, trans. Richard Nice (Cambridge, MA: Harvard University Press, 1984).

42. For an excellent discussion of the way the government and media targeted these informal neighborhoods as hotbeds of Islamic militancy, see Kuppinger, "Cracks in the Cityscape," 185–207. These views were widely disseminated in the print media and even found their way into political campaigns such as that of television writer Fathiyya Al-'Assal, discussed in the conclusion.

43. Anderson, *Imagined Communities*.

44. For a good description of changes in consumption habits in a rural area in the north, see Kirsten Haugaard Bach, "The Vision of a Better Life: New Patterns of Consumption and Changed Social Relations," in *Directions of Change in Rural Egypt*, eds. Kirsten Westergaard and Nicholas Hopkins (Cairo: American University in Cairo Press, 1998), 184–200.

45. See Fred Myers, ed., *The Empire of Things*, for exciting discussions of regimes of value and circulations among them (Santa Fe: School of American Research Press, 2001).

46. Silverstone, *Television and Everyday Life*, 104, has argued that a telling feature of advertisements' links with desire and consumption is that they display little about the processes of production.

47. Even in Cairo among industry professionals, according to a personal communication from Dalia Wihdan, this last ad was thought to have backfired; it exuded so much elegance that people mistakenly assumed that the tiles would be too expensive for them, even though they cost no more than other quality brands.

48. Diase in "Egyptian Television Serials, Audiences, and *The Family House*," p. 235, makes the good point that viewers' lack of criticism of the affluent clothing and homes in the television serial she studied was due to the prevalence of these styles in serials.

CONCLUSION

1. This is discussed in my article "The Objects of Soap Operas."

2. Stephen Hinerman sees some of the pleasures stars give as deriving from audiences' senses that, through the production of their private and public lives as well as through watching them in many roles, they "know" the stars well. Stephen Hinerman, "Star Culture," in *Culture in the Communication Age*, ed. James Lull (London: Routledge, 2001), 193–211.

3. 'Ali Al-Sawi, "Al-mar'a wa intikhabat majlis al-sha'b 1995: halat da'irat imbaba" [Women and the 1995 parliamentary elections: The situation of Imbaba District], in *Al-mar'a*

wa intikhabat majlis al-sha'b 1995 [Women and the 1995 parliamentary elections], ed. Waduda Badran (Cairo: Friedrich Ebert Stiftung and Cairo University's Faculty of Economics and Political Science, 1996), 181–200.

4. Ra'uf Tawfiq, "Al-kalima hiyya al-batal" [The word is the hero], *Sabah al-Khayr,* March 10, 1994, pp. 40–43.

5. 'A'isha Salih, "Harim al-Haj Mitwalli" [The harem of Haj Mitwalli], *Al-Musawwar,* December 7, 2001, pp. 40–42.

6. 'Ala' Al-Shafi'i, "Thawrat al-nisa' 'ala al-Haj Mitwalli" [The revolt of women against Haj Mitwalli], *Al-Ahram al-'Arabi,* December 8, 2001, pp. 80–81.

7. Ayman Al-Hakim, "Al-za'ima al-nisa'iyya allati tutalib bi ra's al-Haj Mitwalli" [The feminist leader who calls for the head of Haj Mitwalli], *Al-Qahira,* December 25, 2001, p. 14.

8. Usama Anwar 'Ukasha, "Al-mutatarrif al-'azim" [The great extremist], *Ruz al-Yusuf,* January 19, 1998, pp. 78–79.

9. Interview with author, April 15, 1990.

10. Usama Anwar 'Ukasha, "Lughuz najah musalsalat al-sabun" [The puzzle of the success of soap operas], *Ruz al-Yusuf,* January 18, 1993, pp. 8–10.

11. Using a different food metaphor than Fadil's pumpkin-seed munching, 'Ukasha contrasted *Oshin,* a natural drama with no food preservatives or artificial flavors, to the "hawawshi bread" of *The Bold and the Beautiful.* (Hawawshi bread is a kind of meat pie whose strong spices are known to mask poor-quality mincemeat.) Instead of striking women showing off their bodies and male mannequins smiling promiscuously, *Oshin* tells the profound story of an ordinary Japanese woman who overcomes great obstacles. Usama Anwar 'Ukasha, "Intabahu ayuha al-sada: 'Oshin' tuwajah al-jari' wa al-jamila" [Pay attention gentlemen: "Oshin" confronts "The Bold and the Beautiful"], *Ruz al-Yusuf,* June 26, 1993, pp. 52–53. Ironically, under public pressure, *The Bold and the Beautiful* was eventually reduced from nightly broadcasts and *Oshin* brought back on the air in late 1993. Only a few months later, however, *Oshin* had become the subject of tremendous criticism in the media because of its relentlessly depressing character. *Oshin* was wildly popular elsewhere in the Middle East. Shahla Haeri reports the anecdote that it was taken off the air in Iran after women interviewed on the day meant to commemorate the Prophet's daughter Fatima replied "Oshin" when asked who their role model was. Shahla Haeri, "Obedience versus Autonomy: Women and Fundamentalism in Iran and Pakistan," in *Fundamentalisms and Society: Reclaiming the Sciences, the Family, and Education,* eds. Martin E. Marty and R. Scott Appleby (Chicago: University of Chicago Press,1993), 181–213.

12. On state feminism and its demise in Egypt, see Hatem, "Economic and Political Libera(liza)tion in Egypt and the Demise of State Feminism."

13. For more on the marvelous *The White Flag,* see L. Abu-Lughod, "Finding a Place for Islam" and Armbrust, *Mass Culture and Modernism in Egypt.*

14. Various studies have shown this. Soha Abdel Kader's study, "The Image of Women in Drama and Women's Programs in Egyptian Television," for example, shows that there was a bias toward portraying the urban upper classes. Of 14 serials and 12 short plays sampled during a six-month period in 1980, none were set in rural areas (unpublished report, Population Council, 1985, p. 36). See also Diase, "Egyptian Television Serials, Audiences, and *The Family House,* a Public Health Enter-Educate Serial."

15. L. Abu-Lughod, "The Objects of Soap Operas."

16. Her clearest example comes in her analysis of several women's appropriation of Draupadi, the disrobed heroine on the televised *Mahabharata.* Mankekar, *Screening Culture, Viewing Politics.*

17. Jackie Stacey has developed a complex typology, based on a study of British women who were fans of female Hollywood stars in the 1940s and 1950s, about "the forms of intimacy between femininities" that the relationship entailed. I have not done careful work on women's relationship with television and film stars in Egypt, but I imagine that the forms of identification and desire may be somewhat different because of the more cosmopolitan identities of the stars and the strong moral language that surrounds them. One of Stacey's interesting findings, however, was that for British women, there was a historical shift such that in the 1950s, with the growth of consumer markets in Britain and greater Americanization, the stars seemed closer and were therefore easier to identify with. One wonders if such a process might not occur in Egypt as well. See Jackie Stacey, *Star Gazing: Hollywood Cinema and Female Spectatorship* (London: Routledge, 1994).

18. Geraghty, *Women and Soap Opera*, 15.

19. So wedded did the actors become to their roles that, after the conclusion of the serial, many of them complained that they felt trapped by their characters in *Hilmiyya Nights*. As in American soap operas, stars also quit the show before its conclusion and had to be replaced, so audiences had to cope with the separation of character from actor.

20. For more on the moral evaluation of performers in Egypt, see Karin van Nieuwkerk, *A Trade Like Any Other: Female Singers and Dancers in Egypt* (Austin: University of Texas Press, 1995); Kathryn E. Zirbel, "Playing It Both Ways: Local Egyptian Performers between Regional Identity and International Markets," in *Mass Mediations*, ed. Armbrust; Susan Slyomovics, *The Merchant of Art;* and Sherifa Zuhur, *Asmahan's Secrets: Woman, War, and Song* (Austin: University of Texas Press, 2001).

21. Jad al-Haq 'Ali Jad al-Haq, "Simat al-halal wa al-haram" [The characteristics of the permitted and forbidden], *Majallat al-Azhar,* August/September–July 1988–89, Free Supplement, p. 10.

22. Interview with the author, March 14, 1997. Yet by 2003 she had a fan club and Web site: see http://monazaki.proboards17.com.

23. See my "Movie Stars and Islamic Moralism in Egypt."

24. Armbrust, "Manly Men on a National Stage (and the Women Who Make Them Stars)," 247–75; and Danielson, *The Voice of Egypt.*

25. Armbrust, "The Riddle of Ramadan," 335–48.

26. Salvatore, "Introduction: The Problem of the Ingraining of Civilizing Traditions into Social Governance," 14.

27. Magdi Kamil, *Fannanat wara' al-hijab* [Artists behind the veil] (Cairo: Markaz al-raya li-l-nashr wa al-i'lam, MR, 1993).

28. Fawzi, *'Umar 'Abd al-Kafi,* 57–58. I want to thank Farha Ghannam for bringing this and another book on the Shaykh to my attention.

29. For more on Huda Sultan and her public relationship (as constructed in fan magazines) with her husband, Farid Shauqi, who became a national figure and star after marrying her, see Armbrust, "Manly Men on a National Stage (and the Women Who Make Them Stars)."

30. "Al-sitt Huda Sultan ba'd an ta'atiqat wa ihlawwit" [Madam Huda Sultan after she matured and got more beautiful], *Nusf al-Dunya,* March 20, 1994, pp. 64–65.

References

'Abd al-Rahim, Ashraf bin 'Abd al-Maqsud bin. 1994. *Musalsal al-'a'ila: Al-irhab al-fanni wa al-hujum 'ala al-islam* [The serial *The Family:* Artistic terrorism and the attack on Islam]. Cairo: Maktabat al-turath al-islami.

Abdel Kader, Soha. 1985. The image of women in drama and women's programs in Egyptian television. Unpublished report, Population Council.

Abelmann, Nancy. 2003. *The melodramas of mobility: Women, talk, and class in contemporary South Korea.* Honolulu: Univ. of Hawaii Press.

Abu El-Haj, Nadia. 2002. *Facts on the ground: Archaeological practice and territorial self-fashioning in Israeli society.* Chicago: Univ. of Chicago Press.

Abu-Lughod, Ibrahim. 1963. The mass media and Egyptian village life. *Social Forces* 42:97–104.

Abu-Lughod, Janet. 2004. Cairo: Too many people, not enough land, too few resources. In *World cities beyond the West,* ed. Josef Gugler, 258–313. Cambridge: Cambridge Univ. Press.

Abu-Lughod, Lila. 1986/2000. *Veiled sentiments: Honor and poetry in a Bedouin society.* Berkeley and Los Angeles: Univ. of California Press.

———. 1989. Zones of theory in the anthropology of the Arab world. *Annual Review of Anthropology* 18:267–306.

———. 1990a. The romance of resistance: Tracing transformations of power through Bedouin women. *American Ethnologist* 17:41–55.

———. 1990b. Shifting politics in Bedouin love poetry. In Abu-Lughod and Lutz 1990a, 24–45.

———. 1991. Writing against culture. In Fox 1991, 137–62.

———. 1993a. Editorial comment: On screening politics in a world of nations. *Public Culture* 5:465–69.

———. 1993b. *Writing women's worlds: Bedouin stories.* Berkeley and Los Angeles: Univ. of California Press.

———. 1993c. Finding a place for Islam: Egyptian television serials and the national interest. *Public Culture* 5:493–513.

———. 1993d. Islam and the gendered discourses of death. *International Journal of Middle East Studies* 25:187–205.

———. 1995a. The objects of soap operas. In *Worlds apart: Modernity through the prism of the local,* ed. Daniel Miller, 191–210. London: Routledge.

———. 1995b. Movie stars and Islamic moralism in Egypt. *Social Text* 42 (spring): 53–67.

———. 1995c. A tale of two pregnancies. In *Women writing culture,* ed. Ruth Behar and Deborah Gordon, 339–49. Berkeley and Los Angeles: Univ. of California Press.

———. 1997a. The interpretation of culture(s) after television. *Representations* 59:25–50.

———. 1997b. Dramatic reversals. In *Political Islam: Essays from* Middle East Report, ed. Joel Beinin and Joe Stork, 269–82. Berkeley and Los Angeles: Univ. of California Press.

———. 1998a. Introduction: Feminist longings and postcolonial conditions. In Abu-Lughod 1998c, 3–31.

———. 1998b. The marriage of feminism and Islamism in Egypt: Selective repudiation as a dynamic of postcolonial cultural politics. In Abu-Lughod 1998c, 243–69.

———, ed. 1998c. *Remaking women: Feminism and modernity in the Middle East.* Princeton, NJ: Princeton Univ. Press.

———. 1999. Comments on "Writing for Culture." *Current Anthropology* 40:S13–S15.

———. 2001. *Orientalism* and Middle East feminist studies. *Feminist Studies* 27 (spring): 101–13.

———. 2003. Asserting the local as national in the face of the global: The ambivalence of authenticity in Egyptian soap opera. In *Localizing knowledge in a globalizing world: Recasting the area studies debate,* ed. Ali Mirsepassi, Amrita Basu, and Frederick Weaver, 101–27. Syracuse, NY: Syracuse Univ. Press.

Abu-Lughod, Lila, and Catherine Lutz, eds. 1990a. *Language and the politics of emotion.* Cambridge: Cambridge Univ. Press.

———. 1990b. Introduction: Emotion, discourse, and the politics of everyday life. In Abu-Lughod and Lutz 1990a, 1–23.

Adorno, Theodor. 1991. *The culture industry: Selected essays on mass culture.* Ed. J. M. Bernstein. London: Routledge.

Ahmed, Leila. 1992. *Women and gender in Islam: Historical roots of a modern debate.* New Haven, Conn.: Yale Univ. Press.

Al-Ali, Nadje. 2000. *Secularism, gender and the state in the Middle East: The Egyptian women's movement.* Cambridge: Cambridge Univ. Press.

Al-Hakim, Tawfiq. 1985. *'Awdat al-wa'i* [Return of consciousness]. 1st English ed. New York: New York Univ. Press.

———. 1990. *'Awdat al-ruh* [Return of the spirit]. 1st English ed. Washington, DC: Three Continents Press.

Ali, Kamran Asdar. 2002a. *Planning the family in Egypt: New bodies, new selves.* Austin: Univ. of Texas Press.

———. 2002b. Faulty deployments: Persuading women and constructing choice in Egypt. *Comparative Studies in Society and History* 44 (2): 370–92.

Allen, Robert C. 1985. *Speaking of soap opera.* Chapel Hill: Univ. of North Carolina Press.

———, ed. 1995. *To be continued . . .: Soap operas around the world.* New York: Routledge.

Al-Sawi, 'Ali. 1996. Al-mar'a wa intikhabat majlis al-sha'b 1995: Halat da'irat imbaba [Women and the 1995 parliamentary elections: The situation of Imbaba District]. In *Al-mar'a wa intikhabat majlis al-sha'b 1995* [Women and the 1995 parliamentary elections], ed. Waduda Badran, 181–200. Cairo: Friedrich Ebert Stiftung and Cairo Univ. Faculty of Economics and Political Science.

Al-Sholkamy, Hania. 1999. Why is anthropology so hard in Egypt? Seteny Shami and Linda Herrera, eds., *Cairo Papers in Social Science* 22:119–38.

Altorki, Soraya. 1999. Patriarchy and imperialism: Father-son and British-Egyptian relations in Najib Mahfuz's trilogy. In *Intimate selving in Arab Families,* ed. Suad Joseph, 214–34. Syracuse, NY: Syracuse Univ. Press.

Amin, Hussein. 1996. Egypt and the Arab world in the satellite age. In *New patterns in global television: Peripheral vision,* ed. John Sinclair, Elizabeth Jacka, and Stuart Cunningham, 101–25. Oxford: Oxford Univ. Press.

Anderson, Benedict. 1991. *Imagined communities.* London: Verso.

Ang, Ien. 1985. *Watching "Dallas": Soap opera and the melodramatic imagination.* London: Methuen.

———. 1990. Melodramatic identifications: Television fiction and women's fantasy. In *Television and women's culture: The politics of the popular,* ed. Mary Ellen Brown, 75–88. London: Sage.

———. 1991. *Desperately seeking the audience.* London: Routledge.

———. 1996. *Living room wars: Rethinking media audiences for a postmodern world.* London: Routledge.

Appadurai, Arjun. 1986a. Is homo hierarchicus? *American Ethnologist* 13:745–61.

———. 1986b. Theory in anthropology: Center and periphery. *Comparative Studies in Society and History* 28:356–61.

———. 1988. Putting hierarchy in its place. *Cultural Anthropology* 3:36–49.

———. 1996a. Global ethnoscapes: Notes and queries for a transnational anthropology. In Appadurai 1996b.

———. 1996b. *Modernity at large: Cultural dimensions of globalization.* Minneapolis: Univ. of Minnesota Press.

Armbrust, Walter. 1996. *Mass culture and modernism in Egypt.* Cambridge: Cambridge Univ. Press.

———. 1998. Terrorism and kabab: A Capraesque view of modern Egypt. In *Images of enchantment: Visual and performing arts of the Middle East,* ed. Sherifa Zuhur, 283–99. Cairo: American Univ. in Cairo Press.

———. 1999. Bourgeois leisure and Egyptian media fantasies. In *New media in the Muslim world,* ed. Dale Eickelman and Jon Anderson, 106–32. Bloomington: Indiana Univ. Press.

———, ed. 2000a. *Mass mediations: New approaches to popular culture in the Middle East and beyond.* Berkeley and Los Angeles: Univ. of California Press.

———. 2000b. The riddle of Ramadan: Media, consumer culture, and the "Christmasization" of a Muslim holiday. In *Everyday life in the Muslim Middle East,* ed. Donna Lee Bowen and Evelyn A. Early, 335–48. Bloomington: Indiana Univ. Press.

———. 2002a. Islamists in Egyptian cinema. *American Anthropologist* 104 (3): 922–31.

———. 2002b. Manly men on a national stage (and the women who make them stars). In *Histories of the modern Middle East: New directions,* ed. Israel Gershoni, Hakan Erdem, and Ursula Wokock, 247–75. Boulder, CO: Lynne Rienner Publishers.

Asad, Talal. 1993. *Genealogies of religion.* Baltimore: Johns Hopkins Univ. Press.

———. 2003a. *Formations of the secular: Christianity, Islam, modernity.* Stanford, CA: Stanford Univ. Press.

———. 2003b. Reconfigurations of law and ethics in colonial Egypt. In Asad 2003a, 205–56.

Bach, Kirsten Haugaard. 1998. The vision of a better life: New patterns of consumption and changed social relations. In *Directions of change in rural Egypt,* ed. Kirsten Westergaard and Nicholas Hopkins, 184–200. Cairo: American Univ. in Cairo Press.

Badran, Margot. 1993. Gender activism: Feminists and Islamists in Egypt. In *Identity politics and women: Cultural reassertions and feminism in international perspective,* ed. Valentine Moghadam, 202–27. Denver: Westview Press.

———. 1995. *Feminists, Islam, and nation: Gender and the making of modern Egypt.* Princeton, NJ: Princeton Univ. Press.

Bakr, Salwa. 1992. *Such a beautiful voice.* Trans. Hoda El-Sadda. Cairo: General Egyptian Book Organization.

———. 1997. *The wiles of men.* Trans. Denys Johnson-Davies. Cairo: American Univ. in Cairo Press.

Balibar, Etienne. 1991. *Race, nation, class: Ambiguous identities.* London: Verso.

Baron, Beth. 1991. The making and breaking of marital bonds in modern Egypt. In *Women in Middle Eastern history,* ed. Nikki Keddie and Beth Baron, 275–91. New Haven, Conn.: Yale Univ. Press.

———. 1994. *The women's awakening in Egypt: Culture, society, and the press.* New Haven, Conn.: Yale Univ. Press.

———. 1997. Nationalist iconography: Egypt as a woman. In *Rethinking nationalism in the Arab Middle East,* ed. James Jankowski and Israel Gershoni, 105–24. New York: Columbia Univ. Press.

Baudrillard, Jean. 1988. *Selected writings.* Ed. Mark Poster. Stanford, CA: Stanford Univ. Press.

Behar, Ruth. 1990. Rage and redemption: Reading the life story of a Mexican marketing woman. *Feminist Studies* 16: 223–58.

Berger, John. 1992. *Pig earth.* Rev. ed. New York: Vintage Books.

Bhabha, Homi. 1990. DissemiNation: Time, narrative, and the margins of the modern nation. In *Nation and narration,* ed. Homi Bhabha, 297–99. London: Routledge.

———. 1994. *The location of culture.* London: Routledge.

Bhargava, Rajeev, ed. 1998. *Secularism and its critics.* Delhi: Oxford Univ. Press.

Booth, Marilyn. 1998. The Egyptian lives of Jeanne d'Arc. In Abu-Lughod 1998c, 171–211.

———. 1990. *Bayram al-Tunisi's Egypt: Social criticism and narrative strategies.* Oxford: Ithaca Press.

———. 2001. *May her likes be multiplied: Biography and gender politics in Egypt.* Berkeley and Los Angeles: Univ. of California Press.

Bourdieu, Pierre. 1977. *Outline of a theory of practice.* Trans. Richard Nice. Cambridge: Cambridge Univ. Press.

———. 1984. *Distinction: A social critique of the judgment of taste.* Trans. Richard Nice. Cambridge, MA: Harvard Univ. Press.

Boyd, Douglas. 1999. *Broadcasting in the Arab world.* Ames: Iowa State Univ. Press.

Braman, Sandra, and Annabelle Sreberny-Mohammadi, eds. 1996. *Globalization, communication and transnational civil society.* Cresskill, NJ: Hampton Press.

Brooks, Peter. 1976. *The melodramatic imagination: Balzac, Henry James, melodrama, and the mode of excess.* New Haven, Conn.: Yale Univ. Press.

Brown, Mary Ellen, ed. 1990. *Television and women's culture: The politics of the popular.* London: Sage.

Brown, Nathan. 1990. *Peasant politics in modern Egypt: The struggle against the state.* New Haven, Conn.: Yale Univ. Press.

Brumann, Christoph. 1999. Writing for culture. *Current Anthropology* 40:S1–S13.

Brunsdon, Charlotte. 1995. The role of soap opera in the development of feminist television scholarship. In Allen 1995, 49–55. New York: Routledge.

———. 1997. *Screen tastes: Soap opera to satellite dishes.* London: Routledge.

CEDEJ. 1987. *Anciens et nouveaux médias en Egypte: Radio, télévision, cinéma, vidéo. Bulletine de CEDEJ* 21: Premiere semestre.

———. 1988. Renseignements égyptiens: Le héros, la pécheresse et l'agent double. *Revue de la presse Ègyptienne* 32/33, 2ème semestre: 109–54.

Chakrabarty, Dipesh. 1994/1997. The difference-deferral of a colonial modernity: Public debates on domesticity in British Bengal. In *Subaltern studies VIII*, ed. David Arnold and David Hardiman, 50–88. Delhi: Oxford Univ. Press. Repr. in *Tensions of empire: Colonial cultures in a bourgeois world*, ed. Frederick Cooper and Ann Laura Stoler, 373–40. Berkeley and Los Angeles: Univ. of California Press, 1997.

———. 2000. Witness to suffering: Domestic cruelty and the birth of the modern subject in Bengal. In *Questions of modernity*, ed. Timothy Mitchell, 49–86. Minneapolis: Univ. of Minnesota Press.

———. 2002. *Habitations of modernity: Essays in the wake of subaltern studies*. Chicago: Univ. of Chicago Press.

Chatterjee, Partha. 1993. *The nation and its fragments*. Princeton, NJ: Princeton Univ. Press.

———. 1995. Religious minorities and the secular state: Reflections on an Indian impasse. *Public Culture* 8:11–39.

———. 1998. Secularism and tolerance. In Bhargava 1998, 345–79. Delhi: Oxford Univ. Press.

Chih, Rachida. 2000. *Le soufisme au quotidien: Confréries d'Egypte au XXe siècle*. Arles: Actes Sud-Sindbad.

Clifford, James. 1988. *The predicament of culture: Twentieth-Century ethnography, literature, and art*. Cambridge, MA: Harvard Univ. Press.

———. 1992. Travelling cultures. In *Cultural studies*, ed. Lawrence Grossberg, Cary Nelson, and Paula Treichler, 96–112. New York: Routledge.

Colla, Elliott. 2000. Shadi Abd al-Salam's *al-Mumiya*: Ambivalence and the Egyptian nation-state. In *Beyond colonialism and nationalism in the Maghreb*, ed. A. Ahmida, 109–43. New York: Palgrave.

———. 2001–2. The stuff of Egypt: The nation, the state and their proper objects. *New Formations* 45 (winter): 72–90.

Cooper, Frederick, and Ann Laura Stoler, eds. 1997. *Tensions of empire: Colonial cultures in a bourgeois world*. Berkeley and Los Angeles: Univ. of California Press.

Crehan, Kate. 2002. *Gramsci, culture and anthropology*. Berkeley and Los Angeles: Univ. of California Press.

Cvetkovich, Ann. 1992. *Mixed feelings: Feminism, mass cultures, and Victorian sensationalism*. New Brunswick, NJ: Rutgers Univ. Press.

Daniel, E. Valentine. 1996. *Charred lullabies: Chapters in an anthropography of violence*. Princeton, NJ: Princeton Univ. Press.

Danielson, Virginia. 1997. *The voice of Egypt: Umm Kulthum, Arabic song, and Egyptian society in the twentieth century*. Chicago: Univ. of Chicago Press.

Das, Veena. 1995. On soap opera: What kind of anthropological object is it? In *Worlds apart: Modernity through the prism of the local*, ed. Daniel Miller, 169–89. London: Routledge.

———. 2000. The making of modernity: Gender and time in Indian cinema. In *Questions of modernity*, ed. Timothy Mitchell, 166–88. Minneapolis: Univ. of Minnesota Press.

Davila, Arlene. 1999. El Kiosko Budweiser. *American Ethnologist* 25:452–70.

———. 2001. *Latino Inc.: The marketing and making of a people*. Berkeley and Los Angeles: Univ. of California Press.

Deng, Francis Mading. 1973. *The Dinka and their songs*. Oxford: Clarendon Press.

Diase, Martha. 1996. Egyptian television serials, audiences, and *The Family House*, a public health enter-educate serial. Ph.D. diss., Univ. of Texas at Austin.

Dirks, Nicholas, Sherry Ortner, and Geoffrey Eley, eds. 1993. *Culture/power/history: A reader in contemporary social theory*. Princeton, NJ: Princeton Univ. Press.

Early, Evelyn. 1993. *Baladi women of Cairo: Playing with an egg and a stone*. Boulder, CO: Lynne Reiner Publishers.

Eickelman, Dale, and Jon Anderson, eds. 1999. *New media in the Muslim world: The emerging public sphere.* Bloomington: Indiana Univ. Press.

El-Bakly, Sawsan, and Ronald Hess. 1994. Mass media makes a difference. *Integration* 41 (September): 13–15.

El-Gawhary, Karim. 2001. An interview with Heba Ra'uf Ezzat. In *Women and power in the Middle East,* ed. Suad Joseph and Susan Slyomovics, 99–102. Philadelphia: Univ. of Pennsylvania Press.

El-Guindi, Fadwa. 1999. *Veil: Modesty, privacy, and resistance.* Oxford: Berg.

El-Hamamsy, Laila Shukry. 1982. The assertion of Egyptian identity. In *Ethnic identity: Cultural continuities and change,* ed. George DeVos and Lola Romanucci-Ross, 2nd ed., 276–306. Chicago: Univ. of Chicago Press.

El-Kholy, Heba Aziz. 2002. *Defiance and compliance: Negotiating gender in low-income Cairo.* New York: Berghahn Books.

El-Messiri, Sawsan. 1978. *Ibn al-Balad: A concept of Egyptian identity.* Leiden: Brill.

El Shakry, Omnia. 2002. The great social laboratory: Reformers and utopians in twentieth century Egypt. Ph.D. diss., Princeton Univ.

Elsheikh, Ibrahim Abdelwahab. 1977. *Mass media and ideological change in Egypt (1950–1973): An inquiry into the relation between media activities and the ideological change process as illustrated by the propagation of socialism.* Amsterdam: Univ. of Amsterdam.

Evans-Pritchard, E. E. 1969. *The Nuer: A description of the modes of livelihood and political institutions of a Nilotic people.* Rev. ed. New York: Oxford Univ. Press.

Fakhreddine, Jihad. 2002. National versus pan-Arab reach: Which way for Egypt's private commercial TV channels? *TBS* 9 (fall/winter), http://www.tbsjournal.com/Archive/Fall02/Fakhreddine.html.

Fallers, Lloyd A. 1974. *The social anthropology of the nation-state.* Chicago: Aldine Publishing Co.

Faria, Vilmar E., and Joseph E. Potter. 1999. Television, *telenovelas,* and fertility change in Northeast Brazil. In *Dynamics of value in fertility change,* ed. Richard Leete, 252–72. Oxford: Oxford Univ. Press.

Fawzi, Mahmud. 1993. *'Umar 'Abd al-Kafi . . . wa fatawa sakhina . . . fi-l-din wa al-siyasa wa al-fann!* ['Umar 'Abd al-Kafi and hot fatwas (legal opinions) . . . on religion, politics, and art!]. Cairo: Al-jadawi li-l-nashr.

Fernandez, Leela. 2000. Nationalizing "the global": Media images, cultural politics and the middle class in India. *Media Culture and Society* 22:611–28.

———. 2001. Rethinking globalization: Gender and the nation in India. In *Feminist locations: Global and local, theory and practice in the 21st century,* ed. Marianne de Koven, 147–67. New Brunswick, NJ: Rutgers Univ. Press.

Fernea, Elizabeth. 1998. *In search of Islamic feminism: One woman's global journey.* New York: Doubleday.

Feuer, Jane. 1984. Melodrama, serial form and television today. *Screen* 25:4–16.

Fiske, John. 1987. *Television culture.* London: Methuen.

Foster, Robert. 1991. Making national cultures in the global ecumene. *Annual Review of Anthropology* 20:235–60.

———. 1999. The commercial construction of "new nations." *Journal of Material Culture* 4:263–82.

———. 2002. *Materializing the nation: Commodities, consumption and media in Papua New Guinea.* Bloomington: Indiana Univ. Press.

Foucault, Michel. 1978. *Discipline and punish.* Trans. Alan Sheridan. New York: Random House.

———. 1982. Afterword: The subject and power. In *Michel Foucault: Beyond structuralism and hermeneutics,* ed. Hubert Dreyfus and Paul Rabinow, 208–26. Chicago: Univ. of Chicago Press.

———. 1985. *The history of sexuality.* Vol. 2, trans. Robert Hurley. New York: Random House.

———. 1988. Technologies of the self. In *Technologies of the self,* ed. L. Martin, H. Gutman, and P. Hutton, 16–49. Amherst: Univ. of Massachusetts Press.

———. 1993. About the beginning of the hermeneutics of the self. *Political Theory* 21:198–227.

Fox, Richard, ed. 1990. *Nationalist ideologies and the production of national cultures.* Washington, DC: American Anthropological Association.

———. 1991. *Recapturing anthropology: Working in the present.* Santa Fe: School of American Research Press.

Friedman, Jonathan. 1994. *Cultural identity and global process.* London: Sage.

Gaffney, Patrick. 1994. *The prophet's pulpit: Islamic preaching in contemporary Egypt.* Berkeley and Los Angeles: Univ. of California Press.

Gasper, Michael. 2001. 'Abdallah al-Nadim, Islamic reform, and "ignorant" peasants: State-Building in Egypt? In *Muslim traditions and modern techniques of power,* ed. Armando Salvatore, 75–92. *Yearbook of the Sociology of Islam,* vol. 3, ed. Helmut Buchholt and Georg Stant. Munster:Lit.

Geertz, Clifford. 1973a. Deep play: Notes on the Balinese cockfight. In *The interpretation of cultures,* 412–14. New York: Basic Books.

———. 1973b. Thick description: Toward an interpretive theory of culture. In Geertz 1973a, 3–30.

———. 1988. *Works and lives.* Stanford, Calif.: Stanford Univ. Press.

———. 1995. *After the fact: Two centuries, four decades, one anthropologist.* Cambridge, MA: Harvard Univ. Press.

Geraghty, Christine. 1991. *Women and soap opera: A study of prime-time soaps.* Cambridge: Polity Press.

Ghannam, Farha. 2002. *Remaking the modern: Space, relocation, and the politics of identity in a global Cairo.* Berkeley and Los Angeles: Univ. of California Press.

Ghazoul, Ferial. 1988. Balaghat al-ghalaba [The eloquence/rhetoric of the downtrodden]. Paper presented at "Women and Contemporary Arab Thought," Second International Conference of the Arab Women's Solidarity Association, November 3–5, Cairo.

Gillespie, Marie. 1995. *Television, ethnicity, and cultural change.* London: Routledge.

Ginsburg, Faye. 1994. Culture/media: A (mild) polemic. *Anthropology Today* 10:5–15.

Ginsburg, Faye, Lila Abu-Lughod, and Brian Larkin, eds. 2002. *Media worlds: Anthropology on new terrain.* Berkeley and Los Angeles: Univ. of California Press.

Gledhill, Christine, ed. 1994. *Melodrama: Stage, picture, screen.* London: British Film Institute.

Gordon, Joel. 1998. Becoming the image: Words of gold, talk television, and Ramadan nights on the little screen. *Visual Anthropology* 10:247–63.

———. 2000. Nasser 56/Cairo 96: Reimaging Egypt's lost community. In Armbrust 2000a, 161–81.

———. 2001. Golden boy turns bête noire: Crossing boundaries of unscripted television in Egypt. *Journal of Middle East and North African Intellectual and Cultural Studies* 1:1–18.

———. 2002. *Revolutionary melodrama: Popular film and civic identity in Nasser's Egypt.* Chicago: Chicago Studies on the Middle East, Center for Middle Eastern Studies, Univ. of Chicago.

Guillermoprieto, Alma. 1993. Letter from Brazil: Obsessed in Rio. *New Yorker,* August 16, 44–55.

Gupta, Akhil. 1998. *Postcolonial developments: Agriculture in the making of modern India.* Durham, NC: Duke Univ. Press.

Gupta, Akhil, and James Ferguson, eds. 1997. *Culture, power, place: Explorations in critical anthropology.* Durham, NC: Duke Univ. Press.

Haeri, Shahla. 1993. Obedience versus autonomy: Women and fundamentalism in Iran and Pakistan. In *Fundamentalisms and society: Reclaiming the sciences, the family, and education,* ed. Martin E. Marty and R. Scott Appleby, 181–213. Chicago: Univ. of Chicago Press.

Hamburger, Esther. 1999. Politics and intimacy in Brazilian telenovelas. Ph.D. diss., Univ. of Chicago.

Hamdan, Jamal. 1970. *Shakhsiyat misr: dirasa fi 'abqariyyat al-makan* [The character of Egypt: A study in the genius of place]. Cairo: Maktabat al-nahda al-misriyya.

Hamdy, Naila. 2002a. El Mehwar the mercurial. *TBS* 9 (fall/winter), http://www.tbsjournal .com/Archives/Fall02/Mehwar.html.

———. 2002b. A dream TV come true. *TBS* 8 (spring/summer), http://www.tbsjournal.com/ Archives/Spring02/sirhan.html.

Handler, Richard. 1988. *Nationalism and the politics of culture in Québec.* Madison: Univ. of Wisconsin Press.

Hannerz, Ulf. 1992. *Cultural complexity.* New York: Columbia Univ. Press.

———. 1996. *Transnational connections.* New York: Routledge.

Hatem, Mervat. 1992. Economic and political libera(liza)tion in Egypt and the demise of state feminism. *International Journal of Middle East Studies* 24:231–51.

———. 1998. Secularist and Islamist discourses on modernity in Egypt and the evolution of the post-colonial nation-state. In *Islam, gender and social change,* ed. Yvonne Haddad and John Esposito, 85–99. New York: Oxford Univ. Press.

Heider, Karl G. 1991. Indonesian cinema: National culture on screen. Honolulu: Univ. of Hawaii Press.

Herrera, Linda. 2001. Accommodating disco and Quran: Lay female pedagogues and the education of metropolitan Muslims. In Salvatore 2001, 225–39.

Herzfeld, Michael. 1997. *Cultural intimacy: Social poetics in the nation-state.* New York: Routledge.

Himpele, Jeff. 2002. Arrival scenes: Complicity and media ethnography in the Bolivian public sphere. In Ginsburg, Abu-Lughod, and Larkin 2002, 301–16.

Hinerman, Stephen. 2001. Star culture. In *Culture in the communication age,* ed. James Lull, 193–211. London: Routledge.

Hirschkind, Charles. 2001. Civic virtue and religious reason: An Islamic counterpublic. *Cultural Anthropology* 16:3–34.

Hoffman, Valerie. 1995. *Sufism, mystics, and saints in modern Egypt.* Columbia: Univ. of South Carolina Press.

Hoodfar, Homa. 1997. *Between marriage and the market: Intimate politics and survival in Cairo.* Berkeley and Los Angeles: Univ. of California Press.

Illouz, Eva. 2003. *Oprah Winfrey and the glamour of misery: An essay on popular culture.* New York: Columbia Univ. Press.

Jansen, Willy. 1987. *Women without men: Gender and marginality in an Algerian town.* Leiden: E. J. Brill.

Joyrich, Lynne. 1992. All that television allows: TV melodrama, postmodernism, and consumer culture. In *Private screenings: Television and the female consumer,* ed. Lynne Spigel and Denise Mann, 227–51. Minneapolis: Univ. of Minnesota Press.

Kamel, Bouthayna. 1999. Night confessions: Social boundaries of talk radio. Paper presented at the Middle East Studies Association Annual Meeting, Washington, DC.

Kamil, Magdi. 1993. *Fannanat wara' al-hijab* [Artists behind the veil]. Cairo: Markaz al-raya li-l-nashr wa al-i'lam, MR.

Kandil, Heba. 2000. The media free zone: An Egyptian media production city finesse. *Transnational Broadcasting Journal* 5 (fall), http://www.tbsjournal.com/Archives/Falloo/Kandil.htm.

Karthigesu, Ranggasamy. 1988. Television as a tool for nation-building in the third world. In *Television and its audience,* ed. Phillip Drummond and Richard Paterson, 306–26. London: British Film Institute.

Kashak, Marwan. 1987. *Al-Usra al muslima amam al-fidiyu wa al-tilifizyun* [The Muslim family in front of video and television]. Cairo: Dar al-kalima al-tayyiba.

Kelly, John D., and Martha Kaplan. 2001. *Represented communities: Fiji and world decolonization.* Chicago: Univ. of Chicago Press.

Kendall, Laurel. 1988. *The life and hard times of a Korean shaman.* Honolulu: Univ. of Hawaii Press.

Khalifa, 'Abd al-Latif Muhammad, and Sha'ban Jaballah Radwan. 1998. *Al-shakhsiya al-misriyya: Al-malamih wa al-abad* [The Egyptian personality: Features and dimensions]. Cairo: Dar gharib.

Kienle, Eberhard. 2001. *A grand delusion: Democracy and economic reform in Egypt.* London: I. B. Tauris.

Kuppinger, Petra. 2001. Cracks in the cityscape: Traditional spatial practices and the official discourse on "informality" and *irhab* (Islamic terrorism). In Salvatore 2001, 185–207.

Lane, Sandra. 1997. Television minidramas: Social marketing and evaluation in Egypt. *Medical Anthropology Quarterly* 11 (2): 164–82.

Larkin, Brian. 1996. The social space of media. Panel organized for the American Anthropological Association Annual Meeting, San Francisco.

Lerner, Daniel. 1958. *The passing of traditional society.* Glencoe, IL: Free Press.

Levy, Marion Jr. 1966. *Modernization and the structure of societies.* Princeton, NJ: Princeton Univ. Press.

Liebes, Tamar, and Elihu Katz. 1990. *The export of meaning: Cross-Cultural readings of "Dallas."* New York: Oxford Univ. Press.

Lomnitz-Adler, Claudio. 1992. *Exits from the labyrinth: Culture and ideology in the Mexican national space.* Stanford, CA: Stanford Univ. Press.

Lopez, Ana. 1995. Our welcomed guests: Telenovelas in Latin America. In Allen 1995, 256–75.

Lull, James. 1990. *Inside family viewing: Ethnographic research on television's audience.* London: Routledge.

———. 1995. *Media, communication, culture: A global approach.* New York: Columbia Univ. Press.

Lutz, Catherine. 1986. Emotion, thought, and estrangement: Emotion as a cultural category. *Cultural Anthropology* 1: 405–36.

———. 2001. *Homefront: A military city and the American twentieth century.* Boston: Beacon Books.

Machado-Borges, Thaïs. 2003. *Only for you! Brazilians and the telenovela flow.* Stockholm: Stockholm Studies in Social Anthropology.

MacLeod, Arlene. 1991. *Accommodating protest: Working women, the new veiling, and change in Cairo.* New York: Columbia Univ. Press.

Mahfouz, Naguib. 1989/1956. *Palace Walk.* Trans. William M. Hutchins and Olive E. Kenny. New York: Doubleday.

Mahmood, Saba. 1998. Women's piety and embodied discipline: The Islamic resurgence in contemporary Egypt. Ph.D. diss., Stanford Univ.

———. 2001a. Feminist theory, embodiment, and the docile agent: Some reflections on the Egyptian Islamic revival. *Cultural Anthropology* 16:202–36.

———. 2001b. Rehearsing spontaneity and the conventionality of ritual: Disciplines of Salat. *American Anthropologist* 8:827–53.

———. 2004. *Politics of piety: The Islamic revival and the feminist subject.* Princeton, NJ: Princeton Univ. Press.

Malkki, Liisa. 1995. *Purity and exile: Violence, memory, and national cosmology among Hutu refugees in Tanzania.* Chicago: Univ. of Chicago Press.

Malkmus, Lizbeth, and Roy Armes. 1991. *Arab and African film making.* London: Zed Books.

Mandel, Ruth. 2002. A Marshall Plan of the mind: The political economy of a Kazakh soap opera. In Ginsburg, Abu-Lughod, and Larkin 2002, 211–28.

Mankekar, Purnima. 1993a. National texts and gendered lives: An ethnography of television viewers in a north Indian city. *American Ethnologist* 20:543–63.

———. 1993b. Television tales and a woman's rage. *Public Culture* 5:469–92.

———. 1999. *Screening culture, viewing politics: An ethnography of television, womanhood, and nation in postcolonial India.* Durham, NC: Duke Univ. Press.

Marcus, George. 1998a. Ethnography in/of the world system: The emergence of multi-sited ethnography. In Marcus 1998b.

———. 1998b. *Ethnography through thick and thin.* Princeton, NJ: Princeton Univ. Press.

———. 2003. On the unbearable slowness of being an anthropologist now: Notes on a contemporary anxiety in the making of ethnography. *Xcp: Cross-Cultural Poetics* 12 (April): 7–20.

Martin, Emily. 1994. *Flexible bodies: Tracking immunity in American culture from the days of polio to the age of AIDS.* Boston: Beacon Press.

Mead, Margaret, and Rhoda Metraux, eds. 2000. *The study of culture at a distance.* New York: Berghahn Books.

Merritt, Russell. 1983. Melodrama: Postmortem for a phantom genre. *Wide Angle* 5:25–31.

Meskell, Lynn. 2001. The practice and politics of archaeology in Egypt. In *Ethics and anthropology: Facing future issues in human biology, globalism, and cultural property,* ed. A.-M. Cantwell, E. Friedlander, and M. L. Tram, 146–69. New York: Annals of the New York Academy of Sciences.

Miller, Daniel. 1992. The young and the restless in Trinidad: A case of the local and the global in mass consumption. In *Consuming technologies: Media and information in domestic spaces,* ed. Roger Silverstone and Eric Hirsch, 163–82. London: Routledge.

———, ed. 1995a. *Acknowledging consumption.* London: Routledge.

———. 1995b. Consumption as the vanguard of history. In Miller 1995a, 1–57.

———. 1995c. Consumption studies as the transformation of anthropology. In Miller 1995a, 264–95.

———. 2001. *The dialectics of shopping.* Chicago: Univ. of Chicago Press.

Miller, Toby. 1993. *The well-tempered self.* Baltimore: Johns Hopkins Univ. Press.

Mitchell, Timothy. 1990. The invention and reinvention of the Egyptian peasant. *International Journal of Middle East Studies* 28:129–50.

———. 1995. Worlds apart: An Egyptian village and the international tourism industry. *Middle East Report* 196 (September-October): 8–11, 23.

———. 2000. The stage of modernity. In *Questions of modernity,* ed. Timothy Mitchell, 1–34. Minneapolis: Univ. of Minnesota Press.

———. 2002a. *Rule of experts: Egypt, technopolitics, economy.* Berkeley and Los Angeles: Univ. of California Press.

———. 2002b. Heritage and violence. In Mitchell 2002a, 179–205.

———. 2002c. McJihad: Islam in the U.S. global order. *Social Text* 73:1–18.

Modleski, Tanya. 1982. *Loving with a vengeance: Mass produced fantasies for women.* Hamden, CT: Archon Books.

———. 1983. The rhythms of reception: Daytime television and women's work. In *Regarding television,* ed. E. Ann Kaplan, 67–75. American Film Institute Monograph. Frederick, MD: Univ. Publications of America.

Moody, Sherin. 1999. Pay-TV in Egypt: Impediments and developments. *TBS* 2 (spring), http://www.tbsjournal.com/Archives/Spring99/Documents/Sherin/sherin.html.

Morley, David. 1986. *Family television.* London: Comedia.

Morley, David, and Charlotte Brunsdon. 1999. *The nationwide television studies.* London: Routledge.

Moustafa, Tamir. 2000. Conflict and cooperation between the state and religious institutions in contemporary Egypt. *International Journal of Middle East Studies* 32:3–22.

Mulvey, Laura. 1986. Melodrama in and out of the home. In *High theory/low culture,* ed. Colin McCabe, 80–100. Manchester: Manchester Univ. Press.

Mumford, Laura Stempel. 1995. *Love and ideology in the afternoon.* Bloomington: Indiana Univ. Press.

Myers, Fred, ed. 2001. *The empire of things.* Santa Fe: School of American Research Press.

Najmabadi, Afsaneh. 1998. Crafting an educated housewife in Iran. In Abu-Lughod 1998c, 91–125. Princeton, NJ: Princeton Univ. Press.

Negus, Steve. 1994. Militant repents on TV: Soap or sincere? *Civil Society* 3 (29): 6–8. (May.)

Neiburg, Federico, and Marcio Goldman. 1998. Anthropology and politics in studies of national character. *Cultural Anthropology* 13:56–81.

Nelson, Cynthia. 1996. *Doria Shafik, Egyptian feminist: A woman apart.* Gainesville: Univ. Press of Florida.

Ortner, Sherry. 1995. Resistance and the problem of ethnographic refusal. *Comparative Studies in Society and History* 37:173–93.

Peacock, James. 1966. *The rites of modernization.* Chicago: Univ. of Chicago Press.

Petty, Sheila. 1994. Miseria: The evolution of a unique melodramatic form. *Passages: A Chronicle of the Humanities* 8:19–20.

Piterburg, Gabriel. 1997. The tropes of stagnation and awakening in nationalist historical consciousness: The Egyptian case. In *Rethinking nationalism in the Arab Middle East,* ed. James Jankowski and Israel Gershoni, 42–62. New York: Columbia Univ. Press.

Press, Andrea L., and Elizabeth R. Cole. 1999. *Speaking of abortion: Television and authority in the lives of women.* Chicago: Univ. of Chicago Press.

Public Information Agency Center for Media, Education and Communication. 1992. Mu'shirat sari'a awwaliyya nahw musalsal 'wa ma zala al-nil yajri' [Quick initial findings about the serial *And the Nile Flows On*]. Unpublished report. Cairo: Al-Hay'a al-'amma li-l-isti'lamat, markaz al-i'lam wa al-ta'lim wa al-ittisal [The Public Information Agency Center for Media, Education and Communication].

Rabinow, Paul. 1986. Representations are social facts. In *Writing Culture,* ed. James Clifford and George Marcus, 234–61. Berkeley and Los Angeles: Univ. of California Press.

Radwan, Nadya. 1997. *Dawr al-drama al-tilifizyuniyya fi tashkil wa'i al-mar'a: dirasa ijtima'iyya maydaniyya* [The role of television drama in forming women's consciousness/awareness: A field-based social study]. Cairo: Al-hay'a al-misriyya al-'amma l-il-kitab [The Egyptian General Book Organization].

Radway, Janice. 1984. *Reading the romance: Women, patriarchy, and popular literature*. Chapel Hill: Univ. of North Carolina Press.

Rajagopal, Arvind. 1999a. Advertising, politics and the sentimental education of the Indian consumer. *Visual Anthropology Review* 14:1–18. (fall-winter.)

———. 1999b. Thinking through emerging markets. *Social Text* 60:131–49. (fall.)

———. 2001. *Politics after television: Hindu nationalism and the reshaping of the public in India*. Cambridge: Cambridge Univ. Press.

Rajan, Rajeswari Sunder. 2000. Women between community and state: Some implications of the uniform civil code debates in India. *Social Text* 65, vol. 18 (4): 55–82. (winter.)

Raouf, Heba. 2001. The silent Ayesha: An Egyptian narrative. In *Globalization, gender and religion: The politics of women's rights in Catholic and Muslim contexts*, ed. Jane H. Bayes and Nayereh Tohidi, 231–57. New York: Palgrave.

Rapp, Rayna. 1999. *Testing women, testing the fetus: The social impact of amniocentesis in America*. New York: Routledge.

Reiker, Martina. 1996. The Sa'id and the city: The politics of space in the making of modern Egypt. Ph.D. diss., Temple Univ.

Reynolds, Dwight. 1995. *Heroic poets, poetic heroes: The ethnography of performance in an Arabic oral epic tradition*. Ithaca, NY: Cornell Univ. Press.

———, trans. Forthcoming. *The Epic of Bani Hilal*.

Robbins, Bruce. 1993. *Secular vocations: Intellectuals, professionalism, culture*. London: Verso.

Rofel, Lisa. 1994. Yearnings: Televisual love and melodramatic politics in contemporary China. *American Ethnologist* 21:700–22.

Roseberry, William. 1994. Hegemony and the language of contention. In *Everyday forms of state formation*, ed. Gilbert Joseph and Daniel Nugent, 170–209. Durham, NC: Duke Univ. Press.

Saad, Reem. 1998. Shame, reputation and Egypt's lovers: A controversy over the nation's image. *Visual Anthropology* 10:401–12.

———. 1999. State, landlord, parliament and peasant: The story of the 1992 tenancy law in Egypt. In *Agriculture in Egypt from Pharaonic to modern times*, ed. Alan Bowman and Eugene Rogan, 387–404. *Proceedings of the British Academy*, vol. 96. Oxford: Oxford Univ. Press.

Sahlins, Marshall. 1995. *How "natives" think: About Captain Cook, for example*. Chicago: Univ. of Chicago Press.

Said, Edward. 1978. *Orientalism*. New York: Pantheon Books.

Sakr, Naomi. 2001. *Satellite realms: Transnational television, globalization and the Middle East*. London: I. B. Tauris.

Sakseid, Geir. 2000. Values in conflict: A study of the values in the Egyptian television serial "A woman from the time of love." Unpublished paper.

Salamandra, Christa. 1999. Moustache hairs lost: Ramadan television serials and the construction of identity in Damascus, Syria. *Visual Anthropology* 10:227–46.

Salvatore, Armando. 1999. *Islam and the political discourse of modernity*. Reading, UK: Ithaca Press.

———. 2000. Social differentiation, moral authority and public Islam in Egypt. *Anthropology Today* 16:12–15. (April.)

————, ed. 2001a. *Muslim traditions and modern techniques of power. Yearbook of the sociology of Islam*, vol. 3, ed. Helmut Buchholt and Georg Stauth. Munster: Lit.

————. 2001b. Introduction: The problem of the ingraining of civilizing traditions into social governance. In Salvatore 2001a, 9–42.

————. 2001c. After the state: Islamic reform and the "implosion" of Shari'a. In Salvatore 2001a, 123–40.

Sangari, Kumkum. 1995. Politics of diversity: Religious communities and multiple patriarchies. *Economic and Political Weekly* 30, nos.(51, 52): 3287–310; 3381–89. (December 23 and 30.)

Sassen, Saskia. 1999. Cracked casings: Notes toward an analytics for studying transnational processes. In *Sociology for the twenty-first century*, ed. Janet Abu-Lughod, 134–45. Chicago: Univ. of Chicago Press.

Schudson, Michael. 1984. *Advertising, the uneasy persuasion: Its dubious impact on American society.* New York: Basic Books.

Seiter, Ellen, Hans Borchers, Gabrielle Kreutzner, and Eva-Maria Warth, eds. 1989. *Remote control: Television, audiences, and cultural power.* London: Routledge.

Seymour-Jorn, Caroline. 2002. A new language: Salwa Bakr on depicting Egyptian women's worlds. *Critique: Critical Middle Eastern Studies* 12 (2): 151–76.

Shafik, Viola. 1998. *Arab cinema: History and cultural identity.* Cairo: American Univ. in Cairo Press.

Shakry, Omnia. 1998. Schooled mothers and structured play: Child rearing in turn-of-the-century Egypt. In Abu-Lughod 1998c, 126–70.

Silj, Alessandro, et al. 1988. *East of "Dallas": The European challenge to American television.* London: British Film Institute.

Silverstone, Roger. 1994. *Television and everyday life.* London: Routledge.

Singerman, Diane. 1995. *Avenues of participation: Family, politics, and networks in urban quarters of Cairo.* Princeton, NJ: Princeton Univ. Press.

Skovgaard-Petersen, Jakob. 1997. *Defining Islam for the Egyptian state.* Leiden: Brill.

Skursi, Julie. 1996. The ambiguities of authenticity in Latin America: Dona Barbara and the construction of national identity. In *Becoming national: A reader,* ed. Geoff Eley and Ronald Grigor Suny, 371–402. New York: Oxford Univ. Press.

Slyomovics, Susan. 1986. *The merchant of art.* Berkeley and Los Angeles: Univ. of California Press.

————. 1987. The death-song of 'Amir Khafaji: Puns in an oral and printed episode of Sirat Bani Hilal. *Journal of Arabic Literature* 18:62–78.

————. 1997. The epic of the Bani Hilal: The birth of Abu Zayd II (southern Egypt). In *Oral epics from Africa: Vibrant voices from a vast continent,* ed. John William Johnson, Thomas A. Hale, and Stephen Belcher, 240–51. Bloomington: Indiana Univ. Press.

————. 2004. Praise of God, praise of self, praise of the Islamic people: Arab epic narrative in performance. In *Classical and popular medieval Arabic literature: A marriage of convenience,* ed. Jareer Abu-Haidar and Farida Abu-Haidar. London: Curzon Press.

Sommer, Doris. 1991. *Foundational fictions: The national romances of Latin America.* Berkeley and Los Angeles: Univ. of California Press.

Spitulnik, Debra. 1993. Anthropology and mass media. *Annual Review of Anthropology* 22: 293–315.

————. 1999. *Producing national publics.* Durham, NC: Duke Univ. Press.

Spivak, Gayatri Chakravorty. 1998. Cultural talks in the hot peace: Revisiting the "global village." In *Cosmopolitics*, ed. Pheng Cheah and Bruce Robbins, 329–48. Minneapolis: Univ. of Minnesota Press.

Sreberny-Mohammadi, Annabelle, and Ali Mohammadi. 1994. *Small media, big revolution: Communication, culture, and the Iranian revolution*. Minneapolis: Univ. of Minnesota Press.

Stacey, Jackie. 1994. *Star gazing: Hollywood cinema and female spectatorship*. London: Routledge.

Starrett, Gregory. 1995. Political economy of religious commodities in Cairo. *American Anthropologist* 91:8–13.

———. 1998. *Putting Islam to work: Education, politics and religious transformation in Egypt*. Berkeley: Univ. of California Press.

Sulayman, Sabir Sulayman 'Asran. 1987. Al-qiyam al-islamiyya al-lati yatadammanuha al-musalsal al-'arabi fi-l-tilifizyun [Islamic values included in Arabic television serials]. M.A. thesis, Faculty of Mass Communication, Cairo Univ.

Taher, Bahaa'. 1996. *Aunt Safiyya and the monastery*. Trans. Barbara Romaine. Berkeley: Univ. of California Press.

Talaat, Shahinaz. 1987. *Mass media and rural development in Egypt*. Cairo: The Anglo-Egyptian Bookshop.

Talhami, Ghada. 1996. *The mobilization of Muslim women in Egypt*. Gainesville: Univ. Press of Florida.

Tauxe, Caroline. 1993. The spirit of Christmas: Television and commodity hunger in a Brazilian election. *Public Culture* 5:593–604.

Thompson, John B. 1995. *The media and modernity*. Stanford, Calif.: Stanford Univ. Press.

Tomlinson, John. 1999. *Globalization and culture*. Chicago: Univ. of Chicago Press.

Tsing, Anna. 1993. *In the realm of the diamond queen: Marginality in an out-of-the-way place*. Princeton, NJ: Princeton Univ. Press.

Tucker, Judith. 1985. *Women in nineteenth century Egypt*. Cambridge: Cambridge Univ. Press.

Turner, Terence. 2002. Representation, politics, and cultural imagination in indigenous video: General points and Kayapo examples. In Ginsburg, Abu-Lughod, and Larkin 2002, 75–89.

Underwood, Carol, Louise F. Kemprecos, Bushra Jabre, and Muhamed Wafai. 1994. *"And the Nile Flows On"*: The impact of a serial drama in Egypt. Johns Hopkins Center for Communication Programs Project Report (May).

Uthman, Nader K. and Leah Ida Harris. 2002. Zii'! (Broadcast it!): Reading the construction of cultural negotiation in the Egyptian TV show "Hidden Camera." Paper presented at the Middle East Studies Association Meetings, Washington, DC.

van der Veer, Peter. 2001. *Imperial encounters: Religion and modernity in India and Britain*. Princeton, NJ: Princeton Univ. Press.

van Niewkerk, Karin. 1995. *A trade like any other: Female singers and dancers in Egypt*. Austin: Univ. of Texas Press.

Verdery, Katherine. 1991. *Nationalist ideology under socialism: Identity and cultural politics in Ceausescu's Romania*. Berkeley and Los Angeles: Univ. of California Press.

Vitalis, Robert. 2000. American ambassador in Technicolor and Cinemascope: Hollywood and revolution on the Nile. In Armbrust 2000a, 269–91.

Watson, Helen. 1992. *Women in the city of the dead*. London: Hurst & Company.

Weber, Max. 1949. Objectivity in social science and social policy. In *The methodology of the social sciences*. New York: Free Press.

Westergaard, Kirsten, and Nicholas Hopkins. 1998. *Directions of change in rural Egypt*. Cairo: American Univ. in Cairo Press.

Wickett, Elizabeth. 1993. "For our destinies": The funerary laments of Upper Egypt. Ph.D. diss., Univ. of Pennsylvania.

Wikan, Unni. 1980. *Life among the poor in Cairo*. London: Tavistock Publications.

———. 1996. *Tomorrow, God willing: Self-made destinies in Cairo*. Chicago: Univ. of Chicago Press.

Wilk, Richard. 1993. "It's destroying a whole generation": Television and moral discourse in Belize. *Visual Anthropology* 5:229–44.

———. 2002. Television, time, and the national imaginary in Belize. In Ginsburg, Abu-Lughod, and Larkin 2002, 171–186.

Willemen, Paul. 1993. Negotiating the transition to capitalism: The case of Andaz. In *Melodrama and Asian cinema*, ed. Wimal Dissanayake, 179–88. Cambridge: Cambridge Univ. Press.

Williams, Brackette. 1993. The impact of the precepts of nationalism on the concept of culture: Making grasshoppers of naked apes. *Cultural Critique* 24:143–91.

Williams, Raymond. 1975. *Television: Technology and cultural form*. New York: Schocken Books.

———. 1989. Drama in a dramatised society. In *Raymond Williams and Television*, ed. A. O'Connor, 3–13. London: Routledge.

Winegar, Jessica. 2003. Claiming Egypt: The cultural politics of artistic practice in a postcolonial society. Ph.D. diss., New York Univ.

Wolf, Eric. 1982. *Europe and the people without history*. Berkeley and Los Angeles: Univ. of California Press.

Yanagisako, Sylvia, and Carol Delaney, eds. 1995. *Naturalizing power: Essays in feminist cultural analysis*. New York: Routledge.

Yang, Mayfair. 2002. Mass media and transnational subjectivity in Shanghai: Notes on (re)cosmopolitanism in a Chinese metropolis. In Ginsburg, Abu-Lughod, and Larkin 2002, 189–210. Berkeley and Los Angeles: Univ. of California Press.

Zeghal, Malika. 1996. *Gardiens de l'Islam: Les Oulémas d'Al Azhar dans l'Egypte Contemporaine*. Paris: Presses de la Fondation Nationale des Sciences Politiques.

Zirbel, Kathryn E. 2000. Playing it both ways: Local Egyptian performers between regional identity and international markets. In Armbrust 2000a. Berkeley and Los Angeles: Univ. of California Press.

Zuhur, Sherifa. 1992. *Revealing reveiling: Islamist gender ideology in contemporary Egypt*. Albany: State Univ. of New York Press.

———, ed. 1998. *Images of enchantment: Visual and performing arts of the Middle East*. Cairo: American Univ. in Cairo Press.

———. 2001. *Asmahan's secrets: Woman, war, and song*. Austin: Univ. of Texas Press.

PERIODICALS (SEE ENDNOTES FOR REFERENCES TO SPECIFIC ARTICLES)

Akhbar al-Adab
Akhbar al-Yawm
Akhir Sa'a
Al-Ahali
Al-Ahram al-'Arabi
Al-Ahram al-Iqtisadi
Al-Ahram Weekly
Al-Hilal
Al-Idha'a wa al-tilifizyun
Al-Musawwar

Al-Qahira
Al-Sha'b
Al-Wafd
Cairo Today
Egyptian Gazette
Egyptian Mail
El-Wekalah
Guardian Weekly
Majallat al-Azhar
Middle East Times
New York Times
Nusf al-Dunya
Ruz al-Yusuf
Sabah al-Khayr

Index